Why Do You Need This New Edition?

If you're wondering why you should buy this Thirteenth Edition of *Writing About Literature*, here are 6 good reasons!

1. **NEW Chapter I** centers on Alice Walker's "Everyday Use," a short story to which students relate.

2. **Updated MLA-Style Student Papers:** All illustrative student essays have been reformatted to conform to the new MLA Guidelines.

3. **Updated MLA Section:** The updated MLA section includes visual document maps to help students see citation information.

4. **NEW Student Essays:** Nine illustrative student essays are new to the Thirteenth Edition.

5. **NEW Fiction Selection:** Alice Walker's "Everyday Use."

6. **NEW Poetry Selections:** Christina Rossetti's "Echo" and John Keats's "On First Looking into Chapman's Homer."

PEARSON

Boston Columbus Indianapolis New York San Francisco Upper Saddle River
Amsterdam Cape Town Dubai London Madrid Milan Munich Paris Montréal Toronto
Delhi Mexico City São Paulo Sydney Hong Kong Seoul Singapore Taipei Tokyo

Contents

PART II   Writing Essays on Designated Literary Topics

ADDITIONAL SELECTIONS FROM EANTHOLOGY ON MYLITERATURELAB

The following selections are referenced throughout *Writing About Literature* but do not physically appear in the text:

Susan Glaspell, *Trifles*
Katherine Mansfield, "Miss Brill"
Guy de Maupassant, "The Necklace"
Edgar Allan Poe, "The Cask of Amontillado"
William Shakespeare, *Hamlet*

However, these selections are available in the eAnthology featured in *MyLiteratureLab* (www.myliteraturelab.com), along with more than 200 additional literary works. Please refer to the inside front and back cover for a complete listing of available selections. For more information on packaging this text with *MyLiteratureLab*, refer to page xvi.

To the Instructor

What's New in the Thirteenth Edition

All changes in the Thirteenth Edition of *Writing About Literature*, as in earlier editions, are designed to help students read, study, think, plan, organize, draft, and write. Many other features are designed to improve the Thirteenth Edition. In making the many revisions, alterations, rearrangements, and additions (as well as subtractions), I have tried to clarify, improve, and freshen the underlying information and examples.

- The most noteworthy change is in the first chapter, where Walker's "Everyday Use" has replaced Maupassant's "The Necklace." The subsequent discussion and illustrative material is based on "Everyday Use," thus altering virtually every part of this first chapter.
- In a number of chapters the writing sections headed "Raise Questions to Develop Ideas" are augmented, and to the various "Writing Topics about . . ." sections I have designed topics to help students when they go to the library or, these days, to search the Web.
- Additions to Appendix C are Rossetti's "Echo," and Keats's "On First Looking into Chapman's Homer."
- The Thirteenth Edition features nine new illustrative student essays.
- All illustrative student essays in the Thirteenth Edition have been reformatted to conform to the 2009 MLA Guidelines.
- The updated MLA section includes visual document maps to help visualize citation information.

In addition to new essays, many of the titles, headings, and subheadings have been retained to make them crystalize the discussions that follow them. My hope is that these informative headings will assist students in their understanding of the various topics.

Questions throughout the book are mainly keyed to the works anthologized in Appendix C ("Works Used for Illustrative Essays and References"), but I encourage you to adapt them to the selections in whatever full anthologies you may be using. In a number of chapters, there are short related topics that are boxed and shaded to set them apart for emphasis. These discussions—such as "Referring to Names of Authors When Writing About Literature," "Essays and Paragraphs—Foundation Stones of Writing," "Vehicle and Tenor," and "Plagiarism: An Embarrassing but Vital Subject—and a Danger to Be Overcome," to name just a few—are designed as short notes to help students think about and develop their own powers of analysis and writing. Users of previous editions have found these boxed discussions helpful.

Aside from the extensive revisions and improvements, the chapters are internally different because of a number of changes in Appendix C. The Thirteenth Edition of *Writing About Literature* is not planned as a full-scale anthology, for the selections have been designed to accompany the discussions and illustrative materials within the various chapters. It was not possible, however, to include in the anthology every selection referenced. Nevertheless, an excellent alternative is readily available in Pearson's electronic anthology in MyLiteratureLab.com. The eAnthology contains over 200 literary works, including "The Necklace," "The Cask of Amontillado," *Trifles*, and *Hamlet*—all of which are referred to extensively in *Writing About Literature*. MyLiteratureLab.com is conveniently available with *Writing About Literature* at no additional cost by ordering the package ISBN 0205245293. With all the changes, the Thirteenth Edition of *Writing About Literature* remains a comprehensive guide for composition courses in which literature is introduced, and also for literature courses at any level.

The glossary, based on terms set in boldface in the text, is an innovation that has been retained ever since the Sixth Edition. The increasing number of students taking entrance examinations and the GRE has justified this continuation. To help students acquaint themselves with important literary terms and concepts, the glossary includes brief independent definitions together with text-page numbers for further reference.

In the Thirteenth Edition of *Writing About Literature*, I have kept and strengthened those features that you have valued over the years. While the constant emphasis in the book is on writing complete essays (and paragraphs) about literature, the chapters may be used as starting points for classroom study and discussion, and may be adapted for shorter and paragraph-length writing assignments. In a one-semester course the book offers selective choices for study and writing, whereas in a two- or three-semester sequence, it is extensive enough to offer the possibility of complete or close-to-complete use.

The various chapter discussions were originally developed as essay assignments. Many years ago, when I was just starting out as a teacher of literature and writing, I learned that there was a direct connection between the ways I made my assignments and the quality of student work. The more I described to my students what I wanted, and the longer I took to explain things, the better their final essays turned out to be. Soon, however, I found myself spending close to entire periods in assigning essays, and it was then that I began to hand out written directions, thus saving much valuable classroom time. I tried and tested each assignment in a number of separate classes, and I constantly made changes based on both student questions and student writing. When I was able to put everything together, *Writing Themes About Literature*, now *Writing About Literature*, was the result, first published in 1964.

Revisions, Changes, and Other Additions

For the Thirteenth Edition, Chapter 1 is the major introductory section. A feature that was new in the Twelfth Edition, now continued in the Thirteenth Edition, is an extra chapter-title line indicating which genres might be most suitable for the approach discussed in the chapter. Some of the topics—such as setting ("Fiction, Drama,

Narrative Poems"), point of view ("Fiction, Narrative Poetry"), and rhyme ("Poetry")—lend themselves naturally to particular genres. Of course, for many of the assignments, all three genres are, and always have been, relevant. The comparison-contrast chapter (Chapter 15), for example, illustrates the ways in which the earlier techniques may be focused on any of the chapter-title topics in the book. This chapter also illustrates how a longer comparison-contrast essay may consider many of the genres simultaneously, as a group.

As in past editions, each chapter on literary topics consists of two parts. The first part is a discussion of a particular analytical approach—such as character, structure, or imagery—and the second consists of suggestions for writing, together with an illustrative paragraph, essay, or essays showing how students might wish to adapt the approach for their own assignments. A major characteristic preserved in this edition is that, after the general introduction of Chapter 1, the subsequent chapters are arranged in a loose order of increasing difficulty. Thus the chapters on Rhyme (Chapter 13) and research (Chapter 19) are increasingly detailed and complex, but they also build on the various techniques of analysis presented in the earlier chapters. Chapter 16, on literary works as they are related to their historical period, might work best if students acquire knowledge and understanding, either through study or discussion, of some of the issues that were important when particular works were published.

In the appendixes, Appendix A is a brief introduction to various critical approaches to literary study. Appendix B concerns the perennially essential topic of documentation. A brief collection of works used for references and illustrative essays is contained in Appendix C. This appendix is not intended as a full-scale anthology, but is to be understood as a brief collection designed to assist in making the discussions and the illustrative essays self-contained.

Although you might assign the chapters in sequence throughout your course, you may also choose them according to your objectives and needs. For example, you might wish to pass over the earlier chapters and go directly to the later ones. You might also choose the chapter on comparison-contrast (Chapter 15) as the basis of separate assignments such as symbolism, structure, character, or point of view. Or you might concentrate on just a few of the chapters, assigning them two or more times until students overcome initial difficulties. No matter how the chapters are used, the two parts of each chapter—discussion followed by illustration—are designed to encourage students to improve their skills as readers and writers.

The illustrative essays concluding the chapters are offered in the belief that the word *imitation* need not be preceded by adjectives like *slavish* and *mere*. I mean this. In the Thirteenth Edition there are nine illustrative essays that were not a part of the Twelfth Edition. The purpose of these and all the other essays is to show what *might* be done—not what *must* be done—on particular assignments. It is clear that students writing about literary works are facing a complex task. First, they must read a new work for the first time; second, they must attempt to understand it; and third, they must then apply new or unfamiliar concepts to that work as they begin to write about it. By guiding them in developing a thematic form in which to express their ideas, the illustrative essays, along with illustrative paragraphs along the way, are intended to help them overcome the third difficulty. *Guidance* and *help* are keys here, not *prescriptiveness*. At first, of course, some students may want to follow the illustrative essays closely, whereas others may adapt them or else use them as points of departure. My hope is that students will free themselves to go their own ways as they gain more writing experience.

Following the illustrative essays are commentaries, something students recommended that I include in the Fourth Edition way back in 1976 and that I have included ever since. These are designed to connect the principles in the first part of each chapter to the interpretive writing in the second part.

Writing and Literature

The Thirteenth Edition brings into focus something that has been true of *Writing About Literature* since its first publication. The book is primarily a practical guide for writing; the stress throughout is on how thinking and writing skills may be improved through the reading of literature. This emphasis is made to help students not only in composition and literature but also in most of their other classes. In subjects such as biology, economics, history, political science, psychology, and sociology, instructors use texts and ask students to develop essays from raw data. Writing is based on external, written materials, not on the student's own experiences or on opinions. Writing is intended to help students think about their reading.

Yet we instructors of writing and literature face the problems we have always faced. In our colleges and universities, the demand for good student writing has gone beyond a requirement and now has ascended to the degree of a clamor. The needs of other departments have been brought into strong focus by the creation of programs for writing across the curriculum. Such demands have correspondingly imposed a wide diversification of subject matter, straining the general knowledge of English department staffs and also creating topical and thematic pressure on composition and literature courses. Writing programs that stress internalized subject matter, such as personal experiences or occasional topic materials, have little bearing on writing for other courses. We, as English faculty with our background in literary study, have the task of meeting the service needs of our institutions without compromising our own disciplinary commitment.

The approach in *Writing About Literature* is aimed at these problems. English teachers can work within their own discipline—literature—while also fulfilling a major and usually required responsibility of teaching writing that is externally, not internally, directed. The book thus keeps the following issues in perspective:

- The requirement by our institutions for thinking and writing skills

- The need of students to develop as writers through the study of written texts

- The responsibility of the English faculty to teach writing while still working within their own expertise

It is, therefore, gratifying to claim that, for the last 47 years, *Writing About Literature* has been offering assistance to meet these needs. The approach works, but I believe it is still novel. It gives coherence to the sometimes fragmented composition course. It also provides for adaptation and, as I have stressed, variety. Using the book, you can develop a virtually endless number of new topics for essays. One obvious benefit is the possibility of entirely eliminating not only the "theme barrels" of infamous memory but also the newer interference from "enterprises" that provide critical and research essays through the Internet. I do not have words to express my contempt for such "business" ventures.

Although *Writing About Literature* is designed as a rhetoric of practical criticism for students, it is based on profoundly held convictions. Simply to make assignments based on the word "discuss," and let students do with them what they will is to invite frustration for students and instructors alike. If students develop knowledge of specific approaches to literary subject material, however, they can begin to improve their expertise as readers, thinkers, and writers. As Alexander Pope said so well and so wittily in *An Essay on Criticism* (lines 362–63):

> True   in Writing comes from Art, not Chance,
> As those move easiest who have learn'd to dance.

I have a concluding article of faith. We who are devoted to the teaching of literature are committed to our belief in its value. The study of literature, together with the lifelong love of literature, is valid in and for itself. But literature as an art form employs techniques that can be fully appreciated only through study, understanding, reflection, discussion, and analysis—in short, through systematic and disciplined effort. In the pursuit of a liberal education, no one can become mentally free without intensive intellectual discipline. It is axiomatic that the development of writing skill in one area (in this instance, the interpretation of literature) has an enabling and creative effect upon skills in other areas: The search for information with a particular goal in mind; the asking of pointed questions; the testing, rephrasing, and developing of ideas—all these and more are transferable skills for students to build on throughout their college years and beyond. Thus my aim in *Writing About Literature* is to help students read and write systematically about individual literary works and, thereby, to develop the confidence, power, and freedom that are the close bosom-friends of professional mastery in any and all subjects.

Acknowledgments

As I complete the Thirteenth Edition of *Writing About Literature*, I renew my deepest thanks to all of you who have been loyal to the earlier editions. Your approval of the book is a great honor. As I think about the revisions for this new edition, I note that *Writing About Literature* has been influenced by the collective wisdom of many students and teachers. Those who have been particularly helpful for the Thirteenth Edition are: Natalia Andrievskikh, Binghamton University; William Davis, College of Notre Dame of Maryland; Adrienne Eastwood, San Jose State University; Frederic Giacobazzi, Kirtland Community College; Barbara Howard, Central Bible College; and Lynne Lerych, Grays Harbor College.

Conversations and discussions with many others have influenced my changes in innumerable and immeasurable ways. At Pearson, I thank Vivian Garcia, Senior Acquisitions Editor, for her constant thoughtfulness, encouragement, and helpfulness; Phil Miller has given me firm and friendly support over many years. I salute him as he leaves for retirement. I also thank Managing Editor Donna DeBenedictis, Production Manager Savoula Amanatidis, and Senior Manufacturing Buyer Dennis J. Para. In addition, I am especially grateful to Judith Bucci of Nesbitt Graphics; Sean Strathy, Editorial Assistant; Heather Vomero, Editorial Assistant; Joyce Nilsen, Executive Marketing Manager; Megan Zuccarini, Marketing Assistant; and Katie Huha, Text Permissions Researcher. Special thanks go to Barbara Willette, who diligently copyedited the manuscript and offered many, many corrections and improvements, and to Erin Reilly of Pearson, whose efforts on behalf of the book have been wonderfully creative and extensive. I am also especially grateful to Brooke Mitchell. I particularly thank Jonathan Roberts for his skilled and patient help in preparing the disks of the halting and tentative drafts leading to the final copy. Thank you, each and every one.

Edgar V. Roberts

Chapter 1

The Process of Reading, Responding to, and Writing About Literature

Fiction, Poetry, and Drama

Writing About Literature introduces a number of analytical approaches that are important in the study of literature, along with guidance for writing informative and well-focused essays based on these approaches. The chapters will help you to fulfill two goals of composition and English courses: (1) to write good essays and (2) to understand and assimilate great works of literature.

The premise of the book is that no educational process is complete until you can *apply* what you study. That is, you have not learned something—really *learned* it—until you talk or write about it. This does not mean that you retell a story, state an undeveloped opinion, or describe an author's life but rather that you deal directly with topical and artistic issues about individual works. The need to write requires that you strengthen your understanding and knowledge through the recognition of where your original study might have fallen short. Thus, it is simple for you to read the chapter on point of view (Chapter 3), and it is easy to read Alice Walker's story "Everyday Use." Your grasp of point of view as a concept will not be complete, however, nor will your appreciation of the technical artistry of this story be complete, until you have prepared yourself to write about Walker's technique. As you do so, you will need to reread parts of the work, study your notes, and apply your knowledge to the problem at hand; you must check facts, grasp relationships, develop insights, and try to express yourself with as much exactness and certainty as possible.

Primarily, then, this book aims to help you improve your writing skills through the use of literature as subject matter. After you have finished a number of essays derived from the following chapters, you will be able to approach just about any literary work with the confidence that you can understand it and write about it.

What Is Literature, and Why Do We Study It?

We use the word **literature**, in a broad sense, to mean compositions that tell stories, dramatize situations, express emotions, and analyze and advocate ideas. Before the invention of writing five thousand or more years ago, literary works were necessarily spoken or sung, and they were retained only as long as living people continued to repeat them. In some societies, the oral tradition of literature still exists, with many poems and stories designed exclusively for spoken delivery. Even in our modern age of writing, printing, and electronic communication, much literature is still heard as told by living speakers. Parents delight their children with stories and poems read or recited aloud; poets and storywriters read their works directly before live audiences; plays and scripts are interpreted on stages and before movie and television cameras for the benefit of a vast public.

No matter how we assimilate literature, we gain much from it. In truth, readers often cannot explain why they enjoy reading, for goals and ideals are not always easily articulated. There are, however, areas of general agreement about the value of systematic and extensive reading.

Literature helps us to grow, both personally and intellectually. It opens doors for us. It stretches our minds. It develops our imagination, increases our understanding, and enlarges our power of sympathy. It helps us to see beauty in the world around us. It links us with the cultural, philosophical, and religious world of which we are a part. It enables us to recognize human dreams and struggles in different places and times. It helps us to develop mature sensibility and compassion for all living beings. It nurtures our ability to appreciate the beauty of order and arrangement—gifts that are also bestowed by a well-structured song, a beautifully painted canvas, or a skillfully chiseled statue. Literature enables us to see worthiness in the aims of all people. It exercises our emotions through interest, concern, sympathy, tension, excitement, regret, fear, laughter, and hope. It encourages us to assist creative and talented people who need recognition and support. Through our cumulative experience in reading, literature shapes our goals and values by clarifying our own identities—both positively, through acceptance of the admirable in human beings, and negatively, through rejection of the sinister. It enables us to develop perspectives on events that are occurring locally and globally, and thereby it gives us understanding and control. It is one of the shaping influences of our lives. It makes us human.

Types of Literature: The Genres

Literature may be classified into four categories or *genres:* (1) prose fiction, (2) poetry, (3) drama, and (4) nonfiction prose. Usually the first three are classified as **imaginative literature**.

The genres of imaginative literature have much in common, but they also have distinguishing characteristics. **Prose fiction**, or **narrative fiction**, includes **myths**, **parables**, **romances**, **novels**, and **short stories**. Originally, *fiction* meant anything made up, crafted, or shaped, but today the word refers to prose stories based in the imaginations of authors. The essence of fiction is **narration**, the relating or recounting of a sequence of events or actions. Fictional works usually focus on one or a few major characters who change and grow (in their ability to make decisions, their awareness or insight, their intellect, their attitude toward others, their sensitivity, and their moral capacity) as a result of how they deal with other characters and how they attempt to solve their problems. Although fiction, like all imaginative literature, can introduce true historical details, it is not real history, for its main purposes are to interest, stimulate, instruct, and divert, not to create a precise historical record.

If prose is expansive, **poetry** tends toward brevity. It offers us high points of emotion, reflection, thought, and feeling in what the English poet Wordsworth called "narrow room[s]." Yet in this context, poetry expresses the most powerful and deeply felt experiences of human beings, often awakening deep responses of welcome recognition: "Yes, I know what that's like. I would feel the same way. That's exactly right." Poems make us think, make us reflect, and generally instruct us. They can also stimulate us, surprise us, make us laugh or cry, inspire us, exalt us. Many poems become our lifelong friends, and we visit them again and again for insight, understanding, laughter, or the quiet reflection of joy or sorrow.

Poetry's power lies not only in its words and thoughts but also in its music, using rhyme and a variety of rhythms to intensify its emotional impact. Although poems themselves vary widely in length, individual lines are often short because poets distill the greatest meaning and imaginative power from their words through rhetorical devices such as **imagery** and **metaphor**. Though poetry often requires many **formal** and **metrical** restrictions, it is paradoxically the very restrictiveness of poetry that provides poets with great freedom. Traditionally important poetic forms include the fourteen-line **sonnet**, as well as **ballads**, **blank verse**, **couplets**, **elegies**, **epigrams**, **hymns**, **limericks**, **odes**, **quatrains**, **songs** or **lyrics**, **tercets** or **triplets**, **villanelles**, and the increasingly popular **haiku**. Many songs or lyrics have been set to music, and some were written expressly for that purpose. Some poems are long and **discursive**, like many poems by the American poet Walt Whitman. **Epic poems**, such as those by Homer and Milton, contain thousands of lines. Since the time of Whitman, many poets have abandoned rhymes and regular rhythms in favor of **free verse**, a far-ranging type of poetry that grows out of content and the natural rhythms of spoken language.

Drama is literature designed for stage or film presentation by people—actors—for the benefit and delight of other people—an audience. The essence of drama is the development of **character** and **situation** through **speech** and **action**. Like fiction, drama may focus on a single character or a small number of characters, and it enacts fictional (and sometimes historical) events as if they were happening right before our eyes. The audience, therefore, is a direct witness to the ways in which characters are influenced and changed by events and by other characters. Although most modern plays use prose **dialogue** (the conversation of two or more characters), on the principle that the language of drama should resemble the language of ordinary people as much as possible, many plays from the past, such as those of ancient Greece and Renaissance England, are in poetic form.

Nonfiction prose consists of news reports, feature articles, essays, editorials, textbooks, historical and biographical works, and the like, all of which describe or interpret facts and present judgments and opinions. The goal of nonfiction prose is to present truths and conclusions about the factual world. Imaginative literature, although also grounded in facts, is less concerned with the factual record than with the revelation of truths about life and human nature. Recently, another genre has been emphasized within the category of nonfiction prose. This is **creative nonfiction**, a type of literature that is technically nonfiction, such as essays, articles, diaries, and journals, but that nevertheless introduces carefully structured form, vivid examples, relevant quotations, and highly creative and imaginative insights.

Reading Literature and Responding to It Actively

Sometimes we find it difficult, after we have finished reading a work, to express thoughts about what we have read and to answer pointed questions about it. But more active and thoughtful reading gives us the understanding to develop well-considered answers. Obviously, we need to follow the work and to understand its details, but just as important, we need to respond to the words, get at the ideas, and understand the implications of what is happening. We rely on our own fund of knowledge and experience to verify the accuracy and truth of situations and incidents, and we try to articulate our own emotional responses to the characters and their problems.

To illustrate such active responding, we will examine the story "Everyday Use" (1973), by the American writer Alice Walker.[1] "Everyday Use," one of the more popular stories of recent decades, is included here, with right-hand marginal notes like those that any reader might make during original and follow-up readings. Many of the notes record details about the action and the movement of the story. But as the action progresses and relationships among the characters become clearer, the marginal comments also become focused on the reader's interpretations of the story's meaning. Toward the end of the story, the marginal comments result not only from first responses but also from considered thought. Here, then, is Alice Walker's "Everyday Use."

---

[1]Alice Walker was born in Georgia and attended Spellman College in Georgia and Sarah Lawrence College in Bronxville, New York. In addition to teaching at Yale, Wellesley, and other schools, she has written and edited fiction, poetry, and biography. She received a Guggenheim Fellowship in 1977. For her collection of poems *Revolutionary Petunias and Other Poems* (1973), which contains the poem "Revolutionary Petunias," she received a Wall Book Award nomination. Her best-known novel, *The Color Purple* (1982), was awarded the Pulitzer Prize for Fiction in 1983 and was made into a movie that won an Academy Award in 1985. Walker's more recent fictional works include *The Temple of My Familiar* (1989), *Possessing the Secret of Joy* (1992), and *By the Light of My Father's Smile* (1998). In 1994, she published her *Collected Stories*, and in 2005, her *Collected Poems* appeared. Her main hobby is gardening.

Alice Walker   (b. 1944)

Everyday Use (1973)

I will wait for her in the yard that Maggie and I made so clean and wavy yesterday afternoon. A yard like this is more comfortable than most people know. It is not just a yard. It is like an extended living room. When the hard clay is swept clean as a floor and the fine sand around the edges lined with tiny, irregular grooves, anyone can come and sit and look up into the elm tree and wait for the breezes that never come inside the house.

Something is about to happen. The Narrator and Maggie, who is not otherwise identified, have straightened and swept the yard, which is "like an extended living room."

Maggie will be nervous until after her sister goes; she will stand hopelessly in corners, homely and ashamed of the burn scars down her arms and legs, eying her sister with a mixture of envy and awe. She thinks her sister has held life always in the palm of one hand, that "no" is a word the world never learned to say to her.

They are waiting for Maggie's sister. Maggie is a "homely and ashamed" woman, unlike her more daring sister.

You've no doubt seen those TV shows[2] where the child who has "made it" is confronted, as a surprise, by her own mother and father, tottering in weakly from backstage. (A pleasant surprise, of course: What would they do if parent and child came on the show only to curse out and insult each other?) On TV mother and child embrace and smile into each other's faces. Sometimes the mother and father weep, the child wraps them in her arms and leans across the table to tell how she would not have made it without their help. I have seen these programs.

The Narrator thinks of herself as being like the parent of a successful child who has "made it." She compares her situation to the TV show This Is Your Life.

Sometimes I dream a dream in which Dee and I are suddenly brought together on a TV program of this sort. Out of a dark and soft-seated limousine I am ushered into a bright room filled with many people. There I meet a smiling, gray, sporty man like Johnny Carson[3] who shakes my hand and tells me what a fine girl I have. Then we are on the stage and Dee is embracing me with tears in her eyes. She pins on my dress a large orchid, even though she has told me once that she thinks orchids are tacky flowers.

The Narrator imagines a sentimental scene almost like those on TV, hosted by someone like Johnny Carson.

---

[2]In the early days of television (i.e., the 1950s), a popular show was *This is Your Life*, which the narrator accurately describes here.
[3]Johnny Carson (1925–2005) was an amateur magician, actor, and radio announcer before he began hosting the late-night television show *Tonight*, a role in which he continued for thirty years. He amused and pleased huge national audiences, gained many awards, and was known as "the king of late night." He did not host *This Is Your Life*.

5   In real life I am a large, big-boned woman with rough, man-working hands. In the winter I wear flannel nightgowns to bed and overalls during the day. I can kill and clean a hog as mercilessly as a man. My fat keeps me hot in zero weather. I can work outside all day, breaking ice to get water for washing; I can eat pork liver cooked over the open fire minutes after it comes steaming from the hog. One winter I knocked a bull calf straight in the brain between the eyes with a sledge hammer and had the meat hung up to chill before nightfall. But of course all this does not show on television. I am the way my daughter would want me to be: a hundred pounds lighter, my skin like an uncooked barley pancake. My hair glistens in the hot bright lights. Johnny Carson has much to do to keep up with my quick and witty tongue.

She then goes back to reality. She describes her very practical and robust appearance and her skills in slaughtering livestock, but she carries on her fantasy about pleasing her daughter, idealizing her own slenderness and wittiness before the imaginary audience of someone like Johnny Carson.

But that is a mistake. I know even before I wake up. Who ever knew a Johnson with a quick tongue? Who can even imagine me looking a strange white man in the eye? It seems to me I have talked to them always with one foot raised in flight, with my head turned in whichever way is farthest from them. Dee, though. She would always look anyone in the eye. Hesitation was no part of her nature.

She comes back to "reality." She contrasts her slowness of wit with the boldness of Dee (her daughter?). She also brings up the issue of color, and says her role is always to speak with whites as though she is ready to flee. This, she says, was never true of Dee. The family name is Johnson, and so the Narrator may be called "Mrs. Johnson."

A new section in the story.

"How do I look, Mama?" Maggie says, showing just enough of her thin body enveloped in pink skirt and red blouse for me to know she's there, hidden by the door.

"Come out into the yard," I say.

Maggie appears. She must be the daughter who stays at home. Dee is clearly the daughter who has been away and who is returning.

Have you ever seen a lame animal, perhaps a dog run over by some careless person rich enough to own a car, sidle up to someone who is ignorant enough to be kind to him? That is the way my Maggie walks. She has been like this, chin on chest, eyes on ground, feet in shuffle, ever since the fire that burned the other house to the ground.

Maggie seems to have been hurt in some way and is very much in need of kindness. Her physical carriage suggests need.

10   Dee is lighter than Maggie, with nicer hair and a fuller figure. She's a woman now, though sometimes I forget. How long ago was it that the other house burned? Ten, twelve years? Sometimes I can still hear the flames and feel Maggie's arms sticking to me, her hair smoking and her dress falling off her in little black papery flakes. Her eyes seemed stretched open, blazed open by the flames reflected in them. And Dee, I see her standing off under the sweet gum tree she used to dig gum out of; a look of concentration on her face as she watched the last dingy gray board of the house fall in toward the red-hot brick

The Narrator remembers the past and the burning of the previous house. Maggie was burned, and Mrs. Johnson, the mother, rescued her. Dee had not liked that earlier house and seems not to have made any effort to rescue either her mother or her sister but simply stood by while the house burned. Is Mrs. Johnson saying that Dee might have set the fire?

chimney. Why don't you do a dance around the ashes? I'd wanted to ask her. She had hated the house that much.

I used to think she hated Maggie, too. But that was before we raised the money, the church and me, to send her to Augusta[4] to school. She used to read to us without pity; forcing words, lies, other folks' habits, whole lives upon us two, sitting trapped and ignorant underneath her voice. She washed us in a river of make-believe, burned us with a lot of knowledge we didn't necessarily need to know. Pressed us with the serious way she read, to shove us away at just the moment, like dimwits, we seemed about to understand.

Dee wanted nice things. A yellow organdy dress to wear to her graduation from high school; black pumps to match a green suit she'd made from an old suit somebody gave me. She was determined to stare down any disaster in her efforts. Her eyelids would not flicker for minutes at a time. Often I fought off the temptation to shake her. At sixteen she had a style of her own; and knew what style was.

I never had an education myself. After second grade the school was closed down. Don't ask me why: in 1927 colored asked fewer questions than they do now. Sometimes Maggie reads to me. She stumbles along good-naturedly, but can't see well. She knows she is not bright. Like good looks and money, quickness passed her by. She will marry John Thomas (who has mossy teeth in an earnest face) and then I'll be free to sit here and I guess just sing church songs to myself. Although I never was a good singer. Never could carry a tune. I was always better at a man's job. I used to love to milk till I was hooked in the side in '49.[5] Cows are soothing and slow and don't bother you, unless you try to milk them the wrong way.

I have deliberately turned my back on the house. It is three rooms, just like the one that burned, except the roof is tin; they don't make shingle roofs any more. There are no real windows, just some holes cut in the sides, like the portholes on a ship, but not round and not square, with rawhide holding the shutters up on the outside. This house is in a pasture, too, like the other one. No doubt when Dee sees it she will want to tear it down. She wrote me one that no matter where we "choose" to live, she will manage to come see us. But she will never bring her friends. Maggie and I thought about this and Maggie asked me, "Mama, when did Dee ever *have* any friends?"

Dee has attended college away from home but has spent time in reading "without pity" to her mother and to Maggie. Does it seem that the Narrator, Mrs. Johnson, seems to distrust Dee because Dee might have been doing her reading not out of love but out of contempt? Here is an indication that Mrs. Johnson might distrust Dee, even though Dee is her daughter. Background about Dee. She wanted to be stylish and was willing to remake an old dress. Dee had a sense of color, even when young. But Mrs. Johnson seems to have been annoyed by Dee, also.

Mrs. Johnson describes her education. She didn't get beyond the second grade because her school was closed down. The race issue emerges to indicate that the speaker's parents were not able to challenge the decision to close her school. Mrs. Johnson, the Narrator, carries on the theme of paragraph 5: She is strong. But when Maggie leaves, she will have nothing to do but sing. She was hurt when a cow gored her at one time. The home of the Johnsons. It is small and inexpensive. Mrs. Johnson thinks that Dee will be ashamed of her past and will not bring friends to see her family.

---

[4]Augusta, Georgia, the second largest city in the state, is the home of Augusta State University and of Paine College, traditionally a "black" school.

[5]i.e., gored by a cow.

15   She has a few. Furtive boys in pink shirts hanging about on washday after school. Nervous girls who never laughed. Impressed with her they worshiped the well-turned phrase, the cute shape, the scalding humor that erupted like bubbles in lye. She read to them.

When she was courting Jimmy T she didn't have much time to pay to us, but turned all her faultfinding power on him He *flew* to marry a cheap city girl from a family of ignorant flashy people. She hardly had time to recompose herself.

When she comes I will meet—but there they are!

Maggie attempts to make a dash for the house, in her shuffling way, but I stay her with my hand. "Come back here," I say. And she stops and tries to dig a well in the sand with her toe.

It is hard to see them clearly through the strong sun. But even the first glimpse of leg out of the car tells me it is Dee. Her feet were always neat-looking, as if God himself had shaped them with a certain style. From the other side of the car comes a short, stocky man. Hair is all over his head a foot long and hanging from his chin like a kinky mule tail. I hear Maggie suck in her breath. "Uhnnnh," is what it sounds like. Like when you see the wriggling end of a snake just in front of your foot on the road. "Uhnnnh."

20   Dee next. A dress down to the ground, in this hot weather. A dress so loud it hurts my eyes. There are yellows and oranges enough to throw back the light of the sun. I feel my whole face warming from the heat waves it throws out. Earrings gold, too, and hanging down to her shoulders. Bracelets dangling and making noises when she moves her arm up to shake the folds of the dress out of her armpits. The dress is loose and flows, and as she walks closer, I like it. I hear Maggie go "Uhnnnh" again. It is her sister's hair. It stands straight up like the wool on a sheep. It is black as night and around the edges are two long pigtails that rope about like small lizards disappearing behind her ears.

"Wa-su-zo-Tean-o!"[6] she says, coming on in that gliding way the dress makes her move. The short stocky fellow with the hair to his navel is all grinning and he follows up with "Asalamalakim,[7] my mother and my sister!" He moves to hug Maggie but she falls back, tight up against the back of my chair. I feel her trembling there and when I look up I see the perspiration falling off her chin.

The Narrator recalls Dee's friendships in the past. She compares Dee's past humor with "bubbles in lye." The narrator really doesn't like her daughter, Dee.

Dee's past, according to the narrator's memory. Dee drove Jimmy T away with her "faultfinding."

A new section of the story. A shift here, from the past to the present. Dee is coming, but she is a part of "they." She is not alone. The Narrator stops Maggie from leaving, but Maggie is clearly nervous.

The car: Dee is accompanied by a short, stocky man whom Mrs. Johnson does not know but who has long and unkempt hair. Maggie's response is fear, as though she is seeing a wriggling snake.

The descriptions here are funny. Dee and her friend are using phrases from the culture of Black Power, but Mrs. Johnson and Maggie don't know how to respond to them.

---

[6]A phrase from the Lugandan dialect, meaning "Good morning" or "I hope you had a good night."
[7]Arabic phrase meaning "Peace be with you."

"Don't get up," says Dee. Since I am stout it takes something of a push. You can see me trying to move a second or two before I make it. She turns, showing white heels through her sandals, and goes back to the car. Out she peeks next with a Polaroid.[8] She stoops down quickly and lines up picture after picture of me sitting there in front of the house with Maggie cowering behind me. She never takes a shot without making sure the house is included. When a cow comes nibbling around the edge of the yard she snaps it and me and Maggie *and* the house. Then she puts the Polaroid in the back seat of the car, and comes up and kisses me on the forehead.

Continuation of the comedy of the story. Dee photographs everything, making sure to get the house in the background of all her instant photos. It appears that she is trying to record some of the poverty of the place where she was brought up.

Meanwhile Asalamalakim is going through motions with Maggie's hand. Maggie's hand is as limp as a fish, and probably as cold, despite the sweat, and she keeps trying to pull it back. It looks like Asalamalakim wants to shake hands but wants to do it fancy. Or maybe he don't know how people shake hands. Anyhow, he soon gives up on Maggie.

"Well," I say, "Dee."

"No, Mama," she says. "Not 'Dee.' Wangero Leewanika Kemanjo!"[9]

More comedy. Asalamalakim wants to shake Maggie's hand, but Maggie is unable to respond, even though he has called her "sister." His gesture is probably a version of a "soul handshake," given the fact that Mrs. Johnson thinks that his action is 'fancy.'

Dee has changed her American name, in the manner of Black Muslims.   25

"What happened to 'Dee'?" I wanted to know.

"She's dead," Wangero said. "I couldn't bear it any longer, being named after the people who oppress me."

"You know as well as me you was named after your aunt Dicie," I said. Dicie is my sister: She named Dee. We called her "Big Dee" after Dee was born.

"But who was *she* named after?" asked Wangero.

"I guess after Grandma Dee," I said.

Dee, now Wangero, thinks of her past life as being dead. What does Mrs. Johnson think of this?

Even if Mrs. Johnson has to guess   30
about the tradition of the family, she nevertheless believes in it.

"And who was she named after?" asked Wangero.

Dee's questions seem to indicate that she is trying to establish a new family tradition, her own. She is also challenging whether "Dee" is a name of "theirs" that was imposed by the "oppressors" of past generations.

"Her mother," I said, and saw Wangero was getting tired. "That's about as far back as I can trace it," I said. Though, in fact, I probably could have carried it back beyond the Civil War through the branches.

Mrs. Johnson is now remembering the name "Dee" and thinks that it extends into the remote past.

---

[8]The Polaroid Land Camera was an "instant camera" that in the 1960s and beyond provided fully developed photographs a minute after the picture was taken.
[9]Dee apparently mispronounces "Wanjiro" and "Kamenjo," her adopted African names.

"Well," said Asalamalakim, "there you are."

Asalamalakim's comment indicates not much intelligence.

"Uhnnnh," I heard Maggie say.

35 "There I was not," I said, "before 'Dicie' cropped up in our family, so why should I try to trace it that far back?"

He just stood there grinning, looking down on me like somebody inspecting a Model A car.[10] Every once in a while he and Wangero sent eye signals over my head.

"How do you pronounce this name?" I asked.

"You don't have to call me by it if you don't want to," said Wangero.

Dee's comment may suggest that she thinks she might have offended her mother.

"Why shouldn't I?" I asked. "If that's what you want us to call you, we'll call you."

40 "I know it might sound awkward at first," said Wangero.

"I'll get used to it," I said. "Ream it out again."

Well, soon we got the name out of the way. Asalamalakim had a name twice as long and three times as hard. After I tripped over it two or three times he told me to just call him Hakim-a-barber.[11] I wanted to ask him was he a barber, but I didn't really think he was, so I didn't ask.

This is a funny paragraph. Mrs. Johnson, who has said that Asalamalakim has hair "a foot long," remarks that she doesn't think he is a barber.

"You must belong to those beef-cattle peoples down the road," I said. They said "Asalamalakim" when they met you, too, but they didn't shake hands. Always too busy: feeding the cattle, fixing the fences, putting up salt-lick shelters,[12] throwing down hay. When the white folks poisoned some of the herd the men stayed up all night with rifles in their hands. I walked a mile and a half just to see the sight.

Mrs. Johnson describes a serious and dangerous situation. There was a Black Muslim group, whom she calls "beef-cattle peoples." "White folks" poisoned some of the cattle, and the men guarded the rest with rifles. Mrs. Johnson herself wanted to see black men opposing oppression.

Hakim-a-barber said, "I accept some of their doctrines, but farming and raising cattle is not my style." (They didn't tell me, and I didn't ask, whether Wangero (Dee) had really gone and married him.)

45 We sat down to eat and right away he said he didn't eat collards and pork was unclean. Wangero, though, went on through the chitlins and corn bread, the greens and everything else. She talked a blue streak over the sweet potatoes. Everything delighted her. Even the fact that we still used the benches her daddy made for the table when we couldn't afford to buy chairs.

They have a meal, and Dee is happy with the home-cooked food that she had obviously liked when she was living at home. She had even liked the homemade benches that "her daddy" had made for the family.

---

[10]The Model A was the Ford car that replaced the Model T in the late 1920s. The Model A was proverbial for its quality and durability.

[11]A mistake in hearing "Hakim Akbar," meaning, in Arabic, "The wise man is great."

[12]Salt-lick shelters were designed to keep rain from dissolving the large blocks of rock salt put on poles for cattle.

"Oh, Mama!" she cried. Then turned to Hakim-a-barber. "I never knew how lovely these benches are. You can feel the rump prints," she said, running her hands underneath her and along he bench. Then she gave a sigh and her hand closed over Grandma Dee's butter dish. "That's it!" she said. "I knew there was something I wanted to ask you if I could have." She jumped up from the table and went over in the corner where the churn stood, the milk in it clabber[13] by now. She looked at the churn and looked at it.

Dee is noticing "how lovely these benches are." Is she thinking of how to blend her old tradition with her new tradition? She seems to have an idea about how the butter churn would fit into her life.

"This churn top is what I need," she said. "Didn't Uncle Buddy whittle it out of a tree you all used to have?"

Yes, Dee wants the churn top, which, in fact, is an essential part of the entire butter churn.

"Yes," I said.

"Uh huh," she said happily. "And I want the dasher,[14] too."

Dee doesn't ask but states instead that she wants to take the dasher of the butter churn. She is making a demand for it.

"Uncle Buddy whittle that, too?" asked the barber.

Dee (Wangero) looked up at me.

"Aunt Dee's first husband whittled the dash," said Maggie so low you almost couldn't hear her. "His name was Henry, but they called him Stash."

Maggie is able to provide some of the family history. Does this suggest that Maggie is brighter than people in her family have thought?

"Maggie's brain is like an elephant's." Wangero said, laughing. "I can use the churn top as a centerpiece for the alcove table," she said, sliding a plate over the churn, "and I'll think of something artistic to do with the dasher."

It's clear that Dee thinks of the family artifacts not as things of use, but rather as things to be displayed. Here is one of the details fitting into the story's title.

When she finished wrapping the dasher, the handle stuck out. I took it for a moment in my hands. You didn't even have to look too close to she where hands pushing the dasher up and down to make butter had left a kind of sink in the wood. In fact, there were a lot of small sinks; you could see where thumbs and fingers had sunk into the wood. It was beautiful light yellow wood, from a tree that grew in the yard where Big Dee and Stash had lived.

The connection of the dasher with the family, with the past, and with the imprints left by past family members.

After dinner Dee (Wangero) went to the trunk at the foot of my bed and started rifling through it. Maggie hung back in the kitchen over the dishpan. Out came Wangero with two quilts. They had been pieced by Grandma Dee and then Big Dee and me had hung them on the quilt frames on the front

Dee is now going after two quilts that are in a trunk at the foot of the Narrator's bed. It seems that Dee is planning on "raiding" her mother's home.

50

55

---

[13]i.e., clabbered: curdled.
[14]A dasher is used for agitating and blending together the ingredients of butter (and also ice cream).

porch and quilted them. One was in the Lone Star
paten. The other was Walk Around the Mountain. In
both of them were scraps of dresses Grandma Dee
had worn fifty and more years ago. Bits and pieces of
Grandpa Jarrell's Paisley shirts. And one teeny faded
blue piece, about the size of a penny matchbox, that
was from Great Grandpa Ezra's uniform that he wore
in the Civil War.

"Mama," Wangero said sweet as a bird. "Can I have
these old quilts?"

I heard something fall in the kitchen, and a minute
later the kitchen door slammed.

It is clear that Maggie, who over-hears this conversation, had planned on having the quilts herself and planned to use them. Maggie is not as quiet and as shy as we were led to believe earlier in the story.

"Why don't you take one or two of the others?"
I asked. These old things was just done by me and Big
Dee from some tops your grandma pieced before she
died."

"No," said Wangero. "I don't want those. They are
stitched around the borders by machine."

60   "That'll make them last better," I said.

Mrs. Johnson offers a strong rea-son for the superiority of the other quilts in the house.

Dee wants the hand-sewn quilts, on the grounds that "Grandma" wore the dresses that were used for the quilts.

"That's not the point," said Wangero. "These are
all pieces of dresses Grandma used to wear. She did all
this stitching by hand. Imagine!" She held the quilts
securely in her arms stroking them.

"Some of the pieces, like those lavender ones,
come from old clothes her mother handed down
to her," I said, moving up to touch the quilts. Dee
(Wangero) moved back just enough so that I couldn't
reach the quilts. They already belonged to her.

A small conflict. Dee moves the quilts out of her mother's grasp, as though they "already belonged to her." Mrs. Johnson brings out arguments for the family tradition connected with the other quilts.

"Imagine!" she breathed again, clutching them
closely to her bosom.

"The truth is," I said, "I promised to give them
quilts to Maggie, for when she marries John Thomas."

65   She gasped like a bee had stung her.

"Maggie can't appreciate these quilts!" she said.
"She'd probably be backward enough to put them to
everyday use."

"I reckon she would," I said. "God knows I been saving 'em for long enough with nobody using 'em. I hope
she will!" I didn't want to bring up how I had offered
Dee (Wangero) a quilt when she went away to college.
Then she had told me they were old-fashioned, out of
style.

"But they're *priceless*!" she was saying now, furiously,
for she has a temper. "Maggie would put them on the
bed and in five years they'd be in rags. Less than that!"

"She can always make some more," I said. "Maggie knows how to quilt."

Dee (Wangero) looked at me with hatred. "You just will not understand. The point is these quilts, *these* quilts!"

"Well," I said, stumped. "What would *you* do with them?"

"Hang them," she said. As if that was the only thing you *could* do with quilts.

Maggie by now was standing in the door. I could almost hear the sound her feet made as they scraped over each other.

"She can have them, Mama," she said, like somebody used to never winning anything, or having anything reserved for her. "I can 'member Grandma Dee without the quilts."

I looked at her hard. She had filled her bottom lip with checkerberry snuff[15] and it gave her face a kind of dopey, hangdog look. It was Grandma Dee and Big Dee who taught her how to quilt herself. She stood there with her scarred hands hidden in the folds of her skirt. She looked at her sister with something like fear but she wasn't mad at her. This was Maggie's portion. This was the way she knew God to work.

When I looked at her like that something hit me in the top of my head and ran down to the soles of my feet. Just like when I'm in church and the spirit of God touches me and I get happy and shout. I did something I never had done before: hugged Maggie to me, then dragged her on into the room, snatched the quilts out of Miss Wangero's hands and dumped them into Maggie's lap. Maggie just sat there on my bed with her mouth open.

"Take one or two of the others." I said to Dee.

But she turned without a word and went out to Hakim-a-barber.

"You just don't understand," she said, as Maggie and I came out to the car.

"What don't I understand?" I wanted to know.

"Your heritage," she said. And then she turned to Maggie, kissed her, and said, "You ought to try to make something of yourself, too, Maggie. It's really a new day for us. But from the way you and Mama still live you'd never know it."

Mrs. Johnson makes a practical suggestion: Maggie can make more quilts.

This is new. Dee is now looking at her mother with "hatred." This indicates a deep division between the two. Dee wants to have her own way and hates anyone opposing her.
    70

Maggie appears. It seems that she has heard the previous conversation.

Maggie is generous and self-effacing. She agrees to give the quilts to Dee.

The Narrator is filled with a sense   75
of deep sympathy for Maggie, who asks for little, gives much, and is resigned to the ways of Fate.

The Narrator gives the quilts, just like that, to Maggie, snatching them out of the hands of "Miss Wangero." Mrs. Johnson is certainly annoyed at Dee.

Interesting. Dee leaves the house without a word, but the Narrator and Maggie come out to her. Who   80
is superior?

---

[15]A snuff flavored with wintergreen.

She put on some sunglasses that hid everything above the tip of her nose and her chin.

The sunglasses, hiding much of Dee's face, suggest that she is living in another world from her mother and sister.

Maggie smiled; maybe at the sunglasses. But a real smile, not scared. After we watched the car dust settle I asked Maggie to bring me a dip of snuff. And then the two of us sat there just enjoying, until it was time to go in the house and go to bed.

Maggie finally smiles. Her mother has given her a vote of confidence.

Questions

1. Describe the Narrator, Mrs. Johnson. Who is she? What is she like? Where and how does she live? What kind of life has she had? How does the story bring out her judgments about her two daughters?
2. Describe Dee and Maggie. How are they different physically and mentally? How have their lives been different? How do they change during the story?
3. Why did Dee change her name? How is this change important, and how is it reflected in her desire for the family artifacts?
4. Describe the importance of the title "Everyday Use" in the story (paragraph 65). How does this phrase highlight the conflicting values in the story?

Reading and Responding in a Computer File or Notebook

The marginal comments printed with "Everyday Use" demonstrate the active reading-responding process you might try to apply to everything you read. Use the margins in your text similarly to record your comments and questions, but plan also to record your more lengthy responses in a notebook, on note cards, on separate sheets of paper, or in a computer file. Be careful not to lose anything; keep all your notes. As you progress from work to work, you will find that your written or saved comments will be immensely important to you as your record, or journal, of your first impressions together with your more carefully considered and expanded thoughts.

In keeping your notebook, your objective should be to learn assigned works inside and out and then to say perceptive things about them. To achieve this goal, you need to read the work more than once. Develop a good note-taking system so that as you read, you will create a "memory bank" of your own knowledge. You can make withdrawals from this fund of ideas when you begin to write. As an aid in developing your own procedures for reading and "depositing" your ideas, you may wish to begin with the following Guidelines for Reading. Of course, you will want to modify these suggestions and add to them as you become a more experienced and disciplined reader.

Guidelines for Reading

1. Observations for basic understanding
   a. Explain words, situations, and concepts. Write down words that are new or not immediately clear. Use your dictionary, and record the relevant

meanings in your notebook. Write down any special difficulties so that you can ask your instructor about them.

b. Determine what is happening in the work. For a story or play, where do the actions take place? What do they show? Who is involved? Who is the major figure? Why is he or she major? What relationships do the characters have with one another? What concerns do the characters have? What do they do? Who says what to whom? How do the speeches advance the action and reveal the characters? For a poem, what is the situation? Who is talking and to whom? What does the speaker say about the situation? Why does the poem end as it does and where it does?

2. Notes on first impressions
    a. Make a record of your reactions and responses. What did you think was memorable, noteworthy, funny, or otherwise striking? Did you worry, get scared, laugh, smile, feel a thrill, learn a great deal, feel proud, find a lot to think about?
    b. Describe interesting characterizations, events, techniques, and ideas. If you like a character or an idea, explain what you like, and do the same for characters and ideas you don't like. Is there anything else in the work that you especially like or dislike? Are parts easy or difficult to understand? Why? Are there any surprises? What was your reaction to them? Be sure to use your own words when writing your explanations.

3. Development of ideas and enlargement of responses
    a. Trace developing patterns. Make an outline or a scheme: What conflicts appear? Do these conflicts exist between people, groups, or ideas? How are the conflicts resolved? Is one force, idea, or side the winner? How do you respond to the winner or to the loser?
    b. Write expanded notes about characters, situations, and actions. What explanations need to be made about the characters? What is the nature of the situations (e.g., young people discover a damaged boat, and themselves, in the spring; a prisoner tries to hide her baby from cruel guards; and so on)? What is the nature of the actions (e.g., a platoon of soldiers carries out actions during the Vietnam War, a woman is told that her husband has been killed in a train wreck, a group of children are taken to a fashionable toy store, a young boy is taken by his mother to the dentist, and so on)? What are the people like, and what are their habits and customs? What sort of language do they use?
    c. Memorize important, interesting, and well-written passages. Copy them in full on note cards, and keep these in your pocket or purse. When walking to class, riding public transportation, or otherwise not fully occupying your time, learn them by heart. Please take memorization seriously.
    d. Always write down questions that come up during your reading. You may raise these in class, and trying to write out your own answers will also aid your own study.

Sample Notebook Entries on Walker's "Everyday Use"

The following entries demonstrate how you can use the foregoing guidelines in your first thoughts about a work. You should try to develop enough observations and responses to be useful later, both for additional study and for developing essays. Notice that the entries are not only comments but also questions.

> The Narrator is Mrs. Johnson. She tells about the brief homecoming of her daughter, Dee, and about her reaction and the reaction of her other daughter, Maggie. Mrs. Johnson tells the story, and, therefore, we hear a lot about how she feels.

> Mrs. Johnson has had a tough life. She is a big, husky woman and is good at doing jobs like butchering, not what is expected of a woman.

> She has had little education, because support of her public elementary school ended when she was in second grade.

> The issue of black/white relationships is important. The whites, in control of the school financing, closed the school for blacks when Mrs. Johnson was very little. She never knew why the school was closed and never dared to ask.

> Even though Mrs. Johnson had little education, she still speaks pretty well, with some occasional grammatical issues.

> When Dee comes, we see that she is a person who likes to hog people's attention. She has always assumed that she should be on top, and she behaves like it.

> Dee's companion is a short fellow with hair a foot long, whose name Mrs. Johnson believes to be Asalamalakim or "Hakim-a-barber." They are committed to Black Power and have changed their American names to names taken from Africa.

> It's kind of funny that Dee takes pictures of the place in such a way that she always gets the plain and rustic Johnson home into view. Is Dee making some kind of point?

> Dee wants to take away some of the basic but primitive things, such as parts from the family butter churn, together with two homemade quilts, to display at her present home, but just to display, not to use.

> Maggie is shy and retiring and apparently simple. When little, she received burns when the previous Johnson home was destroyed by fire. She believes that she is always second, never first. She is generous and is willing to give Dee the quilts that had been saved for her.

> Mrs. Johnson gets annoyed at some of the things that Dee is saying and doing. When Dee demands the quilts, Mrs. Johnson believes that Dee is speaking with hatred. This is big in their relationship.

> When Mrs. Johnson gives the quilts to Maggie rather than Dee, Dee leaves. As a result of being allowed to keep the quilts, Maggie seems to have become stronger and more self-possessed than she was earlier in the story.

> *Questions:* Is this story more about Dee, or Maggie, or both? Or is it about Mrs. Johnson, the Narrator? Which of these characters do we learn the most about? Why is Dee's companion, Asalamalakim, brought into the story? Are some of these details supposed to be comic? Why is such a fuss made about the two quilts? Why does Mrs. Johnson give the quilts to Maggie rather than to Dee? Does Dee go through any change in the story? Why does Mrs. Johnson speak negatively about Dee when recalling her girlhood? How important is the story's title?

These are reasonable—and also fairly full—remarks and questions about "Everyday Use." Use your notebook or journal similarly for all reading assignments. If your assignment is simply to learn about a work, general notes like these should be enough. If you are preparing for a test, you might write pointed observations that are more in line with what is happening in your class and also write and answer your own questions. If you have a writing assignment, observations like these can help you to focus more closely on your topic—such as character, idea, or setting. Whatever your purpose, always take good notes, and put in as many details and responses as you can. The notes will be invaluable to you as a mind refresher and as a wellspring of thought.

Major Stages in Thinking and Writing About Literary Topics: Discovering Ideas, Preparing to Write, Making an Initial Draft of Your Essay, and Completing the Essay

Finished writing is the sharpened, focused expression of thought and study. It begins with the search for something to say—an idea. Not all ideas are equal; some are better than others, and getting good ideas is an ability that you will develop the more you think and write. As you discover ideas and explain them in words, you will also improve your perceptions and increase your critical faculties.

In addition, because literature itself contains the subject material (though not in a systematic way) of philosophy, religion, psychology, sociology, and politics, learning to analyze literature and to write about it will also improve your capacity to deal with these and other disciplines.

Writing Does Not Come Easily—to Anyone

A major purpose of your being in college, of which your composition and literature course is a vital part, is to develop your capacities to think and to express your thoughts clearly and fully. However, the process of creating a successfully argued essay—the actual process itself of writing—is not automatic. Writing begins in uncertainty and hesitation, and it becomes certain and confident—accomplished— only as a result of great care, applied thought, a certain amount of experimentation, the passage of time, and much effort. When you read complete, polished, well-formed pieces of writing, you might assume, as many of us do, that the writers wrote their successful versions the first time they tried and never needed to make any changes and improvements at all. In an ideal world, perhaps, something like this could happen, but not in this one.

If you could see the early drafts of writing you admire, you would be surprised and startled—and also encouraged—to see that good writers are also human and that what they first write is often uncertain, vague, tangential, tentative, incomplete, and messy. Good writers do not always like their first drafts; nevertheless, they work with their efforts and build upon them. Good writers reconsider their ideas and try to restate them, discard some details, add others, chop paragraphs in half and reassemble the parts elsewhere, throw out much (and then maybe recover some of it), revise or completely rewrite sentences, change words, correct misspellings, sharpen expressions, and add new material to tie all the parts together in a smooth, natural flow.

The Goal of Writing: To Show a Process of Thought

As you approach the task of writing, keep in mind that your goal should always be to *explain* the work you are analyzing. You should never be satisfied simply to restate the events in the work. Too often, students fall easily into a pattern of retelling a story or play or summarizing the details of a poem. But nothing could be further from what is expected from good writing. **Good writing should be the embodiment of your thought; it should show your thought in action.** Thinking is an active process that does not happen accidentally. Thinking requires that you develop ideas, draw conclusions, exemplify them and support them with details, and connect everything in a coherent manner. Your goal should constantly be to explain the results of your thinking—your ideas, your play of mind over the materials of a work, your insights, your conclusions.

Approach each writing assignment in light of the following objectives: You should consider your reader to be a person who has read the work, just as you have done. This person knows what is in the work and, therefore, does not need you to restate what she or he already knows. Instead, your reader wants to learn from you what to think about it. Therefore, always, your task as a writer is to explain something about the work, to describe the thoughts that you can develop about it. Let us consider again Walker's "Everyday Use." Early in the story we learn that the narrator, Mrs. Johnson, along with her younger daughter Maggie, is anticipating a visit from her older daughter, Dee. We know this, but if we are reading an essay about the story we will want to learn more from you, as the essay writer. Let us then suppose that a first goal of one of your paragraphs is to explain the uneasiness that Mrs. Johnson feels about her daughter's return. Your paragraph might go as follows:

> In the story's first part, Walker establishes that Mrs. Johnson is not totally delighted by her daughter Dee's returning visit. That, in itself, is a surprise, and readers might wonder why she feels this way. Mrs. Johnson's thoughts go back to details about her early life with the daughters. Maggie, the younger, was badly burned in a house fire many years before, which Dee escaped. Mrs. Johnson's memory of the fire, when she rescued Maggie only to encounter Dee waiting safely outside, suggests, but only suggests, that Dee might have had something to do with the fire (6). This incident, strong in Mrs. Johnson's mind, however, might explain some of her ambiguous feelings. The same hesitation applies to her memory that Dee as an adolescent was always trying to command, always trying to be No. 1. She had a "scalding humor" (8), even in the family. She also almost literally drove away a boy, Jimmy T, who could not stand Dee's criticism and who fled to marriage with another young woman (8). It is clear that in these early paragraphs of the story, Walker is providing details that prepare readers for Mrs. Johnson's refusal of Dee's request later on—demand, really—for the two quilts that had been promised to Maggie.

Notice that this paragraph does not simply retell the story's introductory details but rather refers to the details to explain to us, as readers, the causes for Mrs. Johnson's ambiguous feelings about her elder daughter's returning visit. In short, the paragraph illustrates a process of thought involving the story's details and is not a restatement of the narrative. Here is another way in which you might use a thought to connect the same materials:

In the opening paragraphs of "Everyday Use," Walker points out the negative qualities of Dee's character. Dee has always tried to be in command and has the habit of staring people down who might disagree with her. In the judgment of the narrator, Mrs. Johnson, Dee's mother, Dee has always felt that she held things in the "palm of one hand" (2) and seems to expect that the "world never learned to say no to her" (2). As an adolescent girl, she had a strongly negative humor that, in her mother's words, were "like bubbles in lye" (8). At a time when Dee was seeing a boy, Jimmy T, she criticized and antagonized him, and he then got married to another young woman whom he would have thought of as being less critical. These details indicate that Dee, who is to appear later in the story and exhibit some of these same qualities, has a strong character but has a negative bearing that brings out opposition in others.

Here, the details are not unlike the details in the first paragraph, but they are unified by a different idea: the difficult and proud traits of the character Dee. What is important is that neither paragraph tells only the details. Instead, the paragraphs illustrate the goal of writing with a purpose. Whenever you write, you should always be trying, as in these examples, to use a dominating thought or thoughts to shape and explain the details in the work you are analyzing.

For practiced and beginning writers alike, there are four stages of thinking and writing, and in each of these, there are characteristic activities. In the beginning stage, writers try to find the details and thoughts that seem to be right for eventual inclusion in what they are hoping to write. The next (or middle) stage is characterized by written drafts, or sketches—ideas, sentences, paragraphs. An advanced stage of writing is the forming and ordering of what has previously been done—the creation and determination of final paragraphs and a final essay. Although these stages occur in a natural order, they are not separate and distinct but merge with each other and in effect are fused together. However, when you think you are close to finishing a piece of writing, you may find that you are not as close as you might have thought. You are now in the finishing or completing stage, when you need to include something else, something more, something different, and something to make things complete. At this point, you can easily go back to an earlier stage to discover new details and ideas. Your writing is always open for change and improvement until you regard it as finished or until you need to turn it in.

Discovering Ideas ("Brainstorming")

With the foregoing general goal in mind, let us assume that you have read the work about which you are to write and have made notes and observations on which you are planning to base your thought. You are now ready to consider and plan what to include in your paragraphs and essays. This earliest stage of writing is unpredictable and somewhat frustrating because you are on a search. You do not know quite what you want, for you are reaching out for ideas and you are not yet sure what they are and what you might say about them. This process of searching and discovery, sometimes called **brainstorming**, requires you to examine any and every subject that your mind can produce.

Just as you are trying to reach for ideas, however, you also should try to introduce purpose and resolution into your thought. You have to zero in on something specific and develop your ideas through this process. Although what you first write may seem indefinite, the best way to help your thinking is to put your mind, figuratively, into specific channels or grooves and then to confine your thoughts within these boundaries. What matters is to get your mind going on a particular topic and to get your thoughts down on paper or onto a computer screen. Once you can see your thoughts in front of you, you can work with them and develop them. The following drawing can be helpful to you as an illustration of the various facets of a literary work, and it will help you with discovering ways of talking about it.

Consider the work you have read—story, poem, play—as the central circle from which a number of points, like the rays of a star, shine out, some of them prominently, others less so. These points, or rays, are the various subjects, or topics, that you might decide to select in exploration, discovery, and discussion. Because some elements in a work may be more significant than others, the points are not all equal in size. Notice also that the points grow larger as they get nearer to the work, suggesting that once you have selected a point of discussion, you may amplify that point with details and your own observations about the work.

You can consider literary works in many ways, but for now, as a way of getting started, you might choose to explore (1) the work's characters, (2) its historical period and background, (3) the social and economic conditions it depicts, (4) its major ideas, (5) any of its artistic qualities, or (6) any additional ideas that seem important to you. These topics, of course, have many subtopics, but any one of them can help you in the concentration you will need for beginning your essay (and for classroom discussion). All you need is one topic, just one; don't try everything at the same time. Let us see how our illustration can be revised to account for these topics. This time the number of points is reduced to illustrate the points or approaches we have just raised (with an additional and unnamed point to represent all the other approaches that might be used for other studies). These points represent your ways of discovering ideas about the work.

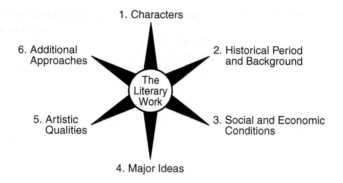

Study the Characters in the Work

You do not need to be a professional psychologist to discuss the people or characters that you find in a work. You need only to raise issues about the characters and what they do and what they represent. What are the characters like at the beginning of the work? What happens to them? Do they change in any way? What sort of change occurs, such as an alteration of personal condition or an alteration or modification of an attitude or attitudes? Does the change occur because of what the characters do? Is the change for good or for bad? What brings about the change? For example, in Walker's "Everyday Use," the narrator, Mrs. Johnson, undergoes a shift in her attitudes toward her two daughters. At the beginning, she speaks deferentially about her older daughter, Dee, and makes apologies about her younger daughter, Maggie. When the story develops to show just how demanding and possessive Dee really is, however, Mrs. Johnson bristles at Dee's demand for the quilts and refuses to give them up, giving them to Maggie instead. When Dee feels affronted and immediately leaves, it is clear that relationships between mother and daughters have changed.

In discussing character, you might also wish to raise the issue of whether the characters in the work do or don't do what might normally be expected from people in their circumstances. Do they correspond to type? The idea here is that certain attitudes and behaviors are typical of people at particular stages of life (e.g., children behaving like children, lovers dealing with their relationship, a young couple coping with difficult finances). Therefore, we might ask questions about whether the usual circumstances experienced by the characters affect them, either by limiting them in some way or by freeing them. What attitudes seem typical of the characters? How do these attitudes govern what the characters do or do not do? For example, in life, parents typically try to treat their children equally, both when the children are small and dependent and when they become adults. Life being what it is, however, along with the literature about it, both real and fictional parents sometimes have favorites among their children. Mrs. Johnson clearly has admired her daughter Dee (or perhaps respected her or felt awe toward her), but in the course of "Everyday Use," Mrs. Johnson shifts her favor to her younger daughter Maggie. One might, therefore, ask whether her change is logical or illogical—a parental attitude that is within the limits of what we think of as normality.

Determine the Work's Historical Period and Background

An obvious topic is the historical circumstances of the work. When was the work written? How well does it portray details about life at the time it appeared or the time it depicts? What is historically unique about it? To what degree does it help you learn something about the past—or the present—that you did not previously know? What actions in the work are like or unlike actions going on at the present time? What truthfulness to life do you discover in the work? "Everyday Use," for example, brings us many details about the life of poor blacks during the time of the Black Power movement following the sit-ins of the 1960s. The story revolves around the differences between a young woman who has accepted the precepts of Black Power and her mother, who has stayed in the rural South and who has also accepted her inequality as a black woman in a predominantly white society. Discussing matters like these might also help you with works written during more recent times, because even the latest assumptions, artifacts, and habits will bear analysis and discussion.

Analyze the Work's Economic and Social Conditions

Closely related to the historical period, and perhaps integral to it, an obvious topic to pursue in many works is the economic and social condition of the characters. To what level of life, economically, do the characters belong? How are events in the work related to their condition? How does their money, or lack of it, limit what they do? How do their economic circumstances either restrict or liberate their imaginations? How do their jobs and their apparent income determine their way of life? If we apply some of these issues to "Everyday Use," we can see that Mrs. Johnson and her daughter Maggie are greatly hindered by their lowly economic status. Mrs. Johnson sustains herself through much hard work that is more befitting a powerful man. She and Maggie live in Mrs. Johnson's tiny, tin-roofed home. To be comfortable, they go outside to her yard that is "like an extended living room" (5). They have few modern conveniences, or none, and instead still actively use many old-fashioned homemade objects in her household. Finally, Mrs. Johnson's lowly social status brings about a consequent acceptance of her political and social inequality as a black woman.

An important part of the economic and social analysis of literature is the consideration of female characters and what it means to be a woman. This is the feminist analysis of literature, which asks questions like these: Generally, how do female literary characters fare because of their sex? To what degree do they conform to gender typing, and to what degree are they able to be free (e.g., Mrs. Johnson does what is normally considered a man's work)? What is their relationship to the men who happen to be a part of their lives? What difficulties are imposed on them as a result of their being women? Contrastingly, what opportunities or benefits do they gain because they are women? What role are female characters able to take as a result of their sex and their family background? To what degree is their imaginative life either enhanced or restricted? Should female characters be considered as an aspect of political arguments for greater freedom for women? Once you start asking questions like these, you will find that your thinking is developing along with your ideas for writing.

The feminist approach to the interpretation of literature has been well established, and it will usually provide you with a way to discuss a work. It is also possible, of course, to analyze what a work says about the condition of being a man or being a child. Depending on the kind of literature you are reading, many of the questions that are important in a feminist approach are not dissimilar to those you might use if you are dealing with childhood or male adulthood.

One of the most important social and economic topics is that of race and ethnicity. What happens in the work that seems to occur mainly because of the race of the characters? Is the author pointing out any deprivations, any absence of opportunity, any oppression? What do the characters do under such circumstances? Do they succeed or not? Are they negative? Are they angry? Are they resolute and determined, as seems to be the outlook of Dee, Mrs. Johnson's older daughter? Your aim in an inquiry of this type should be to concentrate on actions and ideas in the work that are clearly related to race.

Explain the Work's Major Ideas

One of the major ways of focusing on a work is to zero in on various ideas, values, or issues to be discovered there. What ideas might we gain from Mrs. Johnson's recollections of her headstrong and self-absorbed daughter Dee? One idea is that when making requests from others, it is more important to be considerate than demanding. This is an idea that we might illustrate and expand in an entire essay, not to mention a paragraph. Here are some other ideas that we might also pursue, all of them based on the story's actions:

- Childhood behavior is sometimes carried over into adulthood.
- Too much enthusiasm for a cause often skews one's judgment.
- Adversity may bring out a character's good qualities.
- Many things are to be used for service, not style.

These ideas are all to be found in Walker's "Everyday Use." In other works, of course, we may find similar ideas, in addition to other major ideas and issues.

Describe the Work's Artistic Qualities

A work's artistic qualities provide many possible choices for study, but basically, here you might want to consider matters such as (1) the author's narrative method or writing style and (2) the work's plan or organization. Thus, if we discuss the narrative method of "Everyday Use," we observe that the narrator, Mrs. Johnson, begins her description of Dee with a good deal of detail, but at the same time, she provides less detail about Dee's sister Maggie. Thus, at first, the story focuses our attention on Dee, for we learn about Dee's childhood, adolescence, and present appearance and circumstances—no matter how amusing Dee may at first seem. As the story progresses, however, and as the characters interact, Mrs. Johnson tells about Dee more objectively while at the same time we learn more personal details about Maggie. For this reason, we become increasingly sympathetic to Maggie, who emerges as the more likable sister at the story's end, after Dee has departed. Another artistic approach might be to discuss the author's use of chronology in the story. Through Mrs. Johnson's narration, for example, Walker permits us to follow Dee as she sets about ransacking the Johnson family's possessions, especially the chest containing the quilts. We, therefore, understand Mrs. Johnson's developing disapproval of Dee, if not anger against her, and we also understand Mrs. Johnson's increasing favor toward Maggie. An additional aspect of Walker's artistic skill in the story is her inclusion of symbols to explain Mrs. Johnson's attitudes. A strong symbol is the earlier house fire when, we learn, Dee did nothing to help her mother and sister. Another detail that we may understand symbolically is Mrs. Johnson's "rough, man-working hands" (6), for she has needed to do heavy labor to make ends meet during her lengthy life as a single mother.

Explain Any Other Approaches That Seem Important

Additional ways of looking at a work might occur to you beyond those just described. One reader might want to deal with some of the comic or humorous parts of a story, such as those in "Everyday Use." One comically presented situation is that Dee makes sure to include the tiny house in all her photographs of the surroundings, along with Mrs. Johnson's responses to this action. Another somewhat comic element is that Mrs. Johnson and Maggie enjoy snuff together at the end of the story. Another reader might want to consider the character of Maggie alone, although she is clearly not the story's major focus. But we watch Maggie undergo change as we learn more about her, and this change would be of definite interest. It would also be of interest to track Mrs. Johnson's exact views of Dee and deal with the problem of whether Dee always put her mother off the way she does in this story—and the implications for the subject of parent-child relationships. The point here is that additional ideas may suggest themselves to you, and you should keep yourself open to explore and discuss any of these other ways of seeing and thinking.

ESSAYS AND PARAGRAPHS—FOUNDATION STONES OF WRITING

Throughout this book, there are many directions and guides for various assignments requiring either fairly full essays or shorter paragraphs. The basic idea underlying an **essay** is that the writer of an essay tries to present a comprehensive treatment of a particular idea, question, subject, issue, or topic. Originally, the word "essay" referred to an *attempt*, or *exploration*, and it was associated with "trial" in the phrase "trial and essay." That meaning is still in play, but the word is usually considered today as a writer's explorations and conclusions about a subject based on a number of connected subtopics. In short, an essay is a focused and full presentation.

In a finished essay, the major subtopics are presented not only in single sentences but also in a pattern of related sentences designed to sustain a major idea—a **paragraph**, which is a separate subpresentation in itself, but which may also be a connected section of a larger essay. Sentences build up to a paragraph; paragraphs build up to an essay; essays—as essential parts of further developing thought—build up to a section or chapter; and sections and chapters may be built up to a complete book.

A major requirement in many if not most courses is for students to write full essays for both out-of-class and in-class assignments. Essays are evaluated on how well you state an idea and on your success in creating a related pattern of argument that explores and expands on the idea. Quite often also, you may be asked for a single, stand-alone paragraph that explores just one aspect of an idea. These are the two major elements of writing that are stressed in this book. For each of the chapters, you will be asked to develop essays and paragraphs in relation to the works of literature that will be assigned for your reading, understanding, enjoyment, and benefit.

Depending on the available time for both out-of-class and in-class writing (including the writing of tests), your instructor may designate either full-scale essays or single paragraphs for your assignments. Writing a single paragraph helps you to build up your preparation for essays. Accordingly, the writing of paragraphs will help you to control topic sentences and immediately related topical development, meaning that you include details that illustrate the ideas you have stated at the beginnings of your paragraphs. You should constantly be practicing this habit of mind as you develop your analytical skills for all your courses, not just for those in reading and writing about literature. Throughout this book, therefore, each of the writing sections will be directed toward possible assignments for either single paragraphs or full-scale essays. The successful writing of paragraphs leads naturally toward the buildup of paragraphs in full essays, just as the successful writing of essays depends on the proper development and ordering of individual paragraphs.

Preparing to Write

By this time, you will already have been focusing on your topic and will have assembled much that you can put into your essay. You should now aim to develop paragraphs and sketches of what you will eventually include. You should think constantly of the point or argument you want to develop, but invariably, digressions will occur, together with other difficulties—false starts, dead ends, total cessation of thought, digressions, despair, hopelessness, and general frustration. Remember, however, that it is important just to start. Jump right in and start writing anything at all—no matter how unacceptable your first efforts might seem—and force yourself to deal with the materials. Get going. The writing down of ideas does not commit you. You should not think that these first ideas are untouchable and holy just because you have written them on paper or on your computer screen. You can throw them out in favor of new ideas; you can make cross-outs and changes; and you can move paragraphs or even sections around as you wish. However, if you do not start writing, your first thoughts will remain locked in your mind, and you will have nothing to work with. You must learn to accept the uncertainties in the writing process and make them work *for* you rather than *against* you.

Build Ideas from Your Original Notes

You need to get your mind going by mining your notebook or computer file for useful things you have already written. Thus, let us use an observation in our original set of notes—"When Dee comes, we see that she is a person who likes to hog people's attention."—in reference to the ways in which Dee comes to her mother's home and immediately begins to take charge. With such a note as a start, you might develop a number of ideas to support an argument about Dee's character, as in the following:

> When Dee comes, we see that she is a person who likes to hog people's attention. She has always assumed that she should be on top, and she behaves like it. Her dress is so loud that her mother claims that it hurts her eyes. Dee is also wearing flashy gold earrings and noisy bracelets.

> On Dee's first appearance, she grabs her Polaroid camera and takes pictures of her mother's home. Dee snaps her mother and sister, Maggie, and makes sure to get the home into the background of each picture. She even manages to get a cow to stand still long enough to picture the animal in front of the house. It isn't until she has taken enough pictures that she kisses her mother on the forehead, something she should have done right away.

> When her mother addresses her as "Dee," Dee immediately denies the name. She also states that Dee is "dead," certainly a bombshell to her mother. Then, to indicate her status or her individuality, or whatever, she announces that she has taken a new name in place of the old, and she indicates that she now has three names: "Wangero Leewanika Kemanjo." It is fair to say that Dee's mother is surprised and shocked by this news.

In this way, even in an assertion as basic as "she is a person who likes to hog people's attention," the process of putting together details is a form of concentrated thought that leads you creatively forward. You can express thoughts and conclusions that you could not express at the beginning. Such an exercise in stretching your mind leads you to put elements of the work together in ways that create ideas for good paragraphs and essays.

Trace Patterns of Action and Thought

You can also discover ideas by making a list or scheme for the story or main idea. What conflicts appear? Do these conflicts exist between people, groups, or ideas? How does the author resolve them? Is one force, idea, or side the winner? Why? How do you respond to the winner or to the loser? Using this method, you might make a list similar to this one:

The story's beginning describes past conflicts or contrasts between Mrs. Johnson and her daughter Dee.

After Dee enters with Asalamalakim, does it seem that Dee is slightly ashamed of her family? Why does she want to assert herself about being given household objects that will be of no use to her?

A number of Dee's actions seem to produce negative reactions in Mrs. Johnson, whose joy at seeing Dee is replaced as the story develops.

The argument over household possessions marks a high point of the family antagonism. Dee wants the butter churn dasher and the quilts as objects to be displayed on a wall or on a shelf, as an emblem of outmoded but quaint family objects that are to be seen as part of a past and outmoded age.

These conflicts revolve around Dee, but you might wish to trace other patterns that you find in the story. If you start planning an essay about another pattern, be sure to account for all the actions and scenes that relate to your topic. Otherwise, you might miss a piece of evidence that could lead you to new conclusions.

THE NEED FOR THE ACTUAL PHYSICAL PROCESS OF WRITING

Thinking and writing are interdependent processes. If you don't get your thoughts into words that are visible to you on a paper or computer screen, your thinking will be impeded. It is, therefore, vital for you to use the writing process itself as an essential means of developing your ideas. If you are doing an assignment in class—tests or impromptu essays—write your initial responses on a single side of your paper. So elementary a strategy will enable you to see everything together and to spread your materials out to get an actual physical overview of them when you begin writing. Everything will be open to you; none of your ideas will be hidden on the other side of the paper.

Outside of class, however, when you are at home or otherwise able to use a computer or other word processor, your machine is an indispensable tool for your writing. It will help you to develop ideas, for it quickly enables you to eliminate unworkable thoughts and to replace them with others. You can move sentences and paragraphs into new contexts, test how they look, and move them somewhere else if you choose.

In addition, with the rapid printers that are now available, you can print even the initial and tentative stages of writing. Using the printed draft, you can make additional notes, corrections, and suggestions for further development. With the marked-up draft as a guide, you can go back to the word processor and fill in your changes and improvements, repeating this procedure as often as you can. This facility makes the machine an incentive for improvement, right up to your final draft.

Word processing also helps you in the final preparation of your essays. Studies have shown that errors and awkward sentences are frequently found at the bottoms of pages that are prepared by hand or with a conventional typewriter. The reason is that writers hesitate to make improvements when they get near the end of a page because they want to avoid the dreariness of writing or typing the page over. Word processors eliminate this difficulty completely. Changes can be made anywhere in the draft, at any time, without any ill effect on the final appearance of your work.

Regardless of your writing method, you should always remember that unwritten thought is incomplete thought. You cannot lay everything out at once on the word processor's screen. You can see only a small part of what you are writing. Therefore, somewhere in your writing process, you need to prepare a complete draft of what you have written. A clean, readable draft permits you to gather everything together and to make even more improvements through revision.

Raise and Answer Your Own Questions

A habit that you should always cultivate is to raise your own questions and try to answer them yourself as you consider your reading. The guidelines for reading will help you to formulate questions (pp. 14–17), but you can raise additional questions like these:

- What is happening as the work unfolds? How does an action at the beginning of the work bring about later actions and speeches?
- Who are the main characters? What seems unusual or different about what they do in the work?
- What conclusions can you draw about the work's actions, scenes, and situations? Explain these conclusions.
- What are the characters and speakers like? What do they do and say about themselves, their goals, the people around them, their families, their friends, their work, and the general circumstances of their lives?
- What kinds of words do the characters use: formal or informal words, slang or profanity?
- What literary conventions and devices have you discovered, and how do these affect the work? (When an author addresses readers directly, for example, that is a convention; when a comparison is used, that is a device, which might be either a metaphor or a simile.)

Of course, you can raise other questions as you reread the piece, or you can be left with one or two major questions that you decide to pursue.

A Plus-Minus, Pro-Con, or Either-Or Method for Ideas

A common and very helpful method of discovering ideas is to develop a set of contrasts: plus-minus, pro-con, either-or. Let us try a plus-minus method of considering the following question about Dee: Is she likable (plus) or not likable (minus)?

Plus: Likable	**Minus: Not likable**
Dee is self-confident and dresses to attract attention. Her bracelets make a noise as she moves her arms. She expresses her thoughts and opinions freely.	Dee's self-confidence makes her somewhat inconsiderate of others, even her sister and her mother, who mentions that Dee when younger was characterized by "faultfinding" (8).
She does appreciate the past, for she fondly praises the benches that had been made by "her daddy" (10). She knows about, and likely appreciates, her past relatives who had made the objects in her mother's home.	She thinks that the "new day for us" (13) of Black Power denies the meaning and vitality of the past. In this respect, her thinking is contradictory.
She is artistic and is able to visualize where some of the homemade objects, which she considers her "heritage" (13), would fit artistically into her present home.	Her artistic appreciation limits her vision, so she thinks the past objects have no place in modern ways of living. Thus, she thinks that the family quilts would be spoiled by "everyday use" (12).
Even as a child, Dee believed strongly in what she was learning and would read to her family with great and demanding enthusiasm.	The things she read were impractical, and she "washed" her family "in a river of make-believe" (10).

By putting contrasting observations side by side in this way, you will find that ideas will start to come naturally and will be helpful to you when you begin writing, regardless of how you finally organize your essay or your paragraph. It is possible, for example, that you might develop either column as the argumentative basis of an essay, or you might use your notes to support the idea that Dee is too complex to be considered either as wholly negative or wholly positive. You might also want to introduce an entirely new topic of development, such as that Dee might not understand the effects she has on others or that she might be a character who is dominated by her own self-esteem. In short, arranging materials in the plus-minus pattern is a powerful way to discover ideas—a truly helpful habit of promoting thought—that can lead to ways of development that you do not at first realize.

Originate and Develop Your Thoughts Through Writing

Always write down what you are thinking for, as a principle, unwritten thought is incomplete thought. Make a practice of writing your observations about the work in addition to any questions that occur to you. This is an exciting step in preliminary writing because it can be useful when you write later drafts. You will discover that looking at what you have written can not only enable you to correct and improve the writing you have done but also lead you to recognize that you need more. The process goes like this: "Something needs to be added here—important details that my reader will not have noticed, new support for my argument, a new idea that has just occurred to me, a significant connection to link my thoughts." If you follow such a process, you will be using your own written ideas to create new ideas. You will be advancing your own abilities as a thinker and writer.

The processes just described of searching for ideas, or brainstorming, are useful for you at any stage of composition. Even when you are fairly close to finishing your essay, you might suddenly recognize that you need to add something more (or subtract something you don't like). When that happens, you may return to the discovery or brainstorming process to initiate and develop new ideas and new arguments.

Making an Initial Draft of Your Assignment

As you use the brainstorming and focusing techniques, you are also in fact beginning your essay, or your paragraph. You will need to revise your ideas as connections among them become clearer and as you reexamine the work to discover details to support the argument you are making. By this stage, however, you already have many of the raw materials you need for developing your topic.

Base Your Writing on a Central Statement, Argument, or Idea

By definition, an essay *is an organized, connected, and fully developed set of paragraphs that expand on a* **central idea, central argument,** or **central statement**. All parts of an essay should contribute to the reader's understanding of the idea. To achieve unity and completeness, each separate paragraph refers to the argument and demonstrates how selected details from the work relate to it and support it. The central idea helps you to control and shape your essay, just as it also provides guidance for your reader.

A successful essay about literature is a brief but thorough (not exhaustive) examination of a literary work in light of topics like those we have already raised: character, background, and economic conditions to circumstances of gender, major ideas, artistic qualities, and any additional topic such as point of view and symbolism. Central ideas or arguments might be (1) that a character is strong and tenacious, or (2) that the story shows the unpredictability of action, or (3) that the point of view makes the action seem "distant and objective," or (4) that a major symbol governs the actions and thoughts of the major characters. In essays on these topics, all materials must be tied to such central ideas or arguments. Thus, it is a fact that Dee in "Everyday Use," after being away after a period of time, has returned home to visit her mother and sister. This is of course true, but it is not relevant to an essay or paragraph development about her character unless you connect it to a central argument showing how it demonstrates one of her major traits: her adoption of a new way of life in comparison to a different set of ideas she might have believed when younger.

Look through all of your ideas for one or two that catch your eye for development. In all the early stages of preliminary writing, the chances are that you have already discovered at least a few ideas that are more thought provoking or more important than the others.

Once you have chosen an idea that you think you can work with, write it as a complete sentence that is essential to the argument of your essay. A simple phrase such as "appearance and character" does not focus thought the way a sentence does.

THE NEED FOR A SOUND ARGUMENT
IN WRITING ABOUT LITERATURE

As you write about literature, you should always try to connect your explanations to a specific argument; that is, you are writing about a specific work, but you are trying to prove—or argue or demonstrate—a point or idea about it. This book provides you with a number of separate subjects relating to the study of literature. As you select one of these and begin writing, however, you are not to explain just that such-and-such a story has a character who changes and grows or that such-and-such a poem contains the thought that nature creates great beauty. Rather, you should assert the importance of your topic to the work as a whole in relation to a specific point or argument. One example of an argument might be that a story's first-person point of view permits readers to draw their own conclusions about the speaker's character. Another argument might be that the poet's thought is shown in a poem's details about the bustling sounds and sights of birds and other animals in springtime.

Let us, therefore, repeat and stress that your writing *should always have an argumentative edge*—a goal of demonstrating the truth of your conclusions and clarifying and illuminating your idea about the topic and about the work. It is here that the accuracy of your choices of details from the work, the soundness of your conclusions, and the cumulative weight of your evidence are essential. You cannot allow your main ideas to rest on one detail alone but must support your conclusions by showing that the bulk of material leads to them and that they are linked in a reasonable chain of fact and logic. It is such clarification that is the goal of argumentation.

The following sentence moves the topic toward new exploration and discovery because it combines a topic with an outcome: "Dee's dress and manner in 'Everyday Use' reflect her character." You can choose to be even more specific: "Dee's dress and speech in "Everyday Use" show her as a positive but perhaps heedless person."

Now that you have phrased a single, central idea or argument, you have also established a guide by which you can accept, reject, rearrange, and change the ideas you have been planning to develop. You can now draft a paragraph (for a single paragraph) or a few paragraphs (for a complete essay). Naturally, you may base your drafts on some of the sketches you have already made, for you should always adapt as much as you can from your first observations. Try to determine whether your idea seems valid or whether it would be more helpful to make an outline or a list before you do more writing. In either case, you should use your notes for evidence to connect to your central idea. If you need to bolster your argument with more supporting details and ideas, go once again to the techniques of discovery and brainstorming.

Using the central idea that Dee's dress and speech in "Everyday Use" reveal the nature of her character, a paragraph might be written as the following, which presents observations originally taken and somewhat changed from the list about her likable qualities:

> The description of Dee's way of dressing in "Everyday Use" shows her as a positive person. She is self-confident and attracts attention through her colorful clothes. Her "loud" dress, about which her mother says, "I like it" (9), goes to the ground and makes her seem to flow as she walks. Her dangling bracelets make a noise when she moves her arms.

In such a beginning draft, in which the purpose is to connect details and thoughts to the major idea, a number of details from the story are used in support. In all stages of writing, such use of details essential.

Create a Thesis Sentence as Your Guide to Organizing Your Essay

With your central idea or argument as your focus in a developing essay, you can decide which of the earlier observations and ideas can be developed further. Your goal is to establish a number of major topics to support your argument and to express them in a **thesis sentence** or **thesis statement**—an organizing sentence that contains the major topics you plan to develop in your essay. Suppose you choose three ideas from your discovery stage of development. If you put the central idea at the left and the list of topics at the right, you have the shape of the thesis sentence. Note that the first two topics below are taken from the discovery paragraph.

Central Idea	Topics
Dee, of "Everyday Use," is positive but also overbearing.	1. Dress and jewelry
	2. Plans for home decoration
	3. Quilts and butter churn parts

This arrangement can be fashioned to the following thesis statement or thesis sentence

> Dee's positive but overbearing character is connected to her dress and jewelry, her genuine plans for home decoration, and her wish to be given parts from the family butter churn along with two home-sewn quilts.

You can revise the thesis sentence at any stage of the writing process if you find that you do not have enough evidence from the work to support it. Perhaps a new topic will occur to you, and you can include it, appropriately, as a part of your thesis sentence.

As we have seen, the central idea or central argument is the *glue* of the essay. The thesis sentence lists the parts to be fastened together—that is, the topics in which the central idea is to be demonstrated and argued. To alert your readers to your essay's structure, the thesis sentence is usually placed at the end of the introductory paragraph, just before the body of the essay.

As you write your first draft, you need to support the points of your thesis sentence with your notes and discovery materials. You can alter, reject, and rearrange ideas and details as you wish, as long as you change your thesis sentence to account for the changes (a major reason why many writers write their introductions last). The thesis sentence just shown contains three topics (it could be two, or four, or more) to be used in forming the body of the essay.

Begin Each Paragraph with a Topic Sentence

Just as the organization of the *entire essay* is based on the thesis, the form of each *paragraph* is based on a **topic sentence**—an assertion about how one of the topics in the predicate of the thesis statement supports the argument contained or implied in the central idea. The first topic in our example is the relationship of Dee's character to her dress and jewelry, and the resulting paragraph should emphasize this relationship. If your topic is the relationship of her character to her plans for home decoration, you can then form a topic sentence by connecting the trait with the location, as follows:

> Her plans, or hopes, for home decoration show that she has a positive sense of developing her own home.

Beginning with this sentence, the paragraph should contain details that argue how Dee's behavior after dinner shows that she, too, has a sense of home that is like the sense of home and stability that is shown by her mother.

REFERRING TO THE NAMES OF AUTHORS

As a general principle, for both men and women writers, you should regularly include the author's *full name* in the *first sentence* of your essay. Here are model first sentences.

> Shirley Jackson's "The Lottery" is a story featuring suspense and horror.
>
> "The Lottery," by Shirley Jackson, is a story featuring suspense and horror.

For all later references, use only last names, such as *Jackson, Walker, Lawrence,* or *Porter.* However, for the "giants" of literature, you should use the last names exclusively. In referring to writers like Shakespeare and Dickinson, for example, there is no need to include *William* or *Emily.*

In spite of today's informal standards, never use an author's first name alone, as in "*Shirley* skillfully creates suspense and horror in 'The Lottery.'" Also, do not use a courtesy title before the names of dead authors, such as "*Ms.* Jackson's 'The Lottery' is a suspenseful horror story" or "*Mr.* Shakespeare's idea is that information is uncertain." Use the last names alone.

As with all conventions, of course, there are exceptions. If you are referring to a childhood work of a writer, the first name might be appropriate, but be sure to shift to the last name when referring to the writer's mature works. If your writer has a professional or a noble title, such as "*Lord* Byron" or "*Queen* Elizabeth," it is not improper to use the title. Even then, however, the titles are commonly omitted for males, so most references to Lord Byron and Alfred, Lord Tennyson, should be simply to "Byron" and "Tennyson."

Referring to living authors is problematic. Some journals and newspapers regularly use the courtesy titles *Mr.* and *Ms.* in their reviews. However, scholarly journals, which are likely to remain on library shelves and Web sites for many decades, follow the general principle of beginning with the entire name and then using only the last name for later references.

Select Only One Topic—No More—for Each Paragraph

You should treat each separate topic in a single paragraph: one topic, one paragraph. This principle holds true for both paragraph-length and essay-length assignments. However, if a topic seems especially difficult, long, and heavily detailed, you can divide it into two or more subtopics, each receiving a separate paragraph of its own: two or more subtopics, two or more separate paragraphs. Should you make this division, your topic then is really a section, or part, and each paragraph in the section should have its own topic sentence.

THE USE OF VERB TENSES IN THE DISCUSSION OF LITERARY WORKS

Literary works spring into life with each and every reading. You may, therefore, assume that everything happening takes place in the present, and when writing about literature, you should use the *present tense of verbs*. It is correct to say, "After Dee and Asalamalakim leave [not 'left'], Mrs. Johnson and Maggie sit outside [not 'sat outside'] for the rest of the evening, 'just enjoying' snuff and each other's company."

When you consider an author's ideas, the present tense is also proper, on the principle that the words of an author are just as alive and current today (and tomorrow) as they were at the moment of writing, even if this author might have been dead for hundreds or even thousands of years. Indeed, one of the plays that is regularly read and discussed by American students, *Oedipus the King* by the ancient Greek dramatist Sophocles, was written just about 2500 years ago. It is still proper to speak of events in this drama in the present tense.

Because it is incorrect to shift tenses inappropriately, you may encounter a problem when you refer to actions that have occurred before the time of the main action. An instance is Glaspell's short play *Trifles*, in which the main character, Minnie Wright (who is described but never actually appears), is the principal suspect in the murder of her husband. As the play develops, we learn much about the lonely and miserable life she led on a lonely Iowa farm with her husband, who was unkind, insensitive, uncommunicative, and in fact cruel. The play's dialogue provides the narrative details that point to Minnie as the actual murderer, but the details also suggest that Minnie's action was her understandable reaction to her isolated farm life. In fact, the play makes the case for understanding Minnie and not condemning her. In discussing such a complex play, it would be important to keep details of the past and the present in order, and if you are discussing the causes and effects, it would be necessary to introduce the past tense, as long as you make the relationship clear between past and present, as in the following sentences: "Minnie is in fact guilty of her husband's murder [present]. She clearly did it [past]. But the dialogue of the two principal women on stage during the play [present] shows Minnie's mental state [present] about her past life and leads us to conclude that her thoughts had been dwelling on the endlessly isolated and dreary life she *knew* [past] at her own home with her cold and hateful husband." This commingling of past and present situations and tenses is suitable as the basis of a discussion because it corresponds to the pattern of time brought out in the reconstruction of Minnie's solitary, painful, and dreary life.

A problem also arises when you introduce historical or biographical details about a work or author. It is appropriate to use the *past tense* for such details if they genuinely do belong to the past. Thus, it is correct to state, "Shakespeare *lived* from 1564 to 1616" or "Shakespeare *wrote* his tragedy *Hamlet* in about 1600–1601." It is also permissible to mix past and present tenses when you are treating historical facts about a literary work and are also considering it as a living text. Of prime importance is to keep things straight. Here is an example showing how past tenses (in bold) and present tenses (in italic) may be used when appropriate:

> Because *Hamlet* **was** first **performed** in about 1601, Shakespeare most probably **wrote** it shortly before this time. In the play, a tragedy, Shakespeare *treats* an act of vengeance, but more importantly he *demonstrates* the difficulty of ever learning the exact truth. The hero, Prince Hamlet, *is* the focus of this difficulty, for the task of revenge *is assigned* to him by the Ghost of his father. Though the Ghost *claims* that his brother, Claudius, *is* his murderer, Hamlet *is* not able to verify this claim during most of the play.

> Here, the historical details are in the past tense, while all details about the play *Hamlet*, including Shakespeare as the creating author whose ideas and words are still alive, are in the present.

> As a general principle, you will be right most of the time if you use the present tense exclusively for literary details and the past tense for historical details. When in doubt, consult your instructor.

Use Your Topic Sentences as the Arguments for Your Paragraph Development

Once you have created a topic sentence, you can use it to focus your observations and conclusions. Let us see how our topic (see p. 32) about Dee's clothes and her character can be developed persuasively within a paragraph. Such a paragraph may stand alone, depending on your assignment, or it may be fitted in as part of a larger essay.

Illustrative Paragraph

> In "Everyday Use," Dee's way of dressing shows her positive nature. She self-confidently attracts attention through her colorful clothes, for she is obviously dressing to be noticed. Her "loud" dress, about

which her mother says, "I like it," goes "down to the ground" and makes her seem almost to flow as she walks. She wears earrings "down to her shoulders," and her dangling bracelets make a distinct noise when she moves her arms. Even her hair shows her self-confidence, for it "stands straight up" like "wool on a sheep," and her two long pigtails "rope about like small lizards" (9). A shy and retiring woman would not draw attention to herself in this way, but Dee, with her strong views about herself, truly clamors to be seen and noticed.

Here, as in the earlier paragraph, details from the story are introduced to provide support for the topic sentence's assertion that Dee is a strongly (and also overly) positive person. All the paragraph's details—the flamboyantly loud dress, the earrings, the bracelets, and the self-conscious hair—are introduced not to retell the story but rather to exemplify the argument the writer is making about Dee's character.

Develop an Outline as the Means of Organizing Your Essay

So far, we have been creating a de facto **outline**—that is, a skeletal plan of organization. Some writers never use any outline at all but prefer informal lists of ideas; others always rely on outlines; still others insist that they cannot make an outline until they have finished writing. Then there are those writers who simply hate outlines. Regardless of your preference, your final essay should have a tight structure that can stand up to the rigor of an outline. Therefore, you should use a guiding outline to develop and shape your essay.

The outline on which we focus here is the **analytical sentence outline**. This type is easier to create than it sounds. It consists of (1) an introduction, including the central idea and the thesis sentence, together with (2) topic sentences that are to be used in each paragraph of the body, followed by (3) a conclusion. When applied to the subject we have been developing, such an outline looks like this:

Title: Mrs. Johnson's Overly Self-Assured Daughter, Dee, in Walker's "Everyday Use"

1. **Introduction**
   a. *Central idea:* Walker uses ordinary details to show Dee's overly self-assured character.
   b. *Thesis statement:* Dee's characteristics are shown by her dress and jewelry, her passion for home decoration, and her demand to be given some of the Johnson family's homemade things.

2. **Body:** *Topic sentences* a, b, and c (and d, e, and f, if necessary)
   a.   Details about Dee's way of dressing show her sense of self-awareness.
   b.   Dee's plans for using family things in her own home indicate her sense of home decoration and also her sense of heritage.
   c.   Her demand to take the homemade quilts away, however, reflects her sense that her wishes should be considered first, certainly a selfish quality.
3. **Conclusion**
   Topic sentence: The dramatic development of the story hinges on Dee's sense of wanting things for herself.

The conclusion is generally the freest part of an outline. It may be a summary of the body of he essay; it may evaluate the main idea; it may briefly suggest further points of discussion; or it may be a reflection on the details of the body.

The illustrative essays that are included throughout this book are organized according to the structure of the analytical sentence outline. To emphasize the shaping effect of these outlines, all central ideas, thesis sentences, and topic sentences are underlined. In your own writing, you may wish to underline or italicize these "skeletal" sentences as a demonstration of your organization. Unless your instructor requires such markings, however, remove them in your final drafts.

1. **A PARAGRAPH ASSIGNMENT: What is the attitude of Dee (Wangero) toward the handmade quilts in her mother's storage chest? How are her feelings different from those of her sister Maggie?**

> Although underlined sentences are not recommended by MLA style, underlines are used in this illustrative paragraph as a teaching tool to emphasize the topic sentence of the paragraph.

[1] Dee (Wangero) asks for the hand-made quilts so that she may keep them as showpieces, but her sister Maggie has expected to have them for "everyday use" (12). [2] Wangero sees the quilts as artworks that represent the past culture of her family, and she says that she would like to hang the quilts for display because they are "priceless" (12). [3] When Mrs. Johnson offers other quilts as substitutes, Wangero rejects them because they "are stitched around the borders by machine" (12). [4] On the other hand, for Maggie, just as for Mrs. Johnson, the quilts are things that are still useful and, therefore, still vital in their lives. [5] This concern is shown in the fact that Mrs. Johnson has offered the quilts to Maggie for when she marries John Thomas and starts her own home (12). [6] To Wangero, this practical view has nothing to do

with the artistic importance of the handmade quilts as a sign of an old-fashioned way of life. [7] But for Maggie, inheriting the handmade quilts for practical use is a sign of her mother's love that links Maggie to her ancestors. [8] Even so, Maggie shows her family love—something that Wangero does not show—when she volunteers to give up Mrs. Johnson's gift because, as she says, "I can 'member Grandma Dee without the quilts" (13).

Commentary on the Paragraph

The first sentence, the topic sentence, announces in general terms the different attitudes of the two sisters toward the handmade quilts. By pointing to specific evidence from the story, sentences 2 and 3 amplify Wangero's view of the quilts and why they are so important to her. Sentences 4, 5, and 6 contrast Maggie's interests in the quilts with those of Wangero, offering evidence particularly of Maggie's practical and "everyday" view as opposed to Wangero's "artistic" view. Sentences 7 and 8 assert the importance of love of family by Maggie, a love that is lacking in Wangero.

> 2. AN ESSAY ASSIGNMENT: Write an essay describing the character of Dee in Walker's "Everyday Use."

The following illustrative full essay is designed to illustrate the qualities of writing that have been presented so far in this chapter. It follows our outline, and it includes details from the story in support of the various topics. However, it is by no means as good a piece of writing as it could be. In the discussion following this essay, there will be details about how writing may be improved by various specific means. The discussion reveals how benefits may be made through additional brainstorming and discovery-prewriting techniques. On page 49, you will find an advanced version of the following essay, showing how improvements have been carried out.

Although underlined sentences are not recommended by MLA style, they are used in this illustrative essay as teaching tools to emphasize the central idea, thesis sentence, and topic sentences.

Mrs. Johnson's Overly Self-Assured Daughter,
Dee, in Walker's "Everyday Use"

In "Everyday Use," Alice Walker vividly presents her four [1]
major characters: Mrs. Johnson, Dee, Maggie, and Asalamalakim.
The narrator, Mrs. Johnson, describes herself fully, well enough to
give readers a strong understanding of what she is actually like.
Even more vivid, however, is the presentation of the older daughter
Dee, who is coming back home for a visit after having been away at
college and elsewhere for a number of years. To those at home, Dee
is like a returning heroine, and, at first she may really seem to be
one. Walker uses ordinary, everyday details to show her overly
self-assured character.[16] All the details in the story about Dee are
presented to bring out this quality. Her characteristics are shown
by her dress and jewelry, her passion for home decoration, her
demand to be given some of the Johnson family's homemade
things.[17]

Dee's way of dressing shows her positive nature. She self- [2]
confidently attracts attention through her colorful clothes, for she
is obviously dressing to be noticed. Her "loud" dress—about which
her mother says, "I like it" (Walker, 8)—goes "down to the ground"
and makes her seem almost flowing as she walks. Her earrings hang
"to her shoulders," and her dangling bracelets make a distinct noise
when she moves her arms. Even her hair shows her self-confidence,
for it "stands straight up" like "wool on a sheep," and her two long
pigtails "rope about like small lizards" (8). A shy and retiring
woman would not draw attention to herself in this way, but Dee,
with strong views about her own importance, clamors to be seen
and noticed.

Dee's plans for using family things in her own home indicate [3]
her sense of home decoration and also her sense of heritage.
When she praises the kitchen benches that "her daddy made"

---

[16]Central idea.
[17]Thesis sentence.

at some time in the past (10), she speaks respectfully and enthusiastically, and it, therefore, seems reasonable that she would want to take something away with her as a keepsake (11). Her picking the churn top from the family butter churn, together with the churn's dasher, therefore is natural, because these pieces were whittled by Uncle Buddy and by Stash, who were family members—now, presumably, gone. It is fair to say that her wishes for these things show that she can be respectful and likable.

[4]   Her demands to take the homemade quilts away, however, reflect her sense that her wishes should be considered first, certainly a selfish quality. When Dee first speaks of the now dead women in the family who made the quilts, she denies their importance (9). And so her desire for the two quilts is contradictory. Her wish for the quilts is positive, but her demand for them is negative, because it leads to the story's major conflict. Maybe she doesn't know that Mrs. Johnson had promised to give the quilts to Dee's sister, Maggie, the bashful and quiet one, but by her demand, Dee antagonizes her mother. Mrs. Johnson sees Dee's self-assurance in this conflict as selfishness that has reached the point of hatred (13), and, thus, Dee provokes Mrs. Johnson's justifiable anger.

[5]   The dramatic development of the story hinges on Dee's sense of wanting things for herself. Almost immediately, Dee demeans the significance not only of her mother and sister but also of the heritage she claims to value at the story's end. Her denial of her given birth name is a clear slap in the face of her mother, and throughout the story, she constantly belittles her home. When the family enjoys their meal together, Dee seems civil and happy, but almost immediately she begins making demands, and it is the selfishness of her wishes that enables Mrs. Johnson and Maggie to enjoy themselves once she has gone.

Work Cited

Walker, Alice. "Everyday Use." Edgar V. Roberts, *Writing About
Literature*. 13th ed. New York: Pearson, 2012. 5–14. Print.

Completing the Essay: Developing and Strengthening Your Essay Through Revision

After finishing an essay like this one, you might wonder what more you can do. Things might seem to be complete as they are, and that's it. You have read the work several times, have used discovering and brainstorming techniques to establish ideas to write about, have made an outline of your ideas, and have written a full draft. How can you do better?

The best way to begin is to observe that a major mistake writers make when writing about literature is to do no more than retell a story or summarize an idea. Retelling a story shows only that you have read it, not that you have thought about it. Writing a good essay requires you to arrange a pattern of argument and thought.

Make Your Own Arrangement of Details and Ideas

One way to escape the trap of summarizing stories and to set up a pattern of development is to stress your own order when referring to parts of a work. Rearrange details to suit your own central idea or argument. It is often important to write first about the conclusion or the middle. Should you find that you have followed the chronological order of the work instead of stressing your own order, you can use one of the preliminary writing techniques to figure out new ways to connect your materials. The principle is that you should introduce details about the work *only* to support the points you wish to make. Details for the sake of detail are unnecessary.

Use Literary Material as Evidence to Support Your Argument

When you write, you are like a detective using clues as evidence for building a case or a lawyer citing evidence to support an argument. Your goal is to convince your readers of your knowledge and the reasonableness of your conclusions. It is vital to use evidence convincingly so that your readers can follow your ideas. Let us look briefly at two drafts of an additional paragraph to see how writing can be improved by the pointed use of details. These are about the character Dee in Walker's "Everyday Use."

Paragraph 1

A major flaw in Dee's character is that she considers other people to be unimportant. When she first appears in the story, she does not immediately embrace her mother but spends an untold number of minutes taking pictures of the house and the cows wandering around in the pasture. It is only then that she kisses her mother and then only on the forehead. When her mother addresses her as "Dee," she immediately says that she has a new name and that Dee is "dead." Although there is a happier time at the table when everyone is enjoying dinner, Dee immediately begins spoiling things by asking about what she might take away once she and Asalamalakim leave to go back home. She wants some whittled parts of the family butter churn and discovers some quilts that she thinks would look good hanging in her home far away from the house in which her mother and sister live. When her mother refuses to give her the quilts, she gets up and leaves with Asalamalakim. Her last words, however, are that both her mother and sister are living in the past, as though nothing new is happening socially and politically, even though she says that it is "really a new day for us."

Paragraph 2

A major flaw in Dee's character is that she considers other people to be unimportant. For example, when she first gets out of the car, she ignores her family but instead takes photos of the home, as though her closest family is worth less than the home. This same devaluation is shown by her kissing her mother only on the forehead and avoiding an embrace. When she says that she has taken a new name, she surprises her mother, and her denial of her birth name seems to be another slap in the face. She clearly thinks the people in her family are unimportant, and she, therefore, does not ask how they are or what they have been doing but rather asks about homemade family artifacts to take away when she leaves. When she picks the quilts, she assumes that they are rightfully hers, regardless of Maggie's previous claim. After her demand is rejected, she gets up and leaves, but not before telling her mother and sister how to improve their lives, as though they were incapable of any ideas of their own.

A comparison of these paragraphs shows that the first one, on the left, has more words than the second, on the right (212 compared to 183) but that it is more appropriate for a rough draft than for a final draft because the writer does little more than retell the story. Paragraph 1 is cluttered with details that do not support any conclusions. If you try to find what it says about Walker's use of Dee's selfish outlook in "Everyday Use," you will get little help. The writer needs to revise the paragraph by eliminating details that do not support the central idea.

On the other hand, the details in paragraph 2 do support the declared topic. Phrases such as "for example," "as though," "this same devaluation," and "clearly thinks" show that the writer of paragraph 2 has assumed that the audience knows the story and now wants to read an argument in support of a particular interpretation. Paragraph 2, therefore, guides readers by connecting the details to the topic. It uses these details as evidence, not as a retelling of actions. By contrast, paragraph 1 recounts a number of relevant actions but does not connect them to the topic. More details could have been added to the second paragraph, of course, but they are unnecessary because the paragraph develops the argument with the details that are used. Good writing has many qualities, but one of the most important is shown in a comparison of the two paragraphs: *In good writing, no details are included unless they are used as supporting evidence in the development of thought and argument.*

Always Keep to Your Point—Stick to It Tenaciously

To show another distinction between first- and second-draft writing, let us consider a third example. In the following paragraph, which treats the relationship of economic circumstances to character in "Everyday Use," the writer's topic idea is that Mrs. Johnson, the story's narrator, has overcome the disadvantages of her life of poverty. She is a character of great integrity.

> *To emphasize Mrs. Johnson's character strength, Walker describes many details showing that she has overcome poverty in her life.* Mrs. Johnson herself has had no education, for her local school was shut down in 1927, when she was still in second grade, and because it was a school for "colored," there was no one to demand that it be reopened for the colored children (7). Mrs. Johnson now does farmwork, including working as a butcher, which also means that she slaughters large animals, but it additionally seems that the family has made butter with a homemade butter churn—a difficult task—probably for sale. Her house is tiny and spare. It was built in a cow pasture, with cows wandering by as they graze. The house has just three rooms and is covered with no more than a tin roof. In addition, the house has no windows. The furniture is homemade and has been in use for many decades. To be comfortable at home, Mrs. Johnson and her daughter Maggie sit outside, on a hard clay surface, or within a sheltered but also unpleasantly hot room.

This paragraph begins with an effective topic sentence, indicating that the writer has a good plan. The remaining part, however, shows how easily writers can be diverted from their objective. The flaw is that the material of the paragraph, while accurate, is not clearly connected to the topic. Once the second sentence is under way, the paragraph gets lost in a recounting of details from the story, and the promising topic sentence is forgotten. The paragraph shows that the use of detail alone will not support an intended meaning or argument. *As a writer, you must do the connecting yourself and make sure that all relationships are explicitly clear.* This point cannot be overstressed.

Let us see how our specimen paragraph can be made better. If the ideal paragraph can be schematized with line drawings, we might say that the paragraph's topic could be like a straight line, moving toward and reaching a specific goal (the topic or argument of the paragraph), with an exemplifying line moving away from the straight line briefly to bring in evidence but returning to the line to demonstrate the relevance of each new fact. Thus, the ideal scheme looks like this, with a straight line touched a number of times by an undulating line:

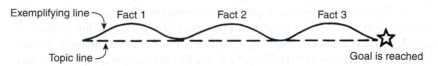

Notice that the exemplifying line, fluctuating to illustrate how documentation or exemplification is to be used, always returns to the topic line. A visual scheme for the faulty paragraph on "Everyday Use," however, looks like this, with the line never returning but flying out into space:

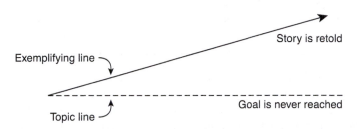

How might the faulty paragraph be improved? The best way is to remind the reader again and again of the writer's argument and to use examples from the text in support of this argument.

As our model wavy-line diagram indicates, each time a new detail is introduced, the undulating line merges with the straight, or central-idea, line. This relationship of argument to illustrative examples should prevail no matter what subject you write about, and you have to be tenacious in forming these connecting relationships. If you are analyzing *point of view*, for example, you should keep connecting your material to the speaker, or narrator, and the same applies to topics such as character, idea, or setting. According to this principle, we might revise the paragraph on Mrs. Johnson's poverty in "Everyday Use" as follows. (Parts of sentences stressing the relationship of the examples to the topic sentence, which is italicized, are underlined.)

To emphasize Mrs. Johnson's character strength, Walker describes many details showing that she has overcome poverty in her life. Early in the story, we learn that Mrs. Johnson herself never had an education, because her local school had been shut down in 1927, when she was still in second grade. Because the school was for "colored," there was no one to demand that it be reopened for the colored children (7). She endured with great effort despite this handicap. To bring up her own two girls, she took her difficult job as a butcher and still keeps it, which also means that she slaughters large animals. In fact, she indicates pride in the hard work she does as a butcher (6). Another mark of being poor is Mrs. Johnson's house, which is tiny and spare. It is situated not in a suburb but in a cow pasture, and it has only three rooms, no windows, and nothing more than a tin roof, with cows wandering by as they graze. But she makes the best of things. Her household furniture—what we are told about it—is homemade, and it is many decades old—another mark of her life as one of the poor. An additional aspect of her difficult life, it seems, is that the family has made butter in a homemade butter churn, probably for sale. Churning butter by hand would be very hard work, but the butter would provide needed income. In those moments when Mrs. Johnson and her daughter Maggie have leisure, they spend it sitting outside, on a hard clay surface, rather than inside, within a sheltered but unpleasantly hot room. Yet with no advantages except the ones she makes for herself, "Everyday Use" shows that Mrs. Johnson has remained strong.

The paragraph now successfully develops the argument promised by the topic sentence. Although it has also been lengthened, the length has been caused not by inessential detail but by phrases and sentences that give form and direction. You might object that if you lengthened all your paragraphs in this way, your essays would grow too bulky. The answer is to reduce the number of major points and paragraphs, on the theory that *it is better to develop a few topics pointedly than many topics pointlessly.* Revising to strengthen central and topic ideas requires you either to throw out some topics or else to incorporate them as subpoints in the topics you keep. Controlling your writing in this way will result in improvement.

Check Your Development and Organization

It bears repeating over and over again that the first requirement of good paragraphs and good essays is to introduce a major idea or argument and then stick to it. Another major step toward excellence is to make your major idea expand and grow. The word *growth* is a metaphor describing the disclosure of ideas that were not at first noticeable, together with the expression of original, new, and fresh interpretations.

Try to Be Original

In everything you write, now and in the future, you should always try to be original. You might claim that originality is impossible because you are writing about someone else's work. "The author has said everything," might be the argument, "and, therefore, I can do little more than follow the story." This claim rests on the mistaken assumption that you have no choice in selecting material and no opportunity to have individual thoughts and make original contributions.

But you do have choices and opportunities to be original. You really do. One obvious area of originality is the development and formulation of your central idea. For example, a natural first response to "Everyday Use" is "The story is about a woman who tells about an afternoon on which her older daughter returns home for a visit." But this response does not promise an argument because it refers only to an outline of the story's narrative and not to any idea. You can point the sentence toward an argument, however, if you call the afternoon "uncomfortable" or "unpleasant" or perhaps "disappointing." Just such words alone demand that you explain the differences between pleasant and unpleasant meetings between people, and your application of these differences to the afternoon's visit could produce an original essay or paragraph. Even better and more original insights could result if the topic of the budding essay were to connect the overinflated and self-absorbed traits of Dee to her mother's offended reactions. A resulting central idea might be "People may unintentionally offend even those who are most dear." Such an argument would require you to consider not only the personal nature but also the representative nature of Dee's actions in "Everyday Use," an avenue of exploration that could produce much in the way of a fresh and original essay.

You might also develop your ability to treat a subject originally if you plan to develop your essay around what you think is the most important and perceptive idea.

As examples of such planning, the following brief outline suggests how a central idea can be widened and expanded:

Argument: Mrs. Johnson Grows as a Character in "Everyday Use"

1. During her lifetime, she has had to overcome difficulties.
2. Although she knows that her daughter Dee can be annoying, she looks forward to Dee's visit.
3. When Dee demands the quilts, Mrs. Johnson has entirely new feelings and rejects Dee's demand by giving the quilts to Maggie.

The list shows how you can enlarge a subject if you treat your exemplifying details in an increasing order of importance. In this case, the order moves from the difficulties in Mrs. Johnson's life to her new feelings about the daughter who has always been on top at everything. The pattern shows how you can meet two primary standards of excellence in writing: organization and growth.

Clearly, you should always try to develop your central idea or argument. Constantly adhere to your topic, and constantly develop it. Nurture it and make it grow. In a short essay or even in a shorter paragraph, you will obviously be able to move only a short distance with an idea or argument, but you should never be satisfied to leave the idea exactly where you found it. To the degree to which you can learn to develop your ideas, you will receive recognition for increasingly original writing.

Writing with Specific Readers as Your Intended Audience

Whenever you write, you must decide how much detail to include for discussion. Usually, you base this decision on a judgment of your readers. For example, if you assume that they have not read the work, you will need to include a short summary as background; otherwise, they might not understand your argument.

Consider, too, whether your readers have any special interests or concerns. If they are particularly interested in politics, psychology, or history, for example, you might need to select and develop your materials along one of these lines.

Your instructor will let you know who your audience is. Usually, it will be your fellow students. They will be familiar with the work and will not expect you to retell a story or summarize an argument. Rather, they will want you to explain and interpret the work in the light of your main assertions about it. Therefore, you can omit details that do not exemplify and support your argument, even if these details are important parts of the work. What you write should always be based on your developing idea together with an assessment of your readers.

Use Exact, Comprehensive, and Forceful Language

In addition to being original, organized, and well developed, the best writing is exact, comprehensive, and forceful. At any stage of the composition process, you should always think about improving your earliest sentences and paragraphs, which usually need to be rethought, reworded, and rearranged.

Try to make each sentence meaningful and exact. First, ask yourself whether your sentences mean what you really intend or whether you can make them more exact and, therefore, stronger. For example, consider these two sentences from essays about "Everyday Use":

1. It seems as though the main character's feelings about her daughter Dee cause her to respond as she does in the story.
2. This incident, although it might seem trivial or unimportant, has substantial significance in the creation of the story; by this, I mean that the incident that occurred is essentially what the story is all about.

These sentences are unclear and vague and are, therefore, unhelpful. Neither of them goes anywhere. Sentence 1 is satisfactory up to the verb *cause*, but then it falls apart because the writer has lost sight of an argumentative or thematic purpose. It would be better to describe what the response *is* rather than to say nothing more than that some kind of response *exists*. To make the sentence more exact, we might try the following revision:

Mrs. Johnson's feelings about her daughter Dee go through a shift in the story, from being in awe to being offended and angry.

With this revision, the writer could readily go on to consider the relationship of the early part of the story to the later parts. Without the revision, it is not clear where the writer might go.

Sentence 2 is vague because the writer has lost all contact with the main thread of argument. If we adopt the principle of trying to be exact, however, we can create more meaning and more promise:

Mrs. Johnson's denial of Dee's demand for the quilts, which might seem trivial or unimportant, is the story's major incident because it brings the simmering mother-daughter antagonism to a head and leads immediately to Dee's departure.

In addition to working for exactness, try to make sentences—all sentences but particularly thesis and topic sentences—complete and comprehensive. Consider the following sentence:

The idea in "Everyday Use" is that Mrs. Johnson has promised the quilts to Maggie for her regular, daily use when she marries John Thomas.

Although this sentence promises to describe an idea, it does no more than state one of the story's major actions. It needs additional rethinking and rephrasing to enable it to lead to further development, as in these two revisions:

1. Walker's rapid ending of "Everyday Use" symbolizes the personal and psychological importance of family objects and traditions.
2. In "Everyday Use," Walker brings out the need for keeping family things within a central home as a way of preserving the memory of parents and relatives.

Both new sentences are connected to the action described by the original phrasing, "Mrs. Johnson has promised the quilts to Maggie for her regular, daily use when she marries John Thomas," although they point toward differing treatments. A key word in the first sentence is *symbolizes*, and an essay or paragraph stemming from it would stress the significance of the objects in Mrs. Johnson's extended family, both past and future. The writer would emphasize that the butter churn and the quilts are unifying symbols and that Mrs. Johnson's refusal of the quilts to Dee might be taken to show her wish to keep her family heritage intact. Comparably, the second sentence concerns the need for preserving family things even when members of the family become dispersed. Both of the revised sentences, therefore, are more comprehensive than the original sentence and thus would help the writer to get on the track toward a thoughtful and analytical composition.

Of course, creating fine sentences is not easy and never will be easy, no matter how often you write. As a mode of improvement, however, you might use some self-testing mechanisms:

- *For story materials.* Always relate the materials to a point or argument. Do not say simply, "Mrs. Johnson has worked hard for most of her life" and nothing else. Instead, blend the material into a point, like this: "Mrs. Johnson's lifelong efforts have enabled her to preserve her home that contains the memories of her family, both present and past" or "The fire that destroyed Mrs. Johnson's previous home made her realize the importance of keeping family things together."
- *For responses and impressions.* Do not say simply, "The story's ending left me with a definite impression." What are you giving your readers with a sentence like this? They want to know what your impression is; therefore, you need to describe it, as in the following: "The story's ending surprised me and also made me sympathetic to the major character" or "The story's ending struck me with the idea that life is unpredictable and unfair."
- *For ideas.* Make the idea clear and direct. Do not say, "Mrs. Johnson lives in a poor household," but rather refer to the story to bring out an idea, as follows: "Mrs. Johnson's story shows that great character strength is needed to overcome poverty."
- *For critical commentary.* Do not be satisfied with a statement such as "I found 'Everyday Use' interesting." What does a comment like this tell the reader? Instead, try to describe *what* was interesting and *why* it was interesting, as in this sentence: "'Everyday Use' is an interesting story because it shows that good people may overcome difficulty despite the handicap of being poor."

Good writing begins with attempts, like these, to rephrase sentences to make them really say something. If you always name and pin down descriptions, responses, and judgments, no matter how difficult that job may seem, your sentences can be strong and forceful because you will be making them exact and comprehensive.

Illustrative Student Essay (Revised and Improved Draft)

If you refer again to the first essay above about the character Dee in Walker's "Everyday Use" (pp. 39–41), you might observe that more thought and revision would make for improvements. Most notable is the fourth paragraph, which concerns Dee's lack of concern for others. The point is developed adequately in this essay, but something is missing, for in fact this quality of selfishness is the most important aspect of Dee's character. Therefore, there is need for more detail and discussion about this quality, particularly to stress the relationship of the central idea to the topics of the various paragraphs. A new paragraph is in order, and this is included in the following reworking of the first essay. In addition to this new paragraph, there are a few major revisions and revisions throughout, most of them in the first and last paragraphs. Remember that new thought and revision are never untimely or out of order anywhere in a composition or at any time. Within the limits of a short assignment, the following essay illustrates all the principles of organization and unity that we have been discussing here.

Although underlined sentences are not recommended by MLA style, they are used in this illustrative essay as teaching tools to emphasize the central idea, thesis sentence, and topic sentences.

Mrs. Johnson's Overly Self-Assured Daughter, Dee, in Alice Walker's "Everyday Use"

In "Everyday Use," Walker presents her four major characters vividly: Mrs. Johnson (the narrator), Dee, Maggie, and Asalamalakim. The narrator, Mrs. Johnson, describes herself fully, well enough to give readers a strong understanding of what she is like. Even more vivid and unusual, however, is the presentation of the older daughter, Dee, who is coming back home for a visit after having been away at college and elsewhere for a number of years. Those waiting at home might at first think that Dee is like a returning heroine, but as the story progresses, she seems less heroic and more fussy. Walker uses ordinary, everyday details to show her overly self-assured character.[18] All descriptions of Dee in the story are presented to bring out this quality. Her overly self-assured nature is shown by her dress and jewelry, her passion for home decoration, her demands for some of the Johnson family's home-made things, and her sense of putting herself before others.[19] **[1]**

Dee's way of dressing shows the more positive side of her self-assurance. She obviously dresses to be noticed, and she self-confidently attracts attention through her colorful clothes. Her "loud" dress—about which Mrs. Johnson says "I like it" (Walker, 8)—goes "down to the ground" and makes Dee seem almost flowing as she walks. Her earrings hang "to her shoulders," and her dangling **[2]**

---

[18]Central idea.
[19]Thesis sentence.

bracelets make a distinct noise when she moves her arms. Even her hair shows her self-confidence, for it has been made to stand "straight up" like "wool on a sheep," and her two long pigtails are fixed to "rope about like small lizards" (8). A shy and retiring woman would not draw attention to herself in this way, but Dee, with strongly positive views about herself, clamors to be seen and noticed.

[3]   Dee's praise of some of the things in the family home, however, seem genuinely to indicate her sense of home decoration and also her sense of heritage. When she praises the kitchen benches that "her daddy made" at some time in the past (10), she speaks respectfully and enthusiastically, and it, therefore, seems reasonable that she would want to have something as a keepsake (11). Her picking the churn top from the family butter churn, together with the churn's dasher, therefore is natural, because they were whittled by Uncle Buddy and by Stash, who were family members but who are now gone. It is fair to say that her wishes for these things show that Dee is capable of being respectful and likable.

[4]   But Dee's demands to take the homemade quilts away show that her self-assurance causes her to be unconcerned about others. When she first speaks of the now dead women in the family who made the quilts, she seems to deny their importance (9). So her desire for the two quilts is contradictory. Her wish for the quilts is positive, but her demand for them is negative, because it leads to the story's major conflict. Maybe she doesn't know that Mrs. Johnson had promised to give the quilts to Maggie, the bashful and quiet sister, but by her demand, Dee antagonizes her mother. Mrs. Johnson sees Dee's self-assurance in this conflict as selfishness that has reached the point of hatred (13), and, thus, Dee provokes Mrs. Johnson's justifiable anger.

[5]   There is an additional aspect of Dee's selfish attitude about the quilts. When she first appears, she tells her mother, who is seated, not to get up (9). Without further greeting, she gets her Polaroid camera and starts to take pictures of the house and surrounding things, including cows, as though it is more important

to put things into photographs than to experience the love and happiness of being home again with her mother and sister. This is definitely strange. Although Dee is delighted with everything at dinner, it is quickly clear that she thinks of her past life as little more than a memory. She therefore talks about what she can take away for herself as a memory, and she tells her mother, "I knew there was something I wanted to ask you if I could have" (11). The height of her lack of interest in her own family is her declaration that the quilts should not be for "everyday use" in current, living time, even though they had originally been made for that purpose. Instead, Dee tries to insist on her own way: She wants to display the quilts on a wall, along with parts of the butter churn (13). When she goes away after being rejected, she tells Maggie to "make something" of herself, in this way showing her idea that Maggie's life is irrelevant to the "new day" that she and Asalamalakim have accepted (13). In short, Dee does not recognize that it is important to live life as a balance of future and past, because the past is not dead but is still as alive as the useful quilts and butter churn.

The dramatic development of the story hinges on Dee's sense of wanting things for herself without concern for others. Her [6] return home could have been the subject of a story about a happy and joyful reunion. But almost immediately, Dee seems to be unconcerned about her mother and sister and about the heritage she claims to value at the story's end. Her denial of her birth name is an outright insult to her mother, and throughout the story, Dee speaks negatively about the circumstances of home. When the family enjoys their meal together, Dee seems civil, and happy, but almost immediately she makes demands that run counter to the life of her mother and sister. Mrs. Johnson and Maggie do not put Dee's contradiction into words, but they do react to the hostility of her wishes, and their relief after she has gone enables the two of them to spend the evening "just enjoying" until bedtime (14).

Work Cited

Walker, Alice. "Everyday Use." Edgar V. Roberts, *Writing About Literature*. 13th ed. New York: Pearson, 2012. 5–14. Print.

Commentary on the Essay

Several improvements to the first version can be seen here. Some of the sentences of the first paragraph have been revised to lay out more clearly the situation of Dee's return to the family home. In addition, the thesis sentence at the paragraph's end has been revised to include the additional material to be included in the new fifth paragraph. Other verbal changes in the essay have been made for a similar purpose. Paragraph 5—not present in the earlier version and new in the improved draft—includes additional details about how Dee, literally from the start of her visit, exhibits the pride and indifference to her mother and sister that are apparent after she makes her demand for the quilts. In short, the second version shows the continuity of Dee's character throughout "Everyday Use" more fully than the first draft, and it, therefore, is the most important part of the essay. Because the writer has revised the first-draft ideas about the story, the final essay is more tightly structured, insightful, and forceful.

Essay Commentaries

Throughout *Writing About Literature*, the illustrative essays and paragraphs are followed by short commentaries that show how the essays embody the chapter instructions and guidelines. For each essay that has a number of possible approaches, the commentary points out which one is used, and when an essay uses two or more approaches, the commentary makes this fact clear. In addition, each commentary singles out one of the paragraphs for more detailed analysis of its argument and use of detail. The commentaries will hence help you to develop the insights that are necessary to use the essays as aids in your own study and writing.

A Summary of Guidelines

To sum up, follow these guidelines whenever you write about stories, poems, and plays:

- Do not simply retell the story or summarize the work. Bring in story materials only when you can use them as support for your central idea or argument.
- Throughout your essay, keep reminding your reader of your central idea.
- Within each paragraph, make sure that you stress your topic idea.

- Develop your subject. Make it bigger than it was when you began.
- Always try to make your statements exact, comprehensive, and forceful.
- This bears repeating: Do not simply retell the story or summarize the work.

Writing Topics About the Writing Process

1. Write a brainstorming paragraph on the topic of anything in a literary work that you find especially good or interesting. Write as the thoughts occur to you; do not slow yourself down in an effort to make your writing seem perfect. You can make corrections and improvements later.
2. Using marginal and notebook notations, together with any additional thoughts, describe the way in which the author of a particular work has expressed important ideas and difficulties.
3. Create a plus-minus table to list your responses about a character or ideas in a work.
4. Raise questions about the actions of characters in a story or play in order to determine the various customs and manners of the society out of which the work is derived.
5. Analyze and explain the way in which the conflicts in a story or play are developed. What pattern or patterns do you find? Determine the relationship of the conflicts to the work's development, and fashion your idea of this relationship as an argument for a potential essay.
6. Basing your ideas on your marginal and notebook notations, select an idea and develop a thesis sentence from it, using your idea and a list of possible topics for an argument or central idea for an essay.
7. Using the thesis sentence you write for Exercise 6, develop a brief analytical sentence outline that could help you in writing a full essay.

A Short Guide to Using Quotations and Making References in Essays About Literature

In establishing evidence for the points you make in your essays and essay examinations, you constantly need to refer to various parts of stories, plays, and poems. You also need to include shorter and longer quotations and to keep the time sequences straight within the works you are writing about. In addition, you might need to refer to biographical and historical details that have a bearing on the work or works you are studying. So that your own writing may flow as accurately and naturally as possible, you must be able to integrate these references and distinctions of time clearly and easily.

Integrate Passages and Ideas into Your Essay

Your essays should reflect your own thought as you study and analyze the characteristics, ideas, and qualities of an author's work. In a typical discussion of literature, you constantly need to introduce brief summaries, quotations, general interpretations, observations, and independent applications of everything you are discussing. It is not easy to keep these various elements integrated and to keep confusion from arising.

Distinguish Your Own Thoughts from Those of Your Author

Often, a major problem is that it is hard for readers to figure out when *your* ideas stop and those of your author begin. You must, therefore, arrange your sentences to make the distinctions clear, but you must also blend your materials so that your reader may follow you easily. Let us look at an example of how such problems can be handled. Here, the writer being discussed is the Victorian poet Matthew Arnold (1822–1888). The passage moves from reference to Arnold's ideas to the essay writer's independent application of the ideas.

> [1] In his poem "Dover Beach," Arnold states that in past times, religious faith was accepted as absolute truth. [2] To symbolize this idea, he refers to the ocean, which surrounds all land, and the surf, which constantly rushes onto the earth's shores. [3] According to this symbolism, religious ideas are as vast as the ocean and as regular as the surf, and these ideas at one time constantly and irresistibly replenished people's lives. [4] Arnold's symbol of the flowing ocean changes, however, to a symbol of the ebbing ocean, thus illustrating his idea that belief and religious certainty were falling away. [5] It is this personal sense of spiritual emptiness that Arnold is associating with his own times, because what he describes, in keeping with the symbolism, is that in the present time the "drear" shoreline has been left vacant by the "melancholy long withdrawing roar" of retreat and reduction (lines 25–27).

This paragraph combines but also separates paraphrase, interpretation, and quotation, and it thereby eliminates any possible confusion about the origin of the ideas and also about who is saying what. In the first three sentences, the writer uses the phrases "Arnold states," "To symbolize this idea," and "According to this symbolism" to show clearly that interpretation is to follow. Although the fourth sentence marks a new direction of Arnold's ideas, it continues to separate restatement from interpretation. The fifth sentence indicates, through the phrase "in keeping with the symbolism," what the writer's judgment is about the major idea of "Dover Beach."

Integrate Material by Using Quotation Marks

It is often necessary, and also interesting, to use short quotations from the author to illustrate and reinforce your ideas and interpretations. Here, the problem of separating your thoughts from the author's is solved by quotation marks. In such an internal quotation, you may treat prose and poetry in the same way. If a poetic quotation extends from the end of one line to the beginning of another, however, indicate the line break with a virgule (/), and use a capital letter to begin the next line, as in the following discussion of "Lines Written in Early Spring" by William Wordsworth (1770–1850):

> In "Lines Written in Early Spring" Wordsworth describes a condition in which his speaker is united with the surrounding natural world. Nature is a combination of the "thousand blended notes" of joyful birds (line 1), the sights of "budding twigs" (17), and the "periwinkle" (10). In the exact words of the speaker, these "fair works" form a direct "link" to "The human soul that through me ran" (5, 6).

Blend Quotations into Your Own Sentences

The use of internal quotations still creates the problem of blending materials, however, for quotations should never be brought in unless you prepare your reader for them in some way. *Do not*, for example, use quotations in the following manner:

> Wordsworth states that his woodland grove is filled with the sounds of birds, the sights of flowers, and the feeling of the light wind, making for the thought that creatures of the natural world take pleasure in life. "The birds around me hopped and played."

This abrupt quotation throws the reader off balance because it is not blended into the previous sentence. It is necessary to prepare the reader to move from your discussion to the quotation, as in the following revision:

> Wordsworth claims that his woodland scene is made joyful by the surrounding flowers and the gentle breeze, causing his speaker to observe that "The birds around me hopped and played." From this joyful scene, his conclusion is that the natural world has resulted from a "holy plan" created by Nature.

Here, the quotation is made an actual part of the first sentence. This sort of blending is satisfactory, provided that the quotation is brief.

Indent and Block Long Quotations

You can follow a general rule for incorporating quotations in your writing: Do not quote within a sentence any passage that is longer than twenty or twenty-five words (but consult your instructor, for the allowable number of words may vary). Longer quotations demand so much separate attention that they interrupt your own sentence and make it difficult if not impossible to understand what you have said. It is possible but not desirable to conclude one of your sentences with a quotation, but you should never make an extensive quotation in the *middle* of a sentence. By the time you finish such an unwieldy sentence, your reader will have forgotten how it began—and how can that be clear writing? When your quotation is long, you should make a point of introducing it and setting it off separately as a block.

The physical layout of block quotations should be this: Leave three blank lines between your own discourse and the quotation. Double-space the quotation (like the rest of your essay, when you have prepared it at home), and indent it five spaces from your left margin to distinguish it from your own writing. You might use fewer spaces for longer lines of poetry, but the goal should always be to create a neat, attractive page. After the quotation, leave a three-line space again, and resume your own discourse. Here is a specimen, from an essay about Wordsworth's "Lines Written in Early Spring":

> In "Lines Written in Early Spring" Wordsworth develops the idea that the world of nature is linked directly to the moral human consciousness. He speaks of no religious systems or books of moral values. Instead, he derives his ideas directly from his experience, assuming that the world was made for the joy of the living creatures in it, including human beings ("man"), and that anyone disturbing that power of joy is violating

"Nature's holy plan" itself. Wordsworth's moral criticism, in other words, is derived from his faith in the integrity of creation:

> If this belief from heaven be sent,
>
> If such be Nature's holy plan,
>
> Have I not reason to lament
>
> What man has made of man?
>
> (lines 21–24)

The concept that morality and life are joined is the most interesting aspect of the poem. It encourages a live-and-let-live attitude toward others, however, not necessarily an active program of direct outreach and help.

When quoting lines of poetry, always remember to quote them *as lines*. Do not run them together as though they were continuous prose. When you create such block quotations, as in the preceding example, you do *not* need quotation marks.

Today, computer usage has become the established means of preparing out-of-classroom papers; therefore, computer styling has become prominent in the handling of the matters discussed here. If you have style features in your menu, such as "Poem Text" or "Quotation," each of which sets block quotations apart from "Normal" text, you may certainly make use of these features. Be sure to explain to your instructor what you are doing, however, to make sure that your computer's features correspond to the styles that have been established for your class.

Use Ellipses to Show Omissions

Whether your quotation is long or short, you will often need to change some of the material in it to conform to your own sentence requirements. You might wish to omit something from the quotation that is not essential to your point or to the flow of your sentence. Indicate such omissions with ellipses (three spaced periods), as follows (from an essay about the story "A Worn Path" by Eudora Welty (1909–2001):

> Welty introduces Phoenix as an aging and impoverished but also lovely and delicate woman. Phoenix's dress, which reaches to "her shoe tops," is protected by a "long apron of bleached sugar sacks." Her skin has "a pattern all its own of numberless branching wrinkles, . . . but a golden color ran underneath." Nevertheless, her hair is shaped "in the frailest of ringlets, . . . with an odor like copper."

If your quotation is very brief, however, do not use ellipses because they might be more distracting than helpful. For example, do not use ellipses in a quotation like this:

> Keats asserts that ". . . a thing of beauty . . ." always gives joy.

Instead, make your quotation without ellipses:

> Keats asserts that "a thing of beauty" always gives joy.

Use Square Brackets to Enclose Words that You Add Within Quotations

If you add words of your own to integrate the quotation into your own train of discourse or to explain words that may seem obscure, put square brackets around these words, as in the following passage:

> In "Lines Written in Early Spring," Wordsworth refers to a past experience of extreme happiness, in which Nature seemed to "link / The human soul that through . . . [him] ran." He is describing a state of mystical awareness in which "pleasant thoughts / Bring [him] sad thoughts," and make him "lament" moral and political cruelty (lines 2–8).

Do Not Overquote

A word of caution: *Do not use too many quotations.* You will be judged on your own thought and on the continuity and development of your own essay. It is tempting to include many quotations on the theory that you need to use examples from the text to illustrate and support your ideas. Naturally, it is important to introduce examples, but realize that too many quotations can disturb the flow of your own thought. If your essay consists of many illustrations linked together by little more than your introductory sentences, how much thinking have you actually shown? Try, therefore, to create your own discussion, using appropriate examples to connect your thoughts to the text or texts you are describing and discussing.

Chapter 2

Writing About Plot: The Development of Conflict and Tension in Literature

Fiction, Drama, and Narrative Poetry

Stories, drama, and narrative and epic poetry (and also films) are made up mostly of actions or incidents that follow one another in chronological order. The same is true of life, but there is a major difference: Fiction must make sense even though life does not always seem to make sense at all. Finding a sequential or narrative order is, therefore, only a first step in our thinking about fiction. What we depend on for the sense or meaning of fiction is **plot**—the elements that govern the unfolding of the actions.

Plot: The Motivation and Causality of Literature

The English novelist E. M. Forster, in *Aspects of the Novel* (1927), presents a memorable illustration of plot. To illustrate a bare set of actions, he proposes the following: "The king died, and then the queen died." Forster points out, however, that this sequence does not form a plot because it lacks *motivation* and *causality*; it's too much like life itself to be fictional. Therefore, he introduces motivation and causality in his next example: "The king died, and then the queen died of grief." The phrase "of grief" shows that one thing (grief) controls or overcomes another (the normal desire to live), and thus motivation and causality enter the sequence to form a plot. In a well-plotted story or play, one thing precedes or follows another not simply because time ticks away but, more important, because *effects* follow *causes*. In a good work of fiction, nothing is irrelevant or accidental; everything is related and causative.

Determining the Conflicts in a Story, Drama, or Narrative Poem

The controlling impulse in a connected pattern of causes and effects is **conflict**, which refers to people or circumstances that a character must face and try to overcome. Conflicts bring out extremes of human energy, prompting characters to engage in the decisions, actions, responses, and interactions that make up fictional literature.

In its most elemental form, a conflict is the opposition of two people. Their conflict may take the shape of anger, hatred, envy, argument, avoidance, political or moral opposition, gossip, lies, fighting, and other possible actions and attitudes. Conflicts may also exist between groups, although conflicts between individuals are more identifiable and therefore more suitable for stories. Conflicts may also be abstract—for example, when an individual opposes larger forces such as public opinion, objectionable rules, modes of behavior, natural objects, ideas, and modes of behavior. A difficult or even impossible *choice*—a dilemma—is a natural conflict for an individual person. A conflict may also be brought out in ideas and opinions that clash. In short, conflict is a very human condition that shows itself in many ways.

Relating Conflict Directly to Doubt, Tension, and Interest

Conflict is the major element of plot because opposing forces arouse *curiosity*, cause *doubt*, create *tension*, and produce *interest*. The same responses are the lifeblood of athletic competition. Consider which kind of athletic event is more interesting: (1) One team gets so far ahead that the outcome is no longer in doubt, or (2) the two teams are so evenly matched that the outcome is uncertain until the final seconds. Obviously, games are uninteresting—as games—unless they develop as contests between teams of comparable strength. The same principle applies to conflicts in stories and dramas. There should be uncertainty about a protagonist's success or failure. Unless there is doubt, there is no tension, and without tension, there is no interest.

Finding the Conflicts to Determine the Plot

To see a plot in operation, let us build on Forster's description. Here is a simple plot for a story of our own: "John and Jane meet, fall in love, and get married." This sentence contains a plot because it shows cause and effect (they get married *because* they fall in love), but with no conflict, the plot is not interesting. However, let us introduce conflicting elements into this common "boy meets girl" story:

> John and Jane meet in college and fall in love. They plan to marry after graduation, but a problem arises. Jane first wants to establish herself in a career, and after marriage she wants to be an equal contributor to the family, which will mean graduate studies so that she can enter a profession. John understands Jane's wishes for equality, but he wants to get married first and let her finish her studies and have her career after they have children. Jane believes that John's plan is unacceptable because she thinks of it as a trap from which she might not escape. As they discuss their options, they find themselves increasingly displeased and unhappy with each other. Finally, they bring their marriage plans to an end, and they part in both anger and sorrow. They go on to marry others and build separate lives and careers. In their new lives, neither is totally happy even though they like and respect their spouses. The years pass, and after children and grandchildren, Jane and John meet again. John is now divorced, and Jane is a widow. They find that there is still a spark of feeling between them. Because their earlier conflict is no longer a barrier, they rekindle their love, marry, and try to make up for the past. Even their new happiness, however, is tinged with regret and reproach because of their earlier conflicts, their unhappy decision to part, their lost years, and their increasing age.

Here we find a true plot because our "boy meets girl" story now contains a major conflict from which a number of related complications develop. These complications embody disagreements, choices, arguments, and ill feelings that produce tension, uncertainty, rupture, and regret. When we learn that John and Jane finally join together at the end, we might still find the story painful because it does not give us a "happily ever after" ending. Nevertheless, the story makes sense—as a story—because its plot brings out the plausible consequences of the understandable aims and hopes of John and Jane during their long relationship. It is the imposition of necessary causes and effects upon a series of events in time that creates the story's plot.

Writing About the Plot of a Particular Work

An essay about plot is an analysis of the conflict and its developments in a story or play. The organization of your essay should not be modeled on sequential sections and principal events, however, because these invite only a retelling of the story. Instead, the organization is to be developed from the important elements of conflict. As you look for ideas about plot, try to answer the following questions.

Questions for Discovering Ideas

- Who are the major and minor characters, and how do their characteristics put them in conflict? How can you describe the conflict or conflicts?
- How does the story's action grow out of the major conflict?
- If the conflict stems from contrasting ideas or values, what are these, and how are they brought out?
- What problems do the major characters face? How do the characters deal with these problems?
- How do the major characters achieve (or not achieve) their major goal(s)? What obstacles do they overcome? What obstacles overcome them or alter them?
- At the end, are the characters successful or unsuccessful, happy or unhappy, satisfied or dissatisfied, changed or unchanged, enlightened or ignorant? How has the resolution of the major conflict produced these results?

Organize Your Essay About Plot

Strategies for Organizing Ideas

To keep your essay brief, you need to be selective. Rather than detailing everything a character does, for example, stress the major elements in the character's conflict. Such an essay on Eudora Welty's "A Worn Path" might emphasize the major character, Phoenix Jackson, as she encounters the various obstacles both in the woods and in town. When there is a conflict between two major characters, the obvious approach is to focus equally on the characters. For brevity, however, emphasis might be placed on just one character. Thus, an essay on the plot of Frank O'Connor's story "First Confession" might stress the thoughts and responses of the major character and narrator, Jackie, but could also deal with the positions of his sister and mother. It might also be possible to consider the position of the priest at Jackie's confession.

In addition, the plot may be analyzed more broadly in terms of impulses, goals, values, issues, and historical perspectives. Thus, you might emphasize the elements of guile and cruelty of the character Montresor, the narrator of Poe's "The Cask of Amontillado." The plot of Poe's story could not develop as we have it without Montresor's complex and somewhat baffling motivation.

The conclusion of your essay might contain a brief summary of the points you have made. It is also a fitting location for a brief consideration of the effect or impact produced by the conflict in the story you have chosen. Additional ideas might focus on whether the author has arranged actions and dialogue to direct your favor toward one character or the other or whether the plot is possible or impossible, serious or comic, fair or unfair, powerful or indifferent, and so on.

Illustrative Essay

The Plot of Eudora Welty's "A Worn Path"[1]

[1] At first, the complexity of Welty's plot in "A Worn Path" is not clear. The main character is Phoenix Jackson, an old, poor, and frail woman; the story seems to be no more than a record of her walk to Natchez through the woods from her rural home. By the story's end, however, the plot is clear: It consists of the brave attempts of a courageous, valiant woman to carry on against overwhelming forces.[2] Her determination despite the great odds against her gives the story its impact. The powers ranged against her are old age, poverty, environment, and illness.[3]

[2] Old age as a silent but overpowering antagonist is shown in signs of Phoenix's increasing senility. Not her mind but her feet tell her where to find the medical office in Natchez. Despite her inner strength, she is unable to explain her errand when the nursing attendant asks her. Instead, she sits dumbly and unknowingly for a time, until "a flame of comprehension" comes across her face (346, 87). Against the power of advancing age, Phoenix is slowly losing. The implication is that soon she will lose entirely.

[3] An equally crushing opponent is her poverty. Because she cannot afford a bus or taxi to take her to town, she must walk. She has no

---

[1]See page 341 for this story.
[2]Central idea.
[3]Thesis sentence.

money and acquires her ten cents for the paper windmill by stealing and begging. The "soothing medicine" she gets for her grandson (346, 92) is given to her out of charity. Despite the boy's need for advanced medical care, she has no money to provide it, and the story, therefore, shows that her guardianship is doomed.

[4]   Closely connected to her poverty is the way through the woods, which during her walk seems to be an almost active opponent. The long hill tires her, the thorn bush catches and snags her clothes, the log endangers her balance as she crosses the creek, and the barbed-wire fence threatens to puncture her skin. Another danger on her way is the stray dog, which topples her over. Apparently not afraid, however, Phoenix carries on a cheerful monologue:

> "Out of my way, all you foxes, owls, beetles, jack rabbits, coons and wild animals! . . . Keep out from under these feet, little bobwhites. . . . Keep the big wild hogs out of my path. Don't let none of these come running my direction. I got a long way." (341, 3)

She prevails for the moment as she enters Natchez, but all the hazards of her walk are still there, waiting for her on her return.

[5]   The force against Phoenix that shows her plight most clearly and pathetically is her grandson's incurable illness. His condition highlights her helplessness, for she is his only support. Her difficulties would be enough for one person alone, but with the grandson, the odds against her are doubled. Despite her care, there is nothing anyone can do for the grandson but take the long worn path to get something to help him endure his pain.

[6]   This brief description of the conflicts in "A Worn Path" only hints at the story's power. Welty layers the details to bring out the full range of the conditions against Phoenix, who cannot win despite her determination and devotion. The most hopeless fact, the condition of the invalid grandson, is not revealed until Phoenix reaches the medical office, and this delayed final revelation makes one's heart go out to her. The plot is strong because it is so real, and Phoenix is a pathetic but memorable protagonist struggling against overwhelming odds.

Work Cited

Welty, Eudora. "A Worn Path." Edgar V. Roberts. *Writing About Literature.* 13th ed. New York: Pearson, 2012. 341. Print.

Commentary on the Essay

The strategy of this essay is to explain the elements of plot in "A Worn Path" selectively, without duplicating the story's narrative order. Thus, the third aspect of conflict, the woods, might be introduced first if the story's narrative order were to be followed, but it is deferred while the more personal elements of old age and poverty are considered. It is important to note that the essay does not deal with the story's other characters as part of Phoenix's conflict. Rather, Phoenix's antagonist takes the shape of impersonal and unconquerable forces, such as the grandson's illness.

Paragraph 1 briefly describes how one's first impressions are changed because of what happens at the end of the story. The thesis statement anticipates the body by listing the four topics about to be treated. Paragraph 2 concerns Phoenix's old age; paragraph 3, her poverty; paragraph 4, the woods; and paragraph 5, her grandson's illness. The concluding paragraph (6) points out that with such a set of conflicts arrayed against her, Phoenix cannot win, except as she lives out her duty and her devotion to help her grandson. Continuing the theme of the introduction, the last paragraph also accounts for the power of the plot: By building up to Phoenix's personal strength against unbeatable forces, the story evokes sympathy and admiration.

Writing Topics About Plot

1. Compare the use of interior scenes in "The Story of an Hour," "First Confession," *The Bear*, or *Trifles*. How do these scenes bring out the various conflicts in the works? How do characters in the interiors contribute to plot developments? What is the relationship of these characters to the major themes of the works?
2. Describe the plot of Jackson's "The Lottery." What is the principal conflict in the story? Who is the principal advocate of the custom of the lottery? How does the town's population enter into the plot as a collective character in support of the lottery?
3. Compare "The Story of an Hour" and "Young Goodman Brown" as stories that develop plots about clashing social or religious values and customs. In what ways are the plots similar? In what ways are they different?
4. Select a circumstance in your life that caused you doubt, difficulty, and conflict. Making yourself anonymous (give yourself a fictitious name and put yourself in

a fictitious location), write a brief story about the occasion, stressing how your conflict began, how it affected you, and how you resolved it. You might describe the details in chronological order, or you might begin the story in the present tense and then introduce details in flashback.

5. Write a brief episode or story that takes place in a historical period that you believe you know well (either a past period or possibly a future one), being as factually accurate as you can. Introduce your own fictional characters as important "movers and shakers," and deal with their public or personal conflicts or both. You may model your characters and episodes on historical people, but you are free to exercise your imagination completely and construct your own characters.

Chapter 3

Writing About Point of View: The Position or Stance of the Work's Narrator or Speaker

Fiction and Poetry (Both Narrative and Lyric)

The term **point of view** refers to the **speaker, narrator, persona,** or **voice** created by authors to tell stories, make observations, present arguments, and express personal attitudes and judgments. Literally, point of view deals with how action and dialogue have been seen, heard, or generally perceived. How does the speaker learn about the situation? Is the speaker a participant in the situation or no more than a witness, either close or distant? How close to the action is she or he? How much does the speaker know? How accurate and complete are his or her reports? Is the speaker also involved in what happened? How thoroughly? Did he or she see everything or miss anything? How much did she or he understand? Point of view involves not only the speaker's actual position as an observer and recorder but also the ways in which the speaker's social, political, and mental circumstances affect the narrative. For this reason, point of view is one of the most complex and subtle aspects of literary study.

The underlying philosophical issue of point of view is epistemological: How do we acquire information? How can we verify its authenticity? How can we trust those who explain the world to us? What is their authority? Are they partial or impartial? What is their interest in telling us things? How reliable are their explanations? What physical and psychological positions might affect, or even distort, what they are saying? Do they have anything to hide? When they speak, are they trying to justify themselves to any degree?

It is important to recognize that authors try not only to make their works vital and interesting but also to bring their presentations alive. Their situation as writers is similar to a dramatic performance: In a play, the actors are always themselves, but in their roles, they *impersonate* and temporarily *become* the characters they act. In fictional works, not only do authors impersonate or pretend to be characters who do the talking, but also they *create* these characters. One such character is Jackie, the narrator of Frank O'Connor's "First Confession," (See Appendix C) who is telling about events that occurred when he was a child of seven. Because he is the subject as well as the narrator, he has firsthand knowledge of the actions, even though he also says things indicating that he, as an adult, has not fully assimilated his childhood experience.

Because of the ramifications of creating a narrative voice, point of view may also be considered the centralizing or guiding intelligence in a work—the mind that filters the fictional experience and presents only the most important details to create the maximum impact. It may be compared to the perspectives utilized by painters. In other words, the way in which we understand the reality presented in painted pictures—the point of view or guiding intelligence presented by the painter—determines our perceptions and understanding of the painter's ideas. Similarly, the point of view or guiding intelligence created by the author of a literary work determines how we read, understand, and respond, as with Montresor, the narrator of Edgar A. Poe's "The Cask of Amontillado." As Montresor tells his story of revenge, we realize that the actions he describes are an unfolding record of his criminal insanity. We accept the accuracy of his tale, but we become repulsed by the madness of his confession. His concluding wish, that Fortunato rest in peace, is meaningless, perfunctory, and bizarre.

An Exercise in Point of View: Reporting an Accident

As an exercise to show that point of view is derived from lifelike situations, let us imagine that there has been an auto accident. Two cars, driven by Alice and Bill, have collided, and the after-crash scene is represented in the drawing. How might this accident be described? What would Alice say? What would Bill say?

Now assume that Frank, who is Bill's best friend, and Mary, who knows neither Bill nor Alice, were witnesses. What might Frank say about who was responsible? What might Mary say? Additionally, assume that you are a reporter for a local newspaper and have been sent to report on the accident. You know none of the people involved. How will your report differ from the other reports? Finally, to what degree are all the statements designed to persuade listeners and readers that the details and claims made in the respective reports are true?

The likely differences in the various reports may be explained by reference to point of view. Obviously, because both Alice and Bill are deeply involved—each of them is a major participant or what may be called a **major mover**—they will likely arrange their words to make themselves seem blameless. Frank, because he is Bill's best friend, will report things in Bill's favor. Mary will favor neither Alice nor Bill, but let us assume that she did not look up to see the colliding cars until she heard the crash. Therefore, she did not see the accident happening but saw only the immediate aftereffects. Amid all this mixture of partial and impartial views of the action, to whom should we attribute the greatest reliability?

Each person's report will have the hidden agenda of making herself or himself seem honest, objective, intelligent, impartial, and thorough. Thus, although both Alice and Bill may be truthful to the best of their abilities, their reports will not be reliable because they both have something to gain from avoiding responsibility for the accident. Also, Frank may be questionable as a witness because he is Bill's friend and may report things to Bill's advantage. Mary could be reliable, but she did not see everything; therefore, she is unreliable not because of motivation but rather because of her location as a witness. Most likely, your account as an impartial reporter will be the most reliable and objective of all, because your major interest is to learn all the details and to report the truth accurately, with no concern about the personal interests of either Alice or Bill.

As you can see, the ramifications of describing actions are far-reaching, and the consideration of the various interests and situations is subtle. Indeed, of all the aspects of literature, point of view is the most complex because it is so much like life itself. On the one hand, point of view is intertwined with the many interests and wishes of humanity at large; on the other, it is linked to the enormous difficulty of uncovering and determining truth.

Conditions That Affect Point of View

As this exercise in observation and expression demonstrates, point of view depends on two major details. The first is *the physical situation of the narrator, or speaker, as an observer*. How close to the action is the speaker? Is the speaker a major mover or major participant or no more than a witness, either close or distant? How much is he or she privileged to know? How accurate and complete are his or her reports? How do the speaker's characteristics emerge from the narration? What are his or her qualifications or limitations as an observer?

The second detail is *the speaker's intellectual and emotional position*. How might the speaker gain or lose from what takes place in the story? Do these interests color the speaker's observations and words? Does he or she have any persuasive purpose beyond being a straightforward recorder or observer? What values does the speaker impose upon the action?

In a story, as in many poems using narrative, authors take into account all these subtleties. For example, O'Connor's narrator, Jackie, in "First Confession" tells about boyhood family problems and his first experience with the sacrament of confession, but he has not yet fully separated himself from some of his childhood antagonisms. The narrator/speaker of Shelly Wagner's poem "The Boxes" is a mother describing the horror of searching for her lost son, who has drowned, and the anguish of her feelings in the years after the death. For these reasons, these narrators show their own involvement and concern about the events they describe. As readers, we need to determine how such varying modes of presentation determine the effects of these and all other stories and narrative poems.

POINT OF VIEW AND OPINIONS

Because *point of view* is often popularly understood to mean ideas, opinions, or beliefs, it must be stressed that the term is not directly synonymous with any of these. Point of view refers to a work's mode of narration, comprising narrator, language, audience, and perceptions of events and characters, whereas opinions and beliefs are thoughts and ideas that may or may not have anything to do with a narration.

One may grant, however, that the position from which people see and understand things (e.g., established positions of political party, religion, social philosophy, and morality) has a most definite bearing on how they think and, therefore, on their opinions and beliefs. Opinions also affect how people view reality, and opinions affect, if not control, what people say about their perceptions of the world around them. Therefore, opinions stem out of point of view and at the same time have an influence on point of view. People who favor a particular political party will have different things to say about the building of a bridge or about recommending that tolls should be increased for drivers using the bridge.

For purposes of this chapter, however, a discussion of point of view should emphasize how the narration and dramatic situation of a work create and shape the work. If ideas seem to be particularly important in a story, your objective should be not to analyze and discuss the ideas as ideas but rather to consider whether and how these ideas affect what the narrator concludes and says about the story's actions and situations.

Determining a Work's Point of View

In your reading, you will encounter a wide variety of points of view. To begin your analysis, first determine the work's grammatical voice (i.e., first, second, or third person).

Then study the ways in which the subject, characterization, dialogue, and form interact with the point of view.

In the First-Person Point of View, the Narrator Tells About Events That He or She Has Personally Witnessed

If the voice of the work is an "I," the author is using the **first-person point of view**— the impersonation of a fictional narrator or speaker who may be named or unnamed. In our hypothetical accident reports, both Alice and Bill are first-person speakers who are named. Similarly, the first-person narrators of O'Connor's "First Confession" and Poe's "The Cask of Amontillado" are named and clearly identified. By contrast, the first-person narrators of Matthew Arnold's "Dover Beach" and Samuel Taylor Coleridge's "Kubla Khan" are both unnamed, as are the speakers of Thomas Hardy's "Channel Firing" and Shakespeare's "Sonnet 30: When to the Sessions of Sweet Silent Thought." In Mark Twain's "Luck," there are two unnamed first-person speakers (the first "I" introduces the second "I").

First-person speakers report events as though they have acquired their knowledge in a number of ways:

- What they themselves have done, said, heard, and thought (firsthand experience).
- What they have observed others doing and saying (firsthand witness).
- What others have said to them or otherwise communicated to them (secondhand testimony and hearsay).
- What they are able to infer or deduce from the information they have discovered (inferential information).
- What they are able to conjecture about how a character or characters might think and act, given their knowledge of a situation (conjectural, imaginative, or intuitive information).

First-Person Speakers Come in Many Varieties Of all the points of view, the first person is the most independent of the author because, as we have seen, the first-person speaker may have a unique identity, with name, job, and economic and social position. Such a speaker is Jackie, the presumably young adult who tells a story in O'Connor's "First Confession" about troubles with his sister and mother that happened when he was a young child. The vistas of the first-person speaker may also be extended by the occasional use of the "we" personal pronoun. Such a first-person plural point of view lends additional reliability to the account, as in Shelly Wagner's poignant poem "The Boxes" and Matthew Arnold's "Dover Beach," because the characters that are included as "we" and "us," even if they are unidentified by the speaker, may be considered as corroborating witnesses.

Some First-Person Speakers Are Reliable, and Others Are Unreliable When you encounter a first-person narrative (whether a story or narrative poem), determine the narrator's position and ability, prejudices or self-interest, and judgment of his or her readers or listeners. Most first-person speakers describing their own experiences are to be accepted as **reliable** and authoritative. But sometimes first-person speakers are **unreliable** because they may have interests or limitations that lead them to mislead, distort, or even lie. There is reason, for example, to question the reliability of the narrator Jackie of O'Connor's "First Confession." As an adult, he is describing the events within his family and his after-school preparation sessions prior to his attending his first confession, but he is giving us his childhood memories, and he is not including the potential views of others about the ways in which things happened. Whether first-person speakers are reliable or unreliable, however, they are one of the means by which authors confer an authentic, lifelike aura to their works.

In the Second-Person Point of View, the Narrator Is Speaking to Someone Else Who Is Addressed as "You"

The **second-person point of view**, the least common of the points of view and the most difficult for authors to manage, offers two major possibilities. In the first, a narrator (almost necessarily a first-person speaker) tells a listener what he or she has done and said at a past time. The actions might be a simple retelling of events, as when a parent tells a child about something the child did during infancy or when a doctor tells a patient with amnesia about events before the causative injury. Also, the actions might also be subject to dispute and interpretation, as when a prosecuting attorney describes a crime for which a defendant is on trial or when a spouse lists grievances against an alienated spouse in a custody or divorce case. Still another situation of the second-person point of view might occur when an angry person accuses the listener of a betrayal or some other wrong. In such instances, it is worth bearing in mind that the point of view may be considered first person rather than second, for the speaker is likely to be speaking subjectively about his or her own perception or analysis of the listener's actions.

The second possibility is equally complex. Some narrators are obviously addressing a "you" but are instead referring mainly to themselves—and to listeners only tangentially—in preference to an "I," as in the last lines of Hardy's poem "The Man He Killed." In addition, some narrators follow the usage—not uncommon in colloquial speech—of the indefinite "you." In this use of point of view, the *you* (sometimes, particularly older works, *thou*) refers not to a specific listener but rather to anyone at all. In this way, the writer avoids the more formal use of such words as *one, a person,* or *people.* (Incidentally, the selection of *you* is nongender specific because it eliminates the need for the pronouns *he, she; she/he; he/she;* or *he or she.*)

It is not unusual for some narrators to address a listening audience as "you," and in this case, the situation may be categorized at least partially as second person. It is not uncommon in poetry for the speaker to include a "you" as a person being addressed. In addition to Hardy's poem "The Man He Killed," we see the "you" listener in Arnold's "Dover Beach" (the "love"), John Keats's "Bright Star" (a distant star, likely the North Star), and Christina Rossetti's "Echo" (the "love"). Shakespeare imagines a listener in Sonnets 30 and 73. In these works, which are strongly dramatic, the mythical second-person listener is significantly involved in prompting and interacting with the speaker.

In the Third-Person Point of View, the Speaker Emphasizes the Actions and Speeches of Others

If events in the work are described in the third person (*he, she, it, they*), the author is using the **third-person point of view**. It is not always easy to characterize the voice in this point of view. Sometimes the speaker uses an "I," as with the first narrator in Mark Twain's "Luck." Such a narrator may seem to be identical with the author, but at other times, the author creates a distinct **authorial voice**, as in Katherine Mansfield's "Miss Brill." There are three variants of the third-person point of view: *dramatic* or *objective*, *omniscient*, and *limited omniscient*.

The Dramatic or Objective Point of View Is the Most Basic Method of Narration The most direct presentation of action and dialogue is the dramatic or objective point of view (also called third-person objective). It is the basic method of rendering action and speech that all the points of view share. The narrator of the dramatic point of view is an unidentified speaker who reports things in a way that is analogous to a hovering or tracking video camera or to what some critics have called "a fly on the wall (or tree)." Somehow, the narrator/speaker is always on the spot—in rooms, forests, village squares, moving vehicles, or even in outer space—to tell us what is happening and what is being said.

The dramatic presentation is limited only to what is said and what happens. The writer does not overtly draw conclusions or make interpretations because the premise of the dramatic point of view is that readers, like a jury, can form their own judgments if they are shown the right evidence. Thus, Dudley Randall's "Ballad of Birmingham" is a short and powerful poem illustrating the dramatic point of view. It dramatizes a brief and poignant dialogue between a child and her mother, and it follows the mother to the scene of the bombed-out church to which the mother had sent the child. We, the readers, draw a number of conclusions about the situation (i.e., that racism is evil, that brutal violence is inexplicable, that innocent suffering is heart rending), but because of the dramatic point of view Randall does not *state* any of these conclusions for us.

The Narrator of the Omniscient Point of View Can See All, Know All, and Potentially Tell All The third-person point of view is **omniscient** (all-knowing) when the speaker not only presents action and dialogue but also reports the thoughts and reactions of the characters. In our everyday real world, we never know, nor can we ever know, what other people are thinking. For practical purposes, their minds are closed to us. However, we always make assumptions about the thoughts of others, and these assumptions are the basis of the omniscient point of view. Authors use it freely but judiciously to explain responses, thoughts, feelings, and plans—an additional dimension that aids in the development of character. For example, in Guy de Maupassant's story "The Necklace," the speaker takes an omniscient stance to explain the responses and thoughts of the major character and, though to a much lesser degree, of her husband. However, even in an omniscient point of view story, relatively little description is actually devoted to the thoughts of the characters, for most of the narration must necessarily be taken up with objective descriptions.

The Narrator or Speaker in the Limited or Limited-Omniscient Point of View Focuses on Thoughts and Deeds of a Major Character More common than the omniscient and dramatic points of view is the **limited third person** or **limited-omniscient third person**, in which the author concentrates on or *limits* the narration to the actions and thoughts of a major character. In our accident case, Frank, being Bill's friend, would be sympathetic to Bill. Therefore, Frank's report of the collision would likely be third-person limited, with Bill as the center of interest. Depending on whether a narration focuses on action or motivation, the limited third-person narrator may explore the mentality of the major character either lightly or in depth. The name given to the central figure on whom the third-person omniscient point of view is focused is the **point-of-view character**. Thus, Mathilde Loisel in "The Necklace," Miss Brill in "Miss Brill," Louise in Kate Chopin's "The Story of an Hour," and Goodman Brown in Nathaniel Hawthorne's "Young Goodman Brown" are all point-of-view characters. Almost everything in these stories is there because the point-of-view characters see it, hear it, respond to it, think about it, imagine it entirely, do it or share in it, try to control it, or are controlled by it.

Mixed Points of View

In some works, authors mix points of view in order to imitate reality. For example, many first-person narrators use various types of the third-person point of view during much of their narration. Authors may also vary points of view to sustain interest, create suspense, or put the burden of response entirely upon readers. Such shifting occurs at the end of Hawthorne's "Young Goodman Brown," where the narrator objectively and almost brutally summarizes Brown's loveless and morose life after his nightmare about evil. In poetry, the speaker of Arnold's "Dover Beach" speaks mainly for himself, but he also shifts to the "you" whom he is addressing and to "we" in the concluding lines, in reference to both himself and the "you." There is a comparable shift in Hardy's poem "The Man He Killed," in which the speaker shifts from "I" to include the listener as "you," meaning "you" and "I" together.

POINT OF VIEW AND VERB TENSE

Point of view refers to the ways narrators and speakers perceive and report actions and speeches. In the broadest sense, however, point of view may be considered a total way of rendering truth, and for this reason, the *tense* that the narrators choose is important. Most narratives rely on the past tense: The actions happened in the past, and they are now over.

The introduction of dialogue, however, even in a past-tense narration, dramatically brings the story into the present. Such dramatic rendering is accomplished by the dialogue concluding Maupassant's "The Necklace," for example, which emphasizes the immediacy of Mathilde's problems.

The narrator of a past-tense narrative may also introduce present-tense commentary during the narration—a strong means of signifying the importance of past events. Examples are in O'Connor's "First Confession," in which the narrator Jackie makes personal comments about the events he is describing, and in Twain's "Luck," a complex narrative in which the second first-person speaker both begins and ends his past-tense narrative in the present tense. It is also significant to note that the narrators of parables and fables use past-tense narratives as vehicles for teaching current lessons in philosophy and religion.

In recent years, a number of writers have used the present tense as their principal time reference. With the present tense, the narrative story or poem is rendered as a virtual drama that is unfolded moment by moment. In Shelly Wagner's "The Boxes," for instance, the speaker employs the present tense to emphasize that her pain is a constant part of her life.

Some writers intermingle tenses to show how time itself can be merged within the human mind because our consciousness never exists only in the present but instead is a composite made up of past memories cresting upon a present and never-ending wave sweeping us into the future. Thus, Matthew Arnold, in "Dover Beach," mingles the past, the present, and a hope for the future as he treats the difficulty of maintaining love and sincerity at a time of deteriorating faith and encroaching militarism.

Summary: Guidelines for Point of View

The following guidelines summarize and further classify the types of points of view. Use them to distinguish differences and shades of variation in stories and poems.

1. **First person** (*I, my, mine, me*, and sometimes *we, our*, and *us*). First-person speakers are involved to at least some degree in the actions of the work. Such narrators may have (a) complete understanding, (b) partial or incorrect understanding, (c) no understanding at all, or (d) complete understanding with the motive to mislead or lie. Although the narrators described in guidelines a through c are usually **reliable** and tell the truth, they may also sometimes be **unreliable**. The only way to tell is to study the story closely. Obviously, guideline d is by nature unreliable, but nevertheless the mode might possibly be accepted (although critically) on matters of detail.
   a. *Major participant*
      i. Who tells his or her own story and thoughts as a major mover
      ii. Who tells a story about others and about herself or himself as one of the major movers
      iii. Who tells a story mainly about others and about himself or herself only tangentially
   b. *Minor participant*, who tells a story about events experienced and witnessed.
   c. *Nonparticipating but identifiable speaker*, who learns about events in other ways (e.g., listening to participants through direct conversation, overhearing conversation, examining documents, hearing news reports, imagining what might have occurred). The narrative of such a speaker is a combination of fact and conjectural reconstruction.

2. **Second person** (*you* or possibly *thou*). This is a point of view that authors use often enough to justify our knowing about it. Its premise is that the speaker knows more about the actions of a character (the "you") than the character himself or herself does. (a) It is used when the speaker (e.g., lawyer, spouse, friend, sports umpire, psychologist, parent, angry person) talks directly to the listener and explains that person's past actions and statements. More generally, and in a colloquial and informal style, the speaker may also use "you" to mean (b) himself or herself, (c) the reader, or (d) anyone at all.

3. **Third person** (*she, he, it, they*). The speaker is outside the action and is mainly a reporter of actions and speeches. Some speakers may have unique and distinguishing traits even though no separate identity is claimed for them ("the unnamed third-person narrator"). Other third-person speakers who are not separately identifiable may represent the words and views of the authors themselves ("the authorial voice").

   a. *Dramatic or third-person objective.* The narrator reports only what can be seen and heard. The thoughts of characters are included only if they are spoken or written (dialogue, reported or overheard conversation, letters, reports, etc.).

   b. *Omniscient.* The omniscient speaker knows all, sees all, reports all, and when necessary, reveals the inner workings of the minds of any or all characters. Even an omniscient speaker, however, makes a mostly dramatic presentation.

   c. *Limited, or limited omniscient.* The focus is on the actions, responses, thoughts, and feelings of a single major character. Although the narration may concentrate on the character's actions, it may simultaneously probe deep within the consciousness of the character.

Writing About Point of View

In your essay on point of view, you should explain how point of view contributes to making the work exactly as it is. As you prepare to write, therefore, consider language, authority and opportunity for observation, the involvement or detachment of the speaker, the selection of detail, interpretive commentaries, and narrative development. The following questions will help you to get started.

Raise Questions to Discover Ideas

- How is the narration made to seem real or probable? Are the actions and speeches reported authentically, as they might be seen and reported in life?
- Is the narrator/speaker identifiable? What are the narrator's qualifications as an observer? How much of the story seems to result from the imaginative or creative powers of the narrator?
- How does the narrator/speaker perceive the time of the actions? If the predominant tense is the past, what relationship, if any, does the narrator establish between the past and the present (e.g., providing explanations, making conclusions)? If the tense is present, what effect does this tense have on your understanding of the story?
- To what extent does the point of view make the work interesting and effective?

First-Person Point of View

- What situation prompts the speaker to tell the story or explain the situation? What does the story tell us about the experience and interests of the narrator/speaker?
- Is the speaker talking to the reader, a listener, or herself? How does her audience affect what she is saying? Is the level of language appropriate to her and the situation? How much does she tell about herself?
- To what degree is the narrator involved in the action (i.e., as a major participant or major mover, minor participant, or nonparticipating observer)? Does he make himself the center of humor or admiration? How? Does he seem aware of changes he undergoes?
- Does the speaker criticize other characters? Why? Does she seem to report fairly and accurately what others have told her?
- How reliable is the speaker? Does the speaker seem to have anything to hide? Does it seem that he may be using the story for self-justification or exoneration? What effect does this complexity have on the story?

Second-Person Point of View

- What situation prompts the use of the second person? How does the speaker acquire the authority to explain things to the listener? How directly involved is the listener? What is the relationship between the speaker and listener? If the listener is indefinite, why does the speaker choose to use "you" as the basis of the narration?

Third-Person Point of View

- Does the author speak in an authorial voice, or does it seem that the author has adopted a special but unnamed voice for the work?
- What is the speaker's level of language (e.g., formal and grammatical, informal or intimate and ungrammatical)? Are actions, speeches, and explanations made fully or sparsely?
- From what apparent vantage point does the speaker report action and speeches? Does this vantage point make the characters seem distant or close? How much sympathy does the speaker express for the characters?
- To what degree is your interest centered on a particular character? Does the speaker give you thoughts and responses of this character (limited third person)?
- If the work is third-person omniscient, how extensive is this omniscience (e.g., all the characters or just a few)? Generally, what limitations or freedoms can be attributed to this point of view?
- What special kinds of knowledge does the narrator assume that the listeners or readers possess (e.g., familiarity with art, religion, politics, history, navigation, music, current or past social conditions)?
- How much dialogue is used in the story? Is the dialogue presented directly, as dramatic speech, or indirectly, as past-tense reports of speeches? What is your perception of the story's events as a result of the use of dialogue?

Tense

- What tense is used predominantly throughout the story? If a single tense is used throughout (e.g., present, past), what is the effect of this constant use of tense?
- Does the story demonstrate a mixture of tenses? Why are the tenses mixed? What purpose is served by these variations? What is the effect of this mixture?
- Is any special use made of the future tense? What is the effect of this use on the present and past circumstances of the characters?

Organize Your Essay About Point of View

Throughout your essay, you should develop your analysis of how the point of view determines such aspects as situation, form, general content, and language. The questions in the preceding section should help you decide how the point of view interacts with these other elements.

Introduction Begin by briefly stating the major influence of the point of view on the work. (*Example*: "The omniscient point of view permits many insights into the major character," or "The first-person point of view permits the work to resemble an exposé of back-room political deals.") How does the point of view make the work interesting and effective? How will your analysis support your central idea?

Body An excellent way to build your argument is to explore how a different point of view might affect the presentation of the work. Hardy's poem "Channel Firing," for example, uses a first-person speaker—a skeleton long buried in a churchyard cemetery near the ocean. This speaker is awakened by the noise of nearby naval guns, a bizarre situation prompting ironic humor that could not be duplicated with a third-person point of view. Hardy's first-person point of view is essential because we learn, firsthand, about the speaker's feelings. Indeed, the poem is totally dependent on this speaker. Conversely, Mansfield's "Miss Brill" employs the third-person limited point of view, with the speaker presenting an intimate portrait of the major character while also preserving an objective and ironic distance. If Miss Brill herself were the narrator, we would get the intimacy that encourages us to sympathize with her, but we would lose the distance that permits us to see her objectively.

You can see that this approach requires creative imagination, for you must speculate about a point of view that is not present. Considering alternative points of view deeply, however, will greatly enhance your analytical and critical abilities.

Conclusion In your conclusion, evaluate the success of the point of view. Is it consistent, effective, truthful? What does the writer gain or lose (if anything) by the selection of point of view?

Illustrative Essay

Shirley Jackson's Dramatic Point of View in "The Lottery"

[1] The dramatic point of view in Shirley Jackson's "The Lottery" enables her to render horror in the midst of the ordinary. The story, however, is not only one of horror: It may also be called a surprise story, an allegory, or a portrayal of human insensitivity and cruelty. But the validity of all other claims for "The Lottery" hinges on the author's control over point of view to make the events develop out of a seemingly everyday, matter-of-fact situation—a control that could not be easily maintained with another point of view.[1] The success of Jackson's point of view is achieved through her characterization, selection of details, and diction.[2]

[2] Because of the dramatic point of view, Jackson succeeds in presenting the villagers as ordinary folks attending a normal, festive event—in contrast to the horror of their real purpose. The contrast depends on Jackson's speaker, who is emotionally uninvolved and who tells only enough about the three hundred townsfolk and their customs to permit the conclusion that they are ordinary, common people. The principal character is a local housewife, Tessie Hutchinson, but the speaker presents few details about her beyond the fact that she is just as ordinary and common as everyone else—an important characteristic when she, like any other ordinary person being singled out for punishment, objects not to the lottery itself but to the "unfairness" of the drawing. So it is also with the other characters, whose brief conversations are recorded but not analyzed. This detached, reportorial method of making the villagers seem common and one-dimensional is fundamental to Jackson's dramatic point of view, and the cruel twist of the ending depends on the method.

[3] While there could be much description, Jackson's speaker presents details only partially in order to conceal the lottery's horrible purpose. For example, the speaker presents enough

---

[1]Central idea.
[2]Thesis sentence.

information about the lottery to permit readers to understand its rules, but does not disclose that the winning prize is instant death. The short saying "Lottery in June, corn be heavy soon" is mentioned as a remnant of a long-forgotten ritual, but the speaker does not explain anything more about this connection with scapegoats and human sacrifice (330). All such references do not seem unusual as the narrator first presents them, and it is only the conclusion that reveals, in reconsideration, their shocking ghastliness.

[4]   Without doubt, a point of view other than the dramatic would spoil Jackson's concluding horror, because it would require more explanatory detail. A first-person speaker, for example, would not be credible without explaining the situation and revealing feelings that would give away the ending. Such an "I" speaker would need to say something like "The little boys gathered rocks but seemed not to be thinking about their forthcoming use in the execution." But how would such detail affect the reader's response to the horrifying conclusion? Similarly, an omniscient narrator would need to include details about people's reactions (how could he or she be omniscient otherwise?). A more suitable alternative might be a limited omni-scient point of view confined to, say, a stranger in town or to one of the local children. But any intelligent stranger would be asking "giveaway" questions, and any child but a tiny tot would know about the lottery's horrible purpose. Either point-of-view character would, therefore, require revealing the information too soon. The only possible conclusion is that the point of view that Jackson chose—the dramatic—is best for this story. Because it permits her naturally to hold back crucial details, it is essential for the suspense-ful delay of horror.

[5]   Appropriate both to the suspenseful ending and to the simple character of the villagers is the speaker's language. The words are accurate and descriptive but not elaborate. When Tessie Hutchinson appears, for example, she dries "her hands on her apron" (329)—words that define her everyday household status. Most of these simple and straightforward words may be seen as part of Jackson's similar technique of withholding detail to delay the reader's understanding.

A prime example is the pile of stones, which is in truth a thoughtless and cruel preparation for the stoning, yet this conclusion cannot be drawn from the easy words describing it:

> Bobby Martin had already stuffed his pockets full of stones, and the other boys soon followed his example, selecting the smoothest and roundest stones; Bobby and Harry Jones and Dickie Delacroix—the villagers pronounced this name "Dellacroy"—eventually made a great pile of stones in one corner of the square and guarded it against the raids of the other boys. (327)

Both the nicknames and the seeming description of childhood games divert attention and obscure the horrible purpose of the natives and their stones. Even at the end, the speaker uses the word "pebbles" to describe the stones given to Tessie's son Davy (332). The implication is that Davy is playing a game, not participating in the killing of his own mother!

<u>Such masterly control over point of view is a major cause of the creative strength of Jackson's "The Lottery."</u> Her narrative method is to establish the appearance of everyday, harmless reality, which she maintains up to the beginning of the last ominous scene. She is so successful that a reader's first response to the stoning is that "such a killing could not take place among such common, earthy folks." Yet it is this reality that validates Jackson's vision. Horror is not to be found on moors and in haunted castles, but among everyday people like Jackson's three hundred villagers. Without her control of the dramatic point of view, there could be little of this power of suggestion.

[6]

Work Cited

Jackson, Shirley. *The Lottery.* Edgar V. Roberts. *Writing About Literature.* 13th ed. New York: Pearson, 2012. 327. Print.

Commentary on the Essay

The strategy of this essay is to describe how Jackson's dramatic point of view is fundamental to her success in building up to the shocking horror of the ending. Words of tribute throughout the theme are "success," "control," "essential," "appropriate," and "masterly." The introductory paragraph sets out three areas for exploration in the body: character, detail, and diction. In your own essay on point of view, you might well devote all your analysis to any one of these points, but for illustration here they are all included.

The body begins with paragraph 2, in which the aim is *not* to present a full character study (since the essay is not about character but about point of view) but rather to discuss the ways in which the dramatic point of view enables the characters to be rendered. The topic of the paragraph is that the villagers are to be judged not as complete human beings but as "ordinary folks." Once this idea has been established, the thrust of the paragraph is to show how the point of view keeps readers at a distance sufficient to sustain this conclusion.

The second part of the body (paragraphs 3 and 4) emphasizes the sparseness of detail as an essential part of Jackson's purpose of delaying conclusions about the real horror of the drawing. Paragraph 4, which continues the topic of paragraph 3, shows how assertions about alternative points of view may reinforce ideas about the actual point of view that Jackson employs. The material for the paragraph is derived from notes speculating about whether Jackson's technique of withholding detail to build toward the concluding horror (the topic of paragraph 3) could be maintained if the author had used differing points of view. A combination of analysis, thought, and imagination is, therefore, at work in the paragraph. In effect, the supporting details in the paragraph demonstrate a negative: Other points of view would not allow for the withholding technique. (The first-person and the omniscient points of view would require giving away the ending. Even the more congenial limited omniscient point of view would be ineffective because most point-of-view characters would uncover information rather than withhold it.) In light of the less suitable alternatives, therefore, paragraph 4 concludes by confirming the superiority of Jackson's use of the dramatic point of view.

The third section of the body (paragraph 5) emphasizes the idea that the flat, colorless diction defers awareness of what is happening; therefore, the point of view is vital in the story's surprise and horror. The concluding paragraph (6) emphasizes the way in which general response to the story, and its success, are conditioned by the detached, dramatic point of view.

Writing Topics About Point of View

1. Write a short narrative from the first-person point of view of one of these characters:
   - Mathilde Loisel in "The Necklace": How I ruined ten years of my life by not telling the truth.
   - The baker in "Miss Brill": My favorite customer.
   - Fortunato in "The Cask of Amontillado": Why is Montresor telling me about the special wine he keeps in the family vaults?

- Faith in "Young Goodman Brown": I don't understand why my husband is so sour and sullen all the time.
- Nora in "First Confession": My terrible younger brother.

2. How would Hawthorne's story "Young Goodman Brown" be affected if told by a narrator with a different point of view (different knowledge, different interests, different purposes for telling the story), such as the narrators of "The Lottery" or "The Story of an Hour"?

3. Recall a childhood occasion on which you were punished. Write an explanation of the punishment as though you were the adult who was in the position of punishing you. Be sure to consider your childhood self objectively, in the third person. Present things from the viewpoint of the adult, and try to determine how the adult would have learned about your action, judged it, and decided on your punishment.

4. Write an essay about the proposition that people often have something to gain when they speak and that, therefore, we need to be critical about what others tell us. Are they trying to change our judgments and opinions? Are they telling the truth? Are they leaving out any important details? Are they trying to sell us something? In your discussion, you may strengthen your ideas by referring to stories that you have been reading.

5. In the reference section of your library, find two books on literary terms and concepts. How completely and clearly do these works explain the concept of point of view? With the aid of these books, together with the materials in this chapter, describe the interests and views of the narrators in "First Confession," "Young Goodman Brown," "The Man He Killed," "On First Looking into Chapman's Homer," or another work of your choice.

Chapter 4

Writing About Character: The People in Literature

Writers of fiction create narratives that enhance and deepen our understanding of human character and human life. In our own day, under the influences of such pioneers as Freud, Jung, and Skinner, the science of psychology has influenced both the creation and the study of literature. It is well known that Freud buttressed some of his psychological conclusions by referring to literary works, especially plays by Shakespeare. Widely known though now old films such as *Spellbound* (1945) and *The Snake Pit* (1948) have popularized the relationships between literary character and psychology. Without doubt, the presentation and understanding of character are major aims of fiction (and literature generally).

In literature, a **character** is a verbal representation of a human being. Through action, speech, description, and commentary, authors portray characters who are worth caring about, cheering for, and even loving, although there are also characters you may laugh at, dislike, or even hate.

In a story or play emphasizing a major character, you may expect that each action or speech, no matter how small, is part of a total presentation of the complex combination of both the inner self and the outer self that constitute a human being. Whereas in life, things may "just happen," in literature, all actions, interactions, speeches, and observations are deliberate. Thus, you read about important actions such as a young man's convoluted pathway into mistrust and suspicion (Nathaniel Hawthorne's "Young Goodman Brown") or a devoted grandmother's errand of mercy (Eudora Welty's "A Worn Path"). By making such actions interesting, authors help you to understand and appreciate not only their major characters but also life itself.

Character Traits

In studying a literary character, try to determine the character's outstanding traits. A **trait** is a quality of mind or habitual mode of behavior that is evident in both active and passive ways, such as never repaying borrowed money, supplying moral support to friends and loved ones, being a person on whom people always rely, listening to the thoughts and problems of others, avoiding eye contact, taking the biggest portions, or always thinking oneself the center of attention.

Sometimes, of course, the traits that we encounter are minor and, therefore, negligible, but often a trait may be a person's *primary* characteristic (not only in fiction but also in life). Thus, characters may be ambitious or lazy, serene or anxious, aggressive or fearful, thoughtful or inconsiderate, open or secretive, confident or self-doubting, kind or cruel, quiet or noisy, visionary or practical, careful or careless, impartial or biased, straightforward or underhanded, "winners" or "losers," and so on.

With this sort of list, to which you may add at will, you can analyze and develop conclusions about character. For example, Mathilde in Maupassant's "The Necklace" indulges in dreams of unattainable wealth and comfort and is so swept up in her visions that she scorns her comparatively good life with her reliable but dull husband. It is fair to say that this denial of reality is her major trait. It is also a major weakness, because Maupassant shows that her dream life harms her real life. A contrast is seen in the speaker of Lowell's poem "Patterns," who is realistically facing the truth that her hopes for happiness have been destroyed because of her fiancé's battlefield death. By similarly analyzing the thoughts, actions, and speeches of the literary characters you encounter, you can draw conclusions about their nature and their qualities.

Distinguishing Between Circumstances and Character Traits

When you study a fictional person, distinguish between circumstances and character, for circumstances have value *only if you show that they demonstrate important traits.* Thus, if our friend Sam wins a lottery, let us congratulate him on his luck. His win does not say much about his *character*, however, unless you also point out that for years he has been regularly spending hundreds of dollars each week for lottery tickets. In other words, making an extraordinary effort to win the lottery *is* a character trait but winning (or losing) *is not*.

Or let us suppose that an author stresses the neatness of one character and the sloppiness of another. If you accept the premise that people care for their appearance according to choice—and that choices develop from character—you can use these details to make conclusions about a person's self-esteem or the lack of it. In short, when reading about characters in literature, look beyond circumstances, actions, and appearances, and attempt to determine what these things show about character. Always try to get from the outside to the inside, for it is the internal qualities of character that determine external behavior.

How Authors Disclose Character in Literature

Basically, authors rely on five ways of bringing characters to life. Remember that you must use your own knowledge and experience to make judgments about the qualities of the characters.

The Actions of Characters Reveal Their Qualities

What characters *do* is our best clue to understanding what they *are*. For example, walking in the woods is recreation for most people, and it shows little about their characters except a fondness for the outdoors (perhaps a significant trait). But Phoenix's walk through the woods in Eudora Welty's "A Worn Path" is difficult and dangerous for her. Her walk, seen within the context of her age and her mission, can be taken as the expression of her loving, responsible character. Often, characters are unaware of the meanings and implications of their actions. Smirnov in Anton Chekhov's play *The Bear*, for example, would be a fool to teach Mrs. Popov to use her dueling pistol because she has threatened to kill him with it. Even before he recognizes his love for her, he is subconsciously aware of this love, and his potentially self-destructive action shows that his loving nature has overwhelmed his instinct for self-preservation.

Like ordinary human beings, fictional characters do not necessarily understand how they may be changing or why they do the things they do. The strong inner conflict experienced by the two women in Glaspell's short play *Trifles* brings out their character strength. Theoretically, they have an overriding obligation to the law, but they discover that they have an even stronger personal obligation to the accused killer, Minnie. Hence, they show their adaptability and their willingness to alter their behavior as a result of the things they discover in the farmhouse kitchen. In Mansfield's "Miss Brill," the major character is alone—always alone—and she goes to a public park to enjoy the passing crowd (her only weekly entertainment). She eavesdrops on people sitting nearby and draws silent conclusions about them, thus vicariously sharing in their lives. She even supposes that all those in the park are actors, along with herself, performing in a massive drama of life. Her unrealistic daydreams reveal her habitual solitude and pathetic vulnerability.

The Author's Descriptions Tell Us About Characters

Appearance and environment reveal much about a character's social and economic status, and they also tell us about character traits. Mathilde in Maupassant's "The Necklace" dreams about wealth and unlimited purchasing power. Although her unrealizable desires destroy her way of life, they also cause her strength of character to emerge. The descriptions of the rural countryside in Eudora Welty's "A Worn Path" are unique and interesting, but beyond that, they bring out the determination of Phoenix, her loyalty and dedication to her grandson, and her age and softening physical condition.

What Characters Say Reveals What They Are Like

Although the speeches of most characters are functional—essential to keeping the action moving along—they provide material from which you may draw conclusions. When the second traveler in Hawthorne's "Young Goodman Brown" speaks, for example, he reveals his devious and deceptive nature even though he appears friendly. The lawmen in *Trifles* speak straightforwardly but without much understanding of the women in the story. Their speeches suggest that their characters are similarly direct but unimaginative, although their constant belittling of the two women indicates their inability to understand others.

Often, characters use speech to hide their motives, although we as readers should see through such a ploy. The narrator Montresor in Poe's "The Cask of Amontillado," for example, is a vengeful schemer, and we can see this much from his indirect and manipulative language to the equally unpleasant but gullible Fortunato. To Fortunato, Montresor seems friendly and sociable, perhaps unexpectedly so, but to us, he is clearly lurid and demonic.

What Others Say Tells Us About a Character

By studying what characters say about each other, you can enhance your understanding of the character who is being discussed. For example, the major character in Glaspell's *Trifles* is the farmwoman Minnie Wright. But Minnie never appears as a character, and we learn about her only through the conversations between Mrs. Hale and Mrs. Peters. It is from them that her character is revealed as an oppressed woman who has finally snapped and turned on her oppressor, her husband.

Ironically, speeches often indicate something other than what the speakers intend, perhaps because of prejudice, stupidity, or foolishness. Nora in O'Connor's "First Confession" tells about Jackie's lashing out at her with a bread knife, but in effect, she describes the boy's individuality just as she also discloses her own spitefulness.

The Author, Speaking as a Storyteller or an Observer, May Present Judgments About Characters

What the author, speaking as a work's authorial voice, says about a character is usually accurate, and the authorial voice can be accepted factually. However, when the authorial voice interprets actions and characteristics, as in Hawthorne's "Young Goodman Brown," the author himself or herself assumes the role of a reader or critic, whose opinions are, therefore, open to question. For this reason, authors frequently avoid interpretations and devote their skill to arranging events and speeches so that readers can draw their own conclusions.

Types of Characters: Round and Flat

No writer can present an entire life history of a protagonist, nor can each character in a story get equal time for development. Accordingly, some characters grow to be full and alive, while others remain shadowy. The British novelist and critic E. M. Forster, in *Aspects of the Novel,* calls the two major types "round" and "flat."

Round Characters Are Three-Dimensional and Lifelike

The basic trait of **round** characters is that we are told enough about them to permit the conclusion that they are three-dimensional, rounded, authentic, memorable, original, and true to life. They are the centers of our attention in most works of fiction. Their roundness and fullness are characterized by both individuality and unpredictability. It is true that, like all human beings, round characters have inherent qualities that the circumstances of a story bring out; therefore, their full realization as characters is directly connected to the stories in which they live their lives. Jackie, in O'Connor's "First Confession," is round and dynamic. We learn from his adult narration that he has been a normal and typical child, trying to maintain his sense of individuality amid what he considers to be embarrassing family circumstances. His thoughts about "solutions" to his problems are of course greatly in excess, but when the time comes for him to confess his "sins," he does not evade them but dutifully states everything that he has been thinking. As amusing as his story is, his confession about the truth of his inner thoughts constitutes the type of adjustment that characterizes him as a round character.

A complementary quality of round characters is that they are often **dynamic**. Dynamic characters *recognize, change with*, or *adjust to* circumstances. The reverse side of this coin is that circumstances may also bring a dynamic character to ruin. Such changes may be shown in (1) an action or actions, (2) the realization of new strength and, therefore, the affirmation of previous decisions, (3) the acceptance of new conditions and the need for making changes, (4) the discovery of unrecognized truths, or (5) the reconciliation of the character with adverse conditions. We may consider Minnie, in Glaspell's *Trifles*, as dynamic. We learn that as a young woman, she was happy and musical, though shy, but that she has been deprived and blighted by her twenty-year marriage. Finally, however, a particularly cruel action by her husband so enrages her that she breaks out of her subservient role and commits an act of violence. In short, her action shows her as a dynamic character who is capable of radical and earthshaking change. This is not to say that only round characters are dynamic, for less significant characters in a story may also be altered because of circumstances.

Because a round character plays a major role in a story, he or she is often called the **hero** or **heroine**. Some round characters are not particularly heroic, however, so it is preferable to use the more neutral word **protagonist** (the "first actor"). The protagonist is central to the action, moves against an **antagonist** (the "opposing actor"), and exhibits the ability to adapt to new situations.

Flat Characters Are Simple and One-Dimensional

In contrast with round characters, **flat characters** are simple and one-dimensional. They may have no more than a single role to perform in a story, or they may be associated with no more than a single dominating idea. Most flat characters end pretty much where they begin, and for this reason, we may think of them as **static**, not dynamic. Often, their absence of growth or development results from lack of knowledge or understanding or even from stupidity or insensitivity. Flat characters are not worthless in fiction, however, for they highlight the development of the round characters, as with the lawmen in Glaspell's *Trifles* and the characters whom Goodman Brown meets in Hawthorne's "Young Goodman Brown."

Usually, flat characters are minor (e.g., relatives, acquaintances, functionaries), but not all minor characters are necessarily flat. Sometimes flat characters are prominent in certain types of literature, such as cowboy, police, and detective stories, in which the focus is less on character than on performance. Such characters might be lively and engaging, even though they do not undergo significant change and development. They must be strong, tough, and clever enough to perform recurring tasks such as solving a crime, overcoming a villain, or finding a treasure. The term **stock character** is often used to describe characters who appear in these repeating situations. To the degree to which stock characters have many common traits, they are **representative** of their class or group. Such characters, with variations in names, ages, and sexes, have been constant in literature since the ancient Greeks. Some typical stock or representative characters are the insensitive father, the interfering mother, the sassy younger sister or brother, the greedy politician, the harassed boss, the resourceful cowboy or detective, the overbearing or henpecked husband, the submissive or nagging wife, the absent-minded professor, the angry police captain, the lovable drunk, and the town do-gooder.

Stock characters are usually also flat as long as they do no more than perform their roles and exhibit conventional and unindividual traits. When they possess no attitudes except those of their class, they are often called **stereotype** characters, because they all seem to have been cast in the same mold.

When authors bring characters into focus, however, no matter what roles they perform, the characters emerge from flatness and move into roundness. For example, Louise Mallard of Chopin's "The Story of an Hour" is a traditional housewife, and if she were no more than that, she would be flat and stereotypical. After she receives the news that her husband has died, however, the roundness of her character is brought out by her sudden and unexpected exhilaration at the prospect of being widowed and free. One may compare Louise with the title character of Mansfield's "Miss Brill." At first, Miss Brill seems dull. She almost literally has no life, and as a character, she is flat. But the story demonstrates that she protects herself by indulging in her remarkable inner life of imagination and creativity, and for this reason, she is to be judged as round. In sum, the ability to grow and develop and adjust to changing circumstances makes characters round and dynamic. Absence of these traits makes characters flat and static.

Reality and Probability: Verisimilitude

Characters in fiction should be true to life. Therefore, their actions, statements, and thoughts must all be what human beings are *likely* to do, say, and think under the conditions presented in the literary work. This is the standard of **verisimilitude**, **probability**, or **plausibility**. One may readily admit that there are people *in life* who perform tasks or exhibit characteristics that are difficult or seemingly impossible (such as always leading the team to victory, always getting an A+ on every test, always being cheerful and helpful, or always understanding the needs of others). However, such characters in fiction would not be true to life because they do not fit within normal or usual behavior.

You should, therefore, distinguish between what characters may *possibly* do and what they *most frequently* or *most usually* do. When we speak of character, we speak of a person's normal, not exceptional, behavior. Thus, in Guy de Maupassant's story "The Necklace," it is possible that Mathilde could be truthful and tell her friend Jeanne Forrestier about the lost necklace. In light of Mathilde's pride and sense of self-respect, however, it is more normal for her and her husband to hide the loss and borrow money for a replacement, even though they must endure the harsh financial consequences for ten years. Given the possibilities of the story (either self-sacrifice or the admission of a fault or a possible crime), the decision Mathilde makes with her husband is the more *probable* one.

Nevertheless, probability does not rule out surprise or even exaggeration. The sudden and seemingly impossible changes that conclude *The Bear*, for example, are not improbable because early in the play, Chekhov shows that both Mrs. Popov and Smirnov are emotional, somewhat foolish, and impulsive. Even in the face of their unpredictable embraces closing the play, these qualities of character dominate their lives. For such individuals, surprise might be accepted as a probable, or normal, condition of life.

Writers render probability of character in many ways. Works that are more or less mirrors of life, such as Mansfield's "Miss Brill," set up a pattern of ordinary, everyday probability. Less realistic conditions establish different frameworks of probability, in which characters are *expected* to be unusual, as in Hawthorne's "Young Goodman Brown." Because a major way of explaining this story is that Brown is having a nightmarish psychotic trance, his bizarre and unnatural responses are probable. Equally probable is the way in which the doctors explain Louise Mallard's sudden death at the end of Chopin's "The Story of an Hour" even though their smug analysis is totally and comically wrong.

You might also encounter works containing *supernatural* figures such as the second traveler in "Young Goodman Brown." You might wonder whether such characters are probable or improbable. Usually, gods and goddesses embody qualities of the best and most moral human beings, and devils such as Hawthorne's guide take on attributes of the worst. However, you might remember that the devil is often given dashing and engaging qualities so that he can deceive gullible sinners and then drag them screaming in fear into the fiery pits of hell. The friendliness of Brown's guide is, therefore, not an improbable trait. In judging characters of this or any other type, your best criteria are probability, consistency, and believability.

Writing About Character

Usually, when you write about character, your topic will be a major character in a story or drama, although you might also study one or more minor characters. After your customary overview of the story, begin taking notes. List as many traits as you can, and determine how the author presents details about the character through actions, appearance, speeches, comments by others, or authorial explanations. If you discover unusual traits, determine what they show. The following suggestions and questions will help you to get started.

Raise Questions to Discover Ideas

- Who is the major character? What do you learn about this character from his or her actions and speeches? From the speeches and actions of other characters? How else do you learn about the character?
- How important is the character to the work's principal action? Which characters oppose the major character? How do the major character and the opposing character(s) interact? What effects do these interactions create?

- What actions bring out important traits of the main character? To what degree is the character creating events and to what degree is he or she just responding to them?
- Describe the main character's actions: Are they good or bad, intelligent or stupid, deliberate or spontaneous? How do they help you to understand the character? What do they show about the character as a person?
- Describe and explain the traits, both major and minor, of the character you plan to discuss. To what extent do the traits permit you to judge the character? What is your judgment?
- What descriptions (if any) of how the character looks do you discover in the story? What does this appearance demonstrate about him or her?
- In what ways is the character's major trait a strength or a weakness? As the story progresses, to what degree does the trait become more (or less) prominent?
- Is the character round and dynamic? How does the character recognize, change with, or adjust to circumstances?
- If the character you are analyzing is flat or static, what function does he or she perform in the story (for example, by doing a task or by bringing out qualities of the major character)?
- If the character is a stereotype, to what type does he or she belong? To what degree does the character stay in the stereotypical role or rise above it? How?
- What do any of the other characters do, say, or think to give you understanding of the character you are analyzing? What does the character say or think about himself or herself? What does the storyteller or narrator say? How valid are these comments and insights? How helpful are they in providing insights into the character?
- Is the character lifelike or unreal? Consistent or inconsistent? Believable or not believable?

Organize Your Essay About Character

Introduction Identify the character you are studying, and refer to noteworthy problems in determining this character's qualities.

Body Use your central idea and thesis sentence to create the form for the body of your essay. Consider one of the following approaches to organize your ideas and form the basis for your essay.

1. **Develop a central trait or major characteristic,** such as "a single-minded dedication to vengeance" (Montresor in "The Cask of Amontillado") or "the habit of seeing the world only on one's own terms" (Miss Brill in "Miss Brill"). This kind of structure shows how the work embodies the trait. For example, a trait may be brought out in one part through speeches that characters make about the major character (as at the end of Welty's "A Worn Path") and in another part through that character's own speeches and actions (also in Welty's "A Worn Path"). Studying the trait thus enables you to focus on the differing ways in which the author presents the character; it also helps you to focus on separate parts of the work.
2. **Explain a character's growth or change.** This type of essay describes a character's traits at the work's beginning and then analyzes changes or developments. It is important to stress the actual alterations as they emerge but at the same time to avoid retelling the story. Additionally, you should not only describe the

changing traits but also analyze how they are brought out within the work, such as the dream of Goodman Brown or Minnie Wright's long ordeal.

3.   **Organize your essay around central actions, objects, or quotations that reveal primary characteristics.** Key incidents may stand out (such as using a bread knife to strike out against a person), along with objects that are closely associated with the character being analyzed (such as a broken birdcage). There may be important quotations spoken by the character or by someone else in the work. Show how such elements serve as signposts or guides to understanding the character. (See the following illustrative essay for an illustration of this type of development.)

4.   **Develop qualities of a flat character or characters.** If the character is flat (such as the sheriff and county attorney in *Trifles* or the servants in *The Bear*), you might develop topics such as the function and relative significance of the character, the group the character represents, the relationship of the flat character to the round ones, the importance of this relationship, and any additional qualities or traits. For a flat character, you should explain the circumstances or defects that keep the character from being round as well as the importance of these shortcomings in the author's presentation of character.

Conclusion   When bringing your essay to a close, show how the character's traits are related to the work as a whole. If the person was good but came to a bad end, does this misfortune make him or her seem especially worthy? If the person suffers, does the suffering suggest any attitudes about the class or type of which he or she is a part? Or does it illustrate the author's general view of human life? Or both? Do the characteristics explain why the person helps or hinders other characters? How does your essay help to clear up first-reading misunderstandings?

Illustrative Essay

The Character of Minnie Wright of Glaspell's "Trifles"

[1]   Minnie Wright is Susan Glaspell's major character in Trifles. We learn about her, however, not from seeing and hearing her, for she is not a speaking or an acting character in the play, but rather from the secondhand evidence provided by the play's actual characters. Lewis Hale, a neighboring farmer, tells about Minnie's behavior after the body of her husband, John, was found strangled. Mrs. Hale, Hale's wife, tells about Minnie's young womanhood and about how she became alienated from her nearest neighbors because of John's stingy and unfriendly ways. Both Mrs. Hale and Mrs. Peters, the sheriff's wife, make observations about Minnie

based on the condition of her kitchen. <u>From this information, we get a full portrait of Minnie, who has changed from passivity to destructive assertiveness.</u>[1] <u>Her change in character is indicated by her clothing, her dead canary, and her unfinished patchwork quilt.</u>[2]

<u>The clothes that Minnie has worn in the past and in the present indicate her character as a person of charm who has withered during the neglect and contempt of her married life.</u> Mrs. Hale mentions Minnie's attractive and colorful dresses as a young woman, even recalling a "white dress with blue ribbons" (DGL1–10). Mrs. Hale also recalls that Minnie, when young, was "sweet and pretty, but kind of timid and—fluttery" (DGL1–8). In the light of these recollections, Mrs. Hale observes that Minnie had changed—and for the worse—during her twenty years of marriage with John Wright, who is characterized as a "raw wind that gets to the bone" (DGL1–8). As more evidence for Minnie's acceptance of her drab life, Mrs. Peters says that Minnie asked for no more than an apron and shawl when under arrest in the sheriff's home. This modest clothing, as contrasted with the colorful dresses of her youth, suggests her suppression of spirit.

[2]

<u>The end of this suppression of spirit and also the emergence of Minnie's rage is shown by the discovery of her dead canary.</u> We learn that Minnie, who when young had been in love with music, has endured her cheerless farm home for thirty years. During this time, her husband's contempt has made her life solitary, cheerless, unmusical, and depressingly impoverished. But her buying the canary (DGL1–8) suggests the reemergence of her love of song, just as it also suggests her growth toward self-assertion. That her husband wrings the bird's neck may thus be seen as the cause not only of her immediate sorrow (shown by the dead bird in a "pretty box" (DGL1–10) but also of the anger that marks her change from a stock, obedient wife to a person angry enough to kill.

[3]

<u>Like her love of song, her unfinished quilt indicates her creativity.</u> In thirty years on the farm, never having had children, Minnie has

[4]

---

[1]Central idea
[2]Thesis sentence

nothing creative to do except for needlework like the quilt. Mrs. Hale comments on the beauty of Minnie's log-cabin design, and a stage direction draws attention to the pieces in the sewing basket (DGL1–7). The inference is that even though Minnie's life has been bleak, she has been able to indulge her characteristic love of color and form—and also of warmth, granted the purpose of a quilt.

[5]   Ironically, the quilt also shows Minnie's creativity in the murder of her husband. Both Mrs. Hale and Mrs. Peters interpret the breakdown of her stitching on the quilt as signs of distress about the dead canary and of Minnie's nervousness in planning revenge. Further, even though nowhere in the play is it said that John is strangled with a quilting knot, no other conclusion is possible. Both Mrs. Hale and Mrs. Peters agree that Minnie probably intended to knot the quilt rather than sew it in a quilt stitch, and Glaspell pointedly causes the men to learn this detail also, even though they scoff at it and ignore it. In other words, we learn that Minnie's only outlet for creativity—needlework—has enabled her to perform the murder in the only way she can, by strangling John with a slip-proof quilting knot. Even though her plan for the murder is deliberate (Mrs. Peters reports that the arrangement of the rope was "crafty" [DGL1–7]), Minnie is not cold or remorseless. Her passivity after the crime demonstrates that planning to evade guilt, beyond simple denial, is not in her character. She is not so diabolically creative that she plans or even understands the irony of strangling her husband (he killed the bird by wringing its neck). Glaspell, however, makes the irony plain.

[6]   It is important to emphasize again that we learn about Minnie from others. Nevertheless, Minnie is fully realized, round, and poignant. For the greater part of her adult life, she has patiently accepted her drab and colorless marriage even though it is so cruelly different from her youthful expectations. In the dreary surroundings of the Wright farm, she suppresses her grudges, just as she suppresses her prettiness, colorfulness, and creativity. In short, she had been nothing more than a flat character. The killing of the canary, however, causes her to change and to destroy her husband in an assertive rejection of her stock role as the suffering wife. She is a patient woman whose patience finally reaches the breaking point.

Work Cited

Glaspell, Susan. *Trifles. MyLiteratureLab.com.* Pearson. 2010. Web.
    23 Sept. 2010.

Commentary on the Essay

The strategy of this essay is to use details from the play to support the central idea that Minnie Wright is a round, developing character. Hence, the essay illustrates one of the types in the third approach described on page 90. Other plans of organization could also have been chosen, such as the qualities of acquiescence, fortitude, and potential for anger (first approach); the change in Minnie from submission to vengefulness (second approach); or the reported actions of Minnie's singing, knotting quilts, and sitting in the kitchen on the morning after the murder (a type of the third approach).

Because Minnie does not appear in the play but is described only in the words of the major characters, the introductory paragraph of the sample essay deals with the way in which we learn about her. The essay, thus, highlights how Glaspell uses methods 2 and 4 (see pages 89–90) as the ways of rendering the story's main character, while omitting methods 1 and 3.

The body is developed through inferences made from details in the play, namely, Minnie's clothing (paragraph 2), her canary (paragraph 3), and her quilt (paragraphs 4 and 5). The last paragraph summarizes a number of these details; it also considers how Minnie transcends the stock qualities of her role as a farm wife and gains roundness as a result of this outbreak.

As a study in composition, paragraph 3 demonstrates how a specific character trait, together with related details, may contribute to the essay's central idea. The trait is Minnie's love of music (shown by her canary). The connecting details, selected from study notes, are the loss of music in her life, her isolation, her lack of pretty clothing, the contemptibility of her husband, and her grief when putting the dead bird into the box. In short, the paragraph weaves together enough material to show the relationship between Minnie's trait of loving music and the crisis of her developing anger—a change that marks her as a round character.

Writing Topics About Character

1. Compare the ways in which actions and speeches are used to bring out the character traits of Jackie in O'Connor's "First Confession," Mrs. Popov in Chekhov's *The Bear*, and Goodman Brown in Hawthorne's "Young Goodman Brown."
2. Write a brief essay comparing the changes or developments of two major or round characters in stories or plays included in Appendix C or in MyLiteratureLab.

You might deal with issues such as what the characters are like at the beginning; what conflicts they confront, deal with, or avoid; or what qualities are brought out that signal the changes or developments.

3. Compare the qualities and functions of two or more flat characters (e.g., the men in Glaspell's *Trifles* or the secondary characters in Chopin's "The Story of an Hour"). How do they bring out qualities of the major characters? What do you discover about their own character traits?

4. Using Miss Brill (Mansfield's "Miss Brill") or Scoresby (Twain's "Luck") as examples, describe the effects of circumstance on character. Under the rubric "circumstance," you may consider elements such as education, family, economic and social status, wartime conditions, and geographic isolation.

5. Write a brief story about an important decision you have made (e.g., picking a school, beginning or leaving a job, declaring a major, or ending a friendship). Show how your own qualities of character (to the extent to which you understand them), together with your own experiences, have gone into the decision. You might write more comfortably if you give yourself another name and describe your actions in the third person.

6. Topics for paragraphs or short essays:

    a. What characteristics of the speaker who tells the story of Scoresby are brought out by Mark Twain in "Luck"? What qualities does he show that make his narrative possible? What is his interest in Scoresby?

    b. Why does the speaker of Matthew Arnold's "Dover Beach" philosophize about the darkness and the pounding surf nearby? What qualities of character do his thoughts reveal?

    c. Consider this proposition: To our friends, we are round, but to ourselves (perhaps) and to many other people, we are flat.

Chapter 5

Writing About a Close Reading: Analyzing Entire Short Poems or Selected Short Passages from Fiction, Longer Poems, and Plays

An essay based on a close reading is a detailed study of an entire short work, usually a poem or else a passage of prose or verse that is part of a longer work. This type of essay is specific because it focuses on the selected poem or passage. It is also general because you do not consider only a single topic, such as the nature of a character or the meaning of a particular idea; rather, you deal with all the elements you think are important. If the passage describes a person, for example, you might naturally want to discuss character. You might also want to stress the actions that are described in the passage, or noteworthy ideas or expressions of emotion, or descriptions of the location of an action if you decide that these matters are important. In other words, the content of a close-reading essay is variable. The passage you are studying governs what you write.

The Purpose and Requirements of a Close-Reading Essay

Writing a close-reading essay magnifies your abilities and increases your skills. Think of these implications: If you can read and assimilate a single paragraph, you have then developed your power to read and assimilate an entire book. And if you can follow and appreciate a single poem, you will have acquired the skill to comprehend other poems. In addition, if you can understand a single speech by a dramatic character—any speech—you can go on to do the same for the entire play. This is not to say that writing a close-reading essay gives you the magic power instantly to understand every work you read, but what it does give you is the development of abilities on which you can build—an approach toward your comprehension and appreciation of other works.

The essay is designed as an explanation of what is in the assigned passage. General content is the objective, together with anything else that is noteworthy. To write the essay, you do not need to undertake a detailed analysis of diction, grammar, or style. Instead, you should analyze and discuss what you consider the most important aspects of the passage. Although you are free to consider special words and phrases, and should do so if you find them important, your primary aim is to get at the content of your passage.

The Location of the Passage in a Longer Work

Close-reading essays about portions of a work should demonstrate how the passage is connected to the rest of the work. The principle is that all parts are equally important and essential. Analyzing an individual part, therefore, should bring out not only the meaning of the part but also the function of the part within the larger structure of the work.

Expect an Early Passage to Get Things Going

You may reasonably assume that in the early portions of a poem, play, or story, the author is setting things in motion, introducing you to the characters and ideas, and depicting the situations and problems that are going to be dealt with in the work. Therefore, you should try to discover how such early ideas, characterizations, insights, and descriptions are related to later developments. Always assume that everything you find there is connected to everything else in the work, and then analyze and explain that connection.

Expect a Midpoint Passage to Include Anticipations of the Work's Conclusion

In a passage at the work's midpoint, the story or idea usually takes a particular turn—either expected or unexpected. If the change is unexpected, you should explain how the passage focuses the various themes or ideas and then propels them toward the forthcoming conclusion or climax. It may be that the work features surprises, and the passage thus acquires a different meaning on second reading. It may be that the speaker has one set of assumptions while the readers have others and that the passage marks the speaker's increasing self-awareness. In short, your task is to determine the extent to which the passage (a) builds on what has happened previously and (b) prepares the way for the outcome.

Expect a Passage Near the End to Include Details About How Things Are Coming Together

A passage at or near the work's end is designed to solve problems or be a focal point or climax for all the cumulative situations and ideas. You will, therefore, need to show how the passage brings together all details, ideas, and themes. In a narrative work, what is happening? Is any action that is described in the passage a major action or a step leading to the major action? Has everything in the passage been prepared for earlier, or are there any surprises? In a longer narrative poem, such as an epic, what is happening to the topics and ideas introduced earlier in the poem?

Writing About the Close Reading of a Passage
in Prose Work, Drama, or Longer Poem

Focus on the general meaning and impact of the passage or poem. By raising and answering a number of specific questions, you can gather materials for shaping your essay. Once you have created answers, write them in a form that you can adapt in your essay. Try to reach specific and focused conclusions.

Raise Questions to Discover Ideas

- Does the passage (1) describe a scene, (2) develop a character, (3) present an action, (4) reveal a character's thoughts, (5) advance an argument, or (6) introduce an idea? How does all this work?
- What is the situation in the work? Who is the speaker? Who is being addressed? What does the speaker want? What ideas are contained in the work?
- What is the thematic content of the passage? How representative is it of the work as a whole? How does the passage relate to earlier and later parts of the entire text? (To deal with this question, you may assume that your reader is familiar with the entire work.)
- What noticeable aspects of diction and ideas are present in the passage? Do speeches or descriptions seem particularly related to any characterizations or ideas that appear elsewhere in the work?

Organize Your Essay on a Close Reading

Introduction Because the close-reading essay is concerned with details, you might have a problem developing a thematic structure. You can overcome this difficulty if you begin to work with either a generalization about the passage or a thesis based on the relationship of the passage to the work. Suppose, for example, that the passage is factually descriptive or that it introduces a major character or raises a major idea. Any one of these observations may serve as a central idea.

Body Develop the body of the essay according to what you find in the passage. For a passage of character description, analyze what is disclosed about the character together with your analysis of what bearing this information has on the story or play as a whole. For a passage presenting an idea or ideas, analyze the idea and demonstrate how the idea is important for the rest of the work. In short, your aim in this kind of essay is double: first, to discuss the passage itself and, second, to show how the passage functions within the entire work.

Conclusion To conclude, stress the important details of your analysis. In addition, you may want to deal with secondary issues that arise in the passage but do not merit full consideration. The passage may contain specific phrases or underlying assumptions that you have not considered in the body of your essay. The conclusion is the place to mention these matters without developing them fully.

> ## NUMBER THE PASSAGE FOR EASY REFERENCE
>
> In preparing your essay, prepare a copy of the entire passage just as it appears in the text from which you are making your selection. Copy it exactly. Include your copy at the beginning of your essay, as in the following illustrative essays. For your reader's convenience, number the lines in poetry and the sentences in prose.

Illustrative Essay

A Close Reading of a Paragraph from Frank O'Connor's Story "First Confession"[1]

[1] Nora's turn came, and I heard the sound of something slamming, and then her voice as if butter wouldn't melt in her mouth, and then another slam, and out she came. [2] God, the hypocrisy of women! [3] Her eyes were lowered, her head was bowed, and her hands were joined very low down on her stomach, and she walked up the aisle to the side altar looking like a saint. [4] You never saw such an exhibition of devotion, and I remembered the devilish malice with which she had tormented me all the way from our door, and wondered were all religious people like that, really. [5] It was my turn now. [6] With the fear of damnation in my soul I went in, and the confessional door closed of itself behind me.

[1]   This paragraph from O'Connor's "First Confession" appears midway in the story. It is transitional, coming between Jackie's "heartscalded" memories of family troubles and his happier memory of the confession itself. Though mainly narrative, the passage is punctuated by Jackie's recollections of disgust with his sister and fear of eternal punishment for his childhood "sins." It reflects geniality and good nature.[2] This mood is apparent in the comments of the narrator, his diction, the comic situation, and the narrator's apparent lack of self-awareness.[3]

---

[1]See pages 332–38 for this story.
[2]Central idea
[3]Thesis sentence

More impressionistic than descriptive, the paragraph concen-   [2]
trates in a good-humored way on the direct but somewhat exaggerated responses of the narrator, Jackie. The first four sentences
convey Jackie's reactions to Nora's confession. Sentence 1 describes
his recollections of her voice in the confessional, and sentence 3
makes his judgment clear about the hypocrisy of her pious
appearance when she leaves the confessional for the altar. Each of
these descriptive sentences is followed by Jackie's angry reactions,
at which readers smile if not laugh. This depth of feeling is
transformed to "fear of damnation" at the beginning of sentence 6,
which describes Jackie's own entry into the confessional, with the
closing door suggesting that he is being shut off from the world
and thrown into hell. In other words, the paragraph succinctly
presents Jackie's sights and reactions and his confusion about the
scene itself, all of which are part of the story's brief and comic
family drama.

The comic action of the passage is augmented by Jackie's simple   [3]
diction, which enables readers to concentrate fully on his responses.
As an adult telling the story, Jackie is recalling unpleasant childhood
memories, and his direct and descriptive choice of words enables
readers to be both amused and sympathetic at the same time. His
words are neither unusual nor difficult. What could be more
ordinary, for example, than *butter, slam, out, hands, joined, low,
people,* and *closed*? Even Jackie's moral and religious words fall
within the vocabulary of ordinary discussions about sin and
punishment: *hypocrisy, exhibition, devilish malice, tormented,* and
damnation. In the passage, therefore, the diction accurately conveys
Jackie's vision of the oppressive religious forces that he dislikes and
fears and that he also exaggerates. Readers follow these words easily
and with amusement.

It is from Jackie's remarks that the comedy of the passage   [4]
develops. Much of the humor rests on the inconsistency between
Nora's sisterly badgering and her saintly behavior at the confessional.
Since Jackie is careful here to stress her "devilish malice" against him
(sentence 4), readers might smile at the description of her worshipful

pose. But readers surely know that Nora is not unusual; she has been behaving like any typical older sister or brother. So there is also a comic contrast between her normal actions and Jackie's negative opinions. The humor is thus directed more toward the narrator than the sister.

[5]   In fact, it may be that the narrator's lack of self-awareness is the major cause of humor in the passage. Jackie is an adult telling a story about his experience as a seven-year-old. Readers might expect him to be mature and, therefore, to be amused and perhaps regretful about his childhood annoyances and anger. But his child's-eye view seems still to be controlling his responses. Comments about Nora such as "looking like a saint" and "You never saw such an exhibition of devotion" are not consistent with a person who has put childhood in perspective. Hence, readers may smile not only at the obvious comedy of Nora's hypocrisy, but also at the narrator's lack of self-awareness. As he comments on his sister with his still jaundiced attitude, he shows his own limitations and for this reason directs amusement against himself.

[6]   Readers are more likely to smile at Jackie's remarks, however, than to object to his adult character. The focus of the paragraph from "First Confession" is, therefore, on the good-natured comedy of the situation. For this reason, the paragraph is a successful turning point between Jackie's disturbing experiences with his sister, grandmother, and father, on the one hand, and the joyful confession with the kind and genial priest on the other. The child goes into the confessional with the fear of damnation in his thoughts, but after the ensuing farce, he finds the assurances that his fears are not justified and that his anger is normal and can be forgiven. Therefore, in retrospect, Jackie's anger and disgust were unnecessary, but they were important to him as a child—so much so that his exaggerations make him the center of the story's comedy. Jackie's bittersweet memories are successfully rendered and made comic in this passage from O'Connor's story.

> Work Cited
>
> O'Connor, Frank. "First Confession." Edgar V. Roberts. *Writing About Literature*. 13th ed. New York: Pearson, 2012. 332–38. Print.

Commentary on the Essay

A number of central ideas might have arisen about the passage chosen for analysis: that it is dramatic, that it centers on the religious hypocrisy of Jackie's sister, that it brings together the major themes of the story, or that it creates a problem in the character of the narrator. The idea of the illustrative essay as brought out in paragraph 1, however, is that the passage reflects geniality and good nature. The essay does in fact deal with the sister's hypocrisy and with the problem in the narrator's character, but these points are made in connection with the central idea.

In the body of the essay, paragraph 2 shows that the narrator's comments about his sister and his own spiritual condition add to the tone of good nature of the passage. Paragraph 3 deals with the level of diction, noting that the words are appropriate both to the action and to Jackie's anger when he is recollecting it. Paragraph 4 explains the relationship between Jackie's remarks and the comedy being played out in the narration. In paragraph 5, the adult narrator's unwitting revelation of his own shortcomings is related to the good humor and comedy. The final paragraph connects the passage to the latter half of the story, suggesting that the comedy that shines through the passage is, comparatively, like the forgiveness that is believed to follow the act of confession.

Because the essay is based on a close reading, its major feature is the use of many specific details. Thus, the second paragraph stresses the actions and some of Jackie's comments upon it, while the third paragraph provides many examples of his word choices. The fourth paragraph stresses the details about Nora's posturing and Jackie's comments about her. Paragraph 5 provides details of more of Jackie's comments and the limitations of character that they show. Finally, the concluding paragraph includes the detail about Jackie's entering the confessional.

Writing an Essay on the Close Reading of a Poem

The close reading of a poem does not mean that you need to explain everything you find there. Theoretically, a complete or total explication would require you to explain the meaning and implications of each word and every line—a process that obviously would be exhaustive (and exhausting, for both writer and reader). It would also be self-defeating, for writing about everything in great detail would prohibit you from using your judgment and deciding what is important.

A more manageable and desirable technique is, therefore, to devote attention to the meaning of individual parts in relationship to the entire work. You might think of your essay as your explanation or "reading" of the poem. You will need to be selective and to consider only those details that you think are significant and vital to the thematic development of your developing essay.

Raise Questions to Discover Ideas

- What does the title contribute to the reader's understanding?
- Who is speaking? Where is the speaker when the poem is happening or unfolding?
- What is the situation? What has happened in the past, or what is happening in the present, that has brought about the speech?
- What difficult, special, or unusual words does the poem contain? What references need to be explained? How does an explanation assist in the understanding of the poem?
- How does the poem develop? Is it a personal statement? Is it a story?
- What is the main idea of the poem? What details make possible the formulation of the main idea?

Organize Your Essay on the Close Reading of a Poem

In this close-reading essay, you should plan to (1) follow the essential details of the poem, (2) understand the issues and the meaning the poem reveals, (3) explain some of the relationships of content to technique, and (4) note and discuss especially important or unique aspects of the poem.

Introduction In your introduction, use your central idea to express a general view of the poem, which your essay will bear out. A close reading of Arnold's "Dover Beach," for example, might bring out the speaker's understanding that philosophical and religious certainty have been lost and that, therefore, people can find certainty only within trusting individual relationships. In the following illustrative essay describing Hardy's "The Man He Killed," the central idea is that war is senseless.

Body In the body of your essay, first explain the poem's content—not with a paraphrase but with a description of the poem's major organizing elements. Hence, if the speaker of the poem is a first-person "I," you do not need to reproduce this voice yourself in your description. Instead, describe the poem in your own words, with whatever brief introductory phrases you find necessary, as in the second paragraph of the following illustrative essay.

Next, explain the poem's development or growth in relation to your central idea. Choose your own order of discussion, depending on your topics. You should, however, keep stressing your central idea with each new topic. You might wish to follow your description by discussing the poem's meaning or even by presenting two or more possible interpretations. You might also wish to refer to significant techniques. For example, in Dudley Randall's "Ballad of Birmingham," a noteworthy technique is the unintroduced quotations (i.e., quotations appearing without any "she said" or "he said" phrases) as the ballad writer's means of dramatizing the dialogue between mother and "baby."

You might also introduce unique topics, such as the understatements in stanza two of "Ballad of Birmingham" that instruments of violence "Aren't good for a little child." Such a reference to the mother's language underscores adult attempts to shield children from the potential violence of the outside world, and therefore it makes the event described in the poem's conclusion especially ironic. In short, discuss those aspects of meaning and technique that bear upon your central idea.

Conclusion In your conclusion, you may repeat your major idea to reinforce your essay's thematic structure. Because your essay reflects a general but not an exhaustive reading, there will be parts of the poem that you will not have covered. You might, therefore, mention what could be gained from a more complete discussion of various parts of the poem (do not, however, begin an extensive discussion in your conclusion). The last stanza of Hardy's "The Man He Killed," for example, contains the words "quaint and curious" in reference to war. These words are unusual, particularly because the speaker might have chosen "hateful," "senseless," "destructive," or other similarly descriptive words. Why did Hardy have his speaker make such a choice? With brief attention to such a problem, you may conclude your essay.

Illustrative Essay

A Close Reading of Thomas Hardy's "The Man He Killed"[4]

Hardy's "The Man He Killed" exposes the senselessness of [1]
war.[5] It does this through a silent contrast between the needs of
ordinary people, as represented by a young man—the speaker—
who has killed an enemy soldier in battle, and the antihuman and
unnatural deaths that happen in combat. Of major note in this
contrast are the speaker's circumstances, his language, his sense
of identification with the dead man, and his concerns and
wishes.[6]

    The speaker begins by contrasting the circumstances of warfare [2]
with those of peace. He does not identify himself, but his speech
reveals that he is common and ordinary—a person, one of "the
people"—who enjoys drinking in a bar and who prefers friendship
and helpfulness to violence. If he and the man he killed had met in

[4]See page 354 for this poem.
[5]Central idea
[6]Thesis sentence

an inn, he says, they would have shared many drinks together, but because they met on a battlefield, they shot at each other, and he killed the other man. The speaker tries to justify the killing but can produce no stronger reason than that the dead man was his "foe." Once he states this reason, he again thinks of the similarities between himself and the dead man, and then he concludes that warfare is "quaint and curious" (line 17) because it forces a man to kill another man whom he would have befriended if they had met during peacetime.

[3]   To make the irony of warfare clear, the poem uses easy, everyday language to bring out the speaker's ordinary qualities. His manner of speech is conversational, as in "We should have sat us down" (line 3), and "'list" (for "enlist," 13), and his use of "you" in the last stanza. Also, his word choices, shown in words such as "nipperkin," "traps," and "fellow" (4, 15, and 18), are common and informal, at least in British usage. This language is important because it establishes that the speaker is an average man who has been thrown by war into an unnatural role.

[4]   As another means of stressing the stupidity of war, the poem makes clear that the two men—the live soldier who killed and the dead soldier who was killed—were so alike that they could have been brothers or even twins. They had identical ways of life, identical troubles with money, identical wishes to help other people, and identical motives in enlisting in the army. Symbolically, the man who was killed was so much like the speaker himself that the killing seems like a form of suicide. The poem, thus, raises the question of why two people who are so similar should be shoved into opposing battle lines in order to kill each other. This question is rhetorical, for the obvious answer is that there is no good reason.

[5]   Because the speaker (and also, very likely, the dead man) is shown as a person embodying the virtues of friendliness and helpfulness, Hardy's poem represents a strong disapproval of war. Clearly, political justifications for violence as a political policy are irrelevant to the characters and concerns of the men who fight.

They, like the speaker, would prefer to follow their own needs rather than remote and vague ideals. The failure of complex but irrelevant political explanations is brought out most clearly in the third stanza, in which the speaker tries to give a reason for shooting the other man. Hardy's use of dashes stresses the fact that the speaker has no commitment to the cause he served when killing. Thus the speaker stops at the word "because—" and gropes for a reason (9). Not being articulate, he can say only "Because he was my foe. / Just so: my foe of course he was; / That's clear enough" (10–12). These short bursts of words indicate that he cannot explain things to himself or to anyone else except in the most obvious and trite terms, and in apparent embarrassment, he inserts "of course" as a way of emphasizing hostility even though he felt none toward the man he killed.

A close reading thus shows the power of the poem's dramatic argument. Hardy does not establish closely detailed reasons against war as a policy but rather he dramatizes the idea that all political arguments are unimportant in view of the central and glaring brutality of war: killing. Hardy's speaker is not able to express deep feelings; rather, he is confused because he is an average sort who wants only to live and let live and to enjoy a drink in a bar with friends. But this very commonness stresses the point that everyone is victimized by war—not only those who die but also those who pull the triggers and push the buttons.

[6]

Work Cited

Hardy, Thomas. "The Man He Killed." Edgar V. Roberts. *Writing About Literature*. 13th ed. New York: Pearson, 2012. 354. Print.

Commentary on the Essay

This close-reading essay begins by stating a central idea about "The Man He Killed," then indicates the topics to follow that will develop the idea. Although nowhere does the poem's speaker state that war is senseless, the essay takes the position that the poem embodies this idea. A more detailed examination of the poem's themes might develop the idea by discussing the ways in which individuals are caught up in social and political forces or the contrast between individuality and the state. In this essay, however, the simple statement of the idea is enough.

Paragraph 2 describes the major details of the poem, with guiding phrases such as "The speaker begins," "he says," and "he again thinks." Thus, the paragraph explains how things in the poem occur, as is appropriate for a close reading. Paragraph 3 is devoted to the speaker's words and idioms, with the idea that his conversational manner is part of the poem's contrasting method of argument.

Paragraph 4 extends paragraph 3 inasmuch as it points out the similarities of the speaker and the man he killed. If the situation were reversed, the dead man might say exactly the same things about the present speaker. This affinity underscores the suicidal nature of war. Paragraph 5 treats the style of the poem's fourth stanza. In this context, the treatment is brief. The last paragraph reiterates the main idea and concludes with a tribute to the poem as an argument.

The entire essay, therefore, represents a reading and explanation of the poem's high points. It stresses a particular interpretation and briefly shows how various aspects of the poem bear it out.

Writing Topics for a Close-Reading Essay

1. For an Entire Poem
   a. Blake's "The Tyger" or Frost's "Desert Places." Try to establish how the poems bring out the speaker's ideas about evil or spiritual blankness.
   b. Keats's "On First Looking Into Chapman's Homer." How does Keats convey his sense of intellectual excitement and discovery?
2. For a Paragraph from a Story or Play
   a. Jackson's "The Lottery." Try to show how the passage connects the main character's imagination with her real death agony.
   b. Twain's "Luck." Try to show how the passage indicates the speaker's thoughts about the story's major character, Scoresby.
3. For a Single Speech or a Passage of Dialogue from a Play (You Choose)
   a. Glaspell's *Trifles*. Demonstrate how the speech (or speeches) shows the relationship between men and women.
   b. Chekhov's *The Bear*. How does the speech or passage create character as it also conveys the play's humor?

Chapter 6

Writing About Structure: The Organization of Literature

Structure refers to the ways in which writers arrange materials in accord with the general ideas and purposes of their works. Unlike plot, which is concerned with conflict or conflicts, structure defines the layouts of works—the ways in which the story, play, or poem is shaped. Structure is about matters such as placement, balance, recurring themes, true and misleading conclusions, suspense, and the imitation of models or forms such as reports, letters, conversations, or confessions. A work might be divided into numbered sections or parts, or it might begin in a countryside (or one state) and conclude in a city (or another state), or it might develop a relationship between two people from their first introduction to their falling in love.

Formal Categories of Structure

Many aspects of structure are common to all genres of literature. Particularly for stories and plays, however, the following aspects form a skeleton, a pattern of development.

The Exposition Provides the Materials Necessary
to Put the Plot into Operation

Exposition is the laying out, the putting forth, of the materials in the story: the main characters and their backgrounds, characteristics, interests, goals, limitations, potentials, and basic assumptions. Exposition might not be limited to the beginning of the work, where it is most expected, but may be found anywhere. Thus, intricacies, twists, turns, false leads, blind alleys, surprises, and other quirks may be introduced to interest, intrigue, perplex, mystify, and please readers. Whenever something new arises, to the degree to which it is new, it is a part of exposition.

The Complication Marks the Beginning and the Growth of the Conflict

The **complication** is the onset and development of the major conflict—the plot. The major participants are the protagonist and antagonist, together with whatever ideas and values they represent, such as good or evil, freedom or oppression, independence or dependence, love or hate, intelligence or stupidity, or knowledge or ignorance.

The Crisis Marks the Decisions Made to End the Conflict

The **crisis** (a separating, distinguishing, or turning point) marks that part of the action where the conflict reaches its greatest tension. During the crisis, a decision or an action to resolve the conflict is undertaken; therefore, the crisis is the point at which curiosity, uncertainty, and tension are greatest. Usually, the crisis is followed closely by the next stage, the *climax*. Often, in fact, the two are so close together that they are considered the same.

The Climax Is the Conclusion of the Conflict

Because the **climax** (Greek for "ladder") is a consequence of the crisis, it is the story's *high point* and may take the shape of a decision, an action, an affirmation or denial, an illumination or a realization, or a reversal of expectations and intentions. It is the logical, even if sometimes improbable, conclusion of the preceding actions; no new major developments follow it. In most stories and plays, the climax occurs at or close to the end. In Anton Chekhov's play *The Bear*, for example, the climax is that Smirnov suddenly holds and obviously touches the angry Mrs. Popov as he is instructing her in how to hold her dueling pistol, with which she is hoping to shoot him. Everything that happens before this situation leads to it. In this sudden embrace, Smirnov immediately loses all his anger toward Mrs. Popov and impetuously declares his love. This unexpected reversal is magnificently comic. Comparably, but with no such reversal and no such comedy, the climax of Amy Lowell's poem "Patterns" is the very last sentence of the speaker's monologue: "Christ, what are patterns for?" This outburst crystallizes the speaker's developing sorrow, frustration, anger, and hurt.

The Resolution or Dénouement Finishes the Work and Releases the Tension

The **resolution** (a releasing or an untying) or **dénouement** (untying) is the completing of the story or play after the climax, for once the climax has occurred, the work's tension and uncertainty are finished, and most authors conclude quickly to avoid losing their readers' interest. For instance, the dénouement of "Miss Brill" comprises a few short details about the major character's returning home, sitting down, and putting away her muff. Poe ends "The Cask of Amontillado" by the narrator's pointing out that all the events happened fifty years before. Jackson ends "The Lottery" quickly by describing the swiftness with which the townspeople award the "winning" prize. O'Connor ends "First Confession" with a short dialogue between the brother and sister. In other words, after the story's major conflicts are finished, the job of the dénouement is to tie things up as quickly as possible.

Formal and Actual Structure

The structure just described is a *formal* one, an ideal pattern that moves directly from beginning to end. Few narratives and dramas follow this pattern exactly, however. Thus, a typical mystery story holds back crucial details of exposition (because the goal is to mystify); a suspense story keeps the protagonist ignorant but provides readers with abundant details in order to maximize concern and tension about the outcome.

More realistic and less "artificial" stories might also contain structural variations. For example, Welty's "A Worn Path" produces a *double take* because of unique structuring. During most of the story, Phoenix's conflicts seem to be primarily age, solitude, and poverty. Instead of being able to ride on public transportation, for example, she is taking an unaccompanied walk through difficult and dangerous terrain. At the end, however, we are introduced to an additional difficulty—a new conflict—that enlarges our responses to include not just concern but also heartfelt anguish, for what had appeared to be a difficult walk becomes a virtually insurmountable problem involving age and illness. "A Worn Path" is just one example of how a structural variation maximizes the impact of a work.

There are many other possible variants in structure. One of these is called **flashback**, or **selective recollection**, in which present circumstances are explained by the selective introduction of past events. The moment at which the flashback is introduced may be a part of the resolution of the plot, and the flashback might lead you into a moment of climax but then go from there to develop the details that are more properly part of the exposition. Let us again consider our brief story about John and Jane (see also p. 59) and use the flashback method of structuring the story:

> Jane is now old, and the noise of two children squabbling next door causes her to remember the argument that forced her to part with John many years before. They were deeply in love, but their disagreement about her wishes for a career and equality split them apart. Then she pictures in her mind the years that she and John have spent happily together since they married. She then contrasts her present happiness with her memory of her earlier, less happy marriage, and from there she recalls her youthful years of courtship with John before their disastrous conflict developed. Then she looks over at John, sitting beside her on the sofa, and smiles. John smiles back, and the two embrace. Even then, Jane realizes that she is crying.

In this little narrative, the action begins and remains in the present. Important parts of the past flood the protagonist's memory in flashback, though not in the order in which they happened. Memory might be used structurally in other ways. An example is Wagner's poem "The Boxes," which is a narrative spoken by a mother to her dead son. The events of the poem are disclosed through the speaker's memories of the past, but the poem's conclusion depends on the speaker's temporary consideration that time has changed to a point before the death so that she can speak to her son as though he is still living. The poem thus searingly illustrates the poignancy and finality of the situation. In short, the technique of selective recollection permits a narrative that departs significantly from a strictly formal and chronological structural pattern.

Each narrative or drama has a unique structure. Some stories may be structured according to simple geography or room arrangements, as in Layton's poem "Rhine Boat Trip" (a meditation upon castles observed by a tourist on the Rhine leading to thoughts of cattle cars during the World War II Holocaust), in Maupassant's "The Necklace" (movement from a modest apartment to an attic flat to a local street), or in Poe's "The Cask of Amontillado" (a progressive movement downward from the street level to the Montresor family vaults). A story may unfold in an apparently accidental way, with the characters making vital discoveries about the major characters, as in Glaspell's *Trifles*. Additionally, parts of a work may be set out as fragments of conversation, as in O'Connor's "First Confession," or as a ceremony, as in Hawthorne's "Young Goodman Brown," or as an announcement of a party, as in "The Necklace." The possible variations in structuring literary works are literally almost infinite.

You might also aid yourself by drawing a scheme or plan to explain graphically the structure of the work you are analyzing. The story "Miss Brill," by Katherine Mansfield, for example, may be conveniently compared with a person running happily along a narrow path deep in a dark forest and making a turn only to plunge suddenly and unexpectedly off a steep cliff. You might graph this comparison like this:

In writing an essay about the structure of "Miss Brill," you could employ this scheme as a guide. This is not to say that the structure of the story could not be profitably analyzed in another way, but such a scheme might help you to give insight, meaning, and form to your essay.

Sometimes the use of an illustration can create an insight or series of insights that might at first not have been clear to you. For example, Shakespeare's Sonnet No. 73 has three quatrains and a concluding rhymed couplet. Here is the sonnet:

Quatrain I

That time of year thou mayst in me behold,
　　When yellow leaves, or none, or few do hang
Upon those boughs which shake against the cold,
　　Bare ruined choirs, where late the sweet birds sang.

Quatrain II

In me thou seest the twilight of such day,
　　As after sunset fadeth in the West,
Which by and by black night doth take away,
　　Death's second self that seals up all in rest.

Quatrain III

In me thou seest the glowing of such fire,
    That on the ashes of his youth doth lie,
As the death bed, whereon it must expire,
    Consumed with that which it was nourished by.

Concluding Couplet

This thou perceiv'st, which makes thy love more strong.
To love that well, which thou must leave ere long.

We can see a number of links connecting the quatrains and the couplet. Each quatrain refers both to the speaker's present state and to conditions that are passing or will pass—specifically, autumn, sunset, and a dying fire. In addition, the quatrains are grammatically parallel. Each one includes the phrase "in me," together with the parallel phrases "thou mayst behold," "thou seest," and "thou seest" again. In the couplet the phrase "thou perceiv'st" and the word "that" as a pronoun referring to the speaker appear, so that each major unit contains references to the speaker and his listener. In all of the quatrains, death is a common topic. It is spelled out specifically in quatrains II and III, and quatrain I refers to barren branches from which dying and yellowing leaves have fallen. The speaker states that he is in just such circumstances, so his concluding statement "To love that well, which thou must leave ere long" in the concluding couplet is a fitting resumé of the poem.

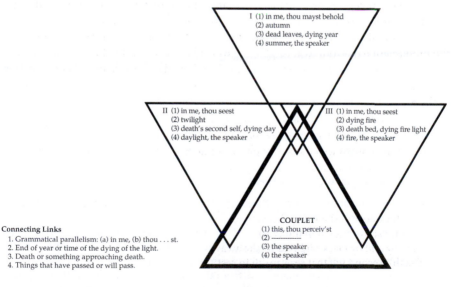

I (1) in me, thou mayst behold
(2) autumn
(3) dead leaves, dying year
(4) summer, the speaker

II (1) in me, thou seest
(2) twilight
(3) death's second self, dying day
(4) daylight, the speaker

III (1) in me, thou seest
(2) dying fire
(3) death bed, dying fire light
(4) fire, the speaker

COUPLET
(1) this, thou perceiv'st
(2) -------------
(3) the speaker
(4) the speaker

Connecting Links
1. Grammatical parallelism: (a) in me, (b) thou . . . st.
2. End of year or time of the dying of the light.
3. Death or something approaching death.
4. Things that have passed or will pass.

We might make these links vivid through a graph, not unlike the well-known Venn diagram method of using circles and ellipses to show connections among sets (after John Venn [1834–1923], an English logician). Allowing for the fact that each part must be independent and distinct as well as connected, a plan or graph might be made of four overlapping triangles, with a list of common elements included within the triangles as a key:

Connecting Links

1. Grammatical parallelism: (a) in me, (b) thou . . . st
2. End of year or time of the dying of the light.
3. Death or something approaching death.
4. Things that have passed or will pass.

In our sketch, interconnecting triangles show the structure of parallels and common topics, but in analyzing another work, you might prefer circles, lines, planes, other geometric figures, or a drawing like the poor fellow falling off the cliff. If you wish, you might make a list, and you always have the option of simply studying carefully and taking good notes. What is important is that you attempt to look at the work you are studying as a structure of some sort so that you can write an essay about this structure. Making a drawing or a graph has the virtue of giving you a visual grasp of the fact that the parts of a unified work are distinct and connected—important discoveries both for your understanding of the work and for your writing of an essay.

Writing About Structure in Fiction, Poetry, and Drama

Your essay should concern arrangement and shape. In form, the essay should not restate or summarize the part-by-part unfolding of the narrative or argument. Rather, it should explain why things are where they are: "Why is this here and not there?" is the fundamental question you need to answer. Thus, it is possible to begin with a consideration of a work's crisis and then to consider how the exposition and complication have built up to it. A vital piece of information, for example, might have been withheld in the earlier exposition, as in Welty's "A Worn Path" and Jackson's "The Lottery," to be introduced only at or near the conclusion. Therefore, the crisis might be heightened because there would have been less suspense if the detail had been introduced earlier. Consider the following questions in planning to write about the story's structure.

Raise Questions to Discover Ideas

- If spaces or numbers divide the story into sections or parts, what is the structural importance of these parts?
- If there are no marked divisions, what major sections can you find? (You might make divisions according to places where actions occur, various times of day, changing weather, or increasingly important events.)
- If the story departs in major ways from the formal structure of exposition, complication, crisis, climax, and resolution, what purpose do these departures serve?
- What variations in chronological order, if any, appear in the story (e.g., gaps in the time sequence, flashbacks or selective recollection)? What effects are achieved by these variations?

- Does the story delay any crucial details of exposition? Why? What effect is achieved by the delay?
- Where does an important action or a major section (such as the climax) begin? End? How is it related to the other formal structural elements, such as the crisis? Is the climax an action, a realization, or a decision? To what degree does it relieve the work's tension? What is the effect of the climax on your understanding of the characters who are involved in it? How is this effect related to the arrangement of the climax?

Organize Your Essay About Structure

Introduction Your essay should show why an entire narrative is arranged the way it is: to reveal the nature of a character's situation, to create surprise, to evoke sympathy, to reveal nobility (or depravity) of character, to unravel apparently insoluble puzzles, to express philosophical or political values, or to bring out maximum humor. However, you might also explain the structure of no more than a part of the story, such as the climax or the complication.

Body Your essay is best developed in concert or agreement with what the work contains. The location of scenes is an obvious organizing element. Thus, essays on the structure of Hawthorne's "Young Goodman Brown" and Mansfield's "Miss Brill" might be based on the fact that both take place outdoors (a dark forest for one and a sunny public park for the other). Similarly, an essay might explore the structure of Maupassant's "The Necklace" by contrasting the story's indoor and outdoor locations. In Glaspell's *Trifles,* much is made of the various parts of a kitchen in an early twentieth-century Iowa farmhouse, and an essay might trace the structural importance of these.

Other ways to consider structure may be derived from a work's notable aspects, such as the growing suspense and horrible conclusion of Poe's "The Cask of Amontillado" or the revelations about the "sinfulness" of Goodman Brown's father and neighbors in Hawthorne's "Young Goodman Brown."

Conclusion The conclusion should highlight the main parts of your essay. You may also deal briefly with the relationship of structure to plot. If the work you have analyzed departs from chronological order, you might explain the causes and effects of this departure. Your aim should be to focus on the success of the work as it has been brought about by the author's choices in development.

Illustrative Essay

The Structure of Eudora Welty's "A Worn Path"[1]

On the surface, Welty's "A Worn Path" is structured simply.
The narrative is not difficult to follow, and things go forward in

[1]

---

[1]See page 341–46 for this story.

straight chronological order. The main character is Phoenix
Jackson, an old, poor black woman. She walks from her rural home
in Mississippi through the woods to Natchez to get a free bottle of
medicine for her grandson, who is a hopeless invalid. Everything
takes place in just a few hours. This action is only the frame,
however, for a skillfully structured plot.[2] The masterly control of
structure is shown in the story's locations and in the way in which
the delayed revelation produces both mystery and complexity.[3]

[2]   The locations in the story coincide with the increasing difficulties faced by Phoenix. The first and most obvious worn path is the
rural woods with all its physical difficulties. For most people, the
obstacles would not be especially challenging, but for an older
woman, they are formidable. In Natchez, the location of the next
part of the story, Phoenix's inability to bend over to tie her shoe
demonstrates the lack of flexibility of old age. In the medical office
where the final scene takes place, two major difficulties of the plot
are brought out. One is Phoenix's increasing senility, and the other is
the disclosure that her grandson is an incurable invalid. This set of
oppositions, the major conflicts in the plot, thus coincide with
locations or scenes and demonstrate the power against Phoenix.

[3]   The most powerful of these conditions, the revelation about the
grandson, makes the story something like a mystery. Because this
detail is withheld until the story's end, the reader wonders for most of
the story what might happen next to Phoenix. In fact, some parts of
the story are false leads. For example, the episode with the young
hunter's dog is threatening, but it leads nowhere; Phoenix, with the
aid of the hunter, is unharmed. That she picks up and keeps his nickel
might seem at first to be cause for punishment. In fact, she thinks it
is, as this scene with the hunter (344, 53–55) shows:

> . . . he laughed and lifted his gun and pointed it at Phoenix.
> She stood straight and faced him.
> "Doesn't the gun scare you?" he said, still pointing it.

---

[2]Central idea.
[3]Thesis sentence.

"No, sir, I seen plenty go off closer by, in my day, and
for less than what I done," she said, holding utterly still.

But the hunter does not notice that the coin is lost, and he does not   [4]
accuse her. Right up to the moment of her entering the medical
building, therefore, the reader is still wondering what might happen.

Hence, the details about the grandson, carefully concealed until
the end, make the story more complex than it at first seems. Because
of this concluding revelation, the reader must go through a double
take, a reconsideration of what has gone on before. Phoenix's
difficult walk into town is then seen not as an ordinary errand but as
a hopeless mission of mercy. Her character also bears reevaluation:
She is not just a funny old woman who speaks to the woods and
animals; she is a brave and pathetic woman carrying on against
crushing odds. These conclusions are not apparent for most of the
story, and the bringing out of the carefully concealed details makes
"A Worn Path" both forceful and powerful.

Thus, the parts of "A Worn Path," while seemingly simple, are   [5]
skillfully arranged. The key to the double take and reevaluation is
Welty's withholding of the crucial detail of exposition until the
very end. The result is that parts of the exposition and complication, through the speeches of the attendant and the nurse, merge
with the climax near the story's end. In some respects, the detail
makes it seem as though Phoenix's entire existence is a crisis,
although she is not aware of this condition as she leaves the office
to buy the paper windmill. It is this complex buildup and emotional peak that make the structure of "A Worn Path" the creation
of a master writer.

Work Cited

Welty, Eudora. "A Worn Path." Edgar V. Roberts. *Writing About
Literature.* 13th ed. New York: Pearson, 2012. 341–46. Print.

Commentary on the Essay

To highlight the differences between essays on plot and structure, the topic of this illustrative essay is Welty's "A Worn Path," also the topic of the illustrative essay on plot (p. 61). Although both essays are concerned with the conflicts of the story, the essay on plot concentrates on the opposing forces, while the essay on structure focuses on the placement and arrangement of the plot elements. Please note that neither essay retells the story, event by event. Instead, these are analytical essays that explain the conflict (for plot) and the arrangement and layout (for structure). In both essays, the assumption is that the reader has read "A Worn Path"; hence, there is no need in the essay to retell the story.

The introduction of the essay points out that Welty's masterly structure accounts for the story's power. The second paragraph develops the topic that the geographical locations are arranged climactically to demonstrate the forces opposing the major character.

In paragraph 3, the subject is how the exposition about the grandson creates uncertainty about the issues and direction of the story. The early absence of this detail is thus vital structurally. As supporting evidence for this topic, the paragraph cites two important details—the danger from the hunter's dog and the theft of his nickel—as structural false leads about Phoenix's troubles. Other structurally important but misleading details could also be used as evidence for the argument, such as the dangers of the woods and the height of the stairs (both of which might cause fatigue or illness). The two conflicts that are cited in the paragraph, however, are enough to make the point about Welty's control of structure; further exemplification is not needed. The quoted passage shows how the reader's concern is pointed toward serious conflicts for Phoenix but not the major conflict brought out at the end by the disclosure of the grandson's condition.

The fourth paragraph deals with the complexity brought about by the delayed information: the necessary reevaluation of Phoenix' character and her mission to town. The final paragraph, 5, also considers this complexity, accounting for the story's power by pointing out how a number of plot elements merge near the end to bring things out swiftly and powerfully.

Writing Topics About Structure

1. What kind of story might "A Worn Path" be, structurally, if readers were initially told about Phoenix's purpose as she struggles on her way to town? How might the early narration of this detail make the story different from the story as we have it?
2. Consider the surprises in "The Story of an Hour," "The Necklace," and *The Bear*. How much preparation is made, structurally, for the surprises? In retrospect, to what degree are the surprises not surprises at all but rather necessary outcomes of the preceding parts of the works?
3. Compare the structuring of the interior scenes in Chopin's "The Story of an Hour" and Maupassant's "The Necklace." How do these scenes bring out the

various conflicts of the stories? How does the presence of characters in the individual rooms contribute to the organization of the stories? What is the relationship of these characters to the major actions of the stories?

4. Compare the ways in which attitudes toward law and military actions are organized in Glaspell's *Trifles,* Browning's "My Last Duchess," Twain's "Luck," and Lowell's "Patterns." How do these works structure your responses toward the people with power and those without power?

5. Write contrasting paragraphs about a character (whom you know or about whom you have read). In the first paragraph, try to make your reader like the character. In the second, try to create a hostile response to the character. Write an additional paragraph explaining the ways in which you tried to organize and shape these opposite responses.

Chapter 7

Writing About Setting: The Background of Place, Objects, and Culture in Literature

Like all human beings, literary characters do not exist in isolation. Just as they become human by interacting with other characters, they gain identity because of their cultural and political allegiances, their possessions, and their jobs, and where they live, and move, and have their being. They are usually involved deeply with their environments, and their surroundings are causes of much of their motivation and many of their possible conflicts. Plays, stories, and many poems must, therefore, necessarily include descriptions of places, objects, and backgrounds—the **setting**.

What Is Setting?

Setting is the natural, manufactured, political, cultural, and temporal environment, including everything that characters know and own. Characters may be either helped or hurt by their surroundings, and they may fight about possessions and goals. Furthermore, as characters speak with each other, they reveal the degree to which they share the customs and ideas of their times.

Authors Use Three Basic Types of Settings

1. **Private homes, public buildings, and various possessions are important in literature, as in life.** To reveal or highlight qualities of character and to make literature lifelike, authors include many details about objects of human construction and manufacture. Houses, both interiors and exteriors, are common, as are possessions such as walking sticks, garden paths, park benches, Christmas trees, necklaces, boxes, pistols, clocks, and hair ribbons. In Maupassant's "The Necklace," the loss of a comfortable home brings out the best in the major character by forcing her to adjust to her economic reversal. In Mansfield's "Miss Brill," the return of the major character to her lonely and shabby room brings out both the economic and emotional poverty of her life. The discovery of a quilt, still in the process of being sewed, explains the major character's feelings and actions in Glaspell's play *Trifles*.

Objects also enter directly into literary action and character. A broken birdcage reveals the pathetic and abusive husband-wife relationship in *Trifles*. The dress worn by the unnamed speaker in Lowell's "Patterns" enters into her thoughts as she contemplates the sudden news of her bereavement.

2. **Outdoor places are scenes of many literary actions.** The natural world is an obvious location for the action of many narratives and plays. It is, therefore, important to note natural surroundings (hills, shorelines, valleys, mountains, meadows, fields, trees, lakes, streams); living creatures (birds, dogs, horses, snakes); and the times, seasons, and conditions in which things happen (summer or winter, morning or evening, sunlight or cloudiness, wind or calmness, rain or shine, sunlight or darkness, snowfall or blizzard, heat or cold)—any or all of which may influence and interact with character, motivation, and conduct. Without the forest in Hawthorne's "Young Goodman Brown," there could be no story, for the events in the story could not have taken place anywhere else just as Hawthorne presents them.

3. **Cultural and historical circumstances are often prominent in literature.** Just as physical setting influences characters, so do historical and cultural conditions and assumptions. O'Connor's "First Confession" is written for an audience of readers who can easily understand the importance of church teachings in modern life. In Arnold's "Dover Beach," the speaker assumes an understanding of the religious skepticism that developed in the nineteenth century. In Chekhov's *The Bear*, the action takes place on an isolated late nineteenth-century Russian estate, and the characters, therefore, see a way of life that is vastly different from current circumstances. The broad cultural setting of Layton's poem "Rhine Boat Trip" brings out the contrast between the beauty of German scenery and mythology, on the one hand, and the ugliness and depravity of Nazi atrocities in World War II, on the other.

The Importance of Setting in Literature

Authors use setting to create meaning, just as painters include backgrounds and objects to render ideas. Such a use of setting is seen in Hawthorne's "Young Goodman Brown," in which a woodland path that is difficult to follow and is filled with obstacles is a major topographical feature. The path is of course no more than ordinary, given the time and conditions in the story, but it also conveys the idea that life is difficult, unpredictable, and mysterious. Similarly, in Glaspell's *Trifles*, the fixtures and utensils in the kitchen of the Wright farm suggest that Midwestern homesteads early in the twentieth century were bleak and isolated. Similarly, in "The Necklace," the relative plainness of a middle-class apartment in late nineteenth-century Paris brings out the major character's dissatisfaction not only with her straitened circumstances but also with the general nature of her existence.

Setting Is Often Essential and Vital in the Story

To study the setting in a narrative (or play), discover the important details and then try to explain their function. Depending on the author's purpose, the amount of detail may vary. Poe provides many graphic and impressionistic details in "The Cask of Amontillado," so we can follow, almost visually, the bizarre action at the story's end. In some works, the setting is so intensely present, like the country estate interior in Chekhov's *The Bear*, that it is a virtual participant in the story's outcome.

Setting Augments a Work's Realism and Credibility

One of the major purposes of literary setting is to establish **realism**, or **verisimilitude**. As the description of location and objects becomes particular and detailed, the events of the work become more believable. Maupassant places "The Necklace" in real locations in late nineteenth-century Paris, and for this reason, the story has all the semblance of having actually happened. Even futuristic, symbolic, and fantastic stories, as well as ghost stories, seem more believable if they include places and objects from everyday experience. Hawthorne's "Young Goodman Brown" and Poe's "The Cask of Amontillado" are such stories. Although these works make no pretense to portray everyday realism, their credibility is enhanced because they take place in settings that have a strong basis in reality.

Setting May Accentuate Qualities of Character

Setting may intersect with character as a means by which authors underscore the influence of place, circumstance, and time on human growth and change. Glaspell's setting in *Trifles* is the kitchen of the lonely, dreary Wright farm. This kitchen is a place of hard work, oppression, and unrelieved joylessness—so much so that it explains the loss of Minnie's early brightness and promise and helps us to understand her angry and destructive act.

The way in which characters respond and adjust to setting can reveal their strength or weakness. In Jackson's "The Lottery," for example, a number of townspeople have grave doubts about the custom of the yearly lottery, but even so, they participate in the concluding mob action. Their acquiescence shows their lack of sensitivity and their inconsistency of thought. In Nathaniel Hawthorne's "Young Goodman Brown," Goodman Brown's Calvinistic religious conviction that human beings are totally depraved, which is confirmed during his nightmarish encounter in the forest, indicates the weakness and gullibility of his character just as it alienates him from family and community.

Setting Is a Means by Which Authors Structure and Shape Their Works

Authors often use setting as one of the means of organizing their stories, as in Maupassant's "The Necklace." The story's final scene is believable because Mathilde leaves her impoverished home to take a nostalgic stroll on the Champs-Elysées, the most fashionable street in Paris. Without this change of setting, she could not have encountered her friend, Jeanne Forrestier, again, for their usual ways of life would no longer bring them together. In short, the structure of the story depends on a normal, natural change of scene.

Another organizational application of place, time, and object is the **framing** or **enclosing setting**, in which an author opens with a particular description or activity and then returns to the same topic at the end. An example is Welty's "A Worn Path," which both begins and ends with a description of the main character's taking a walk along a familiar route through the countryside and the nearby town. The use of objects as a frame is seen in Mansfield's "Miss Brill," which opens and closes with references to the heroine's shabby fur piece. In such ways, framing creates a formal completeness, just as it may underscore the author's depiction of the human condition.

Various Settings May Be Symbolic

If the scenes and materials of setting are highlighted or emphasized, they also may be taken as symbols through which the author expresses ideas. The horse Toby in Chekhov's *The Bear* is such a symbol. Mrs. Popov has made caring for the horse, which was her dead husband's favorite, a major part of her memorial obligations. When she tells the servants not to give oats to this horse, Chekhov is using this ordinary animal to indicate that new commitments replace old ones. In Arnold's poem "Dover Beach," the light that gleams from across the English Channel and that is soon "gone" may be understood as a symbol of the extinguishing of intellectual and religious faith that Arnold believed had taken place during the nineteenth century.

Setting Contributes to Atmosphere and Mood

Most actions *require* no more than a functional description of setting. Thus, taking a walk in a forest needs just the statement that there are trees. However, if you find descriptions of shapes, light and shadows, animals, wind, and sounds, you may be sure that the author is creating an **atmosphere** or **mood** for the action, as in Hawthorne's "Young Goodman Brown." There are many ways to develop moods. Descriptions of bright colors (yellow, white, red, orange) may contribute to a mood of happiness. Colors dimmed by weak light, like the catacombs in Poe's "The Cask of Amontillado," invoke gloom or augment hysteria. References to smells and sounds bring the setting to life further by asking additional sensory responses from the reader. The setting of a story in a small town or a large city, in green or snow-covered fields, or in middle-class or lower-class residences may evoke responses to these places that contribute to the work's atmosphere.

Setting May Underscore a Work's Irony

Just as setting may reinforce character and theme, so it may establish expectations that are the opposite of what occurs, not only in fiction but also in plays and poems. The colorful and orderly garden described in Amy Lowell's "Patterns" emphasizes the irony of the deeply sad and anguished speaker. The dueling pistols in Chekhov's *The Bear* bring out the irony of the developing relationship between the major characters. These guns, which are designed for death, in fact become the means that prompt the characters to fall in love. Hardy creates a heavily ironic situation in the poem "Channel Firing" when the noise of large guns at sea awakens the skeletons buried in an English churchyard. The irony is that those who are engaged in the gunnery practice, if "red war" gets still redder, will soon join the skeletons in the graveyard.

Writing About Setting

In preparing to write about setting, determine the number and importance of locations, artifacts, and customs. Ask questions such as the following.

Raise Questions to Discover Ideas

- How extensive are the visual descriptions? Does the author provide such vivid and carefully arranged detail about surroundings that you could draw a map or plan? Or is the scenery vague and difficult to imagine?
- What connections, if any, are apparent between locations and characters? Do the locations bring characters together, separate them, facilitate their privacy, make intimacy and conversation difficult?
- How fully are objects described? How vital are they to the action? How important are they in the development of the plot or idea? How are they connected to the mental states of the characters?
- How important to plot and character are shapes, colors, times of day, clouds, storms, light and sun, seasons of the year, and conditions of vegetation?
- Are the characters poor, moderately well off, or rich? How does their economic condition affect what happens to them, and how does it affect their actions and attitudes?
- What cultural, religious, and political conditions are brought out in the story? How do the characters accept and adjust to these conditions? How do the conditions affect the characters' judgments and actions?
- What is the state of houses, furniture, and objects (e.g., new and polished, old and worn, ragged and torn)? What connections can you find between these conditions and the outlook and behavior of the characters?
- How important are sounds or silences? To what degree is music or other sound important in the development of character and action?
- Do characters respect or mistreat the environment? If there is an environmental connection, how central is it to the story?
- What conclusions do you think the author expects you to draw as a result of the neighborhood, culture, and larger world of the story?

Organize Your Essay About Setting

Introduction Begin by briefly describing the setting or scenes of the work, specifying the amount and importance of detail. Continue by describing the topics you plan to develop.

Body As you prepare the body of your essay, you might need to combine your major approach with one or more of the others. Whatever topics for development you choose, be sure to consider setting not as an end in itself but rather as illustration and evidence for claims you are making about the particular story.

1. **Setting and action.** Explore the importance of setting in the work. How extensively is the setting described? Are locations essential or incidental to the actions? Does the setting serve as part of the action (e.g., places of flight or concealment, public places where people meet openly or hidden places where they meet privately, natural or environmental conditions, seasonal conditions such as searing heat or numbing cold, customs and conventions)? Do any objects cause inspiration, difficulty, or conflict (e.g., a bridge, a walking stick, a necklace, a mailbox, a dismal room, a hair ribbon, an ordinary box, a dead bird)? How directly do these objects influence the action?

2. **Setting and organization.** How is the setting connected to the various parts of the work? Does it undergo any changes as the action develops? Why are some parts of the setting more important than others? Is the setting used as a structural frame or enclosure for the story? How do objects, such as money or property, influence the characters? How do descriptions made at the start become important in the action later on?

3. **Setting and character.** (For examples of this approach, see the two drafts of the illustrative essay in Chapter 1.) Analyze the degree to which setting influences and interacts with character. Are the characters happy or unhappy where they live? Do they get into discussions or arguments about their home environments? Do they want to stay or leave? Do the economic, philosophical, religious, or ethnic aspects of the setting make the characters undergo changes? What jobs do the characters perform because of their ways of life? What freedoms or restraints do these jobs cause? How does the setting influence their decisions, transportation, speech habits, eating habits, attitudes about love and honor, and general behavior?

4. **Setting and atmosphere.** To what extent does setting contribute to mood? Does the setting go beyond the minimum needed for action or character? How do descriptive words paint verbal pictures and evoke moods through references to colors, shapes, sounds, smells, or tastes? Does the setting establish a mood, say, of joy or hopelessness, of plenty or scarcity? Do events happen in daylight or at night? Do the locations and activities of the characters suggest permanence or impermanence (such as a visit to a park, a walk in the woods, the repair of a battered boat, the description of ocean currents, the building of a fence)? Are things warm and pleasant or cold and harsh? What connection do you find between the atmosphere and the author's expressed or apparent thoughts about existence?

5. **Setting and other aspects of the work.** Does the setting reinforce the story's meaning? How? Does it establish irony about the circumstances and ideas in the story? In what way or ways? If you choose this approach, consult the introductory paragraph on "The Importance of Setting in Literature" earlier in this chapter. If you want to write about the symbolic implications of a setting, please consult Chapter 10.

Conclusion To conclude, summarize your major points or write about related aspects of setting that you have not considered. Thus, if your essay treats the relationship of setting and action, your conclusion might mention connections of the setting with character or atmosphere. You might also point out whether your central idea about setting also applies to other major aspects of the work.

Illustrative Essay

Maupassant's Use of Setting in "The Necklace"
to Show the Character of Mathilde[1]

[1]   In "The Necklace," Maupassant does not present vivid or detailed descriptions of setting. He does not even provide a description of the ill-fated necklace—the central object in the story—but states only that it is "superb." Rather than creating extensive descriptions, he uses the setting of the story to reflect the character and changes in the major figure, Mathilde Loisel.[2] Her character and growth may be related to the first apartment, the dream-life mansion rooms, and the attic flat.[3]

[2]   Details about the modest apartment of the Loisels on the Street of Martyrs (Rue des Martyrs) indicate Mathilde's peevish lack of adjustment to life. Although everything the Loisels own is serviceable, Mathilde is dissatisfied with the "drab" walls, the "threadbare" furniture, and the "ugly" curtains. She has domestic help but wants more than what is provided by the simple country girl who does the household chores. Mathilde's dissatisfaction is also shown by details of her infrequently cleaned tablecloth and the plain and inelegant beef stew that is her husband's favorite dinner dish. Even her best dress, which she wears to the theater, provokes her unhappiness. All these details of setting clearly show that her dominant character trait at the start of the story is maladjustment, and, therefore, she seems unpleasant and unsympathetic.

[3]   Like the real-life apartment, the impossibly expensive setting of her daydreams about wealth and luxury provokes her dissatisfaction and inhibits her capacity to face reality. In these dreams, all her rooms are large, draped in silk, and filled with the expensive furniture and bric-a-brac. Within this setting of her fantasies, she imagines private rooms for intimate talks and big dinners with

---

[1]See MyLiteratureLab for this story
[2]Central idea.
[3]Thesis sentence.

delicacies such as trout and quail. With dreams of such a rich home, she feels even more despair about her apartment. Ironically, this despair, together with her inability to live with actuality, is the cause of her economic and social undoing. It is the root cause of her borrowing the necklace (which, also ironically, is just as unreal as her daydreams of wealth), and it is the loss of this necklace that forces reality on her with the loss of her first apartment and the move to a life of deprivation and endless work in the cheap attic flat.

An additional irony is that the attic flat brings out coarseness in her character while at the same times it brings out her best qualities of cooperativeness, pride, and honesty. There is little detail about this flat except that it is cheap and that Mathilde must walk up many stairs to reach it. Maupassant emphasizes the drudgery of the work she must do to maintain the flat, such as washing floors with large pails of water and haggling about prices with local shopkeepers and tradespeople. Although she speaks loudly, gives up hair and hand care, and wears the cheapest dresses, all her efforts in keeping up the flat make her heroic, as Maupassant's narrator emphasizes. While Mathilde cooperates to help her husband, Loisel, save enough money to pay back the loans, her dreams of a mansion fade, and all she has left of her former life is the memory of that one happy and delightful evening at the Minister of Education's reception. Thus, being forced to live in the attic flat brings out her physical change for the worse at the same time that it brings out her psychological and moral change for the better.

Other details of setting in "The Necklace" have a similar bearing on the character of Mathilde. Thus, the story mentions little about the big party scene but emphasizes only that Mathilde was a great "success"—certainly a detail that shows her ability to shine if given the chance. When she and her husband return to their first apartment and discover the loss of the necklace, Maupassant includes details about the Parisian streets, the visits to loan sharks, and the jewelry and jewelry-case shop, to bring out Mathilde's sense of honesty and pride as she and her husband prepare for the long years to be lived in relative poverty. Anything that is not focused on

[4]

[5]

Mathilde's deprived life is not needed in the story, nor is it included. Thus, in "The Necklace," Maupassant uses setting as a means to highlight Mathilde's maladjustment, her needless misfortune, her loss of youth and beauty, and finally her growth as a responsible human being.

Work Cited

Maupassant, Guy de. "The Necklace." trans. Edgar V. Roberts.
    Edgar V. Roberts. *Literature*. 10th ed. New York: Pearson,
    2012. 200–05. Print.

Commentary on the Essay

This essay illustrates how a writer may relate the setting of a work to a major character (type 3 above). While this approach necessarily requires emphasis on character traits, it is important to note that these traits are brought out only as they are related to details about place and objects. The topic is setting and its relationship to character, not character alone or setting alone.

The introduction of the essay makes the point that Maupassant uses just as much detail as he needs and no more. The essay's central idea is that the details of setting may be directly related to Mathilde's character as it is first shown and as it develops in the story. The thesis sentence does not indicate a plan to deal with all the aspects of setting in the story but mentions only two real places and one imaginary place.

Paragraphs 2 and 3 show how Mathilde's real-life apartment and dream-life mansion bring out her dissatisfaction and inability to face reality. The fourth paragraph connects the Loisels' attic flat in a cheaper neighborhood with both the dulling and coarsening of Mathilde's character and the emergence of her admirable qualities. The idea here is that while better surroundings at the start reinforce her inabilities and lack of adjustment, the poorer surroundings of the ugly flat are associated not only with the expected and predictable loss of her looks and her youth but also with her unexpected development of honesty, cooperation, hard work, and endurance.

The conclusion cites additional examples of Maupassant's use of setting and asserts that all details of setting are focused directly on Mathilde and on her at first unexpected growth because she is the major character and center of interest in "The Necklace."

Writing Topics About Setting

1. Compare and contrast how details of setting are used to establish the qualities and traits of the following characters: Mrs. Popov in *The Bear* and Miss Brill in "Miss Brill" or the speakers in "Desert Places," "That Time of Year Thou Mayst in Me Behold," or "The Boxes."
2. In what ways might we say that the events of both "The Story of an Hour" and "The Necklace" are governed by the settings of the stories? To answer this question, consider the relationship of character to place and circumstance. How could the actions of the stories happen without the locations in which they occur?
3. Compare and contrast how details of setting establish qualities and traits of the following characters: Faith in "Young Goodman Brown," Miss Brill in "Miss Brill," Nora in "First Confession," Mrs. Popov in "The Bear," and Louise in "The Story of an Hour." To add to your comparison, you might introduce details about women in paintings or works of sculpture that you know.
4. Choose a story from Appendix C or in MyLiteratureLab and rewrite a page or two, taking the characters out of their setting and placing them in an entirely new setting or in the setting of another story (you choose). Then write a brief analysis dealing with these questions: How were your characters affected by their new settings? Did you make them change slowly or rapidly? Why? As a result of your rewriting, what can you conclude about the uses of setting in fiction?
5. Write a short narrative as though it is part of a story (which you may also wish to write for the assignment), using one or both of the following options:
   a. Relate a natural setting or type of day to a mood—for example, a nice day to happiness and satisfaction or a cold, cloudy, rainy day to sadness. Or create irony by relating the nice day to sadness or the rainy day to happiness.
   b. Indicate how an object or a circumstance becomes the cause of conflict or reconciliation (such as the lost necklace in "The Necklace," the dead canary in *Trifles*, or the trip through the forest in "Young Goodman Brown").
6. In your library, locate two books on the career of Edgar Allan Poe. On the basis of the information you find in these sources, write a brief account of Poe's uses of setting and place to evoke atmosphere and to bring out qualities of human character.

Chapter 8

Writing About an Idea or Theme: The Meaning and the "Message" in Literature

Fiction, Poetry, and Drama

Idea is a word—not easily defined—that broadly refers to the result or results of thought. Synonymous words are *concept, thought, opinion,* and *principle.* Other words that are sometimes used synonymously are *assertion, assumption, conclusion, conviction, creed, dogma, hypothesis, proposition,* and *supposition.* In short, there are many words that refer to the results of thinking—all of them either tightly or loosely connected to the word *idea.* In literary study, the consideration of ideas relates to *meaning, interpretation, explanation,* and *significance.* Although ideas are usually extensive and complex (and, often, elusive), separate ideas can be named by single words, such as *right, good, love, piety, causality, wilderness,* and, not surprisingly, *idea* itself. President Abraham Lincoln stated that our nation was "conceived in [the idea of] liberty, and dedicated to the proposition [i.e., the idea] that all men are created equal." It would be difficult to overstate the power and importance of these ideas.

Ideas and Assertions

Although single words alone can name ideas, we must put these words into operation in *sentences* or *assertions* before they can advance our understanding. Good operational sentences about ideas are not the same as ordinary conversational statements such as "It's a nice day." An observation of this sort can be true (depending on the weather), but it gives us no ideas and does not stimulate our minds. Rather, a sentence asserting an idea should initiate a thought or argument about the day's quality, such as "A nice day requires light breezes, blue sky, a warm sun, relaxation, and happiness." Because this sentence makes an assertion about the word *nice,* it allows us to consider and develop the idea of a nice day.

In studying literature, always express ideas as assertions. For example, you might state that an idea in Anton Chekhov's *The Bear* is "love," but it would be difficult to discuss anything more unless you make an assertion promising an argument, such as "This play demonstrates the idea that love is irrational and irresistible." This assertion could lead you to explain the unlikely love that bursts out in the play. Similarly, for Eudora Welty's "A Worn Path," you might express the following idea, which would require further explanation: "The story of Phoenix's mission on her walk to town embodies the idea that caring for others gives no reward but the continuation of the duty itself."

Although we have noted only one idea in these two works, most stories contain many ideas. When one of the ideas turns up over and over again throughout a work, we may call this idea the **theme** of the story, play, or poem. In practice, the words *theme* and *major idea* mean the same thing.

Ideas and Values

Literature embodies **values** along with ideas. The word *value*, of course, commonly refers to the price of something, but in the realm of ideas and principles, a value is a standard of what is desired, sought, esteemed, and treasured. For example, *democracy* refers to our political system, but it is also a complex idea of representative government that we esteem most highly, and so do we esteem concepts such as honor, cooperation, generosity, and love. A vital idea or value is *justice*, which, put most simply, involves equality before the law and the fair evaluation of conduct that is deemed unacceptable or illegal. Such an idea of justice is a major topic of Glaspell's play *Trifles*. Glaspell dramatizes the story of a farm wife who for thirty years has endured her husband's intimidation and her abject circumstances of life but finally has risen up against him and strangled him in his sleep. According to a rigid concept of justice as guilt-conviction-punishment, the wife, Minnie Wright, is guilty and should be convicted and punished. But justice as an idea also involves a full and fair consideration of the circumstances and motivation of wrongdoing, and it is such a consideration that the two women in the play make during their examination of Minnie's kitchen. Many of their speeches showing their sympathy to Minnie are equivalent to a jury deliberation. Their final decision is like a verdict, and their final concealment of Minnie's guilt is evidence for the idea that justice, to be most highly valued, should be tempered with understanding, even if the women do not use these exact words in their discussions of Minnie's situation. In short, the idea of justice underlying Glaspell's *Trifles* also involves a deeply held value.

The Place of Ideas in Literature

Because writers of poems, plays, and stories are usually not systematic philosophers, it is not appropriate to go "message hunting" as though their works contained nothing but ideas. Indeed, there is great benefit and pleasure to be derived from just savoring a work—following the patterns of narrative and conflict, getting to know the characters, understanding the work's implications and suggestions, and listening to the sounds of the author's words, to name only a few of the reasons for which literature is treasured.

Nevertheless, ideas are vital to understanding and appreciating literature, for writers have ideas and want to communicate them. For example, in *The Bear*, Chekhov directs laughter at two unlikely people suddenly and unpredictably falling in love. The play is funny, however, not only because it is preposterous but also because it is based on the *idea* that love takes precedence over other resolutions that people might make. Blake in "The Tyger" describes the "fearful symmetry" of a wild tiger in "the forests of the night," but the poem also embodies *ideas* about the inexplicable nature of evil, the mystery of life, and the unsearchability of divine purpose in the universe.

Distinguish Between Ideas and Actions

As you analyze works for ideas, it is important to avoid the trap of confusing ideas and actions. Such a trap is contained in the following sentence about O'Connor's "First Confession": "The major character, Jackie, misbehaves at home and tries to slash his sister with a bread-knife." This sentence successfully describes a major action in the story, but it does not express an *idea* that connects characters and events, and for this reason, it obstructs understanding. Some possible connections might be achieved with sentences like these: "'First Confession' illustrates the idea that family life may produce anger and potential violence" or "'First Confession' shows that compelling children to accept authority may cause effects that are the opposite of adult intentions." A study based on these connecting formulations could be focused on ideas and would not be sidetracked into doing no more than retelling O'Connor's story.

Distinguish Between Ideas and Situations

You should also make a distinction between situations and ideas. For example, in Lowell's poem "Patterns," the narrator describes what is happening to her as a result of her fiancé's death. Her plight is not an idea, but a situation that brings out ideas, such as that future plans may be destroyed by uncontrollable circumstances, that fate strikes the fortunate as well as the unfortunate, or that human institutions often seem arbitrary, capricious, and cruel. If you are able in such ways to distinguish a work's various situations from the writer's major idea or ideas, you will be able to focus on ideas and, therefore, sharpen your own thinking.

How to Locate Ideas

Ideas are not as obvious as characters or setting. To determine an idea, you need to consider the meaning of what you read and then to develop explanatory and comprehensive assertions. Your assertions need not be the same as those that others might make. People notice different things, and individual formulations vary. In Kate Chopin's "The Story of an Hour," for example, an initial expression of some of the story's ideas might take any of the following forms: (1) Even in a good marriage, husbands and wives can have ambivalent feelings about their married life. (2) An accident can bring out negative but previously unrecognized thoughts in a wife or husband. (3) Even those who are closest to a person might never realize that person's innermost feelings. Although any one of these choices could be a basic idea for studying "The Story of an Hour," they all have in common the main character's unexpected feelings of release when she is told that her husband has been killed. In discovering ideas, you should follow a similar process: making a number of formulations for an idea and then selecting one for further development. As you read, be alert to the different ways in which authors convey ideas. One author might prefer an indirect way through a character's speeches; another might prefer direct statement. In practice, authors can employ any or all the following methods.

Study the Authorial Voice

Although authors mainly render action, dialogue, and situation, they sometimes state ideas to guide us and deepen our understanding. In Maupassant's "The Necklace," for example, the speaker/storyteller presents the idea that women have no more than charm and beauty to use to get on in the world (paragraph 2). Ironically, Maupassant uses the story to show that for the major character, Mathilde, nothing is effective, for her charm cannot prevent disaster. Hawthorne, in "Young Goodman Brown," uses the following words to express a powerful idea: "The fiend in his own shape is less hideous than when he rages in the breast of man" (paragraph 53). This statement is made as authorial commentary just when the major character, Goodman Brown, is speeding through "the benighted wilderness" on his way to the satanic meeting. Although the idea is complex, its essential aspect is that the causes of evil originate within human beings themselves, the implication being that we alone are responsible for all our actions.

Study the Character and the Words of the First-Person Speaker

First-person narrators or speakers frequently express ideas along with their depiction of actions and situations, and they make statements from which you can make inferences about ideas. (See also Chapter 3, on point of view.) Because what they say is part of a dramatic presentation, their ideas can be right or wrong, well-considered or thoughtless, good or bad, or brilliant or half-baked, depending on the speaker. The I/we (first-person) speaker of Arnold's "Dover Beach," for example, laments the diminution of vital ideas from the past, concluding that this loss is accompanied by increasing ignorance, uncertainty, and violence in today's world. In Hardy's "Channel Firing," the speaker—a skeleton suddenly awakened by the nearby noise of naval gunfire at sea—implies that warfare has been a constant menace from ancient days to the present. Even if the speaker has dubious characteristics or is making a confession about personal shortcomings—as the speaker of Frost's "Desert Places" is doing—you may nevertheless study and evaluate the work's ideas.

Study the Statements Made by Characters

In many stories, characters express their own views, which can be right or wrong, admirable or contemptible. When you consider such dramatic speeches, you need to do considerable interpreting and evaluating yourself. In Chekhov's *The Bear*, both Smirnov and Mrs. Popov express many silly ideas about love and duty as they begin speaking to each other, and it is the sudden force of their love that reveals to us how wrongheaded their previous ideas have been. Old Man Warner in Jackson's "The Lottery" states that the lottery is valuable even though we learn from the narrator that the beliefs underlying it have long been forgotten. Because Warner is a zealous and insistent person, however, his words show that outdated ideas continue to do harm even when there is strong reason to reevaluate and dismiss them.

Study the Work's Figures of Speech

Figurative language is one of the major components of poetry, but it also abounds in prose fiction (see also Chapter 10). In the sonnet "Bright Star," for example, Keats emphasizes the idea that constancy is necessary in love by referring to a fixed and bright star (probably the North Star). Much metaphorical language is also to be found in both narratives and drama, as at the opening of Mansfield's "Miss Brill," in which a sunny day is compared to gold and white wine. This lovely comparison suggests the idea of the beauty of the earth—an idea that contrasts ironically with the indifference and cruelty that Miss Brill experiences later in the story. Another notable figure of speech occurs in Glaspell's *Trifles*, when one of the characters compares John Wright, the murdered husband, to a "raw wind that gets to the bone" (speech 103). With this figurative language, Glaspell conveys the idea that bluntness, indifference, and cruelty create great personal damage.

Study How Characters Represent Ideas

Characters and their actions can often be equated with certain ideas and values. The power of Mathilde's story in Maupassant's "The Necklace" enables us to explain that she represents the idea that unrealizable dreams can inhibit one's ability to function in the real world. Two diverse or opposed characters can embody contrasting ideas, as with Louise and Josephine of Chopin's "The Story of an Hour." Each woman can be taken to represent differing views about the role of women in marriage. In effect, characters who stand for ideas can assume symbolic status, as in Hawthorne's "Young Goodman Brown," in which the protagonist symbolizes the alienation that inevitably accompanies zealousness. Because characters can be equated directly with particular ideas, talking about the characters should lead naturally to a discussion of the ideas they may be taken to represent.

Study the Work Itself as an Embodiment of Ideas

One of the most important ways in which authors express ideas is to interlock them within all parts and aspects of the work. The art of painting is instructive here, for a painting can be taken in with a single view that comprehends all the aspects of color, form, action, and expression, each of which can also be considered separately. In the same way, when considered totally, the various parts of a work may clearly embody major ideas, as in the poem "Negro" by Langston Hughes. In this poem, Hughes makes objective the idea that black people have been cruelly exploited throughout history. In addition, implicit in the poem is the idea that the urgency of ending racial barriers overrides all socially and politically convenient reasons for which these barriers—and the cruelties they bring about—have been established. Most works represent ideas in a similar way. Even "escape literature," which ostensibly enables readers to forget their immediate problems, contains conflicts between good and evil, love and hate, good spies and bad, earthlings and aliens, and so on. Such works thereby do embody ideas, even though their avowed intention is not to make readers think but rather to help them forget.

Writing About a Major Idea in Literature

Most likely, you will write about what you consider the work's major idea or theme, but you may also get interested in a less obvious idea. As you begin brainstorming and developing your first drafts, consider questions such as those that follow.

Raise Questions to Discover Ideas

General Ideas

- What ideas do you discover in the work? How do you discover them (through action, character depiction, scenes, language)?
- To what do the ideas pertain? To the individuals themselves? To individuals and society? To religion? To social, political, or economic justice?
- How balanced are the ideas? If a particular idea is strongly presented, what conditions and qualifications are also presented (if any)? What contradictory ideas are presented?
- Are the ideas limited to members of any groups represented by the characters (age, race, nationality, personal status)? Or are the ideas applicable to general conditions of life? Explain.
- Which characters in their own right represent or embody ideas? How do their actions and speeches bring these ideas out?
- If characters state ideas directly, how persuasive is the expression of these ideas, how intelligent and well considered? How applicable are the ideas to the work? How applicable to more general conditions?
- With children, young adults, or the old, how do the circumstances express or embody an idea?

Specific Ideas

- What idea seems particularly important in the work? Why? Is it asserted directly, indirectly, dramatically, ironically? Does any one method predominate? If so, why?
- How pervasive in the work is the idea (throughout or intermittent)? To what degree is it associated with a major character or action? How does the structure of the work affect or shape your understanding of the idea?
- What value or values are embodied in the idea? Of what importance are the values to the work's meaning?
- How compelling is the idea? How could the work be appreciated without reference to any idea at all?

Organize Your Essay on a Major Idea or Theme

In well-written stories, poems, and plays, narrative and dramatic elements have a strong bearing on ideas. In this sense, an idea is like a key in music or a continuous thread tying together actions, characters, statements, symbols, and dialogue. As readers, we can trace such threads throughout the entire fabric of the work.

As you study and begin to write about ideas, you may find yourself relying most heavily on the direct statements of the authorial voice or on a combination of these and your interpretation of characters and action, or you might focus exclusively on a first-person speaker and use his or her ideas to develop your analysis. Always make clear the sources of your details, and distinguish the sources from your own commentary.

Introduction As you begin, state your general goal of describing an idea and of showing its importance in the work. Your brief statement of the idea will be your central idea for your essay.

Body Each separate work will invite its own approach, but here are a number of strategies you might use to organize your essay:

1. **Analyze the idea as it applies to characters.** Example: "Minnie Wright embodies the idea that living with cruelty and insensitivity leads to alienation, unhappiness, despair, and even to violence." (Glaspell's *Trifles*)

2. **Show how actions bring out the idea.** Example: "That Mrs. Popov and Smirnov fall in love rather than go their rather foolish and fruitless ways indicates Chekhov's idea that love literally rescues human lives." (*The Bear*)

3. **Show how dialogue and separate speeches bring out the idea.** Example: "The priest's responses to Jackie's confession embody the idea that kindness and understanding are the best means to encourage religious and philosophical commitment." (O'Connor's "First Confession")

4. **Show how the work's structure is determined by the idea.** Example: "The idea that horror can affect a nation's beauty and tradition leads Layton to introduce and conclude the poem by referring to aspects of the World War II Holocaust." ("Rhine Boat Trip")

5. **Treat variations or differing manifestations of the idea. Example:** "The idea that zealousness leads to harm is shown in Brown's nightmarish distortion of reality, his rejection of others, and his dying gloom." (Hawthorne's "Young Goodman Brown")

6. **Deal with a combination of these (together with any other significant aspect).** Example: "Chekhov's idea in *The Bear* that love is complex and contradictory is shown in Smirnov's initial scorn of Mrs. Popov, his self-declared independence of character, and his concluding embrace." (Here, the idea is traced through speech, character, and action.)

Conclusion Your conclusion might begin with a summary of your thoughts, together with your evaluation of the validity or force of the idea. If you have been convinced by the author's ideas, you might say that the author has expressed the idea forcefully and convincingly, or else you might show the relevance of the idea to current conditions. If you are not persuaded by the idea, you should demonstrate the idea's shortcomings or limitations. If you wish to mention a related idea, whether in the story you have studied or in some other story, you might introduce that here, but be sure to stress the connections.

> Although the underlined sentences are not recommended by MLA style, they are used in this illustrative essay as teaching tools to emphasize the central idea, thesis sentence, and topic sentences.

Illustrative Essay

The Idea of the Importance of Minor and "Trifling" Details in Susan Glaspell's *Trifles*[1]

A major idea in Glaspell's short play *Trifles*—and the idea that gives the play its name—is that truth is to be found not through earth-shaking matters but rather through small, insignificant, everyday things. The two women who are onstage during the entire play—Mrs. Hale and Mrs. Peters—wait patiently in the kitchen of the Wright farmhouse while their husbands and the County Attorney search for evidence about the death of John Wright, who has been strangled in his sleep. Wright's wife, Minnie, is the principal suspect, and she has been imprisoned in the nearby town. As the two women wait, they examine the ordinary and small things they find in the kitchen, such as broken jars of preserves, an unfinished quilt, a dirty hand-towel, and a dead canary. Because of their observations, they soon understand that Minnie is guilty of the murder for which she has been arrested. Their discovery is a major phase of the idea that truth is to be found in the buildup of many separate small details. These are not only about the dead man and his wife, however, but also about the lives of the two married couples who are there because of the murder. A number of little details about their lives are discovered and revealed in the kitchen, and these both characterize the play's strong portraits of the wives and lead to the play's unexpected and startling conclusion.

[1]

[1]See MyLiteratureLab for this play.

[2]   An important aspect of the play that might easily be ignored is the
way of life of all three married couples, not just one of the couples alone.
We see two of the couples firsthand (Mr. and Mrs. Hale and Mr. and
Mrs. Peters) and learn about the third (John and Minnie Wright)
through the dialogue and the discoveries made by Mrs. Hale and
Mrs. Peters. It may be said that, in accord with the major idea,
married life is not a series of huge and powerfully significant events
but is rather a day-in, day-out progression of both shorter and
lengthier experiences—many of them small and trifling—that
continue for years, decades, and lifetimes. To form an idea about the
nature of marital relationships, one should consider the nature of the
offhand, ordinary, off-guard talk of husbands and wives.

[3]   In the short scenes of the play in which Mr. Hale and Mr. Peters
are actually present, their conversation is minor and trifling—a
trading of platitudes. These men speak just to say something or
anything, but in their small-minded banter, they expose their
generally negative feelings about women. To them, women are
inferior, even though it is clear that both of them have been married
a long while. Mr. Hale, a farmer, talks dismissively about the
"trifles" that occupy women (DGL 1–3). Mr. Peters, the local
sheriff, disparages "kitchen things" (DGL 1–3), and he also laughs
at the knitting skills of the wives. This male insensitivity is reinforced
by Mr. Henderson, the county attorney, who late in the play states
derisively to the other men: "you know juries when it comes to
women," as though a woman, just because she is a woman, could
never be convicted of a crime by a jury even if guilty (DGL 1–10). It
should be noted that the two women also hear these negative
comments by their husbands. Henderson's patronizing compliment
to women is obviously no praise at all. In speech 31 (DGL 1–3), he
says, "what would we do without the ladies?"

[4]   These superficial remarks by the men—trifling speeches—are
much more significant than they might seem. It is obvious that both
wives have lived with similar condescension as long as they have been
married, for such minor details contained in the men's speeches lead
one to conclude that the two women, secretly at least, might believe

that their marriages are far from ideal. The women do not complain, however, but it is this imperfect situation that lies at the root of the overwhelming decision upon which the women act at the play's end. One may speculate that if the women had felt totally approved and accepted, they would have made their decision more in line with the wishes of their husbands.

    Just as the offhand comments by the men—trifling details— expose the less than ideal marriages of Mrs. Hale and Mrs. Peters, so do similarly small details reveal that the Wrights had by far the worst of all possible marriages. As the two women examine the trifles in Minnie's kitchen, they infer that Minnie endured bitter solitude and rejection during her entire married life. It is fair to conclude that conversations between the Wrights were not loving, but very likely scornful. Things were not always this way for Minnie, however, as we learn from Mrs. Hale, who had known Minnie when she was young, when she wore "pretty clothes," was "lively," and sang in the choir (DGL 1–5). And it is Mrs. Hale who points out that Wright was "a hard man, . . . Like a raw wind that gets to the bone" (DGL 1–8). The ultimate small detail, which is actually immense in the context of the play, is the discovery by the two women of Minnie's dead canary. This canary had been the only thing of beauty that Minnie ever owned in her married life and certainly the only relief she ever knew from the dreariness of life with Wright. Obviously, Wright had disliked the bird's singing, and to show his contempt, he had wrung the bird's neck (DGL 1–9). This arbitrarily cruel act, the women infer, brought Minnie to total grief and despair. Unable to endure things any longer, she murdered Wright in his sleep by strangling him with a rope tied with a quilting knot.

    In line with the major idea about the significance of small details, the women form an unspoken alliance of sympathy for Minnie. Their conversation reveals that both have experienced comparable, though less severe, isolation and loneliness during their lives on early twentieth-century farms. Mrs. Hale says, "I know how things can be—for women" (DGL 1–10). Mrs. Peters tells about the loneliness of life on a homestead in Dakota, when she endured the extreme sorrow of having

[5]

[6]

borne a stillborn child (DGL 1–10). The implication is that her
husband considered her feelings as nothing more than "trifles." It
seems clear that the loneliness and hard life experienced by the two
women, on the one hand, and by Minnie, on the other, are only those
of degree. Because the women sympathize with Minnie's lonely plight
so completely, however, they reach an understanding that the wretched
details of her life actually extenuate her guilt.

[7]   Above this understanding, Mrs. Hale, the stronger and more
independent of the two women, also recognizes that she herself, in
effect, committed a moral crime because she did not make a greater
effort to see and befriend Minnie before things got desperate for her
(DGL 1–10). Mrs. Hale's sense of having fallen short suggests that
explaining the kitchen trifles to the men, and thus revealing Minnie's
guilt, would also be an implicit judgment against herself. So she,
along with Mrs. Peters (who tends to be more deferential to the men
and to the importance of the law), withholds the conclusive evidence
that would confirm the case for murder that the men are trying to
build. It is Mrs. Hale who sews and, therefore, hides the "trifle" of
Minnie's disturbed stitching on the quilt (DGL 1–7), and it is she
who conceals the tiny dead bird in her coat pocket, the last action in
the play (DGL 1–11). By doing away with the evidence, Mrs. Hale,
with the silent consent of Mrs. Peters, illegally but justifiably covers
up Minnie's guilt and baffles the law. This immensely significant
action is based on the conclusion that the women have made about
the idea that real truth—not just legal truth, but human truth—is to
be discovered in the trifling details they have discovered in Minnie
Wright's kitchen.

[8]   The two women are perceptive. They act on deeply felt ideas,
and they understand the meaning of individual details when they see
them. That is the key. Ironically, Mrs. Hale and Mrs. Peters do a
better job of detailed detective work than the lawmen—Mr. Peters
and Mr. Henderson. The men look everywhere in the house, but
they waste their time because they do not look in the kitchen, where
the real "clues" could be uncovered that would lead them to solving
the crime. So they are in fact inept, and they do not learn anything

to confirm their suspicions. By contrast, the women correctly see the true evidence, trifling as it may be, and they discover that their interest is to take sides with Minnie. Glaspell's *Trifles* demonstrates that a gap exists between the interests of men and women, and the idea underlying this division is to be found in how women interpret details and, therefore, discover truth.

Work Cited

Glaspell, Susan. *Trifles. MyLiteratureLab.com.* Pearson. 2010. 23 Sept. 2011.

Commentary on the Essay

This essay follows strategy 6 (p. 134) by showing how various components of the play exhibit the principal idea about the importance of little things, both in the marriage of the Wrights and in the marriages of the two women who have come to the Wright household with their husbands. Throughout, the essay points out that situations, dialogue, and actions are evidence for the various conclusions. Paragraph transitions are effected by phrases such as "These" (paragraph 4), "Just as" (paragraph 5), "In line with" (paragraph 6), and "Above this understanding" (paragraph 7). All these transitions emphasize the continuity of the topic. The first paragraph introduces and stresses the major idea and points out some of the necessary plot detail to substantiate the essay's central idea.

As the operative aspect of Glaspell's principal idea, paragraphs 2 and 3 show how the play develops through the discussion of the contrasting marriage lives of the onstage couples. The idea that truth is to be found in small details is shown in paragraph 2 to be an introduction to paragraph 3, which stresses the trifling conversations of the men. Continuing this development, paragraph 4 draws conclusions about the effect of the men's talk on Mrs. Hale and Mrs. Peters, to both of whom the men are not endeared because of what they have said. Paragraph 5 considers details about the Wright marriage, pointing out that Minnie Wright had reached the end of her endurance when Wright killed her bird. Paragraphs 6 and 7 concentrate on the two women, who develop sufficient sympathy for Minnie to sustain them when they in effect absolve her from guilt in her husband's strangulation. The thinking underlying these two paragraphs and the final one, paragraph 8, is that the women have established a silent bond in supporting Minnie and have seen no persuasive reason to prefer supporting the law, in this case as represented by their husbands.

Paragraph 8 then, beyond being used for a brief summary, considers the detail that the urgency of the need to act forces the women to act almost reflexively in support of Minnie. The major new detail here is the tension between the duty to law of the two women, on the one hand, and their personal allegiance to Minnie and her plight, on the other.

Special Topics for Studying and Discussing Ideas

1. Compare the ideas in two works containing similar themes. Examples: Arnold's "Dover Beach" and Hardy's "Channel Firing," Keats's "Bright Star" and Shakespeare's "Let Me Not to the Marriage of True Minds," Frost's "Desert Places" and Hawthorne's "Young Goodman Brown," Layton's "Rhine Boat Trip" and Poe's "The Cask of Amontillado," or Chopin's "The Story of an Hour" and Chekhov's *The Bear*. For help in developing your essay, consult Chapter 15 on the technique of comparison-contrast.
2. Consider Maupassant's "The Necklace" in terms of the idea of economic determinism. That is, to what degree are the circumstances and traits of the characters, particularly Mathilde, controlled and limited by their economic status? According to the idea, how likely is it that the characters could ever rise above their circumstances?
3. Write an essay criticizing the ideas in a work (from Appendix C or in MyLiteratureLab) that you dislike or to which you are indifferent. With what statements in the work do you disagree? What actions? What characters? How do your own beliefs and values cause you to dislike the work's ideas? How might the work be changed to illustrate ideas with which you would agree?
4. Select an idea that particularly interests you, and outline a brief story showing how characters may or may not live up to the idea. If you have difficulty getting started, try one of these ideas:
    a. Interest and enthusiasm are hard to maintain for long.
    b. Fortune has often given people an abundance of worldly things, but few people ever believe they have received enough.
    c. When people reach adulthood, they put away childish things.
    d. It is awkward to confront another person about a grievance.
    e. Making romantic or career decisions is difficult because they demand fundamental and complete changes in life's directions.
5. Using books that you discover in the card or computer catalogue in your college or local library, search for discussions of only one of the following topics, and write a brief report on what you find.
    a. Thomas Hardy on the power of the working classes.
    b. Nathaniel Hawthorne on the significance of religion, both good and bad.
    c. Keats on the significance of intuition and imagination as creative power.
    d. The ideas underlying Poe's concept of the short story as a form.

Chapter 9

Writing About Imagery: The Literary Work's Link to the Senses

In literature, **imagery** refers to words that trigger your imagination to recall and recombine **images**—memories or mental pictures of sights, sounds, tastes, smells, sensations of touch, and motions. The process is both active and mentally vigorous, for when words or descriptions produce images, you constantly use your personal experiences with life and language to help you give shape and understanding to the works you are reading. In effect, you are re-creating the work *in your own way* through the controlled stimulation produced by the writer's words. Imagery is, therefore, one of the strongest modes of literary expression because it provides a channel to your active imagination, and along this channel, writers bring their works directly to you and into your consciousness. **As you read the words of an author, you draw on your own experiences to re-create the life that these words evoke.**

For example, encountering the word *lake* may bring to your mind your literal memory of a particular lake. Your mental picture—or image—may be a distant view of calm waters reflecting blue sky, a nearby view of gentle waves rippling in the wind, a close-up view of the sandy lake bottom from a boat or a dock, or an overhead view of a sun-drenched shoreline. Similarly, the words *rose, apple, hot dog, malted milk,* and *pizza* all cause you to recollect these objects and, in addition, may cause you to recall their smells and tastes. Active and graphic words such as *row, swim,* and *dive* stimulate you mentally to create moving images of someone performing these actions.

Responses and the Writer's Use of Detail

In studying imagery, we try to comprehend and explain our imaginative perception of the pictures and impressions evoked by the work's images. We let the poet's words simmer and percolate in our minds. To get our imaginations stirring, we might follow Coleridge in this description from the poem "Kubla Khan":

A damsel with a dulcimer
In a vision once I saw:
It was an Abyssinian maid,
And on her dulcimer she played
Singing of Mount Abora. (lines 37–41)

We do not read about the color of the young woman's clothing or anything else about her appearance except that she is playing a dulcimer—a somewhat unusual stringed instrument—and that she is singing a song about a mountain in a foreign, remote land. But Coleridge's image is enough. From it, we can imagine a vivid, exotic picture of a young woman from a distant land, singing a song and accompanying herself on her dulcimer, together with the loveliness of her song (even though we never hear it or understand it). The image lives.

The Relationship of Imagery to Ideas and Attitudes

Images do more than elicit impressions. By the authenticating effects of the vision and perceptions underlying them, they give you new ways of seeing the world and of strengthening your old ways of seeing it. Shakespeare's speaker in "Sonnet 73: That Time of Year Thou Mayst in Me Behold," for example, emphasizes that he is getting older and, therefore, closer to the time of his death. Rather than stating this idea so uninterestingly, however, Shakespeare dramatizes it through the introduction of images of autumn, evening, and a dying fire. In the second quatrain, the speaker describes the approaching evening of life:

> In me thou seest the twilight of such day
> > As after sunset fadeth in the West,
> Which by and by black night doth take away,
> > Death's second self that seals up all in rest. (lines 5–8)

This expanded image, like those in the other quatrains of this sonnet, forms an easily recognized and affirmable link with the experiences of readers, who have seen many sunsets and have known many elderly people. Such uses of imagery comprise one of the strongest means by which literature reinforces themes and interpretations of life.

Types of Imagery

Visual Imagery Is the Language of Sight

Our power of sight is the most significant of our senses, for it is a key to our remembrance of other sense impressions. Therefore, the most frequently occurring literary imagery is of things we can visualize either exactly or approximately—**visual images**, which in fact often operate identically with images of action (see the discussion of kinesthetic imagery below). In the poem "Cargoes," John Masefield asks us to re-create mental pictures or images of oceangoing merchant vessels from three periods of human history. He refers to a large and almost proverbial ancient sailing vessel, a quinquereme, which he associates with the biblical King Solomon. Then he turns to a "stately Spanish galleon" of the Renaissance and finally refers to an early twentieth-century British ship caked with salt, carrying grubby and cheap freight across the English Channel. His images are vivid as they stand and need no further amplification. For us to reconstruct them imaginatively, we do not need ever to have seen the ancient biblical lands or waters or ever to have seen or handled the cheap commodities delivered by a modern merchant ship. We have seen enough in our lives both in reality and in pictures to imagine places and objects like these; hence, Masefield is successful in fixing his visual images in our minds.

Auditory Imagery Is the Language of Sound

Auditory images trigger our experiences with sound. For such images, let us consider Wilfred Owen's "Anthem for Doomed Youth," which is about the death of soldiers in warfare and the sorrow of their loved ones. The poem begins with the question of "what passing-bells" may be tolled for "those who die as cattle." Owen's speaker is referring to the traditional tolling of a church bell or a cemetery bell to announce that a new burial is to take place. Reference to the sounds of such a solemn ceremony suggests a period of peace and order, when there is time to pay respect to the dead. But the poem then points out contrastingly that the only sound for those who have fallen in battle is the "rapid rattle" of "stuttering" rifles—in other words, not the solemn and dignified sounds of peace, but the bloodthirsty and horrifying noises of war. Owen's auditory images evoke corresponding sounds in our imaginations, and they help us to experience the poem and to hate the depravity of war.

Olfactory, Gustatory, and Tactile Imagery Refers to Smell, Taste, and Touch

In addition to sight and sound, you will find images from the other senses. An **olfactory image** refers to smell, a **gustatory image** to taste, and a **tactile image** to touch. A great deal of love poetry, for example, includes *olfactory images* about the fragrances of flowers.

Images derived from and referring to taste—*gustatory images*—are also common, though less frequent than those referring to sight and sound. Lines 5 and 10 of Masefield's "Cargoes," for example, includes references to "sweet white wine" and "cinnamon." Although the poem refers to these commodities as cargoes, the words themselves also register in our minds as gustatory images because they refer to our sense of taste.

Tactile images of touch and texture are not as common because touch is difficult to render except in terms of effects. The speaker of Lowell's poem "Patterns," for example (pages 357–59), uses tactile imagery when imagining a never-to-happen embrace with her fiancé, who, we learn, has been killed in war in Flanders. Her imagery records the effect of the embrace ("bruised"), whereas her internalized feelings are expressed in metaphors ("aching, melting, unafraid"):

> And the buttons of his waistcoat bruised my body as he clasped me
> Aching, melting, unafraid. (lines 51–52)

Tactile images are not uncommon in love poetry, in which references to touch and feeling are natural. Usually, however, love poetry deals with yearning and hope rather than sexual fulfillment (as in Keats's "Bright Star").[1]

Kinetic and Kinesthetic Imagery Refers to Motion and Activity

References to movement are also images. Images of general motion are **kinetic** (remember that *motion pictures* are called "cinema"; note the closeness of *kine* and *cine*), whereas the term **kinesthetic** is applied to human or animal movement and effort. Imagery of motion is closely related to visual images, for motion is most often seen. Masefield's "British coaster" in "Cargoes," for example, is a visual image, but when it goes "Butting through the channel," the reference to motion makes it also kinetic. When Hardy's skeletons sit upright at the beginning of "Channel Firing," the image is kinesthetic, as is the action of Amy Lowell's speaker walking in the garden alone after being informed of her fiancé's death.

 The areas from which kinetic and kinesthetic imagery can be derived are varied and unpredictable. Occupations, trades, professions, businesses, recreational activities—all these might furnish images. One poet introduces references from gardening, another from money and banking, another from modern real estate developments, another from the falling of leaves in autumn, another from life in the jungle. The freshness, newness, and surprise of much poetry result from the many and varied areas from which writers draw their images.

Writing About Imagery

Raise Questions to Discover Ideas

In preparing to write, you should develop a set of thoughtful notes dealing with issues such as the following:

- What type or types of images prevail in the work? Visual (shapes, colors)? Auditory (sounds)? Olfactory (smells)? Tactile (touch and texture)? Gustatory (taste)? Kinetic or kinesthetic (motion)? Or is the imagery a combination of these?
- To what degree do the images reflect the writer's actual observation or the writer's reading and knowledge of fields such as science or history?
- How well do the images stand out? How vivid are they? How is this vividness achieved?
- Within a group of images, say, visual or auditory, do the images pertain to one location or area rather than another (e.g., natural scenes rather than interiors, snowy scenes rather than grassy ones, loud and harsh sounds rather than quiet and civilized ones)?
- What explanation is needed for the images? (Images might be derived from the classics or the Bible, the Revolutionary War or World War II, the behaviors of four-footed creatures or birds, and so on.)

---

[1] But see David Lehman, ed. *The Best American Erotic Poems from 1800 to the Present*. New York: Scribner, 2008.

- What effect do the circumstances described in the work (e.g., conditions of brightness or darkness, warmth or cold, etc.) have upon your responses to the images? What poetic purpose do you think the poet achieves by controlling these responses?
- How well are the images integrated within the poem's argument or development?

Answering questions like these should provide you with a sizable body of ready-made material that you can convert directly to the body of your essay.

Organize Your Essay About Imagery

Introduction Connect a brief overview of the work with your plan of development, such as the statement that the writer uses images to strengthen ideas about war, character, or love or that the writer relies predominantly on images of sight, sound, and action.

Body You might deal exclusively with one of the following aspects, or, equally likely, you may combine your approaches, as you wish.

1. **Images suggesting ideas and/or moods.** Such an essay should emphasize the effects of the imagery. What ideas or moods are evoked by the images? (The auditory images beginning Owen's "Anthem for Doomed Youth," for example, all point toward a condemnation of war's brutal cruelty.) Do the images promote approval or disapproval? Cheerfulness? Melancholy? Are the images drab, exciting, vivid? How? Why? Are they conducive to humor or surprise? How does the writer achieve these effects? Are the images consistent, or are they ambiguous? (For example, the images in the first two stanzas of Masefield's "Cargoes" indicate approval, but in the third stanza, the images unambiguously indicate disapproval.)

2. **The types of images.** Here, the emphasis is on the categories of images themselves. Is there a predominance of a particular type of image (e.g., visual or auditory images), or is there a blending? Is there a bunching of types at particular points in the poem or story? If so, why? Is there any shifting as the work develops (as, for example, in Owen's "Anthem for Doomed Youth" (page 360) in which the auditory images first describe loudness and harshness, but later images describe quietness and sorrow)? Are the images appropriate, given the nature and apparent intent of the work? Do they assist in making the ideas seem convincing? If there seems to be any inappropriateness, what is its effect?

3. **Systems of images.** Here, the emphasis should be on the areas from which the images are drawn. This is another way of considering the appropriateness of the imagery. Is there a pattern of similar or consistent images, such as brightness changing to darkness (Mansfield's story "Miss Brill") or pride in military triumph changing to repentance (Dickinson's "My Triumph Lasted Till the Drums")? Do all the images adhere consistently to a particular frame of reference, such as a sunlit garden (Lowell's "Patterns"), an extensive recreational forest and garden (Coleridge's "Kubla Khan"), a church graveyard (Hardy's "Channel Firing"), the sea in various stages of light (Masefield's "Cargoes"), or a darkened forest (Blake's "The Tyger")? What is unusual or unique about the sets of images? What unexpected or new responses do they produce?

Conclusion Your conclusion, in addition to recapitulating your major points, is the place for additional insights. It is not advisable to strike out in new directions here, but you might briefly take up one or more of the ideas that you have not developed in the body. In short, what do you want your readers to know as a result of your study of imagery in the work?

Illustrative Essay

The Images of Masefield's "Cargoes"[2]

[1]   In the three-stanza poem "Cargoes," John Masefield uses imagery skillfully to create a negative impression of modern commercial life.[3] There is a contrast between the first two stanzas and the third, with the first two idealizing the romantic, distant past and the third demeaning the modern, gritty, grimy present. Masefield's images are thus both positive and lush, on the one hand, and negative and stark, on the other.[4]

[2]   The most evocative and pleasant images in the poem are in the first stanza. The speaker asks that we imagine a "Quinquereme of Nineveh from distant Ophir" (line 1), one of the many-oared oceangoing vessels that were in use in the ancient times of the biblical King Solomon. As Masefield identifies the cargo, the visual images are rich and romantic (3 to 5):

> With a cargo of ivory,
> And apes and peacocks,
> Sandalwood, cedarwood, and sweet white wine.

Ivory suggests richness, which is augmented by the exotic "apes and peacocks" in all their spectacular strangeness. The "sandalwood, cedarwood, and sweet white wine" evoke pungent smells and tastes. The "sunny" light of ancient Palestine (2) not only illuminates the imaginative scene (visual), but invites readers to imagine the sun's warming touch (tactile). The references to animals and birds also suggest the sounds that these creatures would make (auditory).

---

[2]See page 360 for this poem.
[3]Central idea.
[4]Thesis sentence.

Thus, in this lush first stanza, images derived from all the senses are introduced to create impressions of a glorious past.

Almost equally lush are the images of the second stanza, which [3] completes the poem's first part. Here the visual imagery evokes the royal splendor of a tall-masted, full-sailed galleon (6) at the height of Spain's commercial power in the sixteenth century. The galleon's cargo suggests wealth, with sparkling diamonds and amethysts, and Portuguese "gold moidores" gleaming in open chests (10). With cinnamon in the second stanza's bill of lading (10), Masefield includes the image of a pleasant-tasting spice.

The negative imagery of the third stanza is in stark contrast to [4] the first two stanzas. The visual image is a modern "Dirty British coaster" (11), which draws attention to the griminess and suffocation of modern civilization. This spray-swept ship, caked in sea-salt, is loaded with materials that pollute the earth with noise and smoke. The smoke-stack of the coaster (11) and the firewood it is carrying suggest choking smog. The Tyne Coal (13) and road rails (14) suggest the noise and smoke of puffing railroad engines. As if this were not enough, the "pig-lead" (14) to be used in various industrial processes indicates not just more unpleasantness, but also something poisonous and deadly. In contrast to the lush and stately imagery of the first two stanzas, the images in the third stanza invite the conclusion that people now, when the "Dirty British coaster" butts through the English Channel, are surrounded and threatened by visual, olfactory, and auditory pollution.

The poem, thus, establishes a romantic past and ugly present [5] through images of sight, smell, and sound. The images of motion also emphasize this view: In the first two stanzas, the quinquereme is "rowing" and the galleon is "dipping." These kinetic images suggest dignity and lightness. The British coaster, however, is "butting," an image indicating bull-like hostility and stupid force. These, together with all the other images, focus the poem's negative views of modern life. The facts that existence for both the ancient Palestinians and the Renaissance Spaniards included slavery (of those men rowing the quinquereme) and piracy (by those Spanish

"explorers" who robbed and killed the natives of the Isthmus)
should probably not be emphasized as a protest against Masefield's
otherwise valid contrasts in images. His final commentary may,
hence, be thought of as the banging of his "cheap tin trays" (15),
which makes a percussive climax of the oppressive images filling too
large a portion of modern lives.

Work Cited

Masefield, John. "Cargoes." Edgar V. Roberts. *Writing About Literature.* 13th ed. New York: Pearson, 2012. 360. Print.

Commentary on the Essay

This essay illustrates the first strategy for writing about imagery (p. 142), using images to develop ideas and moods. All the examples—derived directly from the
poem—emphasize the qualities of Masefield's images. This method permits the introduction of imagery drawn from all the senses in order to demonstrate Masefield's
ideas about the past and the present. Other approaches might have concentrated
exclusively on Masefield's visual images or upon his images drawn from trade and
commerce. Because Masefield uses auditory and gustatory images but does not
develop them extensively, sound or taste might be appropriately treated in short,
paragraph-length essays.

The introductory paragraph of the illustrative essay presents the central idea that
Masefield uses his images climactically to lead to his negative view of modern commer-
cialism. The thesis sentence indicates that the topics to be developed are those of
(1) lushness and (2) starkness.

Paragraphs 2 and 3 form a unit stressing the lushness and exoticism of the first
stanza and the wealth and colorfulness of the second stanza. In particular, paragraph 2
uses words such as "evocative," "rich," "exotic," "pungent," and "romantic" to characterize the pleasing mental pictures that the images invoke. Although the paragraph
indicates enthusiastic responses to the images, it does not go beyond the limits of the
images themselves.

Paragraph 4 stresses the contrast of Masefield's images in the third stanza with those of the first two stanzas. To this end, the paragraph illustrates the imaginative reconstruction needed to develop an understanding of this contrast. The unpleasantness, annoyance, and even the danger of the cargoes mentioned in the third stanza are therefore, emphasized as the qualities evoked by the images.,

The last paragraph demonstrates that the imagery of motion—not much stressed in the poem—is in agreement with the rest of Masefield's imagery. As a demonstration of the need for fair, impartial judgment, the conclusion introduces the possible objection that Masefield may be slanting his images by including not a full but rather a partial view of their respective historical periods. Thus, the concluding paragraph adds balance to the analysis illustrated in paragraphs 2, 3, and 4.

Writing Topics About Imagery

1. Compare the images of home in Owen's "Anthem for Doomed Youth" (p. 360) and Chopin's "The Story of an Hour" (p. 316) or Maupassant's "The Necklace". Describe the differing effects of the images. How are the images used? How effectively do these images aid in the development of the principal actions described in each poem?

2. On the basis of the poems in Appendix C by Arnold, Blake, Coleridge, Frost, and Layton, write an essay discussing the poetic use of images drawn from the natural world. What sorts of references do the poets make? What attitudes do they express about the details they select? What is the relationship between the images and religious views? What judgments about God and nature do the poets show by their images?

3. Write an essay considering the imagery in Hardy's "Channel Firing, " Shakespeare's "Sonnet 73: That Time of Year Thou Mayst in Me Behold," or Blake's "The Tyger." As you develop your thoughts, be sure to consider the dramatic function of the images in the poem you choose and to account for the impressions and ideas that they create. You may also wish to introduce references to images from other poems that are relevant at various parts of your essay.

4. Write a short poem describing one of the following:
   a. Athletes who have just completed an exhausting run
   b. Children getting out of school for the day
   c. The antics of your dog, cat, horse, llama, or other pet
   d. A cat that always sits down on your schoolwork and then purrs when you try to shoo him or her off
   e. A particularly good meal that you had recently
   f. The best concert that you ever attended
   g. Driving to work/school on a cloudy/rainy/snowy/sunny day
   Then write an analysis of the images you selected for your poem, and explain your choices. What details stand out in your mind? What do you recall best: sight, smell, sound, action? What is the relationship between your images and the ideas you attempt to express in your poem?

5. Write an essay considering the graphic or pictorial nature of the imagery in Coleridge's "Kubla Khan" and Keats's "On First Looking Into Chapman's Homer," along with other works that you may wish to discuss. What similarities

and differences do you find in subject matter, treatment, arrangement, and general ideas? On the basis of your comparison, what relationships do you perceive between sight and literary imagery?

6. Use the retrieval system (computer or card catalogue) in your library to research the topic of imagery in Shakespeare (see *Shakespeare: imagery, Shakespeare: style and imagery*). You might also determine what you can find online. How many titles do you discover? Over how many years have these works been published? Take out one of the works, and write a brief report on any of the chapters. What topics are discussed? What types of imagery are introduced? What relationship does the author make between imagery and content?

Chapter 10

Writing About Metaphor and Simile: A Source of Depth and Range in Literature

Poetry, Fiction, and Drama

Figures of speech, metaphorical language, figurative language, figurative devices, and rhetorical figures are terms describing organized patterns of comparison that deepen, broaden, extend, illuminate, and emphasize meaning. First and foremost, the use of figures of speech is a major characteristic by which great literature provides us with fresh and original ways of thinking, feeling, and understanding. Although metaphorical language is sometimes called "ornate," as though it were somehow inessential and unnecessarily decorative, such language is not uncommon in conversational speech, and it is vitally important in literary thought and expression.

Unlike the writing of the social and "hard" sciences, imaginative literature does not purport to offer a direct correspondence of words and things. Yes, literature often presents specific and accurate descriptions and explanations, but it also moves in areas of implication and suggestiveness through the use of metaphorical language, which enables writers to amplify their ideas while still employing a relatively small number of words. Such language is, therefore, a *sine qua non* in imaginative literature, particularly poetry, in which it compresses thought, deepens understanding, and shapes response.

There are many metaphorical figures, some of which are *paradox, anaphora, apostrophe, personification, synecdoche* and *metonymy, pun* (or *paronomasia*), *synesthesia, overstatement,* and *understatement.* All these figures are modes of comparison, and they may be expressed in single words, phrases, clauses, or entire structures. The two most important and easily recognized figures of speech, with which we will be concerned here, are *metaphors* and *similes.*

Metaphors and Similes: The Major Figures of Speech

A Metaphor Shows That Something Unknown Can Be Understood Because It Is Identical to Something Known

A **metaphor** (a "carrying out [*phor*] of change [*meta*]") *equates* known objects or actions with something that is unknown or to be explained (e.g., "Your words are *music* to my ears," "You are the *sunshine* of my life," "My life is *a squirrel cage*"). The equation of the metaphor not only explains and illuminates the thing—let us choose Keats's star in the poem "Bright Star"(p. 355)—but also offers distinctive and original ways of seeing it, applying it, and thinking about it. Thus, Keats draws his metaphor of the star—the North Star—because of its constancy in the heavens, for this star has remained in its present location from century to century, with little change visible to the unaided human eye. Keats applies this quality to his speaker's wish for love that is unchanging and permanent—both a natural and an appropriate equation of celestial star and human desire.

Metaphors are inseparable from language. In a heavy storm, for example, trees may be said to *bow* constantly as the wind blows against them. *Bow* is a metaphor because, today, the word commonly refers to performers' bending forward to acknowledge the applause of an audience and to indicate their gratitude for the audience's approval. In addition, the metaphor extends further back in history to the bowing of courtiers before a king, emperor, or person of other superior power. The metaphor, therefore, asks us to equate our knowledge of theater life or concepts of political power (something known) to a weather occurrence (something to be explained). A comparable reference to theater life creates one of the best-known metaphors to appear in Shakespeare's plays: "All the world's a stage, / And all the men and women merely players." Here, Shakespeare's character Jacques (*JAY-queez*) from Act 2, scene 7 of *As You Like It*, equates human life directly with stage life. In other words, the things that stage actors say and do are also said and done by living people in real life. It is important to recognize that Shakespeare's metaphor does not state that the world is *like* a stage but that it literally *is* a stage.

A Simile Shows That Something Unknown Can Be Understood Because It Is Similar to Something Known

A **simile** (a "showing of likeness or resemblance") illustrates the *similarity* or *comparability* of the known to something unknown or to be explained. Whereas a metaphor merges identities, a simile focuses on resemblances (e.g., "Your words are *like music* to me," "You are *like sunshine* in my life," "I feel *like a squirrel in a cage*"). Similes are distinguishable from metaphors because they are introduced by *like* with nouns and *as* (also *as if* and *as though*) with clauses. If Keats had written that his speaker's desire for steadfastness is *like* the bright star, his comparison would have been a simile.

Let us consider one of the best-known similes in poetry, from "A Valediction: Forbidding Mourning" by the seventeenth-century poet John Donne. This is a dramatic poem spoken by a lover who is about to go on a trip. His loved one is sorrowful, and he attempts to console her by claiming that even when he is gone, he will remain with her in spirit. The following stanza contains the famous simile embodying this idea.

> Our two souls therefore, which are one,
>   Though I must go, endure not yet
> A breach,[1] but an expansion
>   Like gold to airy thinness beat.

The simile compares the souls of the speaker and his loved one to gold, a metal that is both valuable and malleable. By using the simile, the speaker asserts that the impending departure will not be a separation but rather a thinning out, so the relationship of the

---

[1]Break, separation.

lovers will remain constant and rich even as the distance between them increases. Because the comparison is introduced by "Like," the emphasis of the figurative language is on the *similarity* of the lovers' love to gold (which is always gold even when it is thinned out by the goldsmith's hammer), not on the *identification* of the two.

Characteristics of Metaphors and Similes

Metaphors and similes are based in imagery, which is the means by which literature is made graphic and vivid (see Chapter 9, p. 141–50). That is, by using words that convey images the writer prompts us to recall memories (images) of sights, sounds, tastes, smells, sensations, and motions. Metaphors and similes go beyond literal imagery to introduce perceptions and comparisons that can be unusual, unpredictable, and surprising, as in Donne's simile comparing the lovers' relationship to gold. The comparison emphasizes the bond between the two lovers; the reference to gold shows how valuable the bond is; the unusual and original comparison is a major element that makes the poem striking and memorable.

To see metaphorical language in further operation, let us take a commonly described condition: happiness. In everyday speech, we might use the sentence "She was happy" to state that a particular character was experiencing joy and excitement. The sentence may be accurate, but it is not interesting. A more vivid way of saying the same thing is to use an image of action, such as "She jumped for joy." But another and better way of communicating joy is the following simile: "She felt as if she had just won the lottery." Because readers easily understand or can imagine the disbelief, excitement, exhilaration, and delight that such an event would bring, they also understand—and feel—the character's happiness. It is the *simile* that evokes this perception and enables each reader to personalize the experience, for no simple description could help a reader comprehend the same degree of emotion.

As a parallel poetic example, let us look at Keats's famous sonnet "On First Looking into Chapman's Homer," which Keats wrote soon after reading the translation of Homer's great epics *The Iliad* and *The Odyssey* by the Renaissance poet George Chapman. Keats, one of the greatest of all poets himself, describes his enthusiasm about Chapman's successful and exciting work.

John Keats (1795–1821)

On First Looking into Chapman's Homer[2] *1816*

Much have I travell'd in the realms of gold,[3]
   And many goodly states and kingdoms seen:
Round many western islands[4] have I been
Which bards in fealty to Apollo[5] hold.

---

[2]George Chapman (c. 1560–1634) published his translations of Homer's *Iliad* in 1612 and *Odyssey* in 1614–15.
[3]The world of great art.
[4]Ancient literature.
[5]Writers who are sworn subjects of Apollo, the Greek god of light, music, poetry, prophecy, and the sun.

Oft of one wide expanse[6] had I been told   5
   That deep-brow'd Homer ruled as his demesne;[7]
   Yet did I never breathe its pure serene[8]
Till I heard Chapman speak out loud and bold:
Then felt I like some watcher of the skies
   When a new planet swims into his ken;[9]   10
Or like stout Cortez[10] when with eagle eyes
   He star'd at the Pacific—and all his men
Look'd at each other with a wild surmise[11] —
   Silent, upon a peak in Darien.

As a first step in understanding the power of metaphorical language, we can briefly paraphrase the sonnet's content:

> I have enjoyed much art and read much poetry, and I have been told that Homer is the best writer of all. However, I did not appreciate his works until I first read them in Chapman's loud and bold translation. This discovery was exciting and awe-inspiring.

If all Keats had written had been a paragraph like this one, we would pay little attention to it, for it is bland and gives us no sense of the exploration and wonder that the poem itself provides for us. On the other hand, the poem presents us with two indelibly memorable similes ("like some watcher of the skies" and "like stout Cortez"), which stand out and demand a special effort of imagination. To appreciate these similes fully, we need to imagine what it would be like to be an astronomer as he or she discovers a previously unknown planet and what it would have been like to be one of the first European explorers to see the Pacific Ocean. As we imagine ourselves in these roles, we get a sense of the amazement, excitement, exhilaration, and joy that would accompany such discoveries. With that experience comes the realization that the world—the universe—is far bigger and more astonishing than we had ever dreamed.

In this way, metaphorical language makes strong demands on our creative imaginations. It bears repeating that as we develop our own mental pictures under the stimulation of metaphors and similes, we also develop appropriately associated attitudes and feelings. Let us consider once more Keats's metaphor "realms of gold," which invites us both to imagine brilliant and shining kingdoms and to join Keats in valuing and loving not just poetry but all literature. The metaphorical "realms of gold" act upon our minds, liberating our imaginations, directing our understanding, and evoking our feelings. In such a way, the process of reading and responding to the works of writers such as Keats produces both mental and emotional experiences that were previously hidden to us. Writers constantly give us something new, widening our comprehension, increasing our knowledge, and deepening our imagination.

---

[6]Epic poetry.

[7]Realm, estate.

[8]A clear expanse of air; also grandeur, clarity; rulers were also sometimes called "serene majesty."

[9]Range of vision.

[10]Hernando Cortés (1485–1547), a Spanish general and the conqueror of Mexico. Keats confuses him with Vasco de Balboa (c. 1475–1519), the first European to see the Pacific Ocean (in 1510) from Darien, an early name for the Isthmus of Panama.

[11]Conjecture, supposition.

VEHICLE AND TENOR

To describe the relationship between a writer's ideas and the metaphors and similes that the writer chooses to objectify them, two useful terms have been coined by I. A. Richards (in *The Philosophy of Rhetoric,* 1929). First is the **vehicle**, or the specific words of the metaphor or simile. Second is the **tenor**, which is the totality of ideas and attitudes not only of the literary speaker but also of the author. For example, the tenor of Donne's simile in "A Valediction: Forbidding Mourning" is the inseparable love and unbreakable connection of the two lovers; the vehicle is the hammering of gold "to airy thinness." Similarly, the tenor of the similes in the sestet of Keats's sonnet is awe and wonder; the vehicle is the description of astronomical and geographical discovery.

Writing About Metaphors and Similes

Begin by determining the use, line by line, of metaphors or similes. Obviously, similes are the easiest figures to recognize because they introduce comparisons with *like* or *as.* Metaphors can be recognized because the topics are discussed not as themselves but as other topics. If the poems speak of falling leaves or law courts but the subjects are memory or increasing age, you are looking at metaphors.

Raise Questions to Discover Ideas

- What metaphors and/or similes does the work contain? Where do they occur? Under what circumstances? How extensive are they?
- How do you recognize them? Are they signaled by a single word or phrase, such as "desert places" in Frost's "Desert Places" (p. 352), or are they more extensively detailed, as in Shakespeare's "Sonnet 30: When to the Sessions of Sweet Silent Thought" (p. 157–58)?
- How vivid are the metaphors and similes? How obvious? How unusual? What kind of effort is needed to understand them in context?
- Structurally, how are the metaphors and similes developed? How do they rise out of the situation envisioned in the work? To what degree are they integrated into the work's development of ideas? How do they relate to other aspects of the work?
- Is one type of figure used in a particular section while another type predominates in another section? If so, why?
- If you have discovered a number of metaphors, what relationships can you find among them, such as the judicial and financial connections in Shakespeare's "When to the Sessions of Sweet Silent Thought" (p. 361)?
- How do the metaphors or similes broaden, deepen, or otherwise assist in making the ideas in the poem forceful?
- In general, how appropriate and meaningful is the metaphorical language in the poem? What effect does this language have on the poem's tone and on your understanding and appreciation of the poem?

Organize Your Essay About Metaphors and Similes

Introduction In your introduction, relate the quality of the figures of speech to the general nature of the work. Thus, metaphors and similes of suffering might be appropriate to a religious, redemptive work, while those of sunshine and cheer might be right for a romantic one. If there is any discrepancy between the metaphorical language and the topic, you could consider that contrast as a possible central idea, for it would clearly indicate the writer's ironic perspective. Suppose that the topic of the poem is love but the figures put you in mind of darkness and cold. What would the writer be saying about the quality of this love? You should also try to justify any claims that you make about the figures. For example, the major metaphor of Lowell's "Patterns" is that people are virtually compelled to live their lives controlled by many habits, restrictions, customs, expectations, duties, roles, and services—"patterns." How is this metaphor to be taken? As an outcry for personal freedom? As an expression of rage against restrictions? As a suggestion that customs that restrict may also be customs that provide solace? How do you explain your answer or answers? Your introduction is the place to establish ideas and justifications of this sort.

Body The following approaches for discussing rhetorical figures are not mutually exclusive, and you may combine them as you wish. Most likely, your essay will bring in most of the following classifications.

1. **Interpret the meaning and effect of the metaphorical language.** Here you explain how the metaphors and/or similes enable you to make an interpretation. In lines 17 to 19 of "Kubla Khan," for example (p. 350), Coleridge introduces the following simile:

   And from this chasm, with ceaseless turmoil seething,
   As if this earth in fast thick pants were breathing,
   A mighty fountain momently was forced.

   Coleridge's simile of "fast thick pants" almost literally animates the earth as a moving, working power, panting as it forces the fountain out of the chasm. The idea is that the phenomena of Nature are not dead, but vigorously alive. A directly explanatory approach such as this requires that metaphors and similes be expanded and interpreted, including the explanation of necessary references and allusions.

2. **Analyze the frames of reference and their appropriateness to the subject matter.** Here you classify and locate the sources and types of references and determine their appropriateness to the poem's subject matter. Ask questions similar to these: Does the writer refer extensively to nature, science, warfare, politics, business, reading (e.g., Shakespeare's metaphor equating personal reverie with courtroom proceedings in Sonnet 30)? Does the metaphor seem appropriate? If so, how? Why? If not, why not?

3. **Focus on the interests and sensibilities of the poet.** In a way, this approach is like strategy 2, but the emphasis here is on what the selectivity of the writer might show about his or her vision and interests. You might begin by listing the figures of speech in the work and then determining the sources. But then you should raise questions like the following: Does the writer use metaphors or similes derived from one sense rather than another (i.e., sight, hearing, taste, smell, touch)? Does

he or she record color, brightness, shadow, shape, depth, height, number, size, slowness, speed, emptiness, fullness, richness, drabness? Has the writer relied on the associations of figures of sense? Do metaphors and similes referring to green plants and trees, to red roses, or to rich fabrics, for example, suggest that life is full and beautiful, or do references to touch suggest amorous warmth? This approach is designed to help you draw conclusions about the author's taste or sensibility.

4. **Examine the relationship of one figure to the other figures and ideas of the work.** The assumption of this approach is that each literary work is unified and organically whole, so each part is closely related and inseparable from everything else. Usually, it is best to pick a figure that occurs at the beginning of the work and then determine how this figure influences your perception of the remainder. Your aim is to consider the relationship of part to parts and part to whole. The beginning of Frost's poem "Desert Places," for example, describes "Snow falling and night falling." What is the effect of this opening on the poem's metaphor of human "desert places"? To help you with questions like this, you might substitute a totally different detail, such as, for "Desert Places," the rising sun on a beautiful day or playing with a kitten, rather than the onset of cold and night. Such suppositions, which would clearly be out of place, may help you to understand and then explain the poet's figures of speech.

Conclusion In your conclusion, summarize your main points, describe your general impressions, try to describe the impact of the figures, indicate your personal responses, or show what might further be done along the lines you have been developing. If you know other works by the same writer or other works by other writers who use comparable or contrasting figures, you might explain the relationship of the other work or works to your present analysis.

Illustrative Essay

Shakespeare's Metaphors in "Sonnet 30: When to the Sessions of Sweet Silent Thought"

When to the sessions[12] of sweet silent thought
I summon[13] up remembrance of things past,
I sigh the lack of many a thing I sought,
And with old woes new wail my dear time's waste:
Then can I drown an eye, unused to flow,   5
For precious friends hid in death's dateless[14] night,

---

[12]Courtroom sessions.
[13]Give notice to appear in court.
[14]Endless, eternal.

And weep afresh love's long since canceled woe,
And moan th'expense of many a vanished sight.
Then can I grieve at grievances foregone,
And heavily [15] from woe to woe tell [16] o'er   10
The sad account of fore-bemoanéd moan,
Which I new pay, [17] as if not paid before.
    But if the while I think on thee, dear friend,
    All losses are restored, and sorrows end.

[1]   In this sonnet. Shakespeare stresses the sadness of remembering past regrets and misfortunes. He says, however, through his speaker, that a person with such heavyheartedness may be cheered by present thoughts about a good friend. His metaphors present original and unique ways of seeing personal life in this perspective. [18] He creates metaphors drawn from the public and business world of law courts, money and value, and banking and money-handling. [19]

[2]   In the first quatrain, the speaker presents a metaphor of law and the courtroom to show that memories of past experience are constantly present and influential over a person's present life. Like a judge issuing a subpoena to compel defendants to appear in court, Shakespeare's speaker "summon[s]" his memory of "things past" to stand trial before him. In the context of the sonnet, this courtroom metaphor suggests that people are their own judges and that their ideals and morals are actual laws by which they measure themselves. The speaker finds himself guilty of wasting his time in the past. Removing himself, however, from the strict punishment that a real judge might require, he does not condemn himself because of his "dear time's waste" but instead laments it (line 4). The metaphor is, thus, used to indicate that a person's consciousness is made up just as much of self-doubt and reproach as of more positive qualities.

[3]   By introducing a closely related metaphor of money and value in the second quatrain, Shakespeare implies that living is a lifelong

---

[15]Sadly.
[16]Count, tally.
[17]A double jeopardy payment.
[18]Central idea.
[19]Thesis sentence.

process of continued investment. According to this metaphor, living requires the constant spending of emotions and commitment to others. In other words, friendship and love need regular efforts to keep them alive. When friends invariably move away, however, and loved ones die, it is as though the emotional payments continue in memory though not in actuality. The absent people were prized in life, and they continue to be prized even though they are now gone. In addition, the speaker's dead friends are "precious" because of the time and love he gave to them, and his remembered "sight" of those who have "vanished" causes him to "moan" because of his great "expense" and continued emotional expenditure for them (8).

[4]   Like the money-and-value metaphor, the metaphor of banking and money-handling in the third quatrain emphasizes that memory is a bank in which life's experiences are deposited. All the emotions stimulated by remembered experience are present there, and they may be withdrawn and experienced again in moments of "sweet silent thought," just as a depositor may withdraw money. Interestingly, in the three quatrains, the speaker recalls somber memories of loss rather than things that were joyful. Thus, he counts the melancholy aspect of his experience—his woe—just as a businessman or banker counts money: "And heavily from woe to woe tell o'er" (10). Because strong emotions still accompany his memories of past mistakes, the metaphor extends to borrowing and the payment of interest. The speaker goes on to say that he pays again with "new" woe the accounts that he had already paid with old woe. In such a way, the speaker implies, the recollection of his memories puts him in double emotional jeopardy. The metaphor implies that the past is so much a part of the present that a person never stops feeling pain and regret.

[5]   The courtroom, money-and-value, and money-handling metaphors combine in the sonnet's concluding couplet to show how a happy present life may overcome past regrets. The "dear friend" being addressed in these lines has the resources (financial) to settle all the emotional judgments that the speaker as a self-judge has made against himself (legal). It is as though the friend is a rich patron who rescues

him from emotional bankruptcy (legal and financial) and the doom resulting from a sentence of emotional misery and depression (legal).

[6]   In these metaphors, therefore, Shakespeare's references are drawn from ordinary public and financial actions, but his use of them is creative and entirely new, and it will always be new. In particular, the idea of line 8 ("And moan th'expense of many a vanished sight") stresses that people, as a necessary part of their lives, spend much emotional energy on others. Without such personal investment, one cannot have precious friends and loved ones. In keeping with this metaphor of money and investment, one could measure life not in months or years, but in the spending of emotion and involvement in personal relationships with others. <u>By inviting readers to explore his metaphors of love and friendship, Shakespeare has contributed original and powerful insights into the value of life.</u>

Work Cited

Shakespeare, William. "Sonnet 30: When to the Sessions of Sweet Silent Thought." Edgar V. Roberts. *Writing About Literature.* 13th ed. New York: Pearson, 2012. 157. Print.

Commentary on the Essay

This essay treats the three classes of metaphors that Shakespeare introduces in Sonnet 30. It thus illustrates strategy 2 (p. 156). But the aim of the discussion is not to explore the extent and nature of the comparison between the metaphors and the personal situations described in the sonnet. Instead, the goal is to explain how the metaphors develop Shakespeare's meaning. This essay, therefore, also illustrates strategy 1 (p. 156).

In addition to presenting a brief description of the sonnet, the introduction brings out the central idea and the thesis sentence. Paragraph 2 deals with the meaning of Shakespeare's law and courtroom metaphor. His money metaphor is explained in paragraph 3. Paragraph 4 considers the banking or money-handling metaphor. Paragraph 5 shows how Shakespeare's concluding couplet, by emphasizing the reference to the reader or listener, focuses the three strands of metaphor derived from the past. The essay's conclusion comments generally on the creativity of Shakespeare's metaphors; it also amplifies the way in which the money metaphor leads toward an increased understanding of life.

Throughout the essay, transitions are brought about by the linking words in the topic sentences. In paragraph 3, for example, the words "closely related" and "in the second quatrain" move the reader from paragraph 2 to the new content. In paragraph 4, the words that effect the transition are "Like the money-and-value metaphor" and "in the third quatrain." The opening sentence of paragraph 5 refers collectively to the subjects of paragraphs 2, 3, and 4, thereby concentrating them on the new topic of paragraph 5.

Writing Topics About Metaphors and Similes

1. Consider some of the metaphors and similes in the poems included in Appendix C or in MyLiteratureLab. Write an essay that deals with the following questions: How effective are the figures you select? What insights do the figures provide within the contexts of their respective poems? How appropriate are they? Might they be expanded more fully, and if they were, what would be the effect? You might choose any of the following topics or any others, depending on your wishes:
   a. The "darkling plain" simile in Arnold's "Dover Beach"
   b. The metaphor of constancy in Shakespeare's "Let Me Not to the Marriage of True Minds" or of autumn in his "That Time of Year Thou Mayst in Me Behold"
   c. The metaphor of the quilting knot in Glaspell's *Trifles*
   d. The metaphorical use of the black box in Jackson's "The Lottery"
   e. The metaphor of the shabby fur piece in Mansfield's "Miss Brill"
   f. Metaphor in Blake's "The Tyger"
   g. The metaphor of the Rhine River in Layton's "Rhine Boat Trip"
   h. Similes in Owen's "Anthem for Doomed Youth" or in Coleridge's "Kubla Khan"
   i. The metaphor of "red war" in Hardy's "Channel Firing"
   j. The use of similes in Hughes's "Negro"
   k. The horse Toby as a metaphor in Chekhov's *The Bear*
2. Write a poem in which you create a governing metaphor or simile. An example might be: My girlfriend/boyfriend is like (a) an opening flower, (b) a difficult book, (c) an insoluble mathematical problem, (d) a bill that cannot be paid, (e) a slow-moving chess game. Another example: Teaching a person how to do a particular job is like (a) shoveling heavy snow, (b) climbing a mountain during a landslide, (c) having someone force you underwater when you're gasping for breath. When you finish, describe the relationship between your comparison and the development and structure of your poem.
3. In your library's reference section, find the third edition of J. A. Cuddon's *A Dictionary of Literary Terms and Literary Theory* (1991), or use some other dictionary of literary terms that you find on the shelves. Study the entries for *metaphor* and *simile*, and write a brief report on these sections.

Chapter 11

Writing About Symbolism and Allegory: Keys to Extended Meaning

Symbolism and allegory, like metaphors and similes (see Chapter 10, p. 151–61) are modes that expand meaning. They are literary devices developed from the connections that real-life people make between their own existence and particular objects, places, or occurrences, through experience, reading, and memory. By highlighting details as *symbols*, and stories or parts of stories as *allegories*, writers expand their meaning while keeping their works within reasonable lengths. As examples, let us realize that a bereaved mother may associate personal grief with household boxes and containers. A young man may, upon seeing the North Star, dedicate himself to constant love. A beloved animal may cause a widow to remember her love for her departed husband. A distant view of a vanishing light may cause a man to think that traditional ideas are being lost. The significance of details like these can be meaningful not only at the time they occur but also throughout life. It is as though the memory of such things alone can be the same as pages of explanation and analysis, for merely bringing them to mind or speaking about them unlocks their meanings, implications, and consequences. They become **symbols**, as they in fact are in John Keats's "Bright Star," Anton Chekhov's *The Bear*, and Matthew Arnold's "Dover Beach."

Symbolism and Meaning

The words **symbol** and **symbolism** are derived from the Greek word meaning "to throw together" (*syn*, "together," and *ballein*, "to throw"). A symbol creates a direct meaningful equation between (1) a specific object, scene, character, or action and (2) ideas, values, people, or ways of life. In effect, a symbol is a *substitute* for the elements being signified, much as the flag stands for the ideals of our nation. For this reason, symbolism goes beyond the close referral of word to thing; it is more like a window through which one can glimpse the extensive world outside. It is a shorthand way of referring to extensive ideas or attitudes that otherwise would bog down a story, divert the attention of the audience in a theater, or unreasonably lengthen a poem

The use of symbols is a way of moving outward, a means of extending and crystallizing information and ideas. For example, at the time of William Blake (1757–1827), the word *tiger* meant both a large, wild cat and also the specific animal we know today as a tiger. The word's connotation, therefore, links it with wildness and predation. As a symbol in "The Tyger" (p. 348), however, Blake uses the animal as a stand-in for what he considers cosmic negativism—the savage, wild forces that undermine the progress of civilization. Thus, the tiger as a symbol is more meaningful than either the denotation or the connotation of the word would indicate.

When we first see a symbol in literature, it might seem to carry no more weight than its surface or obvious meaning. It can be a description of a character, an object, a place, an action, or a situation, and it may function normally and usefully in this capacity. What makes a symbol symbolic, however, is its capacity to signify additional levels of meaning: major ideas, simple or complex emotions, or philosophical or religious qualities or values. There are two types of symbols: *cultural* and *contextual.*

Cultural Symbols Are Derived from Our Cultural and Historical Heritage

Many symbols are *generally* or *universally* recognized and are, therefore, **cultural** (also called **universal**). They embody ideas and emotions that writers and readers share as heirs of the same historical and cultural tradition. When using cultural symbols, a writer assumes that readers already know what the symbols represent. An example is the character Sisyphus of ancient Greek myth. As a punishment for trying to overcome death not just once but twice, Sisyphus is doomed by the underworld gods to roll a large boulder up a high hill forever. Just as he gets the boulder to the top, it rolls down, and then he is fated to roll it up again—and again—and again—because the boulder always rolls back. The plight of Sisyphus has been interpreted as a symbol of the human condition: In spite of constant struggle, a person rarely if ever completes anything. Work must always be done over and over from day to day and from generation to generation, and the same problems plague humanity throughout all time. Because of such fruitless effort, life seems to have little or no meaning. Nevertheless, there is hope: People who confront their tasks, as Sisyphus does, stay involved and active, and their tasks make their lives meaningful. A writer referring to Sisyphus would expect us to understand that this ancient mythological figure symbolizes these conditions.

Similarly, ordinary water, because living creatures cannot live without it, is recognized as a symbol of life. It has this meaning in the ceremony of baptism, and it conveys this meaning and dimension in a variety of literary contexts. Thus, a spouting fountain might symbolize optimism (as upwelling, bubbling life), and a stagnant pool might symbolize the pollution and diminution of life. Water is also a universal symbol of sexuality, and its condition or state can symbolize various romantic relationships. For instance, stories in which lovers meet near a turbulent stream, a roaring waterfall, a mud puddle, a beach with high breakers, a stormy sea, a calm lake, or a wide and gently flowing river symbolically represent love relationships that range from uncertainty to serenity.

Contextual Symbols Are Symbolic Only in Individual Works

Objects and descriptions that are not universal symbols can be symbols *only if they are made so within individual works.* These are **contextual** symbols, also sometimes called **private**, or **authorial** symbols. Unlike cultural symbols, contextual symbols derive their meanings from the context and circumstances of individual works. As an example, the "shady seat" mentioned in Amy Lowell's "Patterns" (line 86) takes on powerful symbolic value, for we learn that it was where the speaker and her fiancé had planned, before he was sent off to war, to make love in the open air. As a symbol, the shady seat suggests a wished-for liberation from confining and stultifying cultural expectations and for a total union of love and a desire for personal freedom. A symbolic object in a story is the never-seen cask of Amontillado wine in Poe's "The Cask of Amontillado." It is the promise of trying out the wine that enables Montresor to lure Fortunato into the subterranean wine cellar and that, therefore, is symbolic of Montresor's deceit and lurid ruthlessness.

Like Lowell's shady seat, Poe's unseen wine is a major contextual symbol. But there is not necessarily any carryover from one work to the next. In other works, a shady seat and a case of wine are not symbolic unless the authors who include them deliberately give them symbolic meaning. Furthermore, if such objects actually are introduced as symbols, they can be given meanings that are different from those in the works by Lowell and Poe.

Determine What Is Symbolic (and What Is Not Symbolic)

In determining whether a particular object, action, or character is a symbol, you need to judge the importance that the author gives to it. If the element is prominent and also maintains a consistency of meaning, you can justify interpreting it as a symbol. For example, the jug of porter (beer) carried by Jackie's grandmother in O'Connor's story "First Confession" is one of the things that symbolize for Jackie his grandmother's boorish habits. The porter is symbolic, however, only within the story. In another context, a reference to porter would not carry the symbolic meaning with which Jackie invests it in "First Confession." Comparably, at the beginning of Shelly Wagner's "The Boxes," the speaker refers to "boxes in the house," including footlockers, hampers, and a trunk. Readers will note that such large containers could easily conceal a small boy. At the story's end, however, the speaker states that she still visits the cemetery where her son is buried. The box that she mentions at the end is, therefore, a coffin, and for this reason, the "Boxes" of the poem's title may be construed as a contextual symbol of death.

Allegory

An **allegory** is like a symbol because it transfers and broadens meaning. The term is derived from the Greek word *allegorein*, which means "to say something beyond what is commonly understood" (from *allos,* "other" and *agoreuein,* "to speak in public"). Allegory, however, is more sustained than symbolism. An allegory is to a symbol as a motion picture is to a still picture. In form, an allegory is a complete and self-sufficient narrative, but it also signifies another series of conditions or events. Although some stories are allegories from beginning to end, many stories that are not allegories can nevertheless contain brief sections or episodes that are *allegorical*. Allegories are often concerned with morality and especially with religion, but we may also find political and social allegories. To the degree to which literary works are true not only because of the lives of their main characters but also because of life generally, one might maintain that much literature may be considered allegorical even though the authors did not plan their works as allegories.

Understand the Applications and Meaning of Allegory

Allegories and the allegorical method are more than literary exercises. Without question, readers and listeners learn and memorize stories and tales more easily than moral lessons; therefore, allegory is a favorite method of teaching morality. In addition, thought and expression have not always been free and safe. The threat of censorship and the danger of political or economic reprisal have often caused authors to express their views indirectly in the form of allegory rather than to name names and write openly, thereby risking political prosecution, accusations of libel, or even bodily harm. Hence, the double meanings of many allegories are based not just in the literary form but also in the reality of circumstances in our difficult world.

In considering allegory, determine whether all or part of a work can have an extended, allegorical meaning. The popularity of George Lucas's movie *Star Wars* and its sequels (in videotape and newly refurbished rereleases on DVD) and its "prequel" (*The Phantom Menace*), for example, is attributable at least partly to its being an allegory about the conflict between good and evil. Obi Wan Kenobi (intelligence) assists Luke Skywalker (heroism, boldness) and instructs him in "the Force" (moral or religious faith). Thus armed and guided, Skywalker opposes the powers of Darth Vader (evil) to rescue the Princess Leia (purity and goodness) with the aid of the latest spaceships and weaponry (technology). The story has produced a set of popular adventure films, accompanied by dramatic music and ingenious visual and sound effects. With the obvious allegorical overtones, however, it stands for any person's quest for self-fulfillment.

To apply a part of the allegory more specifically, consider that for a time, the evil Vader imprisons Skywalker and that Skywalker must exert all his skill and strength to get free and overcome Vader. In the allegorical application of the episode, this imprisonment signifies those moments of doubt, discouragement, and depression that people experience while trying to improve themselves through education, work, self-improvement, friendship, marriage, and so on.

Almost from the beginning of recorded literature, similar heroic deeds have been represented in allegorical forms. From ancient Greece, the allegorical hero Jason sails the *Argo* to distant lands to gain the Golden Fleece (those who take risks are rewarded). From Anglo-Saxon England, the hero Beowulf saves King Hrothgar's throne by killing the monster Grendel and his even more monstrous mother (victory comes to those who rely on the forces of good). From seventeenth-century England, John Bunyan's *The Pilgrim's Progress* tells how the hero Christian overcomes difficulties and temptations while traveling from this world to the next (belief, perseverance, and resistance to temptation save the faithful). As long as the parallel connections are close and consistent, such as those mentioned here, an allegorical interpretation is valid.

Fable, Parable, and Myth

Closely related to symbolism and allegory in the ability to extend and expand meaning are three additional forms: *fable*, *parable*, and *myth*.

A Fable Is a Short Tale with a Pointed Moral

The **fable** (from Latin *fabula*, a story or narration) is an old, brief, and popular form. Often but not always, fables are about animals that possess human traits (such fables are called **beast fables**). Past collectors and editors of fables have attached "morals" or explanations to the brief stories, as did Aesop, the most enduringly popular of fable writers. Tradition has it that Aesop was a slave who composed fables in ancient Greece. His fable "The Fox and the Grapes" exemplifies the trait of belittling things we cannot have. More recent popular contributions to the fable tradition include Walt Disney's "Mickey Mouse," Walt Kelly's "Pogo," and Berke Breathed's "Bloom County." The adjective *fabulous* refers to the collective body of fables of all sorts, even though the word is often used as little more than a vague term of approval.

A Parable Is a Short Narrative Illustrating a Religious Concept

A **parable** (from Greek *parabolé*, a "setting beside" or comparison) is a short, simple story with a moral or religious bent. Parables are most often associated with Jesus, who used them to embody unique religious insights and truths. For example, his parables "The Prodigal Son" and "The Good Samaritan," as recorded by Luke, are interpreted to show God's understanding, forgiveness, concern, and love.

A Myth Is a Tale with Social, Political, Religious, or Philosophical Meanings

A **myth** (from Greek *muthos*, a "story" or "plot") is a traditional story that embodies and codifies the religious, philosophical, and cultural values of the civilization in which it was composed. Usually, the central figures of mythical stories are heroes, gods, and demigods, such as the ancient figures Aeneas, Athena, Hera, Hercules, Oedipus, Pandora, Prometheus, Sisyphus, Venus, and Zeus. Although most myths are fictional, many are remotely based in historical truth. They are by no means confined to the past, for the word *myth* can also refer to abstractions and ideas that people today hold collectively, such as the concept of perpetual military supremacy or the idea that future problems can be deferred indefinitely. Sometimes the words *myth* and *mythical* are used with the meaning "fanciful" or "untrue." Such disparagement is misleading because the truths of mythology are to be found not literally in the myths themselves but rather in their symbolic and allegorical interpretations.

Allusion in Symbolism and Allegory

Cultural or universal symbols and allegories often allude to other works from our cultural heritage, such as the Bible, ancient history and literature, and works of the British and American traditions. Sometimes understanding a story requires knowledge of history and current politics.

If the meaning of a symbol is not immediately clear to you, you will need a dictionary or other reference work. The scope of your college dictionary will surprise you. If you cannot find an entry there, however, try one of the major encyclopedias, or ask your reference librarian, who can direct you to shelves loaded with helpful books. A few excellent guides are *The Concise Oxford Companion to Classical Literature* (ed. M. C. Howatson and Ian Chilvers), *The Oxford Companion to English Literature* (ed. Margaret Drabble), *Merriam Webster's Encyclopedia of Literature*, Timothy Gantz's *Early Greek Myth: A Guide to Literary and Artistic Sources*, and Richmond Y. Hathorn's *Greek Mythology*.

Useful aids in finding biblical references are *Cruden's Complete Concordance*, which in various editions has been a reliable guide since 1737, and *The Strongest Strong's Exhaustive Concordance of the Bible* (2001), which has been revised and expanded regularly since it was first published in 1890. These concordances list all the major words used in the King James version of the Bible, so you can easily locate the chapter and verse of any and all biblical passages. If you still have trouble after using sources like these, see your instructor.

Writing About Symbolism and Allegory

As you read, take notes and make all the observations you can about the presence of symbols or allusions or both. Explanatory notes will help you to establish basic information, but you also need to explain meanings and create interpretations in your own words. Use a dictionary for understanding words or phrases that require further study. For allusions, you might check out original sources to determine original contexts. Try to determine the ways in which your poem is similar to, or different from, the original work or source, and then determine the purpose served by the allusion.

Raise Questions to Discover Ideas

Cultural or Universal Symbols

- What symbols that you consider cultural or universal can you discover in names, objects, places, situations, or actions in the work (e.g., the character Faith and the walking stick in "Young Goodman Brown," the funeral bells in "Anthem for Doomed Youth," the snow in "Desert Places," Bethlehem in "The Second Coming")? ·
- How are these symbols used? What do they mean, both specifically, in the poem, and universally, in a broader context? What would the poem be like without the symbolic meaning?

Contextual Symbols

- What contextual symbols can you locate in the work (e.g., boxes, children singing in the choir, yellow leaves in autumn)? How is the symbolism used specifically in the poem? What would the poem be like if the symbols were not taken to be symbolic?

- What causes you to conclude that the symbols are truly symbolic? What is being symbolized? What do the symbols mean? How definite or direct is the symbolism?
- Is the symbolism used systematically throughout the work, or is it used only once? How does the symbolism affect the work's ideas or emotions?

Other Forms

- What enables you to identify the story as a parable or fable? What lesson or moral is either clearly stated or implicit?
- What mythological identification is established in the work? What do you find in the story (names, situations, etc.) that enables you to determine its mythological significance? How is the myth to be interpreted? What symbolic value does the myth have? What current and timeless application does it have?

Organize Your Essay About Symbolism or Allegory

Introduction Relate the central idea of your essay to the meaning of the major symbols or allegorical thrust of the story. An idea about "Young Goodman Brown," for example, is that fanaticism darkens and limits the human soul. An early incident in the story provides symbolic support for this idea. Specifically, when Goodman Brown enters the woods, he resolves "to stand firm against the devil," and he then looks up toward "Heaven above him." As he looks, a "black mass of cloud" appears to hide the "brightening stars" (paragraph 47). Within the limits of our central idea, the cloud can be seen as a symbol, just like the widening path or the night walk itself. Look for ways to make solid connections like this when you designate something as a symbol or allegory.

Also, your essay will need to include justifications for your symbols or allegorical parallels. In Poe's "The Cask of Amontillado," for example, Montresor's underground vaults may be taken as an image of his unexpressed hatred and evil wishes. When Fortunato goes into the vaults with him, we may understand that Fortunato will never be able to free himself from Montresor's diabolical clutches. If you treat the vaults as a symbol, it is important to apply it to the festering hatreds and secret schemes that characterize many people who on the surface may seem calm and in control of their lives. In the same way, in describing the allegorical elements in "Young Goodman Brown," you need to establish a comprehensive statement such as the following: People lose ideals and forsake principles not because these people are evil but because they misunderstand the people around them (see the second illustrative essay that follows).

Body For the body of your essay, there are a number of strategies for discussing symbolism and allegory. You might use one exclusively or a combination.

Symbolism

1. **The meaning of a major symbol.** Identify the symbol and what it stands for. Then answer questions such as these: Is the symbol cultural or contextual? How do you decide? How do you derive your interpretation of the symbolic meaning? What is the extent of the meaning? Does the symbol undergo modification or

new applications if it reappears in the work? How does the symbol affect your understanding of the work? Does the symbol bring out any ironies? How does the symbol add strength and depth to the work?

2. **The development and relationship of symbols.** A good approach is to determine how symbolism is related to the work's narrative structure. Where does the symbol occur? If it is early, how do the following parts relate to the ideas borne by the symbol? What logical or chronological function does the symbol serve in the work's development? Is the symbol repeated, and if so, to what effect? If the symbol is introduced later, has it been anticipated earlier? How do you know? Can the symbol be considered climactic? What might the structure of the work have been like if the symbolism had not been used?

When considering two or more symbols, deal with issues such as these: How do the symbols connect with each other (like night and the cloud in "Young Goodman Brown" as symbols of a darkening mind)? What additional meanings do the symbols provide? What is the function of the symbols in the work's narrative? If the symbol is a person, object, or setting, what physical aspects are described? Why? Are colors included? Shapes? Sizes? Sounds? In light of this description, how applicable is the symbol to the ideas it embodies? How appropriate is the literal condition to the symbolic condition? The answers to questions like these should lead not so much to a detailed account of the meaning of the symbols but rather to an account of their appropriateness to the topics and ideas expressed or implicit in the work.

Allegory

1. **The application and meaning of the allegory.** What is the subject of the story (allegory, fable, parable, myth)? How can it be more generally applied to ideas or to qualities of human character, not only of its own time but also of our own? What other versions of the story do you know, if any? Does the story illustrate, either closely or loosely, particular philosophies or religious views? If so, what are these? How do you know?

2. **The consistency of the allegory.** Is the allegory used consistently throughout the story, or is it used intermittently? Explain and illustrate this use. Would it be correct to call your story *allegorical* rather than an *allegory*? Can you determine how parts of the story are introduced for their allegorical importance? Examples are the events that occur in the darkened church in O'Connor's "First Confession"; the Parisian street (Rue des Martyrs) on which the Loisels first live in Maupassant's "The Necklace," which may correspond to the temptation to live beyond one's means; and the frozen preserves in Glaspell's *Trifles*, which we may take as allegorical equivalents of life's sometimes destructive difficulties.

Conclusion You might summarize main points, describe general impressions, explain the impact of the symbolic or allegorical methods, indicate personal responses, or suggest further lines of thought and application. You might also assess the quality and appropriateness of the symbolism or allegory (such as Hawthorne's "Young Goodman Brown" opening in darkness and closing in gloom). If your poem is rich in symbols or allusions, you might also consider some of the elements that you have not discussed in the body and try to tie these together with those you have already discussed. It would also be appropriate to introduce any new ideas that you developed as a result of your study.

Illustrative Essay (Symbolism in a Poem)

Symbolism in William Butler Yeats's "The Second Coming"

Yeats's "The Second Coming" is a prophetic poem that lays out   [1]
reasons for being scared about the future. The poem's symbolism
combines traditional materials from ancient history and literature
with Yeats's own scheme for visualizing the rise and fall of civiliza-
tions. This scheme is designed to explain both the disruption of our
present but old culture, and also the installation of a frightening new
one. [1] To make his prophecies clear, Yeats uses his symbolism as a
reflection of the horrors of the twentieth century. [2]

Yeats's first major symbol, the gyre or spiral—or rather two   [2]
interconnecting gyres—pervades the poem visually, for it outlines the
cyclical nature of moral and political changes. Flying outward at the
widest point of the gyre, symbolizing our modern times, a falcon is
used by Yeats to introduce the idea that "the center cannot hold."
The "desert birds," hovering around the "lion body and the head of
a man" (the sphinx-like figure), show a tighter circle in a second gyre,
symbolizing a new stage of history. Thus, the widening symbolic gyre
in line 1 is interpenetrating with the narrowing gyre pointing at the
"rough beast." This intersecting and blending show that new things
both emerge and separate from old things. The spatial symbolism,
thus, illustrates that the past is breaking up while the future is about
to take the shape of the past—but at its worst, not at its best.

Embodying this horror-to-be, the second major symbol is the   [3]
sphinx-like creature moving its "slow thighs" in the sands of the desert.
The attributes of the monstrous creature are blankness and pitiless-
ness. Yeats describes it as a "rough beast" (line 16), with the
"indignant desert birds" flying in circles above it like vultures.

---

[1]Central idea.
[2]Thesis sentence.

This description symbolizes the brutal nature of the new age. Yeats wrote the poem in 1919, right after the conclusion of World War I, which had seen both the viciousness and the mindlessness of trench warfare. The disruption of life caused by this war was a disturbing indicator of the repressiveness and brutality to come.

It is this brutality that makes ironic another of the poem's major [4] symbol: the long-awaited "second coming" of Jesus. Yeats alludes to the second coming in the poem's title and also in lines 9 and 10:

> Surely some revelation is at hand;
> Surely the Second Coming is at hand.

The reference is to New Testament prophecies about the return of Jesus at the end of historical time. In the Bible, war and rumors of war are claimed as being the signs indicating that the return, or "Second Coming," is near. Thus far, both the biblical signs and the observations of Yeats coincide. The twist, however, is that Yeats is suggesting through the symbol that after the breakup of the present age, the new age will be marked not by God's Kingdom but by the "rough beast." Because Yeats visualizes the beast as a sphinx, his model is the kind of despotism known in ancient Egypt, when power was held absolutely by the pharaoh.

A unique aspect of Yeats's symbolism is that he fuses his own [5] symbolism with symbolism of paganism and Christianity. The "ceremony of innocence," for example (6), uses the language of Christian communion. By indicating that it is being drowned, however, Yeats asserts that the tradition is being lost and brutalized. The Spiritus Mundi is an abstract allusion to a common human bond of images and characteristics, but because of the image of brutality it produces, as a symbol it demonstrates that horror is now and ever will be a normal condition of human life. In addition, the "blood-dimmed tide" is an allusion to Shakespeare's Macbeth, who symbolically has stained the ocean red with King Duncan's blood. The "blood-dimmed tide," therefore, both allusively and symbolically indicates the global scope of the evil age being born.

[6]   "The Second Coming" is rich in symbols that are both traditional and personal, and there are additional symbols. The most
easily visualized of these is the falcon out of control, flying higher
and higher and farther away from the falconer, to symbolize the
anarchy that Yeats mentions in line 4 as being "loosed" in the world.
An example of a symbol being used ironically is the reference to
Bethlehem, where, according to the Gospels of Matthew and Luke,
Jesus, the "Prince of Peace," was born. In "The Second Coming,"
Yeats asserts instead that the new birth will not lead to peace but
instead will bring about a future age of repression and brutality.
Yeats's poem thus offers a complex and disturbing fabric of
symbolism.

Work Cited

Yeats, William Butler. "The Second Coming." Edgar V. Roberts.
    Writing About Literature. 13th ed. New York: Pearson, 2012.
    364. Print.

Commentary on the Essay

The introduction of this essay briefly characterizes Yeats's poem and asserts that the
arguments are made through the use of symbols. The central idea is about the replacement of the old by the new, and the thesis sentence states that Yeats combines major
symbols to achieve an effect of horror. Paragraph 2 describes the shape of the symbol
as a complex and interconnected set of "gyres," or spirals, indicating that nations are
spinning out of control. Paragraph 3 considers the "rough beast" as a symbol of emerg-
ing brutality. Paragraph 4 treats the title's use of New Testament prophetic symbolism,
showing that Yeats makes his point by reversing the outcome that tradition had pre-
dicted. Paragraph 5 demonstrates the complexity of Yeats's poem by stressing how he
fuses symbolism and allusion. The sixth and last paragraph contains a brief summary
and then proceeds to illustrate the richness of "The Second Coming" with brief references to additional symbols.

Illustrative Essay (Allegory in a Story)

The Allegory of Hawthorne's "Young Goodman Brown"[3]

Nathaniel Hawthorne's "Young Goodman Brown" is a   [1]
nightmarish narrative. It allegorizes the process by which something
good—religion—becomes a justification for intolerance and
prejudice. The major character, Goodman Brown of Salem during
colonial times, begins as a pious and holy person, but he takes a
walk into a nearby darkening forest of both suspicion and sanctimo-
niousness. The process is portrayed by Hawthorne as being origi-
nated by the devil himself, who leads Goodman Brown into the
night. By the end of the allegory, Brown is transformed into an
unforgiving, antisocial, dour, and dreary misanthrope.

Hawthorne's choice of location for the story reminds us that it   [2]
was in historical Salem, in the late seventeenth century, that religious
zealousness became so extreme that a number of witch trials and
public hangings took place solely on the basis of suspicion and false
accusation. This setting indicates that Hawthorne's immediate
allegorical target is the overzealous pursuit of religious principles.
So Goodman Brown's trip not only takes him into the gloom of
night, but also marks a descent into the darkest dungeon of his soul.[4]

While the story directly details elements in the growth of   [3]
religious zealotry, Hawthorne's allegory may also be applied more
generally to the ways in which people uncritically follow any ideal
that leads them to distrust and suspect others. The allegory is, thus,
relevant to those who swallow political slogans, who believe in their
own racial or ethnic superiority, or who justify super patriotism and
super nationalism. As such people persuade themselves of their own
supremacy, they ignore the greater need for understanding, toleration, cooperation, forgiveness, and love. Hawthorne's allegory is a
realistic portrait of how people get into such a mental state, with
Goodman Brown as the example of the attitude. Such people push

---

[3]For the text of this story, see p. 317–26.
[4]Central idea.

ahead even against their own good nature and background, and they develop their prejudices through delusion and suspicion.[5]

[4]   Young Goodman Brown's pathway into the night is not a direct plunge into evil, but Hawthorne shows that Brown is not without good nature because he has misgivings about what he is doing. Many times early in the story, we learn that he has doubts about the "evil purpose" of his allegorical walk. At the very beginning, Faith calls him back and pleads with him to stay the night with her (318, 2), but even so, he leaves her. As he walks away, he thinks of himself as "a wretch" for doing so (318, 7). He excuses himself with a promise that once the evening is over, he will stick with Faith forever after, an "excellent resolve for the future," as the narrator ironically states (318, 8). When Goodman Brown is reproached by the devil for being late—we conclude that Brown's purpose was to keep this diabolical appointment—he gives the excuse "Faith kept me back a while" (318, 12), a sentence of ironic double meaning. Once he has kept his appointment with the devil, he states his intention to go no farther because he has "scruples" that remind him that "it is my purpose now to return whence I came" (319, 15). Even when Goodman Brown is standing before the altar of profanation deep within the forest, he appeals to Faith, "Look up to Heaven, and resist the Wicked One!" (326, 68). All this hesitation represents a true conscience in Goodman Brown even though he ignores it as he progresses deeper into the forest of sin. His failure is his inability or unwillingness to make his own insight and conscience his guides of conduct.

[5]   It is important to remember that Goodman Brown is favored by his background, which might reasonably be expected to have kept him on a path of true goodness. Almost as a claim of entitlement, he cries out, "With Heaven above, and Faith below, I will yet stand firm against the devil" (322, 46). He also cries out for Faith even when he hears a voice resembling hers that is "uttering lamentations" within the darkening woods (322, 47). When he sees

---

[5]Thesis sentence.

Faith's pink ribbon mysteriously flutter down, he exclaims, "My Faith is gone!" (323, 50). These instances show allegorically that Goodman Brown's previous way of life has given him the right paths to follow and the right people in whom to believe. Even as he is tempted when he is standing before the "unhallowed altar" (325, 64), he asks the question "But, where is Faith?" as though he could reclaim the innocence that he has previously known (324, 57). Just as he ignores his conscience, he also ignores the power of his background, and it is this neglect that fuels his change into the "demoniac" who abandons himself to "the instinct that guides mortal man to evil" (323, 50).

Another major element in Goodman Brown's allegorical path into darkness is that he develops the assumption that virtually all the people he knows have yielded their lives to sin and are therefore unworthy. In the grip of this distorted view of others, he believes not what he sees but what he thinks he is seeing. Thus, he witnesses the encounter between the devil and Goody Cloyse shortly after he enters the forest, but what he sees is not the good woman who taught him his catechism but rather a witch who is bent on evil and who is friendly with the devil. He ignores the fact that he too is friendly with the devil (the image of his own father), and, therefore, while ignoring the log in his own eye, he condemns Goody Cloyse for the speck in hers. After his transformation, when he walks back into his village from his allegorical walk into evil, he "snatche[s] away" a child from Goody as though she were preaching the words of the devil and not God (326, 70). He cannot believe that others possess goodness as long he is convinced by the devil's words that "the whole earth [is] one stain of guilt, one mighty blood-spot" (325, 63). For this reason, he condemns both his minister and Deacon Gookin, whose conspiratorial voices he thinks he overhears on the pathway through the forest. In short, the process of Hawthorne's allegory about the growth of harmful pietism demonstrates that travelers on the pathway to prejudice accept suspicion and mistrust without trying to get at the whole truth and without recognizing that judgment is not in human but rather is in divine hands.

[6]

[7]   As Hawthorne allegorizes the development of religious discrimination, he makes clear that, as with any kind of discrimination,
mistrust and suspicion form its basis. Certainly, as the devil claims,
human beings commit many criminal and depraved sins (325, 63), but
this does not mean that all human beings are equally at fault and that
they are beyond love and redemption. The key for Goodman Brown
is that he exceeds his judgmental role and bases his condemnation of
others solely on his own hasty and mistrustful conclusions. As long as
he has faith, he will not falter, but when he leaves his faith or believes
that he has lost his faith, he is adrift and will see only evil wherever he
looks. For this reason, he falls victim to suspicion and loathing, and
he becomes harsh and desperate forever after, as Hawthorne shows
happened to him after the fateful night. The story's conclusion
completes the allegorical cycle beginning with Brown's initiation into
evil and extending to his "dying hour" of "gloom" and his unhopeful
tombstone (326, 72).

[8]   Hawthorne's "Young Goodman Brown" allegorizes the paradox
of how noble beliefs become ignoble. Goodman Brown dies in gloom
because he believes that his wrong vision is true. His form of evil is the
hardest to stop because wrongdoers who are convinced of their own
goodness are beyond reach. In view of such self-righteous evil, whether
cloaked in the apparent virtues of Puritanism or of some other blindly
rigorous doctrine, Hawthorne writes, "the fiend in his own shape is less
hideous than when he rages in the breast of man" (323, 53). As
Hawthorne presents the allegory of Young Goodman Brown, the
"hero" is one of the many who convince themselves that they alone
walk in light but who actually create darkness.

Work Cited

Hawthorne, Nathaniel. "Young Goodman Brown." Edgar V.
    Roberts. *Writing About Literature.* 13th ed. New York: Pearson
    Longman, 2012. 317–26. Print.

Commentary on the Essay

Unity in the essay is achieved by a number of means. For example, paragraph 2 extends a topic in paragraph 1. Also, a phrase in sentence 2 of paragraph 1 is echoed in sentence 1 of paragraph 8. Making additional connections within the essay are individual words such as "another," "while," and "therefore" and the repetition of words throughout the essay that are contained in the thesis sentence.

The first three paragraphs of the essay constitute an extended introduction to the topics of paragraphs 4 through 8, for they establish "Young Goodman Brown" as an allegory. Paragraph 1 briefly treats the allegorical nature of the narrative. Paragraph 2 relates the historical basis of the topic to Hawthorne's purpose in writing the story, and it concludes with the essay's central idea. Paragraph 3 broadens the scope of Hawthorne's allegory by showing that it includes zealousness wherever it might appear. Paragraph 3 also concludes with the essay's thesis sentence.

Paragraph 4 deals with an important aspect of the allegory, one that makes it particularly relevant and timely even today—namely, that people of basically good nature may grow fall into suspicious error under the pretense of goodness. Similarly, paragraph 5 points out that such people usually come from good backgrounds and have benefited from good influences during their lives.

Paragraphs 6 and 7 locate the origins of evil in two major human qualities: the belief in one's own delusions and the mental confusion that results from the conviction that appearance is more real and believable than reality itself. Paragraph 8 concludes the essay on the note that the finished "product"—a person who has become suspicious and misguided—demonstrates how good ideas, when pushed to the extreme by false imagination, can backfire.

Writing Topics About Symbolism and Allegory

1. Compare and contrast the symbolism in Blake's "The Tyger," Arnold's "Dover Beach," Hughes's "Negro," and Poe's "The Cask of Amontillado." To what degree do the works rely on contextual symbols? On universal symbols? On the basis of your comparison, what is the case for asserting that realism and fantasy are directly related to the nature of the symbolism presented in these works?

2. Why do writers who advocate moral, philosophical, or religious issues frequently use symbolism or allegory? In treating this question, you might introduce references from Hawthorne's "Young Goodman Brown," Hardy's "Channel Firing," and Arnold's "Dover Beach."

3. Write an essay on the allegorical method of one or more of the parables included in the Gospel of St. Luke, such as "The Bridegroom" (5:34–35), "The Garments and the Wineskins" (5:36–39), "The Sower" (8:4–15), "The Good Samaritan" (10:25–37), "The Prodigal Son" (15:11–32), "The Ox in the Well" (14:5–6), "The Watering of Animals on the Sabbath" (13:15–17), "The Rich Fool" (12:16–21), "Lazarus" (16:19–31), "The Widow and the Judge" (18:1–8), and "The Pharisee and the Publican" (18:9–14).

4. What is the nature of the symbols pertaining to the role of single and married women in Mansfield's "Miss Brill," Chekhov's The Bear, Glaspell's Trifles, Chopin's "The Story of an Hour," and Browning's "My Last Duchess"?

5. Consider the meaning of the symbols of war in Arnold's "Dover Beach," Hardy's "The Man He Killed," Layton's "Rhine Boat Trip," Lowell's "Patterns," and Owen's "Anthem for Doomed Youth."

6. Compare the use of religious symbols in Randall's "The Ballad of Birmingham," Yeats's "The Second Coming," and Hawthorne's "Young Goodman Brown." What are the locations from which the poets draw their symbols? How do the symbols figure into the ideas and actions of the works?

7. Write a poem in which you develop a major symbol, as Maupassant does in "The Necklace" (with the necklace) and Layton does in "Rhine Boat Trip" (with the cattle cars). To get yourself started, you might think about the meaning of symbols like these:
   a. A littered street or sidewalk
   b. Coffee hour after church
   c. An athletic competition
   d. A computer
   e. The checkout counter at the neighborhood supermarket
   f. The family dog looking out a window as the children leave for school

8. Write your own brief story using a widely recognized cultural symbol such as the flag (patriotism, love of country, a certain type of politics), water (life, sexuality, regeneration), or the population explosion (the end of life on earth). By arranging actions and dialogue, make clear the issues conveyed by your symbol, and try to resolve conflicts the symbol might raise among your characters.

9. Using the card or computer catalogue of your library or online searches, discover a recent critical-biographical work about Hawthorne. Explain what the book says about Hawthorne's uses of symbolism. To what extent does the book relate Hawthorne's symbolism to his religious and family heritage?

Chapter 12

Writing About Tone: The Writer's Control over Attitudes and Feelings

Fiction, Drama, and Poetry

Tone refers to the methods by which writers and speakers reveal attitudes or feelings. It is an aspect of all spoken and written statements, whether earnest declarations of love, requests to pass a dinner dish, letters from students asking parents for money, or official government notices threatening penalties if taxes and fines are not paid. Because tone is often equated with *attitude*, it is important to realize that tone refers not so much to attitudes themselves but rather to those technique and modes of presentation that reveal or create attitudes.

As a literary concept, *tone* is adapted from the phrase *tone of voice* in speech. Tone of voice reflects attitudes toward a particular object or situation and also toward listeners. Let us suppose that our good friend Mary has a difficult assignment on which she expects to work all day. Things go well, and she finishes quickly. She happily tells her friend Anne, "I'm so pleased! I needed only two hours for that." Then she decides to buy tickets for a popular concert and must wait in a long, slow line. After getting her tickets, she tells the people at the end of the line, "I'm so pleased. I needed only *two hours* for that!" The sentences are exactly the same, but by changing her emphasis and vocal inflection, Mary indicates her disgust and impatience with her long wait as she shows her sympathy with the people who are still in line. By controlling the *tone* of her statements, in other words, Mary conveys satisfaction at one time and indignation at another.

As this example indicates, an attitude itself may be summarized with a word or phrase (satisfaction or indignation, love or contempt, interest or indifference, deference or command, and so on), but the study of tone examines those aspects of situation, language, action, and background that bring out the attitude. In the last two lines of Owen's "Anthem for Doomed Youth," for example (p. 360), the speaker refers to the reactions of those at home toward the young men who have died in battle:

Their flowers [shall be] the tenderness of patient minds,
And each slow dusk a drawing-down of blinds.

These words suggest that the immediate anguish is past and that those left at home must endure unending, lifelong, quiet sorrow, indicated by the "drawing down of blinds," which by shutting out light also suggests an end of hope, expectation, and love.

Tone and Attitudes

In most literary works, attitudes point in a number of directions, so tone becomes a highly complex matter. The following things to look for, however, should help you in understanding and describing literary tone.

Determine the Writer's Attitude Toward the Material

By reading a work carefully, we may deduce the author's attitude or attitudes toward the subject matter. In "The Story of an Hour," for example, Chopin sympathetically portrays a young wife's secret wishes for freedom just as she also humorously reveals the unwitting smugness that often pervades the married lives of men and women. In "Echo," Rossetti's speaker addresses a lover who is long dead, and by this means, Rossetti renders attitudes of yearning and sorrow. In a broader perspective, authors may view human beings with amused affection, as in Chekhov's *The Bear*, or with amused resignation, as in Hardy's "Channel Firing." All these works exhibit various degrees of irony, which is one of the most significant aspects of authorial tone.

Discover the Writer's Attitude Toward Readers

Authors recognize that readers participate in the creative act and that all elements of a story—word choice, characterization, allusions, levels of reality—must take readers' responses into account (note the discussion of "Reader Response" criticism in Appendix A). When Hawthorne's woodland guide in "Young Goodman Brown" refers to "King Philip's War," for example, Hawthorne assumes that his readers know that this war was inhumane, greedy, and cruel. By allowing this assumption to stand, he indicates respect for the knowledge of his readers, and he also assumes their essential agreement with him. Chekhov in *The Bear* assumes that readers understand that Smirnov's speeches reveal him as irascible and petulant, but they also show him as both generous and funny. Authors always make such considerations about readers by implicitly complimenting them on their knowledge and by satisfying their curiosity and desire to be interested, stimulated, and pleased.

Determine Other Dominant Attitudes

Beyond general authorial tone, there are many internal and dramatically rendered expressions of attitude. For example, the speaker of Lowell's "Patterns" is a decent and proper upper-class young woman. Yet at the news of her fiancé's death, her sorrowful meditation brings out that she had made a promise to him to make love outside, on a "shady seat" in the garden (lines 86–89). This personal confession symbolically reveals an inner warmth that her social situation does not suggest, and it also makes the poem pathetically poignant.

    In addition, as characters interact, their tone dramatically shows their judgments about other characters and situations. A complicated control of tone occurs at the end of Glaspell's *Trifles*, when the two major characters, Mrs. Hale and Mrs. Peters, cover up incriminating evidence about Minnie Wright. When the two women are examining the things in the kitchen, however, before they actually do the covering up, Mrs. Peters speaks not about illegality, but rather about the possible embarrassment of the action:

> MRS. PETERS. (*Takes the bottle, looks about for something to wrap it in; takes petticoat from the clothes brought from the other room, very nervously begins winding this around the bottle. In a false voice.*) "My, it's a good thing the men couldn't hear us. Wouldn't they just laugh! Getting all stirred up over a little thing like a—dead canary. As if that could have anything to do with—with—wouldn't they laugh! (speech 137)

Notice that her words reveal her knowledge that men scoff at feminine concerns, like Minnie's quilting knots, and therefore, she openly anticipates the men's amusement. The reader, however, is thus prepared for Mrs. Peters to join Mrs. Hale in hiding and covering up the incriminating evidence about Minnie.

Tone and Humor

A major aspect of tone is humor. Everyone likes to laugh, and shared laughter is part of good human relationships; but, not everyone can explain why things are funny. Laughter resists close analysis; it is often unplanned, personal, idiosyncratic, and unpredictable. Nonetheless, there are a number of common elements:

1. **There must be an object to laugh at.** There must be something at which to laugh—a person, a thing, a situation, a custom, a habit of speech or dialect, an arrangement of words, and so on.
2. **Laughter usually stems out of disproportion or incongruity.** People normally know what to expect under given conditions, and anything contrary to these expectations is *incongruous* and may, therefore, generate laughter. When the temperature is 100°F, you expect people to dress lightly, but if you were to see a man wearing a heavy overcoat, a warm hat, a muffler, and large gloves and waving his arms and stamping his feet as though to keep warm, he would violate your expectations. Because his garments and behavior are *inappropriate* or *incongruous*, you would think he was funny. A student in a basic English class once wrote about a "*congregation* of verbs" and about parts of speech as "nouns, verbs, and *proverbs*." The student meant the *conjugation* of verbs, of course, and (maybe) either *adverbs* or *pronouns*, but somehow his understanding slipped, and he created a comic incongruity. Such inadvertent verbal errors are called **malapropisms**, after Mrs. Malaprop, a character in Richard Brinsley Sheridan's eighteenth-century play *The Rivals* (1775). In the literary creation of malapropisms, the tone is directed against the speaker for the amusement of readers and author alike.
3. **Safety and/or good will prevent harm and ensure laughter.** Seeing a person slip on a banana peel and hurtle through the air may cause laughter, but only if we ourselves are not that person, for laughter depends on insulation from danger and pain. In comic situations that involve physical abuse—falling down stairs or being hit in the face by cream pies—the abuse never harms the participants. The incongruity of such situations causes laughter, and the immunity from pain and injury prevents responses of horror. Goodwill enters into humor in romantic comedy or in any other work in which we are drawn into general sympathy with the major figures, such as Smirnov and Mrs. Popov in Chekhov's *The Bear*. As the

author leads the characters toward their unexpected flowering of love at the play's end, our involvement produces happiness, smiles, and sympathetic laughter.

4. **Unfamiliarity, newness, and uniqueness are needed to produce the spontaneity of laughter.** Laughter depends upon seeing something new or unique or experiencing something familiar in a new light. Because laughter is prompted by flashes of insight or sudden revelations, it is always spontaneous, even when readers already know and understand the object of their laughter. Indeed, the task of the comic writer is to develop ordinary materials to that point at which spontaneity frees readers to laugh. Thus, you can read and reread Chekhov's *The Bear* and laugh each time because, even though you know what will happen, the play shapes your acceptance of how reconciliation penetrates a wall of anger and guilt. The concluding embraces by Smirnov and Mrs. Popov are now and always will be comic because they are so spontaneous and incongruous.

Tone and Irony

The capacity to have more than one attitude toward someone or something is a uniquely human trait. We know that people are not perfect, but we love a number of them anyway. Therefore, we speak to them not only with love and praise, but also with banter and criticism. On occasion, you may have given mildly insulting greeting cards to your loved ones, not to affront them but to amuse them. You share smiles and laughs, and at the same time, you remind them of your affection.

The word **irony** describes such contradictory statements or situations. Irony is natural to human beings who are aware of life's ambiguities and complexities. It develops from the realization that life does not always measure up to promise, that friends and loved ones are sometimes angry at each other, that the universe contains incomprehensible mysteries, that the social and political structure is often oppressive rather than liberating, that even those with great love and the best of intentions are frequently imposed upon, that doubt exists even in the certainty of knowledge and faith, and that human character is built through chagrin, regret, and pain as much as through emulation and praise. In expressing an idea ironically, writers pay the greatest compliment to their audience, for they assume that readers have sufficient intelligence and skill to discover the real meaning of quizzical or ambiguous statements and situations.

Understand the Four Major Kinds of Irony:
Verbal, Situational, Cosmic, and Dramatic

Verbal Irony Depends on the Interplay of Words In **verbal irony**, one thing is said, but the opposite is meant. In the example at the beginning of this chapter, Mary's ironic expression of pleasure after her two-hour wait for tickets really means that she is disgusted. There are important types of verbal irony. In **understatement**, the expression does not fully describe the importance of a situation, and for this reason, it makes the point strongly through indirection and implication. During the early days of the American space program, an astronaut was asked what he would think if all his reentry safety equipment failed as he was returning to earth after a space exploration, thus dooming him and all aboard to certain death. His answer was this: "A thing like that could ruin your whole day." Such words—adequate for a minor mishap during ordinary daily living but totally inadequate for a major disaster—demonstrate the nature of understatement, which emphasizes by describing the minimum rather than maximum situation.

By contrast, in **hyperbole**, or **overstatement**, the words are obviously and inappropriately excessive, and readers or listeners, therefore, understand that the true meaning is considerably less than what is said. An example is Smirnov's exaggerated dialogue with Mrs. Popov in Chekhov's *The Bear* (speech 69). Although Smirnov tells about the number of times he has jilted women and women have jilted him, readers understand that he is exaggerating his past romantic life to impress Mrs. Popov. The gulf between his exaggeration and the (probably) more modest reality creates smiles and chuckles.

Often verbal irony is ambiguous, having double meaning, or **double entendre**. Midway through Hawthorne's "Young Goodman Brown," for example, the woodland guide leaves Brown alone while stating, "when you feel like moving again, there is my staff to help you along" (paragraph 40). The word "staff" is ambiguous, for it refers to the staff that resembles a serpent (paragraph 13). The word, therefore, suggests that the devilish guide is leaving Brown not only with a real staff but also with the spirit of evil, unlike the divine "staff" of Psalm 23:4 that gives comfort. Ambiguity, of course, may be used in relation to any topic. Quite often, double entendre is used in statements about sexuality for the amusement of listeners or readers.

Situational Irony Fills the Gap Between Hope and Reality

Situational Irony Fills the Gap Between Hope and Reality **Situational irony**, or **irony of situation**, refers to the chasm between what we hope for or expect and what actually happens. It is often pessimistic because it emphasizes that human beings usually have little or no control over their lives or anything else. The forces of opposition may be psychological, social, cultural, political, or environmental. The situation is not temporary, one might add, but permanent and universal, as in Hardy's "Channel Firing," in which the topic is the omnipresence of war in the past, present, and future. Although situational irony often involves disaster, it need not always do so. For example, a happier occurrence of situational irony is in Chekhov's *The Bear*, for the two characters shift from anger to love as they fall into the grips of emotions that, as the saying goes, are "bigger than both of them."

Cosmic Irony Stems from the Power of Fate, Chance, Kings, and Desperate Men

Cosmic Irony Stems from the Power of Fate, Chance, Kings, and Desperate Men A special kind of situational irony that emphasizes the pessimistic and fatalistic side of life is **cosmic irony**, or **irony of fate**. By the standard of cosmic irony, the universe is indifferent to individuals, who are subject to blind chance, accident, uncontrollable emotions, perpetual misfortune, and misery. Even if things temporarily go well, people's lives end badly, and their best efforts do not rescue them or make them happy. A work that illustrates cosmic irony is Glaspell's *Trifles*, which develops out of the stultifying conditions of farm life that Minnie Wright endured for many years while living with her dour and abusive husband. She has no profession, no other hope, no other life except the lonely, dreary farm—nothing. After thirty years of wretchedness, she buys a canary that warbles for her to make her life somewhat more beautiful. Within a year, her insensitive and boorish husband wrings the bird's neck, and she in turn has an ultimate reaction against him. Her situation is cosmically ironic, for the implication of *Trifles* is that human beings are caught in a web of adverse circumstances from which there is no escape.

Dramatic Irony Results from Misunderstanding and Lack of Knowledge   Like cosmic irony, **dramatic irony** is a special kind of situational irony. It happens when a character either has no information about a situation or else misjudges it, but readers (and often some of the other characters) see everything completely and correctly. The classic model of dramatic irony is found in Sophocles' ancient Greek play *Oedipus the King*. In this play, everyone—other characters and readers alike—knows the truth long before Oedipus knows it. Writers of nondramatic works also make use of dramatic irony, as is seen in Chopin's "The Story of an Hour," in which the doctors are ignorant of Louise's secret response to the report of her husband's death. We readers, however, do indeed know and understand her feelings; therefore, we conclude rightly that the doctors' medical diagnosis for her sudden death shows not their skill but rather their masculine vanity.

Writing About Tone

Begin with a careful reading, noting those elements of the work that convey attitudes. Consider whether the work genuinely creates the attitudes it is designed to evoke. In Hughes's "Negro," for example, are the references to real slavery and wage slavery, together with atrocities committed in the Belgian Congo, sufficiently real to support the poem's underlying sense of rage and threat? In Poe's "The Cask of Amontillado," does the claim by Montresor that Fortunato insulted him explain in any way why Montresor carries out his twisted act of revenge? Depending on the work, your devising and answering such questions will help you to understand an author's control over tone. Similar questions apply when you study internal qualities such as style and characterization.

Raise Questions to Discover Ideas

- How strongly do you respond to the work? What attitudes can you identify and characterize? What elements in the story elicit your concern, indignation, fearfulness, anguish, amusement, or sense of affirmation?
- What causes you to sympathize or not to sympathize with characters, situations, or ideas? What makes the circumstances in the work admirable or understandable (or deplorable)?
- In fiction and drama, what does the dialogue suggest about the author's attitudes toward the characters? How does it influence your attitudes? What qualities of diction permit and encourage your responses?
- To what degree, if any, does the work supersede any previous ideas you might have had about the same or similar subject matter? What do you think changed your attitude?
- What role does the narrator or speaker play in your attitudes toward the dramatic or fictional material? Does the speaker seem intelligent or stupid, friendly or unfriendly, sane or insane, idealistic or pragmatic?

- In an amusing or comic story, what elements of plot, character, and diction are particularly comic? How strongly do you respond to humor-producing situations? Why?
- What ironies do you find in the work (verbal, situational, cosmic)? How is the irony connected to philosophies of marriage, family, society, politics, religion, or morality?
- To what extent are characters controlled by fate, social or racial discrimination, limitations of intelligence, economic and political inequality, and limited opportunity?
- Do any words seem unusual or noteworthy, such as words in dialect, polysyllabic words, or foreign words or phrases that the author assumes the reader will know? Are there any especially connotative or emotive words? What authorial assumptions about the readers do these words suggest?

Organize Your Essay about Tone

Introduction Your introduction should describe the general situation of the work and its dominant moods or impressions, such as that the work leads to cynicism, as in "Channel Firing," or to laughter and delight, as in *The Bear*. Problems connected with describing the work's tone should also be introduced here.

Body Your goal is to show how the author establishes the dominant mood or moods of the work, such as the poignancy of Amy Lowell's "Patterns" or the hilarity of Chekhov's *The Bear*. Some possibilities are the use or misuse of language, the exposé of a pretentious speaker, the use of exact and specific descriptions, the isolation of a major character, the failure of plans, and the continuance of naiveté in a disillusioned world. You might find a convenient approach in one of these:

1. **Audience, situation, and characters.** Is any person or group directly addressed by the speaker? What attitude is expressed (love, respect, condescension, confidentiality, confidence, etc.)? What is the basic situation in the story? Do you find irony? If so, what kind is it? What does the irony show (optimism or pessimism, for example)? How is the situation controlled to shape your responses? That is, can actions, situations, or characters be seen as expressions of attitude or as embodiments of certain favorable or unfavorable ideas or positions? What is the nature of the speaker or persona? Why does the persona speak exactly as he or she does? How is the persona's character manipulated to show apparent authorial attitude and to elicit your responses? Does the story promote respect, admiration, dislike, or other feelings about character or situation? If so, how?
2. **Descriptions and diction.** Descriptions or diction in the work should be related to attitude. *For descriptions*: To what degree do descriptions of natural scenery and conditions (snowstorms, cold, rain, ice, intense sunlight) convey an attitude that complements or opposes the circumstances of the characters? Are there any systematic references to colors, sounds, or noises that collectively reflect an attitude? *For diction*: Do connotative meanings of words control response in any way? Does the range of vocabulary require readers to have a large or technical vocabulary? Do speech patterns or the use of dialect evoke attitudes about speakers or their condition of life? Is the level of diction normal, slang, standard, or substandard? What is the effect of such a level? Are there unusual or particularly noteworthy expressions? If so, what attitudes do these show? Does the author use verbal irony? To what effect?

3. **Humor.** Is the work funny? How funny, how intense? How is the humor achieved? Does the humor develop out of incongruous situations or language or both? Is there an underlying basis of attack in the humor, or are the objects of laughter still respected or even loved even though they cause amusement?

4. **Ideas.** Are any ideas advocated, defended mildly, or attacked? How does the author clarify his or her attitude toward these ideas: directly, by statement, or indirectly, through understatement, overstatement, or a character's speeches? In what ways does the story assume a common ground of assent between author and reader? That is, what common assumptions do you find about history, religion, politics, morality, behavioral standards, and so on? Is it easy to give assent (temporary or permanent) to these ideas, or is any concession needed by the reader to approach the work? (For example, a major subject of *Trifles* is the negative effects on a farm wife caused by the isolation and bleakness of an early twentieth-century farm. Things have changed since the time of the play, and the circumstances for such women are certainly better, but sympathetic modern readers can readily understand the psychological situation of the play and can, therefore, understand Minnie Wright's ultimate reaction to the conditions of her life.)

5. **Unique characteristics of the work.** Each work has unique properties that contribute to the tone. Hardy's "Channel Firing," for example, develops from the comic idea that guns being fired at sea are so loud that they awaken the dead in their coffins. In other works, there might be some recurring word or phrase that seems special, as in Rossetti's "Echo." In this poem, the speaker's anguished memory of her dead lover and her yearning are emphasized through the repetitions of the words "Come," "dream," and "long ago."

Conclusion In your conclusion, first summarize your main points and then go on to redefinitions, explanations, or afterthoughts, together with ideas that reinforce earlier points. You might also mention some other major aspect of the story's tone that you did not develop in the body.

Illustrative Essay

Chopin's Irony in "The Story of an Hour"[1]

[1]   "The Story of an Hour" is a remarkably brief short story that exhibits Kate Chopin's complex control over tone. There are many ironies in the story, which grow out of error, misunderstanding, incorrect expectation, and pompous pride.[2] In addition, the story

---

[1]See pages 316–17 for this story.
[2]Central idea.

raises an ironic question about the nature of marriage as an institution. All this is a great deal for so brief a story, yet it is all there. The
story contains a rich mixture of situational irony, cosmic irony, and
dramatic irony.[3]

[2]

The center of the story's situational irony is Louise Mallard, the
central character. Not much is disclosed about her character, her
major circumstances being that she has been a faithful and dedicated
housewife and that she suffers from heart disease. Her situation
reaches an immediate crisis when she is told that her husband has
died. As a loving wife, she weeps convulsively at the news and then
retreats to her room, presumably to grieve in solitude. A previously
unknown and unsuspected feeling then comes to her: the realization
that she is now "free." In other words, she understands that her
marriage has put her in bondage, even though at the same time she
recognizes that her husband "had never looked save with love upon
her" (317, 13). For the first time in her life, she recognizes the gap
between her life and her hidden hopes and expectations, virtually a
definition of situational irony.

[3]

Both situational and cosmic ironies are focused on the people
closest to Louise, namely, her sister Josephine and Brently Mallard's
friend Richards. They are sympathetic people and have the best
intentions toward her. Richards verifies the truth of the train wreck
before coming to the Mallard household with the news and then tells
Josephine. In turn, Josephine breaks the news gently to Louise, in
"veiled hints that revealed in half concealing" (316, 2), so as to
forestall the shock that could bring on a fatal heart attack. Josephine
is successful, and her concern causes her to beg Louise to come out
of her room, for Josephine believes that Louise will make herself ill
with grief (317, 17). With these best intentions, of course, Josephine
becomes the inadvertent cause of bringing Louise in sight of the
front door just as Brently Mallard, safe all along, enters it, and the
shock of seeing him brings about Louise's fatal heart attack. Thus,

---

[3]Thesis sentence.

through no fault of her own, Josephine brings about the blow of fate that she and Richards have tried to avoid.

[4]   Another major cosmic irony in the story results from the inaccuracy and unreliability of information. At the time of the story (1894), the best and most modern method of sending information over distances was by telegraph. Richards is in the newspaper office "when intelligence of the railroad disaster was received, with Brently Mallard's name leading the list of 'killed'" (316, 2). Since the news could not have come so rapidly in the days before telegraphy was common, we may suppose that Louise would never have had the news of the supposed death in the days before telegraphy and, therefore, would never have experienced the emotional crisis brought about by the inaccurate news. The error of information may be caused by human mistake, but the consequences are cosmic for Louise—and, one might add, for her unsuspecting husband, who enters the house only to witness his wife's sudden death.

[5]   This irony-filled story also contains dramatic irony that may be found in two details. None of the characters understands what Louise begins feeling as she sits upstairs. Their experience and their imagination make it impossible for them to comprehend her feelings. This failure of understanding is particularly sad with regard to Josephine and Richards, for these two are the closest ones to her. Thus, in effect, Louise dies alone even though she is surrounded by the people who love her most. In the case of the doctors who diagnose the cause of Louise's death, the lack of understanding is bitterly ironic:

> When the doctors came they said she had died of heart disease— of joy that kills. (23)

The somewhat pompous doctors find it impossible to imagine the true reason for Louise's shock, for, they obviously think, what other reason than joy at seeing her restored husband could bring about such a powerful assault on her system? "The Story of an Hour" ends on this grim and ironic note.

[6]   The story's crowning situational irony is the discrepancy between normal and conventional ideas of marriage as ideal and the

reality of marriage as fact. One senses the authorial voice insisting strongly on uncomfortable reality when Louise contemplates a future life free of the need for satisfying anyone else:

> There would be no powerful will bending hers in that blind persistence with which men and women believe they have a right to impose a private will upon a fellow-creature. (14)

Louise's marriage has not been bad, but the story at this point straightforwardly goes to the heart of the conflict between personal freedom and marital obligation. Chopin's words "blind persistence" are particularly effective here in establishing an attitude of disapproval if not of protest.

Even though "The Story of an Hour" might be considered a tract against traditional marriage, it is above all a superbly crafted story. In just twenty-three paragraphs, it introduces a complex number of ironies revolving around the crisis created by the mistakes and misunderstandings of a single hour. It is the sudden coming together of all these ironies that crash in on Louise Mallard and destroy her. These ironies come into full focus when she suddenly believes that her husband has been killed, only to learn just as suddenly that he is still alive. In life, for most people, such a crisis will never happen. As a general principle, the story's major irony is that even the best and most enviable circumstances of life contain inherent imperfections, unarticulated frustration, and potential unhappiness.

[7]

Work Cited

Chopin, Kate. "The Story of an Hour." Edgar V. Roberts. *Writing About Literature.* 13th ed. New York: Pearson Longman, 2012. 316–17. Print.

Commentary on the Essay

The topic of this essay on tone is Chopin's complex use of irony in "The Story of an Hour." Throughout the essay, a good deal of the story's action is used to exemplify the sorts of irony being discussed. Links and connections within the essay are brought out by phrases like "even though," "also," "crowning situational irony," "another," and "both."

Paragraph 1, the introduction, contains the central idea that announces the causes producing irony. The thesis sentence indicates that the combination of situational, cosmic, and dramatic irony will be explored in the body. Paragraph 2 demonstrates how situational irony applies to the circumstances of the major character, Louise. Paragraph 3 shows how both situational irony and cosmic irony enter into the story through Louise's sister Josephine and Brently's friend Richards.

An additional element of cosmic irony is discussed in paragraph 4. This irony is made to seem particularly unfortunate because the telegraphic errors are totally modern and could never have occurred in a pre-technological age.

In paragraph 5, the story's dramatic irony is introduced. This irony results from the lack of understanding by those closest to Louise and from the pompous intellectual blindness of the examining physicians. Paragraph 6 introduces Chopin's major idea criticizing marriage as an institution. Connected to the thematic purpose of the essay, however, this idea is shown to be integrated with the story's major situational irony. The final paragraph, 7, pays tribute to the story as a story and speculates about how Chopin deals truthfully with difficult issues of life and marriage.

Writing Topics About Tone

1. Consider a story or poem in which the speaker is the central character (e.g., Arnold's "Dover Beach," Frost's "Desert Places," Hardy's "The Man He Killed," Keats's "Bright Star," Lowell's "Patterns," and Rossetti's "Echo"). Write an essay showing how the language of the speaker affects your attitudes toward him or her (that is, your sympathy for the speaker, your interest in the story or the situation).

2. Write an essay comparing and contrasting attitudes toward two or more of the following female characters: Louise in "The Story of an Hour" (p. 316), Mathilde in "The Necklace," Mrs. Popov in *The Bear*, and Minnie Wright in *Trifles*. How does the author's presentation control your understanding of them? What details of tone might be important in a feminist approach to these works?

3. In "First Confession" (p. 332), the adult narrator, Jackie, is describing events that happened to him as a child. What are your attitudes toward Jackie? What do you think are O'Connor's attitudes toward him? To what degree has Jackie separated himself from his childhood emotions? What does he say that might be considered residual childhood responses? What effect, if any, do such comments create?

4. Write a fragment of a story or play of your own about, for example, a student, a supervisor, or a politician. Treat your main character with dramatic irony; that is, your character thinks that he or she knows all the details about a situation but really does not (e.g., a male student declares interest in a female student without realizing that she is already engaged, a supervisor expresses distrust of one of the

best workers in the firm, a politician accuses an opponent of actions that were done not by the opponent but by a supporter). What action, words, and situations do you think you should choose to make your irony clear, and why?

5. Write either (a) two character sketches or (b) two descriptions of an action as though you were planning to include them as part of a story. For either your sketches or your descriptions, make the first favorable and the second negative. Describe your word choices in the contrasting accounts: What kinds of words do you select, and on what principles? What words might you choose if you wanted a neutral account? On the basis of your answers, what can you conclude about the development of a fiction writer's style?

Chapter 13

Writing About Rhyme in Poetry: The Repetition of Identical Sounds to Emphasize Ideas

Poetry

Rhyme refers to separate words that contain identical syllables—most often final syllables. One type of rhyme involves words with identical concluding vowel sounds, or assonance, as in *day, weigh, grey, say, bouquet, fiancé,* and *matinée.* A second type of rhyme is created by identical vowel sounds combined with identical consonant sounds, as in *ache, bake, sake, take, break,* and *opaque;* or *turn, yearn, fern, spurn,* and *adjourn;* or *apple* and *dapple;* or *pensive* and *extensive;* or *slippery* and *frippery.* Rhymes like these, because their rhyming sounds are identical, are called **exact rhymes**. It is important to note that rhymes result from *sound* rather than *spelling*: Words do not have to be spelled the same way or look alike to rhyme. All the words above that rhyme with *day,* for example, are spelled differently, but because they all contain the same *ay* concluding vowel sound, they rhyme.

The Nature and Function of Rhyme

Rhyme, above all, gives unity, certainty, a certain amount of surprise, and interest. It also strengthens a poem's psychological impact. Through its network of similar sounds that resonate in our minds, rhyme promotes memory by clinching feelings and ideas, and it has been an important feature of much English poetry for hundreds of years. Although many poets have not used rhyme and other poets have shunned it because they find it restrictive and artificial, it is closely connected with how well a given poem moves us or leaves us flat.

Most often, rhymes are placed at the ends of lines. Two successive lines may rhyme, for example, and rhymes may appear in alternating lines. It is also possible to introduce rhyming words at intervals of four, five, or more lines. A problem, however, is that if rhyming sounds are too far away from each other, they tend to lose their connectedness—both of rhythm and of identity of sound—and their effectiveness, therefore, becomes limited.

Poets who are skillful and original rhymers are able to create fresh, unusual, and surprising turns of thought. We may, therefore, judge poets on their use of rhyme. Often, poets become quite creative rhymers, putting together words like "bent 'em" and "Tarentum" or "masterly" and "dastardly." Some rhymers, called a "rakehelly route of ragged rhymers" by a sixteenth-century critic, are satisfied with easy rhymes, or **cliché rhymes**, such as *trees* and *breeze* (a rhyme that the English poet Alexander Pope also criticized in 1711). But good rhymes and good poets go together in creative cooperation. The seventeenth-century poet John Dryden (1632–1700), who wrote volumes of rhyming couplets (two-line units), acknowledged that the need to find rhyming words inspired ideas that he had not anticipated. In this sense, rhyme has been—and still is—a vital element of poetic creativity.

There are few restrictions on English rhymes. Poets may rhyme nouns with other nouns, with verbs and adjectives, or with any other rhyming word, regardless of part of speech. Of course, exact rhymes are to be preferred, but the shortage of truly exact rhymes in English has enabled poets to be creative by rhyming words that almost rhyme but don't exactly (*slant rhyme*) or words that look alike but sound different (*eye rhyme*). Some poets use the same words to complete a rhyming pattern (*identical rhyme*), although this repetition eliminates some of the surprise and interest that good rhymes should produce.

Rhyme and Meter

Heavy-Stress Rhyme The effects of rhyme are closely connected with those of rhythm and meter. Rhymes that are produced with one-syllable words—such as *moon, June, tune,* and *soon*—or with multisyllabic words in which the accent falls on the final syllable—such as *combine, decline, supine,* and *refine*—are called **heavy-stress rhyme**, **accented rhyme**, **rising rhyme,** or **iambic rhyme**. In general, rising rhyme lends itself to serious effects. The accenting of heavy- stress rhyme appears in the concluding lines of Wilfred Owen's "Anthem for Doomed Youth":

> Their flowers the tenderness of patient minds,
> And each slow dusk a drawing-down of blinds.

Here, the rhyming sounds are produced by one-syllable words that occur in the final heavy-stress positions of the feet at the ends of the lines. Thus, "tient minds" is the iambic foot that ends the first line, and "of blinds" is the iambic foot that ends the second line. The heavy stresses—on *minds* and *blinds*—form the rhyming sounds.

Trochaic and Dactylic Rhyme Rhymes within poetic feet of two or more syllables in which the heavy stress falls on any syllable other than the last are called *trochaic* or *double rhyme* for rhymes of two syllables and *dactylic* or *triple rhyme* for rhymes of three syllables. Less technically, these types of rhymes are also sometimes called **falling** or **dying rhymes**, probably because the intensity of pronunciation decreases on the light accent or accents following the heavy accent.

In general, **trochaic** or **double rhymes** are often used in light, amusing, and satiric poetry, as may be seen in lines 2 and 4 of the first stanza of "Miniver Cheevy" by the American poet Edwin Arlington Robinson (1869–1935):

> Miniver Cheevy, child of scorn
>   Grew lean while he assailed the *seasons*;
> He wept that he was ever born,
>   And he had *reasons*.

In this poem, the effect of the double rhyme is humorous, thus helping to make Miniver Cheevy seem ridiculous and pathetic.

Double rhymes can also be a means of emphasizing or underscoring irony or anticlimax in serious poems, as in *a-flying* and *be dying* in the first stanza of "To the Virgins, to Make Much of Time," by the English poet Robert Herrick (1591–1674):

> Gather ye rosebuds while ye may,
>   Old time is still a-flying;
> And this same flower that smiles today
>   Tomorrow will be dying.

Herrick uses falling rhymes in the second and fourth lines of every stanza of this poem. The result is a poignant contrast between pleasures of everyday life and the eternal truth of mortality.

Dactylic or **triple rhyme** is often light or humorous because it tends to divert attention from the subject to the words, as in these lines from "The Pied Piper of Hamelin" by the English poet Robert Browning (1812–1889; italics added here):

> Small feet were *pattering*, wooden shoes *clattering*,
> Little hands clapping and little tongues *chattering*.
> And, like fowls in a farm-yard where barley is *scattering*,

Here, the ending words *clattering, chattering,* and *scattering* are all instances of triple rhymes, with the interior word *pattering* rhyming exactly with all three terminal rhyming sounds. The poem indeed does make a serious point (about the failure to keep a pledge); but in this stanza, which deals with the children following the Pied Piper, the triple rhyme is appropriate to the sounds of running, scurrying children.

Variations in Rhyme

Internal Rhyme   As the stanza from Browning shows, the fourth word in the first line, *pattering*, rhymes with the line-ending rhymes. This is an example of **internal rhyme**—the presence of rhyming words within a line of verse. It is not a common variation, but you should be alert for it and make note of it when it occurs.

Inexact Rhyme   Writers of English poetry have often felt limited in selecting rhymes because our language is short in exactly rhyming words. (Italian, by contrast, in which most words end in vowel sounds, offers virtually endless rhyming possibilities.)

A tradition has, therefore, grown in English that words may be set in rhyming positions even though they may not be exact rhymes.

Rhymes may often be created out of words that have similar but not identical sounds. In most of these instances, either the vowel sounds are different while the consonants are the same or vice versa. This type of rhyme is variously called **slant rhyme, near rhyme, half rhyme, off rhyme, analyzed rhyme,** or **suspended rhyme**. In employing slant rhyme, a poet can pair *bleak* with *broke* or *could* with *solitude*. Amy Lowell creates an interesting slant rhyme in the poem "Patterns." She uses the rhyme of *blossom* and *bosom* twice. A poet who uses slant rhyme extensively is Emily Dickinson. She takes great freedom with inexact rhymes by pairing words such as *bird* and *crowd*, *port* and *chart*, *listens* and *distance*, and *surplice* and *church*.

Another common variation is **eye rhyme**, or **sight rhyme**. In eye rhyme, the sounds to be eye-rhymed are *identical in spelling* but *different in pronunciation*. Entire words may be eye-rhymed; for example, *wind* (verb) may be rhymed with *wind* (noun), and *cóntest* (noun) may be used with *contést* (verb). In most eye rhymes, however, it is only the relevant parts of words that must be spelled identically. Thus, *stove* may pair with *prove* and *above*; and *bough* may match *cough, dough, enough,* and *through,* despite all the differing pronunciations. The following lines are eye-rhymed:

> Although his claim was not to praise but *bury*,
> His speech for Caesar roused the crowd to *fury*.

The different pronunciations of *bury* and *fury* make clear the contrast between exact rhyme and eye rhyme. In exact rhyme, identical sound is crucial; spelling is usually the same but may be different as long as the sounds remain identical. In eye rhyme, the eye-rhyming words or syllables must be spelled identically, but the sounds must be different.

Additional Variations Poets sometimes may use **identical rhyme** (noted earlier); that is, the same words in rhyming positions, such as *veil* and *veil* or *stone* and *stone*. **Vowel rhyme** is the use of any vowels in rhyming positions, as in *day* and *sky* or *key* and *play*.

Rhyme Schemes

A **rhyme scheme** refers to a poem's pattern of rhyming sounds, which are indicated by alphabetical letters. The first rhyming sounds, such as *love* and *dove*, receive an *a*; the next rhyming sounds, such as *swell* and *fell*, receive a *b*; and the next sounds, such as *first* and *burst*, receive a *c*; and so on. Thus, a pattern of lines ending with the words *love, moon, thicket; dove, June, picket;* and *above, croon* and *wicket* may be schematized as *a b c; a b c; a b c.*

To formulate a rhyme scheme or pattern, you need to include the meter and the number of feet in each line as well as the letters indicating rhymes. Here is such a formulation:

> Iambic pentameter: *a b a b, c d c d, e f e f*

This scheme shows that all the lines are iambic, with five feet in each line. Commas separating the units (a b a b, c d c d, etc.) indicate that the poem is developed as a number of stanzas (a **stanza** is a separate group that stands alone as a unit of development), and that the form of each stanza, in this case, is a **quatrain** (a unit of four lines). Stanzas may vary according to the wishes of the poet. Thus, a stanza might take the following form:

Iambic: *4a 3b 4a 3b 5a 5a 4b*

This formulation shows an intricate pattern of rhymes and line lengths in a stanza of seven lines. The first, third, fifth, and sixth lines rhyme, and they vary from four to five feet. The second, fourth, and seventh lines also rhyme, and they vary from three to four feet.

The absence of a rhyme sound is indicated by an *x*. Thus, you formulate the rhyme scheme of **ballad measure** like this:

Iambic: *4x 3a 4x 3a*

This formulation shows that this four-line group (a quatrain) alternates iambic tetrameter with trimeter. In this ballad quatrain, only lines 2 and 4 rhyme; there is no end rhyme in lines 1 and 3.

Writing About Rhyme

For your analysis, select either a short, representative passage from a long poem or an entire shorter poem such as a sonnet or three-stanza song. When you are doing your study for the essay, you should, at the beginning, include a work sheet. This should be a double-spaced copy of the poem or passage, with each line numbered beginning with 1. If the lines are of uniform length, indicate that fact at the beginning, and then you will not need to mark the lengths of individual lines. If there are variants in length, however, you may mark the variations where they occur, within parentheses at the right of the line. Thus, the basic line length of John Keats's "Ode to a Nightingale" is five iambic feet. The rhyme scheme of each stanza, consisting of ten lines, is a, b, a, b, c, d, e, c, d, e. In the second stanza, however, we may note some metrical variants. Here are the final four lines of this stanza:

> With beaded bubbles winking at the brim,
> And purple-stainèd mouth; (3)
> That I might drink, and leave the world unseen
> And with thee fade away into the forest dim. (6)

Note that the parenthetically enclosed numbers designate variants of three and six feet. Note also that the word *stainèd*, which usually consists of one syllable, is designated as two syllables because of the grave accent mark over the e, pronounced "stay-nedd." Underline or otherwise draw attention to any comparably unusual, notable, or outstanding aspect of the rhythm and pronunciation of the poem you are discussing.

Organize Your Essay About Rhyme

Introduction Make any general remarks you wish about the poem, but concentrate on the relationship of the rhyme to the content. That is, does the rhyme seem like no more than a decorative adjunct, or is it integrated in some way? What is the way? Try to define and describe this relationship.

Body Try to discuss any or all the following aspects of rhyme:

- *The major features of the poem's rhymes.* What is the dominant rhyme scheme? What variations do you find? What are the lengths and features of the rhyming words? Are there any unusual rhyming words? Are there any noteworthy characteristics about the rhymes?
- *The grammatical features of the rhymes.* As a general principle, the forms of rhyming words should not be the same but should vary. In your poem, what kinds of words are used for rhymes (i.e., verbs, nouns, etc.). Are they all the same? Does one form predominate? Is there variety? Can you determine the grammatical positions of the rhyming words? How may these characteristics be related to the idea or theme of the poem?
- *The qualities of the rhyming words.* Are there any striking rhymes? Any surprises? Any rhymes that are particularly clever and witty? Do any rhymes give unique comparisons or contrasts? How?
- *Any particularly striking or unique effects in the rhymes.* Without becoming overly subtle or far-fetched, you can make valid and interesting conclusions. Do any sounds in the rhyming words appear in any observable pattern elsewhere in the poem? Do the rhymes enter into any onomatopoeic effects? Broadly, what aspects of rhyme are uniquely effective because they blend so fully with the poem's thought and mood?

Conclusion In your conclusion, try to develop a short evaluation of the poem's rhymes. You might also include any additional observations about the rhymes as well as any comparisons between the rhymes in your poem and in other poems by the same poet or other poets. A short, concluding review of your main ideas is here, as always, appropriate.

Illustrative Essay

The Rhymes in Christina Rossetti's "Echo"

Echo

Come to me in the silence of the night;
Come in the speaking silence of a dream;
Come with soft rounded cheeks and eyes as bright
    As sunlight on a stream;
Come back in tears,   5
O memory, hope, love of finished years.

O dream how sweet, too sweet, too bitter sweet,
Whose wakening should have been in Paradise,
Where souls brimfull of love abide and meet;
Where thirsting longing eyes   10
Watch the slow door
That opening, letting in, lets out no more.

Yet come to me in dreams, that I may live
My very life again though cold in death:
Come back to me in dreams, that I may give   15
Pulse for pulse, breath for breath:
Speak low, lean low
As long ago, my love, how long ago.

[1]   In the three-stanza lyric poem "Echo," Christina Rossetti uses
rhyme as a way of emphasizing that a person might regain in dreams
a love that in reality—most likely because of death—is forever lost. [1]
The speaker's idea is that as the real love is to the dream of love, so is
an original sound to an echo; through the vibrations of the echo, the
original life of the sound is continued. This connection underlies the
poem's title and also Rossetti's unique use of rhyme. Aspects of her
rhyme are the lyric pattern, the forms and qualities of the rhyming
words, and the special use of repetition. [2]

[2]   The rhyming pattern is simple, and, in the context of this poem,
it may be thought of as a pattern of echoes, in keeping with the
poem's title. Each stanza contains four lines of alternating end-of-
line rhymes concluded by a rhyming couplet (a two-line rhyming
group) as follows:

Iambic: 5a, 5b, 5a, 3b, 2c, 5c.

There are nine separate rhymes throughout the poem, three
rhymes in each stanza. Only two words are used for each end
rhyme, and no rhyming word is used twice. Of the eighteen
end-rhyming words, sixteen—in short, almost all the rhymes in
the poem—have only one syllable. The remaining two words
consist of two and three syllables. With such a great number

---

[1]Central idea.
[2]Thesis sentence.

of single-syllable words, the rhymes are all rising ones, on the
accented halves of two-syllable iambic feet, and the end-of-line
emphasis is on simple words.

The grammatical forms and positions of the rhyming words   [3]
lend support to the haunting, internalized, and regretful subject
matter. Although there is variety, more than half the rhyming
words are nouns. In all, there are ten rhyming nouns, and eight are
placed as the objects of prepositions (i.e., *of a dream, on a stream,
of finished years, in death*). The nouns that are not the objects of
prepositions are the subject and object of the same subordinate
clause (lines 10 and 11: Where thirsting, longing eyes / Watch the
slow door . . ."). It seems that much of the poem's verbal energy
occurs in the first parts of the lines, leaving the rhymes to occur in
modifying elements, as in these lines:

> Come to me in the *silence of the night* (1)
> O dream how *sweet*, too *sweet*, too bitter *sweet*, (7)
>
> As sunlight on a *stream*, (4)
> Yet come to me in dreams, *that I may live* (13)

Most of the other rhymes are in similar positions. This careful
arrangement is consistent with the speaker's emphasis on her yearning to relive her love, even if she can have this experience only within
her dreams.

The qualities of the words are also consistent with the poem's   [4]
emphasis on the speaker's internal life. Most of the rhyming words
are impressionistic. Even the specific words—*stream, tears, eyes,
door,* and *breath*—reflect the speaker's mental condition. In this
regard, the rhyming words of lines 1 and 3 are effective. These are
night and *bright*, which contrast the bleakness of the speaker's
solitude with the vitality of her inner life. Another effective contrast
is in lines 14 and 16, where *death* and *breath* are rhymed. This rhyme
underscores the sad fact that even though the speaker's love has
vanished, it lives in present memory just as an echo continues to
have the life of the original sound.

[5]   It is in emphasizing how memory echoes experience that
Rossetti creates her special use of rhyming words in "Echo." She
creates an ingenious repetition of a number of words, or identical
rhyme. One may suppose that these also are the poem's echoes. The
major echoing word is the verb *come*, which appears six times at the
beginnings of lines in stanzas 1 and 3. But some of the rhyming
words are also repeated. The most notable is *dream*, the rhyming
word in line 2. Rossetti repeats the word in line 7 and uses the plural,
dreams, in lines 13 and 15. In line 7, the rhyming word *sweet* is used
three times, thus emphasizing the original experience of love: "how
sweet, too *sweet*, too bitter *sweet*." Concluding the poem, Rossetti
repeats *breath* (16), *low* (17) and the phrase *long ago* (18). These
repeating words illustrate the title, "Echo," and they also stress
Rossetti's major idea that it is through memory that experience has
reality, even if memory can only provide dreams that can never be
anything more than echoes.

[6]   Thus, Rossetti's rhyme is not just ornamental in "Echo," but
integral. If reality has vanished, just as episodes in life have vanished, the recollection, the remembered reality, remains in the echoes
of the thoughts and words that at one time were vital and real. In
"Echo," the insistence of Rossetti's rhymes keeps the focus on
memory and yearning even though the immediacy of life and love no
longer exists. The rhymes aid in reaching into the past, however,
because of the echoes suggested by the rhyming words. "Echo" is a
poem in which rhyme is an essential aspect of the speaker's thought.

Commentary on the Essay

Throughout, illustrative words are italicized, and numbers are used to indicate the lines
from which the illustrations are drawn. The introductory paragraph asserts that rhyme
is vital in Rossetti's poem. It also attempts to explain the title "Echo." The thesis statement indicates the three major topics to be developed in the body.

Paragraph 2 deals with the mechanical, mathematical aspects of the poem's
rhymes. The high number of monosyllabic and stressed rhyming words is used to illustrate the rising rhyme.

Paragraph 3 treats the grammar of the rhymes. For example, an analysis and count
reveal that there are ten rhyming nouns and three rhyming verbs. The verb of com-

mand "come" is mentioned to show that many of the rhyming words appear within groups modifying this word. The grammatical analysis is, thus, related to the internalized nature of the poem's subject.

Paragraph 4 emphasizes the impressionistic nature of the rhyming words and points out instances in which rhymes stress the contrast between real life and the speaker's introspective life. Paragraph 5 deals with how Rossetti repeats five of the poem's rhyming words. This repetition creates a pattern of echoes, in keeping with the poem's title.

In the final two paragraphs, the rhymes in "Echo" show that Rossetti is a skilled rhymer, and poet, because of her deliberate and pointed use of rhyme.

Writing Topics About Rhyme in Poetry

1. For Shakespeare's "Sonnet 73: That Time of Year Thou Mayst in Me Behold," analyze the ways in which Shakespeare uses iambic rhymes. That is, what is the relationship of lightly accented syllables to the heavily accented ones? Where does Shakespeare use articles (*the*), pronouns (*this, his*), prepositions (*upon, against, of*), relative clause markers (*which, that*), and adverb clause markers (*as, when*) in relation to syllables of heavy stress? On the basis of this study, how would you characterize Shakespeare's control of the rhyme?

2. Analyze the rhymes in Coleridge's "Kubla Khan," Arnold's "Dover Beach," or another poem of your choice. What is interesting or unique about the various rhyming words? What relationships can you discover between the rhymes and the topics of the poems?

3. Compare one of the rhyming poems with one of the nonrhyming poems included in this book. What differences in reading and sound can you discover as a result of the use or nonuse of rhyme? What benefits does rhyme give to the poem? What benefits does nonrhyme give?

4. Discuss Hardy's rhymes in "Channel Firing." What effects does he create by rhyming words with trochaic rhythm, such as *hatters* and *matters* and by rhyming three-syllable words (dactylic rhythms) *saner be* and *century*? What is the relationship of such rhymes to the rhymes that fall on heavy stresses in the poem?

5. Write a short poem of your own using double or triple rhymes, with words such as *computer, a shooter; scholastic, fantastic; remarking, embarking; inedible, incredible; anxiously, along with me*, and so on. If you have trouble with exact rhymes, see what you can do with slant rhymes and eye rhymes. The idea is to use your ingenuity. Have fun.

6. Using the topical index in your library, take out a book on prosody and rhyme, such as Harvey Gross's *Sound and Form in Modern Poetry* (1968), *The Structure of Verse* (1966), or Gay Wilson Allen's *American Prosody* (1935, reprinted 1966). Select a topic (e.g., formal or experimental prosody) or a poet (e.g., Frost, Arnold, Shakespeare, Blake), and write a brief report about the ideas and observations that the writers make, if any, about the use of rhyme. What relationship do the writers show between prosody and the poet's ideas? How do rhythm and rhyme enter into the writer's thought? Into the ways in which the poets emphasize ideas and images? If you go online, you will notice that there are hundreds of thousands of entries. Be very selective.

Chapter 14

Writing About a Literary Problem: Challenges to Overcome in Reading

A **problem** is a question that cannot be answered correctly and easily about a body of material that is under consideration. Like many of our English words, "problem" came to us in a circuitous route from the ancient Greeks, and it originally referred to an obstacle—something thrown in one's way. You may think of it as a difficulty to your understanding, to be considered and, if possible, overcome. Ironically, problems are not always easy to recognize and describe, for we may not always be aware that problems exist. Therefore, we need to identify the existence of a problem, to determine what it is, to describe its boundaries and significance, and to deal with it satisfactorily.

It is true that the first step in solving a problem or in dealing with an issue is to explain its dimensions and its extent, and it is also true that if we can clearly describe the nature and extent of a problem, we have gone a good distance down the road toward a solution. Even so, problems are often hard both to see and to explain—in intellectual pursuits generally, not just in literature. Determining the nature of problems occupies much attention and energy of researchers in scientific, social, political, and humanistic fields. The development of solutions and answers must be preceded by an often long and painstaking analysis of why some things are not happening and why other things are not working. When such insights can be developed, then solutions to problems may well be near, looming on the intellectual horizon, ready to shed the light of understanding on us. In short, the attempt to deal with problems is a common effort in all human endeavors. Therefore, one of the most important techniques that you can acquire is to be able to identify problems, to describe them accurately, and then to determine and explain solutions.

Not all questions, of course, are problems. The question "Who is the major character in Shakespeare's tragedy *Hamlet*?" is not a problem, because the obvious answer is Hamlet[1]. Let us go a little further, however, and ask another question: "Why is it *correct* to say that Hamlet is the major character?" This question is not as easy as the first, and for this reason, it is a problem. It requires that we think about our answer, even though we do not need to search very far. Hamlet is the title character.

---

[1]Shakespeare's *Hamlet* may be found in MyLiteratureLab.

He is involved in almost all the actions of the play. He is so much the center of our interest, concern, and liking that his death causes sadness and regret. To "solve" this problem has required a number of responses, all of which provide answers to the question "why?"

More complex, however, and more typical of most problems are questions such as these: "Why does Hamlet talk of suicide during his first major speech in the play?" "Why does he treat Ophelia so coarsely and insultingly?" "Why does he delay in avenging his father's death?" Essays on literary problems are normally concerned with such questions, because they require a good deal of thought, together with a number of interpretations knitted together into an entire essay.

Strategies for Developing an Essay About a Problem

Your first purpose is to convince your reader that your solution is a good one. This you do by using evidence correctly in making sound conclusions. In nonscientific subjects such as literature, you rarely find absolute proofs, so your conclusions will not be *proved* in the way you prove triangles congruent in geometry. But your organization, your use of facts from the text, your interpretations, and your application of general or specific knowledge should all make your conclusions convincing. Therefore, your basic strategy is *persuasion*.

Strategy 1: Demonstrate That Conditions for a Solution Are Fulfilled

Suppose that you are writing about the problem of why Hamlet delays revenge against his stepfather, King Claudius. Suppose also that you make the point that Hamlet delays because he is never sure that Claudius is guilty. This is your "solution" to the problem. In your essay, you support your answer by challenging the credibility of the information that Hamlet receives about the crime (i.e., the visits from the Ghost and Claudius's distress at the play within the play). Once you have "attacked" these sources of data on the grounds that they are unreliable, you have succeeded because your solution is consistent with the details of the play.

Strategy 2: Analyze Significant Words in the Phrasing of the Problem

Your object in this approach is to clarify important words in the statement of the problem and then to decide how applicable they are. This kind of attention to words, in fact, might give you enough material for all or part of your essay. Thus, an essay on the problem of Hamlet's delay might focus in part on a treatment of the word *delay*. What, really, does *delay* mean? For Hamlet, is there a difference between delay that is reasonable and delay that is unreasonable? Does Hamlet delay unreasonably? Is his delay the result of a psychological fault or the result of the imperfect and uncertain information he learns about the real cause of his father's death? Would speedy revenge be more reasonable or less reasonable than the delay? By the time you have answered such pointed questions, you will also have sufficient material for your full essay.

Strategy 3: Refer to Literary Conventions or Expectations

The theory of this aspect of argument is that literary problems can be solved by reference either to the literary mode or conventions of a work or to the limitations of the work itself. In other words, what appears to be a problem is really no more than a normal characteristic. For example, a question might be raised about why Mathilde in Maupassant's story "The Necklace" does not tell her friend Jeanne Forrestier about the loss of the necklace. A plausible answer is that, all motivation aside, the story builds up to a surprise (at least for first-time readers), which could be spoiled by an early disclosure. To solve the problem, in other words, one has recourse to the structure of the story—to the literary convention that Maupassant observes in "The Necklace." Similarly, a student once raised a problem about the impossibility of skeletons speaking in Hardy's "Channel Firing." The answer to this problem is that Hardy is playing with the idea that the noise of naval gunnery blasting away at sea is loud enough to awaken the dead. Once this circumstance is accepted, there is no problem at all.

Strategy 4: Argue Against Possible Objections

With this strategy, you raise your own objections and then argue against them. Called **procatalepsis** ("to consider beforehand"), **anticipation** ("to take before"), or **presupposal** (to consider a topic before it is presented), this approach helps you to sharpen your arguments, because *anticipating* and dealing with objections forces you to make analyses and to use facts that you might otherwise overlook. Although procatalepsis can be used point by point throughout your essay, you might find it most useful at the end.

The situation to imagine is that someone is raising objections to your solution to the problem. It is then your task to show that the objections (1) are not accurate or valid, (2) are not strong or convincing, or (3) are based on unusual rather than usual conditions (on an exception and not the rule). Here are some examples of these approaches.

4.1 The Objection Is Not Accurate or Valid   You reject this objection by showing that either the interpretation or the conclusions are wrong and by emphasizing that the evidence supports your solution.

> Although Hamlet's delay is reasonable, the claim might be made that his duty is to kill Claudius in revenge immediately after the Ghost's accusations. This claim is not persuasive because it assumes that Hamlet knows everything the audience knows. The audience accepts the Ghost's word that Claudius is guilty, but Hamlet has no absolutely certain reasons to believe the Ghost. Would it not seem insane for Hamlet to kill Claudius, who reigns legally, and then to claim he did it because of the Ghost's words? The argument for speedy revenge is not good because it is based on an incorrect view of Hamlet's situation.

4.2 The Objection Is Not Strong or Convincing   You concede that the objection has some truth or validity, but you then try to show that it is weak and that your own solution is stronger.

One might claim that Claudius's distress at "The Murder of Gonzago," the play within the play, is evidence for his guilt and that, therefore, Hamlet should carry out his revenge right away. This argument has merit, and Hamlet's speech after Claudius has fled the scene ("I'll take the Ghost's word for a thousand pound") shows that the "conscience of the king" has been caught. But the king's guilty behavior is not a strong cause for killing him. Perhaps Hamlet could justifiably ask for an investigation of his father's death on these grounds, but he could not justify a revenge killing. Claudius could not be convicted in any court on the testimony that he was disturbed at seeing "The Murder of Gonzago." Even after this play within the play, the reasons for delay are stronger than those for action.

4.3 The Objection Depends on Unusual Rather Than Usual Conditions You reject the objection on the grounds that it could be valid only if normal conditions were suspended. The objection depends on an exception, not a rule.

> The case for quick action is simple: Hamlet should kill Claudius right after seeing the Ghost (1.3), or after seeing the King's reaction to the stage murder of Gonzago (3.2), or after seeing the Ghost again (3.4). Redress under these circumstances, goes the argument, must be both personal and extralegal. This argument wrongly assumes that due process does not exist in the Denmark of Hamlet and Claudius. Nothing in the play indicates that the Danes, even though they carouse a bit, do not value legality and the rules of evidence. Thus, Hamlet cannot rush out to kill Claudius, because he knows that the King has not had anything close to due process. The argument for quick action is poor because it rests on an exception being made from civilized law.

Writing About a Problem

Remember that writing an essay about a problem requires you to argue in favor of a position: Either there is a solution or there is not. To develop your position requires that you show the steps to your conclusion. Your general thematic form is, therefore, (1) to describe the conditions that need to be met for the solution you propose and then (2) to demonstrate that these conditions exist. If you assert that there is no solution, then your form would be the same for the first part, but your second part—the development—would show that these conditions have *not* been met.

Organize Your Essay About a Problem

Introduction Begin with a statement of the problem, and refer to the conditions that must be established for a solution. Your central idea is your answer to the question, and your thesis sentence indicates the main heads of your development.

Body In developing your essay, use one or more of the strategies described in this chapter. These are, again, (1) to demonstrate that conditions for a solution are fulfilled, (2) to analyze the words in the phrasing of the problem, (3) to refer to literary expectations or limitations, and (4) to argue against possible objections. You might combine these. Thus, if we assume that your argument is that Hamlet's delay is reasonable, you might first consider the word *delay* (strategy 2); then you might use strategy 1 to explain the reasons for Hamlet's delay. Finally, to answer objections to your argument, you might show that Hamlet acts promptly when he believes he is justified (strategy 4). Whatever your topic, the important thing is to use the method or methods that best help you to make a good argument for your solution.

Conclusion In your conclusion, try to affirm the validity of your solution in view of the supporting evidence. You might do this by reemphasizing your strongest points by simply presenting a brief summary or by thinking of your argument as still continuing and, thus, using the strategy of *procatalepsis* to raise and answer possible objections to your solution, as is done in the last paragraph of the following illustrative essay.

Illustrative Essay

The Problem of Robert Frost's Use of the Term "Desert Places"
in the Poem "Desert Places"[2]

[1]   In the last line of "Desert Places," the meaning suggested by the title seems to undergo a sudden shift. At the beginning, the title clearly refers to the snowy setting described in the first stanza, but in the last line, it refers to a negative state of soul. The problem is this: Does the change happen too late to be effective? That is, does the new meaning come out of nowhere, or does it really work as a climax of ideas that are seriously considered in the body of the poem? To answer these questions, one must grant that the change cannot be effective if there is no preparation for it before the last line of the poem. But if there is preparation—that is, if Frost does provide hints that the speaker feels an emptiness like that of the bleak, snowy natural world—then the shift is both understandable and effective even though it comes at the very end. It is clear that Frost makes the preparation and, therefore, that the change is effective.[3] The preparation may be traced in Frost's references, word choices, and concluding sentences.[4]

[2]   In the first two stanzas, Frost includes the speaker in his reference to living things being overcome. His opening scene is one

_____

[2]See page 352 for this poem.
[3]Central idea.
[4]Thesis sentence.

of snow that covers "weeds and stubble" (line 4) and of snow that almost literally smothers hibernating animals "in their lairs" (6). The speaker then focuses on his own mental state, saying that he is "too absent-spirited to count" and that the "loneliness" of the scene "includes" him "unawares" (7, 8). This movement—from vegetable to animal to human—shows that everything alive is changed by the snow. Obviously, the speaker will not die like the grass or hibernate like the animals, but he indicates that the "loneliness" of the snowy scene literally overcomes him with loneliness. These first eight lines thus connect the natural bleakness with the speaker.

In addition, a number of words in the third stanza are prepara- [3]
tory because they may be applied to human beings. The words "lonely" and "loneliness" (9), "more lonely" (10), "blanker" and "benighted" (11), and "no expression, nothing to express" (12) may all refer equally to human or to natural conditions. The word "benighted" is most important, because it suggests not only the darkness of night but also intellectual or moral ignorance. Since these words invite the reader to think of negative mental and emotional states, they provide a context in which the final shift of meaning is both logical and natural.

The climax of Frost's preparation for the last two words is to be [4]
found in the sentences of the fourth stanza. All along, the speaker claims to feel an inner void that is similar to the bleakness of the cold, snowy field. This idea emerges as the major focus in the last stanza, where in two sentences the speaker talks about his feelings of emptiness or insensitivity:

> They cannot scare me with their empty spaces
> Between stars—on stars where no human race is.
> I have it in me so much nearer home
> To scare myself with my own desert places. (13–16)

In the context of the poem, therefore, the shift in these last two [5]
words—"desert places"—is not sudden or illogical. It rather pulls together the two parts of the comparison that Frost has been building from the very first line. Just as "desert places" refers to the

[6]   snowy field, it also suggests human coldness, blankness, unconcern, insensitivity, and cruelty. The phrase does not spring out of nowhere but is the strong climax of the poem.

Although Frost's conclusion is effective, a critic might still claim that it is weak because Frost's speaker does not develop the thought about the negativity of the soul. He simply mentions "desert places" and stops. But the poem is not a long psychological study, and to expect more than Frost gives would be to expect much more than sixteen lines can provide. A better claim against the effectiveness of the concluding shift of meaning is that the phrase "desert places" is both vague and perhaps boastfully humble. If the phrase were to be taken away from the poem, this criticism might be acceptable. However, the fact is that the phrase is in the poem and that it must be judged in this context. As a part of the poem, it is vitally connected to the previous fifteen lines, and it makes this connection with freshness and surprise. Thus, the shift of meaning is a major reason for Frost's success in "Desert Places."

Commentary on the Essay

The development of this essay illustrates strategy 1 described earlier in this chapter (p. 203). The attention to the word *effective* in paragraph 1 briefly illustrates the second strategy (p. 203). The concluding paragraph shows two approaches to the fourth strategy (p. 204), using the arguments that the objections are not good because they (4a) are not accurate or valid (here, the inaccuracy is related to strategy 3) and (4c) are based on the need for an exception, namely, that the phrase in question be removed from the context in the poem.

After introducing the problem, paragraph 1 emphasizes that a solution is available only if the poem prepares the reader for the problematic shift of meaning. The central idea is that the poem satisfies this requirement and that the shift is effective. The thesis sentence indicates three subjects for development.

Paragraph 2 asserts that there is preparation even early in the poem. (See the next discussion of the third paragraph.) Paragraph 4 asserts that the concluding sentences build toward a climax of Frost's pattern or development.

The argument of paragraph 3, like that of paragraph 2, is that the texture of the poem, right from the start, demonstrates the central idea (stated in the introductory paragraph) that the conditions for a solution to the problem are met. The method in this paragraph is to show how particular words and expressions, because they are applicable to both nature and human beings, connect the bleak opening scene with the speaker's professed spiritual numbness. The word "benighted" (line 11) is the most illustrative, because it particularly refers to cultural and intellectual bleakness. The paragraph, hence, demonstrates how the careful selection and analysis of key words can be part of a total argument.

Paragraphs 5 and 6 form a two-part conclusion to the essay. Paragraph 5 summarizes the arguments and offers an interpretation of the phrase. Paragraph 6 raises and answers two objections. The essay, thus, shows that a careful reading of the poem eliminates the grounds for claiming that there is any problem about the last line.

Writing Topics About Studying Problems in Literature

1. In Arnold's "Dover Beach," the lines "Ah, love, let us be true / To one another!" have been read to refer not so much to the need for love as for the need for fidelity in personal relationships. Which choice seems more correct? Explain.

2. Coleridge was planning a much longer poem when he began writing "Kubla Khan," but he was interrupted and forgot much of what he had planned to write. Some critics, however, are satisfied that the poem is complete as it stands. Defend the judgment that the poem may be considered finished.

3. Montresor, the narrator of Poe's "The Cask of Amontillado," believes that he is justified in making a victim out of Fortunato. Does this explanation ring true? Should his justification be accepted? Why do you think that he is not more specific about what Fortunato has done to him?

4. To what degree would more details in opposition to war make Wilfred Owen's "Anthem for Doomed Youth" a more or less effective poem?

5. Some readers claim that the speaker's reactions to her fiancé's death in Lowell's poem "Patterns" are too reserved, not sufficiently angry or passionate. What is your response to this judgment about the poem?

6. Even though Chekhov's *The Bear* is a farce, some observers have claimed that the passionate embraces of Smirnov and Mrs. Popov at the end happen too suddenly and unexpectedly. Does this outcome spoil the play by making it too unrealistic, too arbitrary, too unnatural?

7. Because Poe often writes about lurid and sensational subjects, some critics have stated that his works do not embody ideas. Consider whether this observation is true of "The Cask of Amontillado."

8. A view that is sometimes expressed about Shakespeare's sonnets is that the "systems" that Shakespeare introduces, such as comparing the aging speaker to various times of the year and times of day in "Sonnet 73: That Time of Year Thou Mayst in Me Behold," are so affected and pretentious that they detract from the ideas. With reference to this sonnet and to Shakespeare's "Sonnet 30," how valid is this judgment? Do the comparisons add to or detract from the poems?

9. Why do you think that Susan Glaspell, in *Trifles*, places Mrs. Hale and Mrs. Peters on stage continuously throughout the play rather than two or more of the men?

Chapter 15

Writing Essays of Comparison-Contrast and Extended Comparison-Contrast: Learning by Seeing Literary Works Together

Fiction, Poetry, and Drama

Comparison-contrast analysis is the act of putting things side by side—juxtaposing them, looking at them together—for a variety of purposes such as description, enhanced understanding, evaluation, and decision making. The technique underlies other important techniques, specifically (1) the analysis of causes and effects and (2) the scientific method of constant-and-variable analysis. Significant questions of all these methods are "How is *A* both like and unlike *B*?" "What are the causes of *A*?" and "How does a change in *A* affect *B*?" These are all questions that call into play the technique of comparison and contrast.

The educational significance of the technique is to encourage you to make connections—one of the major aspects of productive thought and one of the most important characteristics, generally speaking, of leadership. As long as things *seem* different and disconnected, they *are* different and disconnected. In practice, they are two separate and distinct entities. But when you discover that they have similarities and connections, then you can make relationships clear. You are in a position both to stress points of likeness and to demonstrate just what makes things distinct and unique. For all these reasons, it is vital for you to find similarities and differences through the technique of comparison and contrast.

The immediate goal of a comparison-contrast essay on literary works is to compare and contrast different authors; two or more works by the same author; different drafts of the same work; or characters, incidents, techniques, and ideas in the same work or in a number of separate works. The process of developing and writing a comparison-contrast essay enables you to study works in perspective. No matter what works you consider together, the method helps you to get at the essence of a work or writer. Similarities are brought out by comparison; differences, by contrast. In other words, you can enhance your understanding of what a thing *is* by using comparison-contrast to determine what it *is not*.

For example, our understanding of Shakespeare's "Sonnet 30: When to the Sessions of Sweet Silent Thought" may be enhanced if we compare it with Christina Rossetti's poem "Echo" (see pp. 197 or 361). Both poems treat personal recollections of past experiences, told by a speaker to a listener who is not intended to be the reader. Both also refer to people, now dead, with whom the speakers were closely involved. In these respects, the poems are comparable. In addition to these similarities, there are important differences. Shakespeare's speaker numbers the dead people as friends whom he laments generally, whereas Rossetti refers specifically to one person with whom the speaker was in love. Rossetti's topic is the sorrow of dead love, the irrevocability of the past, and the present loneliness of the speaker. Shakespeare includes the references to dead friends as a way of accounting for present sorrows, but then his speaker turns to the present and asserts that thinking about the "dear friend," the poem's listener, enables him to restore past "losses" and end all "sorrows." In Rossetti's poem, there is no reconciliation of past and present; instead, the speaker focuses entirely on the sadness of the present moment. Although both poems are retrospective in nature, Shakespeare's poem looks toward the present, whereas Rossetti's looks mainly toward the past. The technique of comparison-contrast, in short, unlocks our understanding of the uniqueness of each poem.

Guidelines for the Comparison-Contrast Essay

The preceding example, although brief, shows how the use of comparison-contrast makes it possible to identify leading similarities and distinguishing differences in two works. Frequently, you can overcome the difficulties you might encounter in understanding one work by comparing and contrasting it with another work on a comparable subject. A few guidelines will help to direct your efforts in writing comparison-contrast essays.

Clarify Your Intention

When planning a comparison-contrast essay, first decide on your goal, for you can use the method in a number of ways. One objective is the equal and mutual illumination of two (or more) works. For example, an essay comparing Frost's "Desert Places" with Hawthorne's "Young Goodman Brown" might compare ideas or methods in these works equally, without stressing or favoring either. For most purposes, this method will prove most useful. If you wish to emphasize just one of the works, you might also use the comparison-contrast technique. Thus, you might highlight "Young Goodman Brown" by using comparable material in "Desert Places" (and vice versa). You might also show your preference for a particular story, poem, or play at the expense of another or emphasize a method or idea in one work that you do not find in the other work. The illustrative essay on two works beginning on page 216 shows how the essayist brings out the superiority of one work over the other, at least in certain chosen qualities.

Find Common Grounds for Comparison

The second stage in preparing a comparison-contrast essay is to select and articulate a common ground for discussion. It is pointless to compare dissimilar things, for the resulting conclusions will have little value. Instead, compare like with like: idea with idea, characterization with characterization, setting with setting, point of view with point of view, tone with tone. Nothing much can be learned from a comparison of Frost's view of individuality and Chekhov's view of love; but a comparison of the relationship of individuality with identity and character in Frost's "Desert Places" and Chekhov's *The Bear* suggests common ground, with the promise of significant ideas to be developed through the examination of similarities and differences.

In seeking common ground, you will need to be inventive and creative. For instance, if you compare Maupassant's "The Necklace" and Chekhov's *The Bear*, these two works at first might seem dissimilar. Yet common ground can be discovered, such as the treatment of self-deceit, the effects of chance on human affairs, and the authors' views of women. Although other works might seem even more dissimilar than these, it is usually possible to find common ground for comparison and contrast. Much of your success in an essay of this type depends on your success in finding a workable basis— a common denominator—for comparison.

Integrate the Bases of Comparison

Let us assume that you have decided on your rhetorical purpose and on the basis of your comparison. You have done your reading and have taken notes, and you have a rough idea of what you want to say. The remaining problem is the treatment of your material.

One method that writers sometimes choose is to make your points first about one work and then about the other. Unfortunately, such a comparison makes your paper seem like two separate lumps. ("Work 1" takes up one half of your paper to make one lump, and "Work 2" takes up the other half to make a second lump.) Also, the method involves repetition because you must repeat many points when you treat the second subject.

A better method is to treat the major aspects of your main idea and to refer to the two (or more) works as they support your arguments. Thus, you refer constantly to *both* works, sometimes within the same sentence, and remind your reader of the point of your discussion. There are reasons for the superiority of this method: (1) You do not repeat your points needlessly, for you develop them as you raise them. (2) By constantly referring to the two works, you make your points without requiring a reader with a poor memory to reread previous sections.

As a model, here is a paragraph on "Natural References as a Basis of Comparison in Frost's 'Desert Places' and Shakespeare's 'Sonnet 73: That Time of Year Thou Mayst in Me Behold.'" Both poems are included in Appendix C (pages 352 and 362). The virtue of the paragraph is that it uses material from each of the poems simultaneously as the substance for the development of the ideas, as nearly as the time sequence of sentences allows. In this illustration, each sentence is numbered for easy reference.

(1) Both Shakespeare and Frost link their ideas to events occurring in the natural world. (2) Night as a parallel with death is common to both poems, with Frost speaking about it in his first line and Shakespeare introducing it in his seventh. (3) Along with night, Frost emphasizes the onset of winter and snow as a time of death and desolation. (4) With this natural description, Frost also symbolically refers to empty, secret, dead places in the inner spirit—crannies of the soul where bleak winter snowfalls correspond to selfishness and indifference. (5) By contrast, Shakespeare uses the fall season, with the yellowing and dropping of leaves and the migrations of birds, to stress the closeness of real death and, therefore, the need to love fully during the time remaining. (6) The two poems, thus, share a sense of gloom because both present death as inevitable and final, just like the emptiness of winter. (7) Because Shakespeare's sonnet is addressed to a listener who is also a loved one, however, it is more outgoing than the more introspective poem of Frost. (8) Frost turns the snow, the night, and the emptiness of the universe inward in order to show the speaker's inner bleakness, and by extension, the bleakness of many human spirits. (9) Shakespeare instead uses the bleakness of season, night, and dying fire to state the need for loving "well." (10) The poems, thus, use common references for differing purposes.

This paragraph links Shakespeare's references to nature to those of Frost. Five sentences speak of both authors together; three speak of Frost alone, and two speak of Shakespeare alone, but all the sentences are unified topically. This interweaving of references indicates that the writer has learned both poems well enough to consider them together, and it enables the writing to be more pointed and succinct than it would be if the works were treated separately.

You can learn from this example: If you develop your essay by putting your two subjects constantly together, you will write economically and pointedly (not only for essays but also for tests). Beyond that, if you digest the material as successfully as this method indicates, you demonstrate that you are fulfilling a major educational goal: the assimilation and *use* of material. Too often, because you learn things separately (in separate works and courses, at separate times), you tend to compartmentalize them. Instead, you should always try to relate them, to *synthesize* them. Comparison and contrast help in this process of putting together, of seeing things not as fragments but as parts of wholes.

Avoid the Tennis-Ball Method

As you make your comparison, do not confuse an interlocking method with a "tennis-ball" method, in which you bounce your subject back and forth constantly and repetitively, almost as though you were hitting observations back and forth over a net. The tennis-ball method is shown in the following example from a comparison of the characters Mathilde (Maupassant's "The Necklace") and Mrs. Popov (Chekhov's *The Bear*).

Mathilde is a young married woman; Mrs. Popov is also young but a widow. Mathilde has a limited social life, and she doesn't have more than one friend. Mrs. Popov chooses to lead a life of solitude. Mathilde's daydreams about wealth are responsible for her misfortune, and Mrs. Popov's dedication to the memory of her husband is actually limiting her life. Mathilde is made unhappy because of her shortcomings, but Mrs. Popov is rescued despite her shortcomings. In Mathilde's case, the focus is on adversity not only causing trouble but also strengthening character. Similarly, in Mrs. Popov's case, the focus is on a strong person realizing her strength regardless of her conscious decision to weaken herself.

Imagine the effect of an entire essay written in this invariable 1-2, 1-2, 1-2 order. Aside from the inflexible patterning of subjects, the tennis-ball method does not permit much illustrative development. You should not feel so constrained that you cannot take two or more sentences to develop a point about one writer or subject before you include comparative references to another. If you remember to interlock the two subjects of comparison, as in the paragraph about Frost and Shakespeare, your method will give you the freedom to develop your topics fully.

The Extended Comparison-Contrast Essay

For a longer essay about a number of works—such as a limited research paper, comprehensive exam questions, and the sort of extended essay that is often required at the end of a semester—comparison-contrast is an essential method. You might wish to compare the works on the basis of elements such as ideas, plot, language, structure, character, metaphor, point of view, or setting. Because of the larger number of works, however, you will need to modify the way in which you employ comparison-contrast. Suppose you are considering not just two works but six, seven, or more. You need first to find a common ground to use as your central, unifying idea, just as you do for a comparison of only two works. Once you have established the common ground, you can classify or group your works on the basis of the similarities and differences they exemplify with regard to the topic. The idea is to get two *groups* for comparison and contrast, not just two works.

Let us assume that three or four works treat a topic in one way but that two or three do it in another (e.g., either criticism or praise of wealth and trade, the joys or sorrows of love, the enthusiasm of youth, gratitude for life, or the disillusionment of age). In writing about these works, you might treat the topic itself in a straightforward comparison-contrast method but use details from the works within the groupings as the material that you use for illustration and argument.

To make your essay as specific as possible, it is best to stress only a small number of works in each of your subpoints. Once you have established these points, there is no need to go into details about all the other works. Instead, you need to make no more than brief references to the other works, for your purpose should be to strengthen your points without bulking up your essay with more and more examples. Once you go to another subpoint, you might then use different works for illustration so that by the end of your essay, you will have given due attention to each work in your assignment. In this way—by treating many works in small comparative groups—you can keep your essay reasonably free of excessive detail.

The illustrative essay beginning on page 216 shows how this grouping may be done. In the first part of the body of this essay, six works are used comparatively to show how private needs conflict with social, public demands. A second section shows how three works can be compared and contrasted on the basis of how they treat the topic of public concerns as expressed through law. Finally, three additional works are cited to indicate contrasts between personal demands and the demands upon individuals in time of war.

CITING REFERENCES IN A LONGER COMPARISON-CONTRAST ESSAY

For the longer comparison-contrast essay, you may find a problem in making references to many different works. Generally, you do not need to repeat references. For example, if you refer to Louise of Chopin's "The Story of an Hour" or to Minnie Wright of Glaspell's *Trifles*, you should make the full references only once and then refer later just to the character, story, or author, according to your needs.

When you quote lines or passages or when you cite actions or characters in special ways, you should use parenthetical line, speech, or paragraph references, as in the illustrative essay. Be guided by the following principle: If you make a specific reference that you think your reader might want to examine in more detail, supply the page, line, speech, or paragraph number. If you refer to minor details that might easily be unnoticed or forgotten, also supply the appropriate number. Your intention should be to include the appropriate location numbers whenever you are in doubt about references.

Writing a Comparison-Contrast Essay

In planning your essay, you should first narrow and simplify your topic so that you can handle it conveniently. If your subject is a comparison of two poets (as in the comparison-contrast essay on Amy Lowell and Wilfred Owen beginning on page 216), choose one or two of each poet's poems on the same or a similar topic, and write your essay about these.

Once you have found an organizing principle, along with the relevant works, begin to refine and to focus the direction of your essay. As you study each work, note common or contrasting elements, and use these to form your central idea. At the same time, you can select the most illustrative works and classify them according to your topic, such as war, love, work, faithfulness, or self-analysis.

Organize Your Comparison-Contrast Essay

Introduction Begin by stating the works, authors, characters, or ideas that you are considering; then show that you have narrowed the topic for purposes of comparison and contrast. Your central idea should briefly highlight the principal grounds of discussion, such as that both works treat a common topic, exhibit a similar idea, use a similar form, or develop an identical attitude and that major or minor differences help to make the works unique. You may also assert that one work is superior to the other if you wish to make this judgment and expand on it.

Body The body of your essay is governed by the works and your basis of comparison (presentations of ideas, depictions of character, uses of setting, qualities of style and tone, uses of poetic form, uses of comparable imagery or symbols, uses of point of view, and so on). For a comparison-contrast treatment on such a basis, your goal should be to shed light on both (or more) of the works you are treating. For example, you might examine stories written from a first-person point of view. An essay on this topic might compare the ways in which each author uses point of view to achieve similar or distinct effects; or it might compare poems that employ similar images, symbols, or ironic methods. Sometimes, the process can be as simple as identifying female or male protagonists and comparing the ways in which their characters are developed. Another obvious approach is to compare the *subjects*, rather than the *idea*. You might identify works dealing with general subjects such as love, death, youth, race, or war. Such groupings provide a basis for excellent comparisons and contrasts.

As you develop your essay, remember to keep comparison-contrast foremost. That is, your discussions of point of view, figurative language, or whatever should not so much explain these topics *as topics* but rather should explore *similarities and differences* of the works you are comparing. If your topic is an idea, for example, you need to explain the idea, but just enough to establish points of similarity or difference. As you develop such an essay, you might illustrate your arguments by referring to related uses of elements such as setting, characterization, symbolism, point of view, or metaphor. When you introduce these new subjects, you will be on target as long as you use them in the context of comparison-contrast.

Conclusion In concluding, you might reflect on other ideas or techniques in the works you have compared, make observations about similar qualities, or summarize briefly the grounds of your comparison. If there is a point that you consider especially important, you might stress that point again in your conclusion. Also, your comparison might have led you to conclude that one work—or group of works—is superior to another. Stressing that point again would make an effective conclusion.

Illustrative Essay (Comparing and Contrasting Two Works)

The Views of War in Amy Lowell's "Patterns" and Wilfred Owen's "Anthem for Doomed Youth"[1]

[1]   Lowell's "Patterns" and Owen's "Anthem for Doomed Youth" are both powerful condemnations of war.[2] Owen's short poem speaks generally about the ugliness of war and also about large

---

[1]See pages 357 and 360 for these poems.
[2]Central idea.

groups of sorrowful people. Lowell's longer poem focuses on the personal grief of just one person. In a sense, Lowell's poem begins where Owen's ends, a fact that accounts for both the similarities and the differences between the two works. The antiwar themes can be compared on the basis of their subjects, their lengths, their concreteness, and their use of a common metaphor.[3]

"Anthem for Doomed Youth" attacks war more directly than   [2]
"Patterns" does. Owen's opening line, "What passing-bells for those who die as cattle?" suggests that in war, human beings are depersonalized before they are slaughtered, like so much meat, and his observations about the "monstrous" guns and the "shrill, demented" shells unambiguously condemn the horrors of war. By contrast, in "Patterns," warfare is far away, on another continent, intruding only when the messenger delivers the letter stating that the speaker's fiancé has been killed (lines 63–64). A comparable situation governs the last six lines of Owen's poem, quietly describing how those at home respond to the loss of their loved ones. Thus, the antiwar focus in "Patterns" is the contrast between the calm, peaceful life of the speaker's garden and the anguish of her responses. In "Anthem for Doomed Youth," the stress is more on the external horrors of war that bring about the need for ceremonies honoring the dead.

Another major difference between the poems is their wide   [3]
discrepancy in length. "Patterns" is an interior monologue or meditation of 107 lines, but it could not be shorter and still be convincing. Lowell's speaker thinks of the past and contemplates her future loneliness. Her final outburst, "Christ! What are patterns for?" (107) would make no sense if she did not explain her situation as extensively as she does. "Anthem for Doomed Youth," however, is brief—a fourteen-line sonnet—because it is more general and less personal than "Patterns." Although Owen's speaker shows great sympathy, he or she views the sorrows of others distantly, unlike Lowell, who goes right into the mind and spirit of the grieving speaker. In the last six lines of "Anthem for Doomed Youth,"

---

[3]Thesis sentence.

Owen's use of phrases such as "tenderness of patient minds" and "drawing down of blinds" is a powerful representation of deep grief. He gives no further details even though thousands of individual stories might be told. In contrast, Lowell tells just one of these stories as she focuses on her solitary speaker's ruined hopes and dreams. Thus, the contrasting lengths of the poems are determined by the specific or more general consideration of the effects of war.

[4]   Despite these differences of approach and length, the two poems are similarly concrete and real. Owen moves from the real scenes and sounds of far-off battlefields to the homes of the many soldiers who have been killed in battle, but Lowell's scene is a single place: the garden of her speaker's estate. The speaker steps on real gravel along garden paths that contain daffodils, squills, a fountain, and a lime tree. She thinks of her clothing and her ribboned shoes and also of her fiancé's boots, sword hilts, and buttons. The images in Owen's poem are equally real but are not about specific individuals, as in "Patterns." Thus, Owen's images are those of cattle, bells, rifle shots, shells, bugles, candles, and window blinds. Both poems reflect reality, but Owen's details are more general and public, whereas Lowell's are more personal and intimate.

[5]   Along with this concreteness, the poems share the major metaphor that cultural patterns both control and frustrate human wishes and hopes. In "Patterns," this metaphor is shown in warfare itself (line 106), which is the pinnacle of organized human patterns of destruction. Further examples of the metaphor are found in details about clothing (particularly the speaker's stiff, confining gown in lines 5, 18, 21, 73, and 101 and also the lover's military boots in lines 46 and 49); the orderly, formal garden paths in which the speaker is walking (1, 93); her restraint at hearing about her lover's death; and her courtesy, despite her grief, in ordering refreshment for the messenger (69). Within such rigid patterns, her hopes for happiness have vanished, along with the sensuous spontaneity symbolized by her lover's hope to make love to her on a "shady seat" in the garden (85–89). The metaphor of the constricting pattern is also seen in "Anthem for Doomed Youth," except that in this poem, the pattern

is the funeral, not love or marriage. Owen's speaker contrasts the calm, peaceful tolling of "passing-bells" (1) to the frightening sounds of war represented by the "monstrous anger of the guns," "the stuttering rifles' rapid rattle," and "the demented choirs of wailing shells" (2–8). Thus, while Lowell uses the metaphor to reveal the irony of hope and desire being destroyed by war, Owen uses it to reveal the irony of war's negation of peaceful ceremonies.

Although in these ways, the poems share topics and some aspects of treatment, they are distinct and individual. "Patterns"   [6] includes many references to visible things, whereas "Anthem for Doomed Youth" emphasizes sound (and silence). Both poems conclude on powerfully emotional although different notes. Owen's poem dwells on the pathos and sadness that war brings to many unnamed people, and Lowell's expresses the most intimate thoughts of a woman who is alone in the first agony of her grief. Although neither poem attacks the usual political justifications for war (the needs to mobilize, to sacrifice, to achieve peace through fighting, and so on), the attack is there by implication, for both poems make their appeal by stressing how war destroys the relationships that make life worth living. For this reason, despite their differences, both "Patterns" and "Anthem for Doomed Youth" are parallel anti-war poems, and both are expressions of deeply felt emotions.

Works Cited

Lowell, Amy. "*Patterns*." Roberts 357.

Owen, Wilfred. "Anthem for Doomed Youth." Roberts, 360.

Roberts, Edgar V. *Writing About Literature*. 13th ed. New York: Pearson, 2012. Print.

Commentary on the Essay

This essay shows how approximately equal attention can be given to the two works being studied. Words stressing similarity are *common, share, equally, parallel, both, similar,* and *also.* Contrasts are stressed by *while, whereas, different, dissimilar, contrast, although,* and *except.* Transitions from paragraph to paragraph are not different in this type of essay from those in other essays. Thus, the phrases *despite, along with this,* and *in these ways,* which are used here, could be used anywhere for the same transitional purpose.

The central idea—that the poems mutually condemn war—is brought out in paragraph 1, together with the supporting idea that the poems are comparable because both show responses to news of battle casualties.

Paragraph 2, the first in the body, discusses how each poem brings out its attack on warfare. Paragraph 3 explains the differing lengths of the poems as a function of differences in perspective. Because Owen's sonnet views war and its effects at a distance, it is brief; but because Lowell's interior monologue views death intimately, it needs more detail and greater length.

Paragraph 4, on the topic of concreteness and reality, shows that the two works can receive equal attention without the bouncing back and forth of the tennis-ball method. Three of the sentences in this paragraph (3, 4, and 6) are devoted exclusively to details in one poem or the other; but sentences 1, 2, 5, and 7 refer to both works, stressing points of broad or specific comparison. The scheme demonstrates that the two works are, in effect, interlocked within the paragraph.

Paragraph 5, the last in the body, considers the similar and dissimilar ways in which the poems treat the common metaphor of cultural patterns.

The conclusion, paragraph 6, summarizes the central idea; it also stresses the ways in which the two poems, although similar, are distinct and unique.

II. Illustrative Essay (Extended Comparison-Contrast)

Literary Treatments of the Tension Between Private and Public Life

[1]   The tension and conflict between private or personal life, on the one hand, and public or civic and national life, on the other, is a topic common to many literary works.[4] Authors show that individuals try to maintain their personal lives and commitments even though they are tested and stressed by public and external forces. Ideally, individuals should have the freedom to follow their own

---

[4]Central idea.

wishes independently of the outside world. It is a fact, however, that living itself causes people to venture into the public world and, therefore, to encounter conflicts. Taking a walk, going to school, finding a job, attending a concert, getting married, following a profession—in short, just living from day to day—all draw people into the public world in which rules, regulations, and laws compete with private wishes. To greater and lesser degrees, such conflicts are found in Arnold's "Dover Beach," Chekhov's *The Bear*, Glaspell's *Trifles*, Chopin's "The Story of an Hour," Hardy's "Channel Firing," Hawthorne's "Young Goodman Brown," Keats's "Bright Star," Layton's "Rhine Boat Trip," Lowell's "Patterns," Shakespeare's "Sonnet 73: That Time of Year Thou Mayst in Me Behold," Whitman's "Reconciliation," and Wordsworth's "Lines Written in Early Spring."[5] In these works, clashes are shown between the interests of individuals and those of the social, legal, and military public.[6]

    One of the major private-public conflicts is created by the way in which characters respond to social conventions and expectations. In Chekhov's *The Bear*, for example, Mrs. Popov has given up her personal life to spend her time in remembering her dead husband. She wears black, plans to stay in her house indefinitely, and swears eternal fidelity; and she does all this to fulfill what she considers her public role as a grieving widow. Fortunately for her, Smirnov arrives on the scene and arouses her enough to make her give up this silly pose. Not as fortunate is Goodman Brown in Hawthorne's "Young Goodman Brown." Brown's obligation is much less public and also more philosophical than Mrs. Popov's because his religiously inspired vision of the evil around him fills him with lifelong gloom. Although Mrs. Popov is easily moved away from her position by the prospect of immediate life and vitality, Brown's mindless distrust locks him into a fear of evil from which not even his own faithful wife can shake him. Brown and Mrs. Popov, therefore, go in entirely

[2]

---

[5]See Appendix C for the poems, Chopin's "The Story of an Hour," and Hawthorne's "Young Goodman-Brown." See MyLiteratureLab for *The Bear* and *Trifles*.
[6]Thesis sentence.

different directions—one toward personal fulfillment, the other toward personal destruction.

[3]   <u>A major idea in the various works is that philosophical or religious difficulties such as those of Goodman Brown force a crisis in an individual life.</u> In Arnold's "Dover Beach" the speaker expresses regret about uncertainty and the loss of religious faith that symbolically wear away civilization just like the surf that beats on the shores of Dover Beach. This situation might be expected to make a person as dreary and depressed as Goodman Brown actually is. Arnold's speaker, however, in the lines "Ah, love, let us be true / To one another," finds power in personal fidelity and commitment (lines 29–30). In other words, the public world of "human misery" and the diminishing "Sea of Faith" are beyond control, and therefore all that is left is personal commitment. This is not to say that "Young Goodman Brown," as a story, is negative, for Hawthorne implies that a positive personal life lies in the denial of choices like those made by Brown and in the acceptance of choices like those made by Mrs. Popov and Arnold's speaker.

[4]   <u>To deny or to ignore the public world is a possible option that, under some circumstances, can be chosen.</u> For example, "Dover Beach" reflects a conscious decision to ignore the philosophic and religious uncertainty that the speaker finds in the intellectual and public world. Even more independent of such a public world, Shakespeare's "Sonnet 73: That Time of Year Thou Mayst in Me Behold" and Keats's "Bright Star" bring out their ideas as reflections on purely personal situations. Shakespeare's speaker deals with the love between himself and the listener, whereas Keats's speaker, addressing a distant star, considers his need for comparable stead-fastness in his relationship with his "fair love." Louise Mallard, the major character in Chopin's "The Story of an Hour," embodies an interesting variation on the personal matters brought up in these two sonnets. At first, Louise is overwhelmed with grief by the news coming from the public world, through the medium of telegraph, that her husband has been killed in a train wreck. Her first vision of herself is that of a grieving, private widow. As she thinks about

things, however, she quickly begins to anticipate the liberation and freedom—to become free to explore her newly anticipated personal world—that widowhood will give her. Ironically, it is the reappearance of her husband, who moves freely in the public world, that shocks her into her sudden heart failure and death. What she looks forward to as the free choice to do what she wants and to go where she wishes has suddenly been withdrawn from her by her renewed status within the publicly sanctioned system of marriage, and it is her recognition of her abrupt loss of this private possibility that ends her life.

The complexity of the conflict between private and public life is brought out in the way in which governments secure their power through law and legality. With immense power, the law often acts as an arbitrary form of public judgment that disregards personal needs and circumstances. This idea is brought out on the most personal level in Susan Glaspell's *Trifles*, in which the two major characters, both women, urgently confront the conflict between their personal identification with the accused woman, Minnie, and their public obligation to the law. One of the women, Mrs. Peters, is reminded that she is "married to the law," but she and Mrs. Hale suppress the evidence that they know would condemn Minnie, even though technically—by law, that is—their knowledge is public property. Their way of resolving the conflict is, therefore, to recognize their personal obligations to selfhood rather than to public responsibility. **[5]**

The legal conflict is also treated more generally and philosophically in some works. For example, Wordsworth deals with the morality—or immorality—of the conflict in "Lines Written in Early Spring," when he says, "Have I not reason to lament / What man has made of man?" (15–16). This question in its most extreme form refers to legalized suppression and persecution, but Wordsworth does little more with the topic than to say that he laments it. Layton, however, in "Rhine Boat Trip," deals with the extremity of human cruelty. In this poem, Layton condemns the Nazi exterminations of "Jewish mothers" and "murdered rabbis" during the Holocaust of World War II. Ironically, the exterminations were carried out **[6]** legally, for it has commonly been observed that the Nazis created laws to justify all their moral atrocities. So much for "legality."

[7] <u>Works that deal with war especially highlight the conflict between personal and public concerns.</u> It is a fact that individuals must take up arms when the public demands their wartime service, but the conflict between personal and public values reaches its most disturbing height when individuals and families go through the consequent difficulties in all phases of their lives. A character who is personally caught up by the public demands of war is the speaker of Amy Lowell's "Patterns." Because her fiancé, Lord Hartwell, has been killed fighting abroad, her extreme grief leads her to question those military "patterns" that have destroyed her personal plans for married life as Lady Hartwell (107). A comparable but also comic contrast is dramatized by Hardy in "Channel Firing." In this poem, set in a church graveyard, the skeleton of "Parson Thirdly" views "gunnery practice out at sea" (10) as evidence that his "forty year" dedication to serving his church—in other words, serving in public life—was a total waste. His conclusion is that he would have been better off ignoring his public role and instead following personal interests of "pipes and beer." Whereas Hardy's Parson Thirdly is disturbed by the noises of the publicly approved naval gunfire, Whitman's speaker in "Reconciliation" is moved to final and personal pity by the actual contact with the dead. As the speaker sees his dead enemy, lying "still in the coffin," he touches "lightly" with his lips "the white face in the coffin" in an act of personal reconciliation. Here, as in Lowell's "Patterns," whatever public value warfare might possess is insignificant in the face of the permanence of death. On the subject of warfare, writers generally, without hesitation, assert that public things are negligible when compared with the importance of personal lives, loves, and concerns.

[8] <u>The works compared and contrasted here show varied and powerful conflicts between public demands and personal interests and are in general agreement that, under ideal conditions, private life should be supreme.</u> They also demonstrate that in many ways,

the public world invades the private world with a wide range of demands and expectations, from making people behave foolishly to destroying them utterly. Naturally, the tone of the works is shaped by the degree of seriousness of the conflict. Chekhov's *The Bear* is good-humored and farcical because the characters overcome the social roles in which they are cast. More sober are works such as "Dover Beach" and "Young Goodman Brown," in which characters either are overcome by public commitments or deliberately turn their backs on them. In the highest range of seriousness are works such as "Rhine Boat Trip," "Patterns," and "Reconciliation," in which individuals have been crushed by irresistible public forces.

Work Cited

Selected works. *Writing About Literature*. 13th ed. Edgar V. Roberts. New. York: Pearson, 2013. Print.

Commentary on the Essay

This extended comparison-contrast essay, combining for discussion all three genres of fiction, poetry, and drama, is visualized as an assignment climaxing a unit of study. The expectation prompting the assignment is that a fairly large number of literary works can be profitably compared on the basis of a unifying subject, idea, or technique. For this essay, the works—eight poems, two stories, and two short plays—are compared and contrasted on the common topic of private-public conflicts. It is obviously impossible in a short essay to discuss all the works in detail in every paragraph. The essay, therefore, demonstrates that a writer may introduce a large number of works in a straightforward comparison-contrast method without a need for detailed comparison of each work with every other work on each of the major subtopics (social, legal, military).

Thus, the first section, consisting of paragraphs 2–4, treats six of the works. In paragraph 2, however, only two works are discussed, and in paragraph 3, one of these works is carried over for comparison with only one additional work. The fourth paragraph springs out of the third, utilizing one of the works discussed there and then bringing out comparisons with three additional works.

The same technique is used in the rest of the essay. Paragraph 5 introduces only one work; paragraph 6 introduces two additional works; and paragraph 7 introduces three works for comparison and contrast. Each of the twelve works has then been discussed at least once in terms of how it contributes to the major topic. One might note that the essay concentrates on a relatively small number of the works, such as Chekhov's *The Bear* and Hawthorne's "Young Goodman Brown," but that as newer topics are introduced, the essay goes on to works that are more closely connected to these topics.

The technique of extended comparison-contrast used in this way shows how the various works can be defined and distinguished in relation to the common idea: the contrast between personal and public life. The concluding paragraph summarizes these distinctions by suggesting a continuous line along which each of the works may be placed.

Even so, the treatment of so many texts might easily cause crowding and confusion. The division of the major topic into subtopics, as noted, is a major means of trying to make the essay easy to follow. An additional means is the introduction of transitional words and phrases such as *also*, *choose*, and *one of the major conflicts*.

An extended comparison-contrast essay cannot present a full treatment of each of the works. The works are unique, and they deal independently with many things that are outside the topic of an extended comparison-contrast essay. Ideas that are independently important in Hardy's "Channel Firing," for example, are (1) that human beings need eternal rest and not eternal life, (2) that God is amused by—or indifferent to—human affairs, (3) that religious callings or vocations may be futile, and (4) that war itself is the supreme form of cruelty. All these topics could be treated in another essay, but they do not pertain to the goals of this particular essay. A topic that is compatible with the general private-public topic is needed, and the connection is readily made (paragraph 7) through the character of Hardy's Parson Thirdly. Because the essay deals with the conflicts brought out by Thirdly's comments, Hardy's poem is linked to all the other works for comparative purposes. So it is with the other works, each of which could also be the subject of analysis from many standpoints other than comparison-contrast. The effect of the comparison of all the works collectively, however, is the enhanced understanding of each of the works separately. To achieve such an understanding and to explain it are the major goals of the extended comparison-contrast method.

Writing Topics About Comparison and Contrast

1. The use of the speaker in Arnold's "Dover Beach" and Wordsworth's "Lines Written in Early Spring."
2. The description of fidelity to love in Keats's "Bright Star" and Shakespeare's "Sonnet 73: That Time of Year Thou Mayst in Me Behold," or in Arnold's "Dover Beach" and Amy Lowell's "Patterns."
3. The view of women in Chekhov's *The Bear* and Maupassant's "The Necklace" or in Glaspell's *Trifles* and Mansfield's "Miss Brill."

4. The function and importance of descriptive scenery in Hawthorne's "Young Goodman Brown" and Lowell's "Patterns."
5. Symbols of disapproval in Hardy's "Channel Firing" and Frost's "Desert Places."
6. The treatment of loss in Shakespeare's "Sonnet 30: When to the Sessions of Sweet Silent Thought" and Chopin's "The Story of an Hour."
7. Treatments of racial oppression and suppression in Brooks's "We Real Cool," Layton's "Rhine Boat Trip," and Hughes's "Negro."
8. For an extended comparison-contrast essay, any of the foregoing topics applied to a number of separate works.

Chapter 16

Writing About a Work in Its Historical, Intellectual, and Cultural Context

Fiction, Poetry, and Drama

Everything that is written, spoken, painted, or composed reflects the period of its composition—its historical, intellectual, and cultural context, or milieu. Literature for the moment aside, we cannot open our mouths to speak without consciously or subconsciously taking into account the conditions in which we live, our ways of life, our intellectual goals, and our aims and aspirations. We are always a part of our greater culture, and our observations and thoughts are a constant function of the attitudes, idioms, ideas, and customs of our time and place. All things emerge from their own era, whether as a revolutionary idea, a reaction, or a synthesis; and one of the major tasks of the disciplined reader is to understand the relationship between historical times and artistic works. To study a work of literature in historical and cultural perspective is to determine the degree to which the work belongs in, and perhaps transcends, its period.

To carry out such a study, you need to develop thoughts about the connections of literature to life. You might consider the obvious fact that as circumstances change, writers express attitudes reflecting these changes. You might also consider that artists themselves want to create new ideas from existing ones and to suggest improvements and reforms in government and society. A permanent standard of judging art is, therefore, its newness, that is, its status of being different, and artists are always trying to meet this standard. To the degree to which writers of the past (and present) have been successful, it is possible to place their works in historical perspective, in the light of change at least, if not of definite progress.

The point of reading works in historical and sociological perspective is not to file them away in a historical pigeonhole but to improve understanding of the entire work. The aim is to produce accuracy of reading and of judgments and to avoid errors that result from failure to see that writers, and artists generally, respond to their own times, either by embracing the present or by probing idealistically into the past. An interesting example is Samuel Taylor Coleridge's poem "Kubla Khan" (p. 350) It was published in 1816, a time when it had become an accepted fact that scientists could explore the heavens with telescopes and everyday matter with microscopes. Absolutely new descriptions of the elements and their properties had been made, and the known world was appearing to be less awesome and more regular than it had ever seemed previously. But not everything was yielding to scientific discovery, and Coleridge was interested in evoking a less detailed but more mysterious past. Therefore, he based his poem on the distant, almost magical time of the great emperor Kublai Khan, who had ruled China in the thirteenth century. It is as though Coleridge deliberately created his poem as an antithesis of the increasing scientism of his times.

History, Culture, and Multiculturalism

It is such connections that are formative in literary history, which is in effect the chronicling of the interaction of ideas, events, social and political conditions, and literary modes. Of particularly increasing interest has been the consideration of literature as it reflects the society from which the writers of literature have come and on which they have based their work. Recently, great attention has been devoted to multicultural studies and literary works; that is, works that are based in the stories of people who for the greater portion of modern history have been suppressed and even ignored. The United States is a unique place in the world, which during its relatively short existence has seen a virtually constant immigration of national groups and cultures.

The process is by no means over. The census of 1940 recorded about 130,000,000 Americans. At the present time, our population is close to 309,000,000 and it is increasing daily. In addition to the massive numbers of African Americans, Chinese Americans, Central Europeans, and Scandinavians, much of whose immigration occurred before the twentieth century, new waves of people have come from Asia, the Caribbean Islands, and Central and South America. As with all immigrants, many have arrived with little or no knowledge of English but with strong memories of their native cultures. The second generations of these people have learned English but have experienced many of the traditional difficulties of integrating themselves into American life. They have encountered prejudice, hostility, segregation, and violence, for even though they were born on American soil, they have had much to overcome. A good deal of twentieth and early twenty-first century literature concerns the struggles of immigrants and their descendants as they have lived and worked and found a home in the United States.

As one might expect, this process of movement has stirred a not inconsiderable controversy. Politically, a traditional idea of long duration is that America is a "melting pot" of people of differing races and cultures, involving the blending and merging of the old world to create something entirely new. A contrary concept is that of multiculturalism, namely, the idea that the members of each incoming group—on the basis of race, ethnicity, national origin, and culture—do not shed their unique qualities even though they have become American residents and citizens. Each group seeks to preserve its identity in the new land, and so our culture is pluralistic. It is, therefore, diversity that should be celebrated, not assimilationism. Although this idea has profound political implications, our present focus is on the literature that has risen along with the many changes brought about by our unique nation of immigrants and their descendants.

Literature in Its Time and Place

Analyzing a literary work as a product of cultural and intellectual history is the task, first, of determining what can be clearly deducible as coming directly out of the major issues existing at the time it was written and, second, of deciding what is new and permanent—that is, of determining what has been created by the author of the work from ideas that were prevalent at the time of composition. The concern is to see both the similarity and dissimilarity of a work and its period.

Such a study of literature is valuable because it promotes the realization that ideas and ways of seeing the universe change with time and place. Too often, it is easy to read texts as though they were written last week and to attribute to writers ideas that they never had. Shakespeare, for example, had a number of political ideas, but he had no experience with representative government as we know it today. Therefore, in considering works of his that touch the subject of politics, such as the *Henry IV* plays, *Richard II*, and *Henry V*, you should understand why he dramatizes the importance of a just and strong monarch or the necessity of a moral aristocracy. We can enthusiastically accept his idea that wise rulers and moral people are necessary in the creation of successful government, even though we today apply the principle not to monarchy—the form that Shakespeare knew—but to democracy.

Writing About a Work in Its Historical and Cultural Context

The first part of your task is to decide what is topical about the work on which you are going to write. Usually, there is enough in a work's descriptions, actions, locations, customs, and cultural assumptions to find something that is unique. Layton's "Rhine Boat Trip," for example, is derived from reflections about the unspeakable Nazi atrocities and concentration camps during the Second World War.

Some works, however, offer a special challenge because of their apparent lack of references; that is, they seem to be so closely connected with our own contemporary ideas and assumptions that you might not readily see them in historical and cultural perspective. At first, Arnold's poem "Dover Beach" might give this impression. But "Dover Beach" provides abundant symbolism about the loss of religious certainty in the nineteenth century, and this idea, about a loss that many people today also feel, would provide you with sufficient material with which to begin the thoughts for an essay.

Another problem might arise when the work that is assigned is remote either in history or in place. In such works, however, the subject matter brings out ideals and attitudes of the writer, and these can then be related to the time in which the work was written, just as they may also be related to our own times. Browning's poem "My Last Duchess" is such a work. It was published in 1842, but its subject is a Renaissance Italian nobleman who is callous and self-centered and who wields despotic power. Thus, it is apparent that Browning is exemplifying the idea that absolute power produces destructive results both on the individual who wields it and on those around him. This is an idea that is certainly up to date—in fact, it is up to the minute. Browning's presentation of the duke can, therefore, be analyzed as a good deal more than a dramatic study of a powerful eccentric of past times.

Raise Questions to Discover Ideas

It is important to realize that the major source of your information is the work itself. In your reading, you will discover a great deal about the period of the author, even about our own period, and, more important, about the place of the work in that period. You need to ask and answer a number of questions:

- Are historical circumstances specifically mentioned? If so, what are they? What does the author say about them?
- Does the author describe conditions with photographic detail, or is he or she concerned less with pictorial details and more with human and political issues?
- To what national, ethnic, social, and economic class do the principal characters belong? What is their background? What values do they hold or represent?
- Are the characters religious or not? To what degree do religious or philosophical thoughts govern the actions of the characters?
- Is the principal character (or any character) an important part of the prevailing social and economic system as outlined in the work, or is he or she an outsider? If the principal character is outside the system, what conditions have put and now keep him or her there? Are you made to feel pleased or angry with these conditions?
- Does the character eventually win a place in the system, is he or she left out of the system, or is he or she broken by the system?
- What assumptions do you think the author had about the literary interests of his or her audience? That is, does it seem that the author wrote for a sophisticated audience, a simple-minded one, or a sensation-seeking one?
- What conclusions can you draw, on the basis of your answers to these and like questions, about the author's attitudes toward his or her times? Does the author attempt to give a complete view or a partial view? Does the author seem to be recommending values that are similar, or contrary, to those held during his or her era?

From questions such as these, you will soon discover a suitable topic, for there is need here, as always, for narrowing the focus of your discussion. For example, a question about the fortunes of particular characters can lead to an avenue of inquiry like the following: "How can the characters in Alice Walker's story "Everyday Use" be shown to reflect Walker's views about racial politics in the second half of the twentieth century?" Events or situations themselves can be focused in the same way. The details about Jackie's home life in O'Connor's "First Confession" might suggest a topic such as "The Negative Effect of Dublin Home Life on the Individual." Your creation of topics like these should enable you to develop an interesting and relevant essay.

This use of the work of literature itself as an authority for your remarks in the essay might seem open to the objection that literary works are often not reliable as actual source material for history. Sometimes works contain exaggerations made for comic or satiric effect, and sometimes they develop out of improbable circumstances. As history, therefore, the close study of a literary work is a weak substitute for more accurate documentation.

The answer to this objection—and an important realization—is that the focus of this assignment is the work itself. Your essay is about the historical period only as it is reflected in the work. Your concern is not to use the work for evidence in writing history but rather as evidence of a literary reaction to historical and cultural circumstances. Even if there are exaggerations and caricature or if the conditions that are reported are brighter or darker than life, these very aspects of the work become an important part of the material you bring to your essay. Your aim should not be to use the work as a filter through which you attempt to acquire historical data but to determine the use to which such observable data have been put within the work.

Some types of literature are more readily approached from the historical, intellectual, and cultural point of view than others. Usually, novels, short stories, narrative poems, dramas, and essays are fairly obviously rooted in customs and ideas of their time. Many of these works can be discussed without extensive reading in secondary historical sources. By contrast, many short lyric poems are not obviously connected with their respective periods, and writing about these works may require more inferential efforts.

Organize Your Essay About a Work and Its Context

In the following plan, the introduction might be proportionately longer than usual because of the need for presenting detailed information about the work and what you know about its historical period.

Introduction In addition to defining your central idea and thesis sentence, your aim here should be to place the work in its context. You should identify the work and state the time of its publication and, if known, of its composition. You should include any biographical data that might be relevant to an understanding of the work and its background. You should also state whether there are any special problems in discussing the work, such as that it is a historical novel or a work that is remote in time or that there is some controversy about it.

You should also state the pertinent historical facts concerning the events and ideas that you have selected for discussion. There is no need for extensive explication; mention only those details that are relevant. If the work was written during or shortly after a recent war, for example, you may assume that your readers know as much generally about this war as you do and need only those details that will remind them of their knowledge. Thus, if you are discussing Hardy's "The Man He Killed," you might state that the poem is probably based on a soldier's view stemming out of the trench warfare on the Western front during World War I. You might then go on to state that this war was immensely complex, for it had implications for all the nations of Europe and the United States; that it was fought not only on land but also on the sea; that it was sometimes called the "Great War" and "the war to end all wars"; that it was also seen as an ideological war in which nations felt their prestige to be at stake; that the war highlighted for many people the idea that life and love were impermanent and fleeting; that the war was immensely wasteful and destructive; and that it is difficult to pinpoint the causes of the war and to explain the reasons for which opposing nations took sides. There is nothing unusual about these conclusions; the point about them is that they are general statements about the period rather than detailed descriptions.

Body After dealing with introductory details, you should aim to show how they apply to the work you are studying. You may wish to include both of the following or just one or the other.

1. A discussion of how the work embodies the facts or of how the facts shape the work. Thus, Hardy's "The Man He Killed" not only demonstrates the common-sense quality of the speaker, but also exposes the sham of theoretical warfare when contrasted with the ordinary needs and wants of an average human being. The poem can be seen as an assertion that international political concerns, in human terms, are valueless. Similarly, in discussing Browning's "My Last Duchess," you might show that the Duke's conversational manners (his preempting the discussion of marriage details by reflecting on the portrait of his former duchess and his stating that his "just pretense" for a dowry will be acceptable) can be related to the assertion that the poem is an effective counterargument against nineteenth-century claims that "great men" are needed to perform the great tasks that are required in public and political life. Browning's "great man" is so preoccupied with his own power that he listens to no one and abandons all human kindness.

2. As the first part of the body is concerned with ideas, the second is devoted to a discussion of literary matters (style, structure, tone, point of view, imagery, etc.) that can be related to the period. Thus, ideas about the need for personal freedom may be related to poems written in free verse. An awareness of the horror of discrimination may be related to the ballad structure of Randall's "Ballad of Birmingham," in which the simple poetic structure emphasizes the extreme to which such cruelty can go. The modern stress on psychology may account for the limited point of view in Mansfield's "Miss Brill," in which we as readers directly follow the thoughts and responses of the major character. The compact, brief stanzas of Hughes's "Negro" enables the poet to express a brief world history of the exploitation of blacks. What is important here is to apply the context of the work to its literary characteristics.

Conclusion To conclude, you should try to determine which elements that you have discussed seem out of date and which ones are still relevant and important. For purposes of your conclusion, you may assume that your own point of view is modern and up to date, although on this issue, you should perhaps assert yourself humbly and emphasize your broad-mindedness. Thus, in this section, you might attempt to determine whether Browning's exposé of the ruthless Duke in "My Last Duchess" is still applicable, considering that many people in various nations have invented the title "President for Life" and continue to fill that role. Does Goodman Brown's preoccupation with the evil of others seem to be relevant today, or should we regard his ideas as having passed its time? What should be our responses to those young men of Gwendolyn Brooks's poem who claim that they are "real cool"? It is questions such as these that you might ask and attempt to answer in your conclusion.

Illustrative Essay

Hughes's References to Black Servitude and
Black Pride in Langston Hughes's "Negro"

Negro (1958)

I am a Negro:
   Black as the night is black.
   Black like the depths of my Africa.
I've been a slave:
   Caesar told me to keep his door-steps clean.   5
   I brushed the boots of Washington.
I've been a worker:
   Under my hand the pyramids arose.
   I made mortar for the Woolworth Building.
I've been a singer: 10
   All the way from Africa to Georgia
   I carried my sorrow songs.
   I made ragtime.
I've been a victim:
   The Belgians cut off my hands in the Congo.   15
   They lynch me still in Mississippi.
I am a Negro:
   Black as the night is black,
   Black like the depths of my Africa.

[1]   Langston Hughes was a strong voice of the Harlem Renaissance—the twentieth-century movement that declared that the time had come to recognize the significance of African Americans in all phases of life. In "Negro," Hughes propels this argument by showing that oppression against blacks is as old as human history.[1] He might have developed his idea in a lengthy book study, with many supportive details and many references. Instead, his interest is to be brief and memorable—as though he is providing details for a political agenda—and he chooses to create a poem of six brief

[1]Central idea.

stanzas. The poem demonstrates how eloquent a spokesman and leader Hughes actually was. The poem is built on the contrast between what the heritage of blacks should be—the entitlement to equality and freedom—and what in fact it is and has been—the indignity of slavery and oppression.[2]

The form of "Negro" is both simple and direct. There are six **[2]** stanzas in the poem, each beginning with the pronoun "I" followed by a grammatical form of the verb *to be*. The total number of lines is nineteen. The first and sixth stanzas identify the speaker as a representative Negro whose identity is the same as his race—black— "Black like the depths of my Africa" (lines 3, 19). These opening and concluding stanzas are current in scope, for they are in the present tense and they define the speaker's racial identity and pride in the color of his African heritage.

Stanzas 2, 3, and 5 are historical, however, briefly referring **[3]** to the servitude and suffering that blacks have experienced. The emphasis in these stanzas is on the past, and Hughes's use of the present-perfect tense bears out his continuing historical emphasis. These comprehensive stanzas jump time and place, from the slavery and oppression of ancient Rome and ancient Egypt, on the one hand, to Revolutionary War times and modern industrial times of the United States, on the other. Symbolically, the speaker says that in the palace of Caesar, he was a slave who kept the doorsteps clean, just as he cleaned the boots as a personal servant of America's first president, George Washington. The idea is that the heights that these men (and others like them) reached were achieved by their dependence on the slavery of blacks. Similarly, the Belgian colonial regime in Africa was sustained by oppressive cruelty against blacks, which is symbolized by the cutting off of the hands of slaves in the Congo (15). Hughes goes on to state that such colonial oppression is by no means over, for his speaker refers to the neocolonial oppres-

---

[2]Thesis sentence.

sion of life in Mississippi (in 1958, the date of the poem), where lynching still occurred.

[4]   The most positive section of the poem is stanza 4, in which Hughes tells us that the narrator has sung his "sorrow songs" during the entire history of displacement from "Africa to Georgia" (11–12). This stanza is comparable to stanzas 1 and 6, for in all three stanzas, Hughes declares the positive identity and value of African Americans. In stanza 4, the idea is that there is a vast human talent among blacks that has already been realized, with the implication that there is much more to come. Here Hughes is emphasizing black pride, because the power of making music and providing musical beauty is a capacity that could never be suppressed, even through the long centuries of black oppression that date from the origin of history. The possibility of continued high achievement, Hughes implies, is endless.

[5]   As we have seen, "Negro" concludes and ends on the importance of realizing the promises of history for the present time. The tenses of the verbs bring this out, for everything in the poem implies a current condition. The past has had its day, with its oppression, and is now over, or should be over. The present is now of the greatest concern. The time has come for African Americans to appreciate their own blackness, "like the depths of my Africa" (3, 19). Things are in some respects the same, yet they are changed because the time has come for liberation, of freedom. The idea is that it is time for the end of oppression—a time when African Americans can listen to themselves and their "sorrow songs" and can be themselves as they were meant to be when they were in their original homes in Africa.

[6]   "Negro" is, therefore, a thoroughly modern poem. It recognizes the past but emphasizes the significance of the present. In three of the poem's stanzas, Hughes refers to the past. The final stanza indicates that the present is the same as the past but that African Americans have moved up from slavery and oppression and can build their new identity out of their past history. Even though this last stanza is identical to the first, word for word, it suggests that it is time to move, to claim a new movement of history, a new direction. Hughes's argument is that this direction is forward.

Work Cited

Hughes, Langston. "Negro." Edgar V. Roberts. *Writing About Literature*. 13th ed. New York: Pearson, 2012. 234, 354. Print.

Commentary on the Essay

As an essay about a literary work as it pertains to its historical period, this essay deals with the issues of African-American identity and liberation that became a major idea in American life during earlier generations of Americans. All the descriptions and interpretations of "Negro" are based on this connection. Because the issues of African-American life have such strongly political overtones, the essay treats the poem as a work of exhortation as well as description. The essay makes transitions with the key words *however* (paragraph 3), *most positive* (4), *as we have seen* (5), and *therefore* (6).

In the body of this essay, paragraph 2 deals with the poem's shape and its essential simplicity. Of special interest is the poet's use of the present tense to sustain the argument that the poem is directed at current readers, who can translate their attitudes and interpretations of life into direct political action.

Paragraphs 3 and 4 are the most extensive in the essay, for they focus on Hughes's historical stanzas, showing that he deals here with the historical indignities and horrors of black oppression. The unique analysis here is that the grammar of stanzas 2 through 5 is a major means by which Hughes sustains his argument. The idea in the essay here is to show that the past lives on in the present. Paragraph 4 follows Hughes's argument that the musical nature of African Americans is a positive symbol of their inherent human worthiness.

Paragraphs 5 and 6 emphasize once again the present implications of "Negro." Paragraph 5 especially emphasizes the present, while the concluding paragraph, 6, asserts that the poem is particularly modern. In this way, the essay demonstrates how Hughes's poem has a place in the historical times when it was written. The essay's analysis and its central idea both emphasize this connection.

Writing Topics About Works in Their Historical, Intellectual, and Cultural Context

1. Consider a story or poem in which the topics are connected with philosophy or politics, for example, Arnold's "Dover Beach" (religion, philosophy), Frost's "Desert Places" (the cosmos), Hardy's "The Man He Killed" (politics and war), and Lowell's "Patterns" (war and human relationships). Write an essay about just one of these works showing how the topic reflects ideas and concerns of the time when it was written and of today's times.

2. Consider Blake's use of the image of the "Tyger" in "The Tyger." To what degree is the Tyger a symbol of what Blake considered to be evil? How does Blake seem to define evil? How current is his use of what today is considered an endangered animal? How does his poem speak to today's concerns?

3. In the context of current relationship of human beings to the natural world, how significant is Wordsworth's "Lines Written in Early Spring"? Does the poem meet the same need for today's readers that it probably met for Wordsworth's readers?

4. The circumstances of farm life in the second decade of the twentieth century are reflected in Glaspell's *Trifles*. Consider the loneliness, isolation, lack of communication, and marital abuse that are treated in this play. To what degree are these issues still significant in today's world?

5. Describe the timeliness of the issues Layton brings out in "Rhine Boat Trip."

6. Browning's "My Last Duchess" and Randall's "Ballad of Birmingham" touch upon the issue of political power. How do the works reflect what you take to have been the political concerns of their times? What contrasts between the works are you able to make?

Chapter 17

Writing a Review Essay: Developing Ideas and Evaluating Literary Works for Special or General Audiences

Fiction, Poetry, Poetry Collections, and Drama

The **review** is a general essay on a literary work. It may also be thought of as a "critique," a "critical review," an "evaluation," or simply an "essay." It is a free form, because in a review, virtually everything is relevant: subject matter, technique, social and intellectual background, biographical facts, relationship to other works by the same author or by different authors, historical importance, and everything else. Unless you become a professional writer in the future, a review is the most likely kind of writing about literature that you may ever be called upon to do. Many people, businesses, associations, guilds, and comparable organizations issue regular newsletters or have specially designated meetings or "book groups" in which members are asked to lead discussions about designated works. Often, members of such groups are interested in learning about various works and authors—not only recent ones, but also well-known and well-established ones—and so there is a need for good reviews.

A major aim of writing reviews, and of delivering them to members of a group, is to provide a general overview of the work, especially including an evaluation of the author's performance, together with other elements of the work that you should mention, special difficulties that you explain, and special features that you note.

Since the review provides for freedom of topics and development, it is also a challenge to the skills you have acquired thus far as a disciplined reader. Much of your experience has been *assimilation*—acquiring information and applying skills. Your tasks have been mainly fulfilling assignments that you are given in your classes. But with a review, you are left to your own devices; you must decide what to write about as well as what to say. Freedom of choice should be a constant goal, and it is important for you to realize that your experience is equipping you more and more to know what to do with this freedom. You should know not only how to answer questions but also how to decide on the questions to be asked. You should be able to synthesize the knowledge you have acquired and are continuing to acquire.

Writing a Review Essay

Because reviews can be personal as well as objective, you may experiment with form and development. If you choose to write about only a single topic, be sure to emphasize the various aspects with clear transitions. The third illustrative essay below, for example, shows how the subject of faith or trust may be pursued throughout a review. If you are writing a general review and select a number of topics, as in the first illustrative essay, be sure that your thesis sentence includes these various topics.

Raise Questions to Discover Ideas

- Who are the people for whom you intend your review? Are they a general audience or part of a particular group? What are the special interests of the group? What general interests do people in the group have in common?
- How much detail, special or general, do you think you should include about the work itself? How much knowledge does your audience expect you to demonstrate in your review? Should you introduce references to comparable works by the same author or by different authors?
- Have the people who make up your audience read the work? Should you design your review to be a substitute for their reading the work? Should your review be designed to interest people in reading the work themselves?
- When was the work written—just recently or a long time ago? What is the nationality of the author? What kind of background knowledge is needed so that readers may understand the work? What kind of background knowledge, and how much, is supplied by the author (for example, a knowledge of military circumstances, of "old time" religion, of conditions in rural England or rural America)?
- To what genre does the work belong? What general issues need to be explained before you begin your discussion of the work?
- What parts of the work are significant enough to warrant discussion in your review? What issues does the work bring out? What are the author's thoughts about these issues? How important are these thoughts? How timely is the work for today's readers?
- Do any particular characters, situations, or ideas stand out in the work you are reviewing? If so, what are they? Why are they significant?
- What aspects of the writer's style and presentation are worthy of mention? How fully do you think you can refer to these without losing your audience's interest?

Organize Your Review Essay

Introduction In your introduction, you should place the work in perspective. Although most frequently you will be asked to review a play or novel, it is good to bear in mind that you may also be writing a review about acting techniques or play production. If you are reviewing a new edition of an old work, you may be judging the relevance of the past to the present, and you may also be judging the apparatus supplied by the editor. Always try to show that your work has relevance to the present group of readers.

Body   In the body, you should try either to arouse interest in the work or to discourage readers from reading it if it seems to dictate this conclusion.

Beyond providing introductory information, your principal objective is to describe the strengths and weaknesses of the work. To write such a description, you must call into play just about everything you have learned about analyzing literature for ideas, form, and style. In a sense, the review can be as specific as you wish to make it, because the greatest part of the body should be given to analysis. In this analysis, you should try to bring out your own strengths and interests as a critical reader. It may be, for example, that you have become proficient in discussing ideas. Suppose that you observe intricately developed ideas in the work. You might choose to discuss that element in the body of your review, thereby appealing to your reader's interest in thought and ideas. You should always recognize, however, that your discussion should be of limited extent. There is no need for a detailed, word-by-word analysis. It is not an essay on ideas, style, or artistic qualities that you want, but a review emphasizing such elements.

For specialized reviews, you might call into play those disciplines that have interested you thus far in your college career. For example, you might feel competent in handling ideas connected with sociology. Hence, in your review of a novel you might bring your sociological awareness to bear on the work. Or you might have developed an interest in psychology and might treat the characters in a work according to your understanding of psychological problems.

Whatever your personal interests and specialties may be, however, your best guide for subject matter is the work itself, which might well channel your thinking along definite lines. For example, the second illustrative essay relates the obvious character flaw of the hero of "Young Goodman Brown" to religious concerns (for an audience of people interested in religion). The third illustrative essay adopts the position that the same story literally compels readers to consider the psychological importance of personal certainty and security. In the work you are assigned, you may similarly find that certain features will point you in a specific direction (the humor, a connection with existential philosophy, reflections on economic or social conditions, the nature of life on the frontier, etc.).

Conclusion   Your conclusion should be an attempt to evaluate the work, certainly not extensively, but at least you should give an outline of your responses and a suggestion to your readers of how they might respond—assuming that you have shown that your interests coincide approximately with theirs. If the body of your review has emphasized evaluation, you should close your essay with a simple resumé of your points. If you are ever asked to review a work in, say, no more than 150 words, the greatest part of the review should be devoted to evaluation.

First Illustrative Essay (A Review for General Readers)

Hawthorne's Story "Young Goodman Brown":[1]
A View of Mistaken Zeal

[1]   "Young Goodman Brown" is an allegorical story by
Nathaniel Hawthorne (1804–1864), the major American writer who
probed deeply into the relationships between religion and guilt.
Hawthorne's story is set in colonial Salem, presumably during the
days of religious Puritanism in the seventeenth century. His major
aim is to expose the weakness in the religious view that concentrates
only on the shortcomings and sins of human life.[2] Although this
concern may seem narrow, the story itself is timely, presenting a
dreamlike narrative, a realistic analysis of the growth of intolerance,
and a number of additional questions of permanent importance.[3]

[2]   On the surface, the apparent vagueness and dreamlike nature of
Hawthorne's details may leave some readers a little baffled. The
action is a nighttime trip by Goodman Brown to a mysterious satanic
gathering in a deep forest just outside the village of Salem in Massachusetts. Brown begins his walk as a friendly youth, just three months
married to a young woman named Faith. However, the cult gathering
disillusions and embitters him. He loses his faith, and he spends the
rest of his life in pessimism and gloom. This much is clear, but the
precise nature of Brown's experience is not. Does he really make a trip
into the woods? It would seem so, but by the story's end, Hawthorne
states that the whole episode may have been no more than a dream or
nightmare, and he speaks about it as such. Yet when the morning
comes, Brown walks back into town as though he is returning from an
overnight trip, and he recoils in horror from a number of his fellow
villagers, including his wife. Just as uncertain is the identity of the
stranger whom Brown encounters on the path. The man resembles
Brown's father, but his serpentlike walking stick suggests the devil,
who later presides at the satanic ritual deep within the forest.

---

[1]See pages 317–26 for this story.
[2]Central idea.
[3]Thesis sentence.

The fact is, however, that Hawthorne was clearly not interested   [3]
in producing a realistic imitation of life in detail. Rather, he wanted
to get at the inward, psychological reality of persons like Goodman
Brown, who mistakenly build a wall of anger and bitterness between
themselves and the people around them. From this perspective,
Brown's walk into the forest is a symbol of one of the ways in which
people may turn sour. In Brown's case, he falls under the control of
his will to condemn evil. So strong is his view that he rejects anyone
who does not measure up, even if he must live the rest of his life
spiritually alone as a result. Although he is at the extreme edge, he is
like many people who cannot forgive and get along with anyone who
is different from themselves.

Brown is, thus, anything but heroic, even if he is the story's major   [4]
character. Nevertheless, the story is provocative and compelling, and it
raises many timely questions. For example, how can something that is
designed for human salvation, like the religious system that Brown
inherited, lead its followers into intolerance and short-sightedness?
Does the failure result from the people who misunderstand the basic
message of the system or from the system itself? To what degree can
the religious structure of the story be related to political and social
institutions? Should any religious or political philosophy be given
greater importance than the goodwill that is the essential cornerstone
of society? Could any free society survive for long if it were composed
of people like Goodman Brown after his dream, or would it turn into
some form of absolutism or despotism and soon be reduced to
persecution on moral, religious, or political grounds?

Although the materials of the story belong to Salem during the   [5]
late seventeenth century—the location and time, one might remember, of the infamous witchcraft trials—it has many layers. It is a
memorable study in spiritual deterioration and a vivid example of
the need for trust, goodwill, and generosity in human relationships.
Without such will, life itself would soon resemble the life lived by
Goodman Brown, whose vision makes his world bleak and forbidding—
a place controlled by negation and death rather than understanding
and acceptance.

Work Cited

Hawthorne, Nathaniel. "Young Goodman Brown." Edgar V. Roberts.
  Writing About Literature. 13th ed. New York: Pearson, 2012.
  317–26. Print.

Commentary on the Essay

This general review follows a normal pattern of exposition. The introduction briefly presents essential background, and it states a central idea about the timeliness of Hawthorne's ideas. Paragraph 2 deals with the problem of the dreamlike vagueness of the narrative. Paragraph 3 contains an explanation of the vagueness inasmuch as Hawthorne's point is to dramatize the way in which people become intolerant. Paragraph 4 treats the timeliness of this analysis in terms of important questions raised by the story. The last paragraph is a short tribute to the quality of Hawthorne's insights.

Throughout this illustrative review, the purpose is not to examine any of the points in great depth, but rather to give readers topics to consider in detail when they themselves consider the work.

Second Illustrative Essay (Designed for a Particular Group—Here, a Religious Group)

Religious Intolerance and Hawthorne's Story
"Young Goodman Brown"[4]

[1]   Even though Hawthorne's allegorical story "Young Goodman Brown" is set in late seventeenth-century Massachusetts, it continues to have great significance for religious people today.[5] The tale concerns the shattering of the principal character's illusions about human beings as a result of his witnessing a nightmarish witches' Sabbath in a forest. Brown becomes a despairing person and deprives those around him of love and light. This material could easily be interpreted psychologically or politically, but the Christian

[4]See pages 317–26 for this story.
[5]Central idea.

context of the story invites discussion of Hawthorne's religious ideas. His significant message is both timely and biblically based.[6]

The story is timely because it deals with—rather, exposes—the [2] development of religious intolerance. One would like to dismiss the topic as a dead issue in today's world. The reality is otherwise. Intolerance has not vanished along with seventeenth-century Salem but is still here, in many nations of the world, and will continue to exist as long as misperception and distrust like Brown's can exist. He sets up his own religious standards, and no one else can measure up. Surely this formula makes for intolerance, no matter when and where it happens.

The Bible, a work that is at once both ancient and current, is [3] the basis for "Young Goodman Brown." It is true that scripture can be used to justify intolerant views like those by which Goodman Brown judges his fellow Salem residents. We may presume that people in Brown's day, like many in our own, were often urged to seek perfection (for example, Genesis 17:1; Matthew 5:48). Almost all the letters of Paul, together with the Pastoral and General epistles, give advice to Christians to purify life (see Romans 12; Ephesians 5:6; I Timothy 5:22; James 4:8). There is no shortage of such advice. Indeed, there is so much that one might believe, as Brown does, that people who seemingly ignore it cannot continue to call themselves serious members of the religious community.

More positively, however, the rigorous side of things seems [4] to represent no more than a partial view of the biblical message. Nowhere does the Bible say that those who do not measure up should be condemned by *people*. The task of judgment, and even of vengeance if necessary, belongs to God alone (see Psalms 94:1 and Romans 12:19, for example). For human beings, the Bible constantly stresses forgiveness, and this is what Brown lacks. Here are only two of the many passages emphasizing forgiveness:

> When ye stand praying, forgive, if ye have ought against any; that your Father also which is in heaven may forgive you your trespasses. (Mark 11:25)

---

[6]Thesis sentence.

Forbearing one another, and forgiving one another, if any man
have a quarrel against any: even as Christ forgave you, so also do
ye. (Colossians 3:13)

One can go beyond advice like this to examples such as those of the
Good Samaritan (Luke 10:29–31) and the Samaritan woman at
the well (John 4:7–42). These people were outsiders, not members
of the same community, yet Jesus regarded them lovingly.

[5]   Charity, love, forgiveness, and toleration—these are virtues that
people need today and that were needed in seventeenth-century
Salem, but Goodman Brown ignores them totally. He suffers from
the "holier-than-thou" symptom that does nothing so well as to
alienate others. It is no wonder that the final words of the story
describe his offspring following Brown to his grave but who "carved
no hopeful verse upon his tombstone, for his dying hour was gloom."
Certainly, we should all strive for perfection, but we should also leave
judgment in greater hands and rather spend our time working
toward understanding. In "Young Goodman Brown," Hawthorne
has dramatized this point vividly and powerfully.

Work Cited

Hawthorne, Nathaniel. "Young Goodman Brown." Edgar V. Roberts.
Writing About Literature. 13th ed. New York: Pearson, 2012.
317–26. Print.

Commentary on the Essay

This illustrative review is intended for an audience that is concerned about religious
issues. As such, it considers the story not as a general work of art but as one with religious and moral implications. The essay works in two directions: first, as a presentation
of arguments favoring religious tolerance and, second, as an attempt to supply enough
biblical background to show that the views in Hawthorne's story are based in scripture.
The aim of the review is, thus, just as much persuasion as exposition and argument.

The first paragraph introduces the central idea about the story's religious significance, concluding with the essay's thesis sentence. Paragraph 2 demonstrates that misperceptions such as Brown's can occur at any time. Therefore, the story is, first of all, about a permanent human condition. Paragraphs 3 and 4 deal with biblical passages that possibly have a bearing, first, on explaining Brown's conduct (paragraph 3) and, second, criticizing it (paragraph 4). This material is not the sort that one might bring out in an analysis of, say, the ideas in the work, because it deals more with the relevant biblical ideas than with Hawthorne's story. Nevertheless, the ideas are appropriate here because a review is to be considered as a much freer form than an analysis. The last paragraph utilizes the negative example of Brown as an incentive for tolerance.

Although this illustrative review deals with religious issues, it does so because of the intended audience. For an audience with other interests, a different treatment would be appropriate, even for the same work of literature.

Third Illustrative Essay (A Personal Review for a General Audience)

Security and Hawthorne's Story "Young Goodman Brown,"[7]

    The major prop of life is security and certainty. These elements of [1] stability stem from confidence in the people around us, secure laws, a sound economy, hope, and trust in ourselves and in the world generally. The loss of any of these stabilizing props destroys our security and may produce panic.[8] It is this kind of panic that Nathaniel Hawthorne portrays in his story "Young Goodman Brown." The major character is Goodman Brown, who is a still-youthful resident of seventeenth-century colonial Salem in Massachusetts. Deep in a nighttime forest—either in a dream or in a fantastic spell—he witnesses a nightmarish satanic cult meeting, and because he sees his wife there together with the elders and dignitaries of the town, he loses the security that comes from his confidence in others. His story makes one think about the importance of the many things—personal, political, and natural—that provide us with a secure outlook on life.[9]

---

[7]See pages 317–26 for this story.
[8]Central idea.
[9]Thesis sentence.

[2]   Personal security can depend on almost as many situations as there are people. Vital to Brown is his belief in the personal and religious commitment of his wife, Faith. Many people similarly base their lives on their confidence in those around them. But much can happen to disturb such security. Friends on whom we count might not be helpful when we need them because we badly misjudged them. A serious illness of someone close may have a devastating effect on confidence in the continuity of life itself. And, like Brown, we might imprison ourselves in our own suspicions and never again be able to trust anyone else. Personal security is delicate, even though the example of Brown, who does not try to explore the truth of his shattered illusions, shows that efforts at understanding might help to restore personal security that is mortally threatened.

[3]   If personal security is fragile, political security is even more so. At election times, there are always claims and counterclaims, so we are never absolutely sure about the political wisdom we follow. Like many people, Brown loses faith in the local dignitaries, and he can never participate again with confidence in church and home. Today, on a world scale, we have even greater problems with our security, for happenings both abroad and in our nation disturb financial security and also threaten our very lives with distant hatreds and senseless attacks, which constantly verge on becoming big enough to cause the beginning of general wars. Certainly, political security is worth the many efforts of constant negotiating spent by diplomats in trying to gain it.

[4]   In the natural world, too, we assume a great deal on which we depend absolutely. We could not drive around a blind corner without the confidence that the road will continue, even though we cannot see the bends in the road before we make our turns. We normally assume that the sun will rise and set, that rain will fall, that crops will grow (or at least appear in stores and restaurants), that the air will be breathable, and that the earth generally will be a good place. But often there are fires, famines, tornadoes, earthquakes, floods, hurricanes, and volcanic eruptions. What occurs to Good-man Brown is, to him, a psychological equivalent, for his world is

shattered by the dreams (or nightmares) of a single night. Such events can make people doubt the very ground they walk on.

The upshot of Hawthorne's story about poor Goodman Brown is that security—confidence about the world and people—is subject to accident and to design. It is true, nevertheless, that people can work to make themselves more secure. Perhaps Brown's greatest flaw is that he apparently does not try to get to the bottom of what he has seen. He accepts his vision without question, and with his security destroyed, he descends into a life of "gloom" and depression. It is the possibility that people can always try at least to make things better that provides a gauge by which to measure Brown and also ourselves. One should be grateful to Hawthorne for having so memorably dramatized these ideas in "Young Goodman Brown."

[5]

Work Cited

Hawthorne, Nathaniel. "Young Goodman Brown." Edgar V. Roberts. *Writing About Literature*. 13th ed. New York: Pearson, 2012. 317–26. Print.

Commentary on the Essay

This third illustrative review is a personal essay on a topic—security—suggested by Hawthorne's story. The material from "Young Goodman Brown" is, thus, introduced as a part, although a major part, of the train of thought. The method of development is primarily illustration.

Unlike the religiously based audience that we visualized for the second illustrative essay, the intended audience here is a general one that is concerned with many broad topics, such as the personal, political, and natural ones discussed. The goal is to cause readers to reconsider and redefine the topic of security.

Paragraph 1 introduces security as a topic, attempts a definition, relates the topic to Hawthorne's story, and concludes with the essay's thesis sentence. Even though "Young Goodman Brown" is a religious story about how the hero's perceptions of life are destroyed by satanic representatives in a vague and mysterious nightmarish experience, the body of the illustrative essay does not deal with the story's religious issues but instead goes into separate but connected topics. Paragraph 2 deals with the first of these—special situations that threaten personal security; paragraph 3 considers political threats; and paragraph 4 brings in references to threats from the forces of nature. The concluding paragraph includes additional references to Goodman Brown, relating his passive character transformation to a need for a more aggressive pursuit of security.

Topics for Studying and Discussing the Writing of Reviews

Write a review on any of the following topics, being sure to consider the audience for whom the review is intended.

1. A review of Glaspell's *Trifles* for people who are interested in law and the sentencing of offenders.
2. A review of Layton's "Rhine Boat Trip" for people who are interested in World War II and the Holocaust.
3. A review of Lowell's "Patterns" for a group of women or men whose husbands, wives, sons, or daughters have been killed in war or police work.
4. A review of Chekhov's *The Bear* for people who like to laugh at humor and farce.
5. A review of Poe's "The Cask of Amontillado" for fans of mystery and horror stories.
6. A review of Arnold's "Dover Beach" for a group of philosophers.
7. A review of Blake's "The Tyger" for a group of ministers.
8. A review of Frost's "Desert Places" for a group of psychologists.
9. A review of Hughes's "Negro" for people who are concerned with racial issues.
10. A review of a work that you have recently read and liked for a group of compatible friends with ideas that are similar to your own ideas.

Chapter 18

Writing Examinations on Literature

Getting a good grade on a literature exam, or on any exam, is largely a result of intelligent and skillful preparation. Preparation means that you (1) study the material assigned, in conjunction with the comments made in class by your instructor and by fellow students in discussion; (2) develop and reinforce your own thoughts; (3) anticipate exam questions by creating and answering your own practice questions; and (4) understand the precise function of the test in your education.

First, realize that the test is not designed either to trap you or to hold down your grade. The grade that you receive is a reflection of your achievement in the course. If your grades are high, congratulations; keep doing what you have been doing. If your grades are low, you can improve them through diligent and systematic study. Students who can easily do satisfactory work might do superior work if they improved their habits of study and preparation. From whatever level you begin, *you can increase your achievement by improving your study methods.*

Your instructor has three major concerns in evaluating your tests (assuming the correct use of English): (1) to assess the extent of your command over the subject material of the course (How good is your retention?), (2) to assess how well you respond to a question or deal with an issue (How well do you separate the important from the unimportant? That is, how well do you think?), and (3) to assess how well you draw conclusions about the material (How well are you educating yourself?).

Answer the Questions That Are Asked

Many elements go into writing good answers on tests, but *responsiveness* is the most important. A major cause of low exam grades is that students *often do not answer the questions asked.* Does a lack of responsiveness seem surprising? The problem is that some students do no more than retell a story or restate an argument, and they do not zero in on the issues in the question. This problem is not uncommon. Therefore, if you are asked, "Why does . . . ?," be sure to emphasize the *why* and use the *does* primarily to exemplify the *why.* If the question is about *organization*, focus on organization. If the question is about the *interpretation* of an idea, deal with the interpretation of the idea. In short, *always respond directly to the question or instruction.* Answer what is asked. Compare the following two answers to the same question.

Question: *How is the setting of Shirley Jackson's "The Lottery" important in the story's development?*

Answer A

The setting of Jackson's "The Lottery" is a major element in the development of the story. The scene is laid in the town square of an unnamed American village, between the bank and the post office. There are many flowers blooming, and the grass is green. A pile of stones is set up in the square. Into this place, just before ten o'clock in the morning, come the villagers to hold their annual lottery. There are 300 of them—children, men, and housewives. In the center of the square the black lottery box is set up on a three-legged stool. This box has been around for years, and looks broken and shabby. The setting requires that the villagers gather around the box and that the male head representing each family draw a slip of paper for his family. Once they have all drawn, it is discovered that Bill Hutchinson and his family are the "winners." He is not a lucky winner, however, because his family of five has to draw again individually. Bill's wife Tessie draws the black spot that Bill had drawn before for the entire family. Then all the villagers in the square fall upon her to stone her to death, because that is the fate of the "winner." The setting here is, therefore, all important in the development of the story.

Answer B

The setting of Jackson's "The Lottery is a major element in the development of the story. As a setting for the action, the town square of an unnamed American village is large enough to contain all 300 citizens, a black lottery box, and piles of stones that the people can pick up and hurl. As a setting in time, the entire action takes place within a two-hour period between ten in the morning and noon. As a seasonal setting, the date of June 27, specifically mentioned as the day of the lottery, suggests a thoughtless and cruel early summer ritual of some sort. As a setting in character and society, the ordinary lifestyle of the people suggests only small intelligence. It is not unlikely that such people would preserve a cruel and meaningless custom without thinking about its ghastly and horribly cruel effects. In all respects, the setting in place, time, season, and culture is all important in the development of the story.

Although answer A introduces important elements of the story's setting, it does not stress the *importance* of these elements in the story itself. It is also cluttered with details that have no bearing on the question. Indeed, it does not answer the question at all. By contrast, Answer B focuses directly on the connection, stressing how four aspects of the setting relate to the story's development. Because of this emphasis, Answer B is shorter than Answer A by sixty-two words (224 words to 162). That is, with the focus directly on the issue of the question, there is no need for irrelevant narrative details.

Thus, Answer A is unresponsive and unnecessarily long, whereas Answer B is responsive and includes only enough detail to exemplify the major points. Answer B succeeds in answering the question.

Systematic Preparation

Your challenge is how best to prepare yourself to have a knowledgeable and ready mind at examination time. If you simply cram facts into your head for the test in the hope that you can adjust to the questions, you will likely flounder. You need a systematic approach.

Read and Reread the Material on Which You Are to Be Examined

Above all, recognize that your preparation should begin as soon as the course begins, not on the night before the exam. Complete each assignment by the due date, for you will understand the classroom discussion only if you know the material (see also the guides for study in Chapter 1, pages 14–15). Then, about a week before the exam, review each assignment, preferably rereading everything completely. If particular passages were read and discussed in class, make a special point of studying those passages and referring to the notes you took at the time of the discussions. With this preparation, your study on the night before the exam will be fruitful because it is the climax of your preparation, not your entire preparation.

Construct Your Own Questions: Go on the Attack

To prepare yourself well for an exam, plan to read *actively*, not passively. Read with a goal, and *go on the attack* by anticipating test conditions: Create, and then answer, your own practice questions. Yes, make up your own questions. Don't waste time, however, in trying to guess the questions you think your instructor might ask. Guessing correctly might happen (and wouldn't you be happy if it did?), but do not turn your study into a game of chance. Instead, arrange the subject matter by asking yourself questions that help you to get things straight.

How can you construct your own questions? It is not as hard as you might think. Your instructor may have announced certain topics or ideas to be tested on the exam, and you might develop questions from these, or you might apply general questions to the specifics of your assignments, as in the following examples.

1. **Ideas about a character and the interactions of characters** (see also Chapter 4, 82ff). What is character *A* like? How does *A* grow or change in the work? What does *A* learn or not learn that brings about the conclusion? To what degree does *A* represent a type or an idea? How does character *B* influence *A*? Does a change in character *C* bring about any corresponding change in *A*?

2. **Ideas about technical and structural questions.** These can be broad, covering everything from point of view (Chapter 3, 65ff) to the rhymes of poetry (Chapter 13, 192ff). The best guide here is to study those technical aspects that have been discussed in class, for it is unlikely that you will be asked to go beyond the levels considered in classroom discussion.

3. **Ideas about events or situations.** What relationship does episode *A* have to situation *B*? Does *C's* thinking about situation *D* have any influence on the outcome of event *E*?
4. **Ideas about a problem** (see also Chapter 14, 202ff). Why is character *A* or situation *X* this way and not that way? Is the conclusion justified by the ideas and events leading up to it?

Rephrase Your Notes as Questions

Because your classroom notes are the fullest record you have about your instructor's views, one of the best ways to construct questions is to develop them from these notes. As you select topics and phrase questions, refer to passages from the texts that were studied by the class and stressed by your instructor. If there is time, memorize as many important phrases or lines as you can from the studied works. Plan to incorporate these into your answers as evidence to support the points you make. Remember that it is useful to work not only with main ideas from your notes but also with matters such as character, setting, imagery, symbolism, ideas, and organization.

Obviously, you cannot make questions from all your notes, and you will, therefore, need to select from those that seem most important. As an example, here is a short note written by a student during a classroom discussion of Shakespeare's *Hamlet*: "A study in how private problems get public, how a court conspiracy can produce disastrous national and international consequences." Notice that you can devise practice questions from this note.

1. In what ways is *Hamlet* not only about private problems but also about public ones?
2. Why should the political consequences of Claudius's murder of Hamlet's father be considered disastrous?

The principle here is that most exam questions do not ask just about *what*, but rather get into the issues of *why*. Observe that the first question, therefore, introduces the words "in what ways" to the phrasing of the note. For the second question, the word "Why" has been used. Either qualification creates the need for you to study pointedly, and neither asks you merely to describe events from the play. Question 1 requires you to consider the wider political effects of Hamlet's hostility toward Claudius, including Hamlet's murder of Polonius and the subsequent madness of Ophelia. Question 2, with its emphasis on disaster, leads you to consider not only the ruination of the hopes and lives of the characters in the play but also the importance of young Fortinbras and the eventual establishment of Norwegian control over Denmark after Claudius and Hamlet have died. If you were to spend fifteen or twenty minutes writing practice answers to questions such as these, you could be confident in taking an examination on the material, for you could likely adapt, or even partially duplicate, your study answers to any exam question about the personal and political results of Claudius's murder of his brother.

Make Up and Answer Your Own Questions Even When Time Is Short

Whatever your subject, spend as much study time as possible making and answering your own questions. *Writing practice answers is one of the most important things you can do in preparing for your exam.* Remember also to work with your own remarks and the ideas you develop in the notebook or journal entries that you make when doing your regular assignments (see Chapter 1, p. 14). Many of these will give you additional ideas for your own questions, which you can practice along with the questions you develop from your classroom notes.

Obviously, with limited study time, you will not be able to create your own questions and answers indefinitely. Even so, don't neglect to ask and answer your own questions. If time is too short for full practice answers, write out the main heads, or topics, of an answer. When the press of time (or the need for sleep) no longer permits you to make even such a brief outline answer, keep thinking of questions and their answers as you go to the exam. *Never read passively or unresponsively; always read with a creative, question-and-answer goal.* Think of studying as a preliminary step leading to writing.

The time you spend in this way will be valuable, for as you practice, you will develop control and, therefore, confidence. Often, those who have difficulty with tests, or claim a phobia about them, prepare passively rather than actively. Your instructor's test questions compel responsiveness, organization, thought, and insight. But a passively prepared student is not ready for this challenge and, therefore, writes answers that are unresponsive and filled with summary. The grade for such a performance is low, and the student's fear of tests is reinforced. The best way to break such long-standing patterns of fear or uncertainty is to study actively and creatively.

Study with a Classmate

Often, another person's thoughts can help you understand the material to be tested. Find a fellow student with whom you can work comfortably but also productively, for the two of you together can help each other individually. In view of the need for steady preparation throughout a course, regular discussions about the material are a good idea. You might also make your joint study systematic by setting aside a specific evening or afternoon for work sessions. Many students have said that they encounter problems in taking exams because they are unfamiliar with the ways in which questions are phrased. Consequently, they waste time in understanding and interpreting the questions before they begin their answers, and sometimes they kill all their time because they misunderstand the questions entirely. If you work with a fellow student, however, and trade questions, you will be gaining experience (and confidence) in dealing with this basic difficulty about exams.[1] Working with someone else can be extremely rewarding, just as it can be stimulating and instructive. Make the effort, and you'll never regret it.

---

[1] If you study with a fellow student, it might be advisable to tell your instructor about this and to sit as far away as possible from each other at the time of the exam.

Two Basic Types of Questions About Literature

Generally, there are two types of questions on literature exams. Keep them in mind as you prepare. The first type is *factual*, or *mainly objective*; the second is *general, comprehensive, broad*, or *mainly subjective*. Except for multiple-choice questions, very few questions are purely objective in a literature course.

Anticipate the Kinds of Factual Questions That Might Be Asked

Multiple-Choice Questions Ask You to Pick the Most Accurate and Likely Answers Multiple-choice questions are almost necessarily factual. Your instructor will most likely use them for short quizzes, usually on days when an assignment is due, to make sure that you are keeping up with the reading. Multiple-choice questions test your knowledge of facts and your ingenuity in perceiving subtleties of phrasing. On literature exams, however, this type of question is rare.

Identification Questions Ask for Accuracy, Explanation, and a Certain Amount of Interpretation Identification questions are interesting and challenging because they require you both to know details and to develop thoughts about them. This type of question is frequently used as a check on the depth and scope of your reading. In fact, an entire exam could be composed only of identification questions, each requiring perhaps five minutes for you to answer. Here are some typical examples of what you might be asked to identify:

1. **A character.** To identify a character, it is necessary to describe briefly the character's position, main activity, and significance. Let us assume that Fortunato is the character to be identified, from Poe's "The Cask of Amontillado." Our answer should state that he is the unsuspecting victim whom Montresor leads to death by live imprisonment in the underground vaults of Montresor's family estate (main activity). Fortunato's pride and gullibility are the major causes of the story's action, and he embodies the story's theme that human pride often leads not to success but rather to doom (significance) and, if you wish, that offending others may cause them to retaliate secretly and hurtfully. Under the category of "significance," of course, you might develop as many ideas as you have time for, but the short example here is a general model for most identification questions.

2. **Incidents or situations.** In identifying an incident or a situation (for example, "A woman mourns the death of her husband"), first describe the circumstances and the principal character involved in them (Mrs. Popov's reaction to her widowhood in Chekhov's play *The Bear*). Then describe the importance of this incident or situation in the work. For example, in *The Bear*, Mrs. Popov is mourning the death of her husband, and in the course of the play, Chekhov uses her feelings to show amusingly that life and love with real emotion are stronger than allegiance to the dead.

3. **Things, places, and dates.** Your instructor may ask you to identify a hair ribbon (Hawthorne's "Young Goodman Brown") or a beach (Arnold's "Dover Beach") or the date of Amy Lowell's "Patterns" (1916). For dates, you may be

given a leeway of five or ten years. What is important about a date is not so much exactness as historical and intellectual perspective. The date of Lowell's "Patterns," for example, was the third year of World War I, and the poem consequently reflects a reaction against the protracted and senseless loss of life in war (even though details of the poem itself suggest an eighteenth-century war). To claim "World War I" as the date of the poem would be acceptable as an answer if it happens that you cannot remember the exact date.

4. **Quotations.** You should remember enough of the text to identify a passage taken from it or at least to make an informed guess. Generally, you should (1) locate the quotation, if you remember it, or else describe what you think is the probable location; (2) show the ways in which the quotation is typical of the content and style of the work you have read; and (3) describe the importance of the passage. If you suffer a lapse of memory, write a reasoned and careful explanation of your guess. Even if your guess is not actually correct, the knowledge and cogency of your explanation should give you points.

Technical and Analytical Questions and Problems Require You to Relate Knowledge and Technical Understanding to the Issue In a scale of ascending importance, the third and most difficult type of factual question relates to those matters of writing with which much of this book is concerned: technique and analysis. You might be asked to analyze the *setting, images, point of view,* or *important idea* of a work; you might be asked about the *tone and style* of a story or poem; or you might be asked to *explicate* a poem that may or may not be duplicated for your benefit (if it is not duplicated, woe to students who have not carefully studied their assignments). Questions like these assume that you have technical knowledge; they also ask you to examine the text within the limitations imposed by the directions.

Obviously, technical questions occur more frequently in advanced courses than in elementary ones, and the questions become more subtle as the courses become more advanced. Instructors of introductory courses may ask about ideas and problems but will likely not use many of the others unless they state their intentions to do so in advance or unless technical terms have been studied in class.

Questions of this type require fairly long answers, so allow perhaps fifteen to twenty-five minutes apiece. If you have two or more of these questions, try to space your time sensibly; do not devote 80 percent of your time to one question and leave only 20 percent for the rest.

Understand How Your Responses Will Be Judged and Graded

Identification Questions Probe Your Understanding and Application of Facts In all factual questions, your instructor is testing (1) your factual command and (2) your quickness in relating a part to the whole. Thus, suppose you are identifying the incident "A man kills a canary." It is correct to say that Susan Glaspell's play *Trifles* is the location of the incident, that the murdered farmer John Wright killed the bird, and that the canary belonged to his wife, Minnie. Knowledge of these details clearly establishes that you know the facts. But a strong answer must go further. Even in the brief exam time you have for short answers, you should always connect the facts (1) to major causation in the work, (2) to an important idea or ideas, (3) to the development of the work, and (4) for a quotation, to the style. Time is short, and you must be selective, but if you can make your answer move from facts to significance, you will always fashion superior responses. Along these lines, let us look at an answer identifying the action from *Trifles*:

A Man Kills a Canary

The action is from Glaspell's *Trifles*. The man who kills the bird is John Wright, the dead man, and the owner is his wife, Minnie, who, before the story begins, has been jailed on suspicion of murder. The wringing of the little bird's neck is important because it is shown as an indignity and outrage in Minnie Wright's desperate life, and it obviously makes her angry enough to put a rope around Wright's neck to strangle him in his sleep. It is, thus, the cause not only of the murder but also of the investigation that has brought the two lawmen and their wives to the Wright kitchen. In fact, the killing of the bird makes the story possible because it is the wives who discover the dead bird's remains, and this discovery is the means by which Glaspell highlights them as the major characters of the action. Because the husband's senselessly brutal act shows how bleak the married life of Minnie Wright actually was, it dramatizes the lonely and victimized plight of women in a male-dominated way of life like that on the Wright farm. The discovery also raises the issue of legality and morality, because the women decide to conceal the evidence, thereby protecting Minnie Wright from conviction and punishment.

Any of the points in this answer could be developed as a separate essay, but the paragraph is successful as a short answer because it goes beyond fact to deal with significance. Clearly, such answers are possible at the time of an exam only if you have devoted considerable thought beforehand to the works on which you are to be tested. The more thinking and practicing you do before an exam, the better your answers will be. Remember this advice as an axiom: *You cannot write superior answers if you do not think extensively before the exam.* By ambitious advance study, you will be able to reduce surprise to a minimum.

Longer Factual Questions Probe Your Knowledge and Your Ability to Organize Your Thoughts More extended factual questions also require more thoroughly developed organization. Remember that for these questions, your skill in writing essays is important because the quality of your composition will determine a major share of your instructor's evaluation of your answers. It is, therefore, best to take several minutes to pull your thoughts together before you begin to write. Remember, *a ten-minute planned answer is preferable to a twenty-five-minute unplanned answer*. You do not need to write every possible fact on each particular question. Of greater importance is the use to which you put the facts that you know and the organization and development of your answer. Use a sheet of scratch paper to jot down important facts and your ideas about them in relation to the question. Then put them together, phrase a thesis sentence, and use your facts to exemplify and support your thesis.

It is always necessary to begin your answer pointedly, using key words or phrases from the question or direction if possible, so that your answer will have thematic shape. You should *never* begin an answer with "Because" and then go on from there without referring again to the question. To be most responsive during the short time available for an exam, you should use the question as your guide for your answer. Let us suppose that you have the following question on your test: "How does Glaspell use details in *Trifles* to reveal the character of Minnie Wright?" The most common way to go astray on such a question—and the easiest thing to do also—is to concentrate on Minnie Wright's character rather than on how Glaspell uses detail to bring out her character. The word *how* makes a vast difference in the nature of the final answer; hence, a good method on the exam is to duplicate key phrases in the question to ensure that you make your major points clear. Here is an opening sentence that uses the key words and phrases (italicized here) from the question to organize thought and provide focus:

> Glaspell *uses details* of setting, marital relationships, and personal habits *to reveal the character of Minnie Wright* as a person of great but unfulfilled potential whom anger has finally overcome.

Because this sentence repeats the key phrases from the question and because it promises to show *how* the details are to be focused on the character, it suggests that the answer to follow will be responsive.

General or Comprehensive Questions Require You to Connect a Number of Works to Broader Matters of Idea and Technique

General or comprehensive questions are particularly important on final examinations, when your instructor is testing your total comprehension of the course material. Considerable time is usually allowed for answering this type of question, which can be phrased in a number of ways.

1. A *direct question* asking about philosophy, underlying attitudes, main ideas, characteristics of style, backgrounds, and so on. Here are some possible questions in this category.
   What use do _____, _____, and _____ make of the topic of _____?
   Define and characterize the short story as a genre of literature, using examples from the stories of _____, _____, and _____.
   Describe the use of dialogue by _____, _____, and _____.
   Contrast the technique of point of view as used by _____, _____, and _____.
2. A *"comment" question*, often based on an extensive quotation, borrowed from a critic or written by your instructor for the occasion, asking about a broad class of writers, a literary movement, or the like. Your instructor may ask you to treat this question broadly (taking in many writers) or to apply the quotation to a specific writer.
3. A *"suppose" question*, such as "What advice might Minnie Wright of Glaspell's *Trifles* give the speakers of Lowell's 'Patterns' (p. 357) and Keats's 'Bright Star' (p. 355)?" or "What might the speaker of Rossetti's poem 'Echo' say if she were told that her dead lover was actually a person like Goodman Brown of Hawthorne's 'Young Goodman Brown'?" Although "suppose" questions seem whimsical at

first sight, they have a serious design and should prompt original and radical thinking. The first question, for example, might cause a test writer to bring out, from Minnie Wright's perspective, that the love expressed by both speakers overlooks the possibilities of changes in character over a long period. She would likely sympathize with the speaker of "Patterns," a woman, but she might also say that the speaker's enthusiasm would need to be augmented by the constant exertion of kindness and mutual understanding. For the speaker of "Bright Star," a man, Mrs. Wright might say that the steadfast love he seeks should be linked to thoughtfulness and constant communication as well as passion.

Although "suppose" questions (and answers) are speculative, the need to respond to them requires a detailed consideration of the works involved, and in this respect, the "suppose" question is a salutary means of learning. It is of course difficult to prepare for a "suppose" question, which you can, therefore, regard as a test not only of your knowledge but also of your adaptability, inventiveness, and ingenuity.

Understand How Your Responses to General and Comprehensive Questions Will Be Judged and Graded

When answering broad, general questions, you are dealing with an unstructured situation, and you must not only supply an answer but—equally important—also create a *structure* within which your answer can have meaning. You might say that you make up your own specific question out of the original general question. If you were asked to consider the role of women as seen in works by Lowell, Maupassant, and Glaspell, for example, you would structure the question by focusing a number of clearly defined topics. A possible way to begin answering such a question might be this:

> Lowell, Maupassant, and Glaspell present a view of female resilience by demonstrating the inner control, endurance, and power of adaptation of their major characters.

With this sort of focus, you would be able to proceed point by point, introducing supporting data as you form your answer.

As a general rule, the best method for answering a comprehensive question is comparison-contrast (see also Chapter 15). The reason is that in dealing with, say, a general question on Rossetti, Chekhov, and Keats, it is too easy to write *three* separate essays rather than *one*. Thus, you should try to create a topic such as "the treatment of real or idealized love" or "the difficulties in male-female relationships" and then develop your answer point by point rather than writer by writer. By creating your answer in this way, you can bring in references to each or all of the writers as they become relevant. If you were to treat each writer separately, your comprehensive answer would lose focus and effectiveness, and it would also be repetitive.

Remember that in judging your response to a general question, your instructor is interested in seeing (1) how effectively you perceive and explain the significant issues in the question, (2) how intelligently and clearly you organize your answer, and (3) how persuasively you link your answer to materials from the work as supporting evidence.

Bear in mind that in answering comprehensive questions, you do not have the freedom or license to write about anything at all. You must stick to the questions and must first of all directly answer the questions. The freedom you do have is the freedom to create your own organization and development in response to the questions that your instructor has asked you. The underlying idea of the comprehensive, general question is that you possess special knowledge and insight that cannot be discovered by more factual questions. You must, therefore, demonstrate your power of thinking and of perceiving relationships. You need to formulate your own responses to the material and introduce evidence that reflects your own insights and command of information.

A final thought: Try to enjoy the learning experience that preparing for an exam offers you. You will surprise yourself and, hopefully, discover yourself. Good luck.

Chapter 19

Writing and Documenting the Research Essay; Using Extra Resources for Understanding

B roadly, **research** is the act of systematic investigation, examination, and experimentation. It is the basic tool of intellectual inquiry for anyone engaged in any discipline—physics, chemistry, biology, psychology, anthropology, history, and literature, to name just a few disciplines. With research, our understanding and our civilization grow; without it, they die.

The major assumption of doing research is that the researcher is reaching out into new areas of knowledge. With each assignment, the researcher acquires not only the knowledge gained from the particular task but also the skills needed to undertake further research and thereby to gain further knowledge. Some research tasks are elementary, such as using a dictionary to discover the meaning of a word and thereby enhancing one's understanding of an important passage. More involved research uses an array of resources: encyclopedias, biographies, introductions, critical studies, bibliographies, old newspapers, and histories. When you begin a research task, you usually have little or no knowledge about your topic, but with such resources you can acquire expert knowledge in a relatively short time.

Although research is the animating spark of all disciplines, our topic here is **literary research**—the systematic use of primary and secondary sources in studying a literary problem. In doing literary research, you consult not only individual works themselves (*primary sources*) but also many other works that shed light on them and interpret them (*secondary sources*). Typical research tasks are to learn important facts about a work and about the period in which it was written; to learn about the lives, careers, and other works of authors; to discover and apply the comments and judgments of modern or earlier critics; to learn details that help explain the meaning of works; and to learn about critical and artistic taste.

Selecting a Topic

In most instances, your instructor assigns a research essay on a specific topic. Sometimes, however, the choice of a topic will be left in your hands. For such assignments, it is helpful to know the types of research essays you might find most congenial. Here are some possibilities:

1. **A particular work.** You might treat character (for example, "The Character of Louise in Chopin's 'The Story of an Hour'" or "The Question of Whether Young Goodman Brown Is a Hero or a Dupe in Hawthorne's 'Young Goodman Brown'") or tone, ideas, structure, form, and the like. A research paper on a single work is similar to an essay on the same work, except that the research paper takes into account more views and facts than those you are likely to develop without the research.

2. **A particular author.** A project might focus on an idea or some facet of style, imagery, setting, or tone of the author, tracing the origins and development of the topic through a number of different stories, poems, or plays. Examples are "Poe's Treatment of the Speaker in His Short Stories" and "Frost's Selections of Topics in His Poetry." This type of essay is suitable for a number of shorter works, although it is also applicable for a single major work, such as a longer story, novel, or play.

3. **Comparison and contrast** (see Chapter 15). There are two types.

   A. *An idea or quality common to two or more authors.* Here you show points of similarity or contrast, or else you show how one author's work can be taken to criticize another's. A possible subject is "Contrasting Uses of Dialogue in Chekhov and Glaspell" or "The Theme of Male–Female Relations in Lowell, Chekhov, and Rossetti."

   B. *Different critical views of a particular work or body of works.* Sometimes much is to be gained from an examination of differing critical opinions on topics like "The Meaning of Poe's 'The Cask of Amontillado'" or "Various Views of Hawthorne's 'Young Goodman Brown.'" Such a study would attempt to determine the critical opinion and taste to which a work did or did not appeal, and it might also aim at conclusions about whether the work was in the advance or rear guard of its time.

4. **The influence of an idea, author, philosophy, political situation, or artistic movement on specific works of an author or authors.** An essay on influences can be specific and to the point, as in "Details of Black American Life as Reflected in Hughes's poem 'Negro,'" or it can be more abstract and critical, as in "The Influence of Racial Oppression and the Goal of Racial Equality on the Speaker of Hughes's Poem 'Negro.'"

5. **The origin of a particular work or type of work.** Such an essay might examine an author's biography to discover the germination and development of a work—for example, "'Kubla Khan' as an Outgrowth of Coleridge's Reading." Another way of discovering origins might be to relate a work to a particular type or tradition: "'The Cask of Amontillado' and Poe's Theory of the Short Story" or "Amy Lowell's 'Patterns' and Its Relationship to Antiwar Literature."

If you consider these types, an idea of what to write may come to you. Perhaps you have particularly liked one author or several authors. If so, you might start to think along the lines of types 1, 2, or 3. If you are interested in influences or origins, then type 4 or 5 may suit you better.

If you still cannot decide on a topic after rereading the works you have liked, then you should carry your search for a topic into your school library. Look up your author or authors in the computer or card catalogue. Your first goal should be to find a relatively recent book-length critical study published by a university press. Look for a title indicating that the book is a general one dealing with the author's major works rather than just one work.

Study the chapters that are relevant to the work or works you have chosen. Most writers of critical studies describe their purpose and plan in their introductions or first chapters, so begin with the first part of the book. If there is no separate chapter on the primary text, use the index as your guide to the relevant pages. Reading in this way will give you enough knowledge about the issues and ideas raised by the work to enable you to select a promising topic. Once you make your decision, you are ready to develop a working bibliography.

Setting Up a Working Bibliography

The first step in your research should be to create a working bibliography, a list of sources that you plan to consult during your research. A working bibliography is a tool that will evolve with you as you progress through the research process. For example, you might locate and read a source only to discover that it does not address your research topic, or you might come across a new and promising source to add to your working bibliography. Many instructors may encourage you to develop this bibliography as an annotated bibliography, a list of sources that includes your summary of the source and potentially your commentary on how this source will (or will not) be used in your essay. Either way, the goal of a working bibliography is to create a fairly comprehensive search bibliography to use as a guide when you begin to collect your sources.

Locating Sources

Through computer access, today's libraries are connected to a vast array of local, national, and even international libraries, so by using various online services, you can extend your research far beyond the capacities of your own library. Just a few years ago, the broadness of scope that electronic searches provide for most undergraduate students doing research assignments was not possible. Today, it is commonplace. Even with the astounding possibilities of electronically aided research, however, it is still necessary to read, evaluate, and take notes on your material before you can begin and complete a research essay. This section will teach you to use today's library services to find the materials you are seeking, but these services cannot do your reading, evaluating, note taking, and writing. All these sorts of tasks are still up to you, as they always have been for students doing research.

Searching the Internet

Many students choose to begin their research with the Internet. While Internet research may be familiar and convenient, it is important to be aware of its limitations. Most Web sites lack the type of thorough review to which print sources are subjected; therefore, the content you find online might not have been held to the same quality standards as the content that you would find in traditional research sources such as books or scholarly journals. In fact, with today's technology, anyone with access to the Internet and some basic software can publish a Web site. Therefore, it is essential that you evaluate Web sites carefully before trusting their content.

EVALUATING SOURCES

Evaluating sources is a two-pronged issue that involves assessing both a source's reliability and its relevance to your research topic. When evaluating sources, ask yourself:

- Who is the author of this source? Who is the publisher? Was this source created by an established author and a publisher that has a reputation for accuracy and reliability?
- What is the purpose of this source? To inform? To sell something? To advocate a cause? In other words, is the source biased by political or financial interests?
- Has the source been through a scholarly review process? If not, proceed with caution; ask yourself, does this source cite its own sources? Do its sources appear reliable?
- Does this source's discussion relate to your topic? How does this information address your research question?

While you must evaluate *all* sources for reliability and relevance, sources that are uncovered through Internet searches require extra caution on the part of the researcher. Your search-engine results will likely bring up many so-called free essays on literary topics that were written largely by beginners, not by scholars who have studied particular topics for many years and who have become experts in their analyses. The reason for using books and articles approved by scholarly publishers is that the works have been *refereed* by authorities in the particular field. If these authorities, or referees, have recommended publication, you are entitled to expect that the breadth and depth of the critical analyses will be well considered and reliable. A college-level literary paper should rely on such refereed sources, which are found primarily through the library.

To search the Internet through the use of various search engines, such as Google and Bing, you simply need to enter the name of an author, a title, or a topic, after which you will be linked to a host of resources from all over the world—home pages of specific authors, literary organizations, and works on various topics by contemporary writers. You may want to conduct your search through multiple search engines, because search engines index different sites and report their results in different formats. A useful tool with which you may want to experiment is a metasearch engine, such as Dogpile; metasearch engines allow you to search multiple search engines simultaneously. There are also more specialized search engines that you can utilize; for example, *Google Scholar* allows for broad searches of scholarly research.

The key to successful Internet searches, and really any electronic search, is utilizing appropriate search terms. A search for "Katherine Mansfield" using a general search engine could produce several thousand results, many of which will be unrelated to your topic. To avoid this type of overwhelming or disappointing result, use the advanced search options on your search engine. Most search engines will allow you to use quotation marks to indicate certain phrases or use the search terms *AND,* to limit your results (searches for only sites that include both search terms), *OR* (searches for sites that include only one of the search terms), *BUT NOT* (searches for sites that include the first term but do not include the second).

Using Internet research, you may quickly find a vast range of resources for your essay; however, the importance of evaluating sources found through Internet searches for reliability and relevance cannot be overstated (see the box on p. 267 on Evaluating Sources). Finally, an additional important caveat is that many sources still remain in printed journals and magazines that may be or, more probably, may not be on the Web. To make sure your searches are thorough, therefore, *you must never neglect to search for information that is available only through your library.*

Searching Library Resources

Libraries provide vast amounts of print and electronic resources; however, perhaps the most useful resource in your library is the reference librarian, who will be happy to help you make the most of the library's resources, so be sure to consult your reference librarian if you need any help with the research process.

Although card catalogues are still in use at some small libraries, your library's catalogue is most likely electronic. Using an electronic catalogue, you can search your library's holdings by author name, title, keyword, or in some catalogues, by subject.

An additional convenience is that many associated libraries have pooled their resources. Thus, if you use the services of a network of associated libraries, you can go

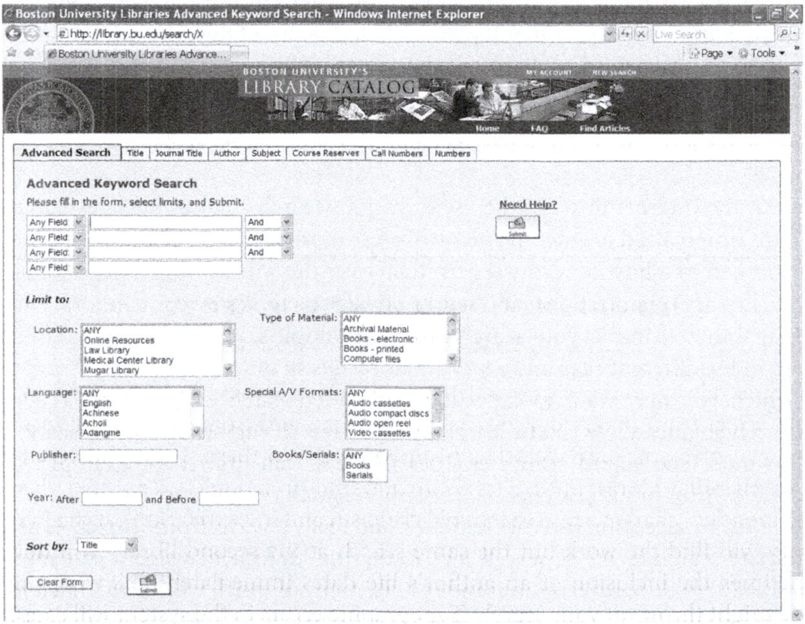

FIGURE 19.1 A major university's library catalog page.

to another library to use materials that are not accessible at your own college or branch. If distances are great and your own library does not have a book that you think is important to your project, you can ask a librarian to get the book for you through the Interlibrary Loan Service. Usually, given time, the libraries will accommodate as many of your needs as they can.

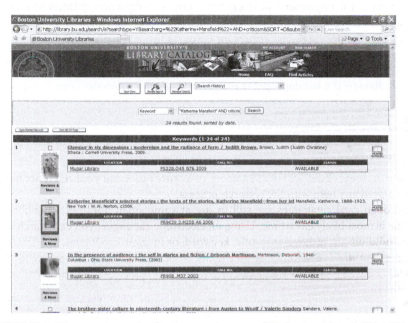

FIGURE 19.2 The search results for the search terms: *"Katherine Mansfield" AND criticism.* Each record lists the author, title, the type of resource, the call number (which indicates where in the library the resource can be found), and finally the availability of the resource (which indicates whether the book has been checked out or is on the shelf).

IMPORTANT CONSIDERATIONS ABOUT COMPUTER-AIDED RESEARCH

You must always remind yourself that online catalogues, such as those you might select from other colleges and universities, and from private organizations, can give you only what has been entered into them. If one university library classifies a work under "criticism and interpretation" and another classifies it under "characters," a search of "criticism and interpretation" at the first library will find the work but the same search at the second library will not. Sometimes the inclusion of an author's life dates immediately following the name might throw off your search. Typographic errors in the system will cause additional search problems, although many programs try to forestall such difficulties by providing "nearby" entries to enable you to determine whether incorrectly entered topics may in fact be helpful to you.

Also, if you use online services, be careful to determine the year when the computerization began. Many libraries have a recent commencement date— 1978, for example, or 1985. For completeness, therefore, you would need assistance in finding catalogue entries for items published before these years.

Review the Bibliographies in Major Critical Studies on Your Topic

One of the best ways to locate relevant and reliable sources for your working bibliography is to begin by finding major critical studies of the writer or writers. Again, use a book or books published by university presses, which will contain comprehensive bibliographies. Be careful to read the chapters on your primary work or works and to look for the footnotes or endnotes, for you can often save time if you record the names of books and articles listed in these notes. Then refer to the bibliographies included at the ends of the books, and select likely-looking titles. Now look at the dates of publication of the scholarly books. Let us suppose that you have found three books, published in 2005, 2007, and 2009. Unless you are planning an extensive research assignment, you can safely assume that the writers of critical works will have done the selecting for you of important works published before the date of publication. These bibliographies will be reliable, and you can use them with confidence. Thus, the bibliography in a book published in 2009 will be complete up through about 2008, for the writer will have finished the manuscript a year or so before the book was published. But such bibliographies will not go up to the present. For that, you will need to search for works published after the most recent of the books.

Consult Bibliographical Guides

Fortunately for students doing literary research, the Modern Language Association (MLA) of America has been providing a complete bibliography of literary studies for years, not only in English and American literatures but also in the literatures of many foreign languages. This is the *MLA International Bibliography of Books and Articles on the Modern Languages and Literatures* ("*MLA Bibliography*"). The *MLA Bibliography* started achieving completeness in the late 1950s. In the volume dated 2008, this comprehensive bibliography lists 71,649 books and articles. The MLA discontinued production of the traditional book format of the *MLA Bibliography* in 2009. However, it may be available at university and college libraries. The most recent version of the bibliography is published electronically and will be accessible to you through your library services.

Using the electronic version of the *MLA Bibliography*, you can search by typing in the name of your author or subject. By whatever means you gain access to the bibliography, be sure to get the complete information—especially volume numbers and years of publication—for each article and book.

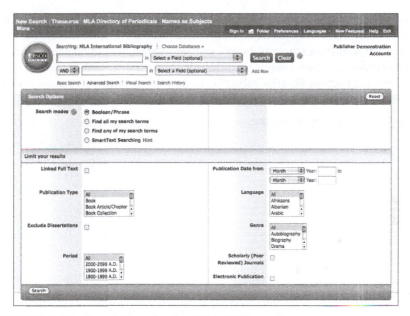

FIGURE 19.3 The Search Page for the MLA Bibliography

There are many other bibliographies that are useful for students doing literary research, such as the *Essay and General Literature Index,* the *Readers' Guide to Periodical Literature,* and various specific indexes. However, with over 2.1 million citations, the *MLA Bibliography* contains far in excess of abundance for your present research purposes.

Gaining Access to Books and Articles Through Databases

Today's libraries subscribe to a number of academic databases that index articles from reliable scholarly journals and other periodicals. Many of these databases include abstracts (brief, nonevaluative summaries), and some even offer the option of accessing the full text of the article. As with any electronic research tool, database searches have some limitations. Many periodicals do not allow their most recent issues into the databases for indexing; furthermore, some periodicals are not indexed through databases at all. Most databases have relatively limited (and recent) dates for which they have indexed articles. Nevertheless, periodical databases are an invaluable resource for your research essay.

A major source is *EBSCOhost,* a multidisciplinary database that includes thousands of scholarly publications, many of which are useful for literary research. For example, "MagillOnLiteraturePlus" has plot summaries and analyses of fictional works, and "Book Index with Reviews" includes excerpts of book reviews along with book summaries. *WilsonWeb* has databases in many disciplines and includes "Book Review Digest Plus," which has summaries of books as well as complete book reviews. *Wilson-Web* also has "Short Story Index," which indexes stories appearing in collections and periodicals since 1984. *Columbia Grangers World of Poetry* has references to many types of poetry. Yet another major electronic source for literary research is *JSTOR* (i.e., *Journal Storage*), a scholarly journal archive. *WorldCat* is a valuable resource that aims to catalogue library resources worldwide. Most college and university libraries and many high school libraries subscribe to database services, and these invaluable resources are available to you as a registered student.

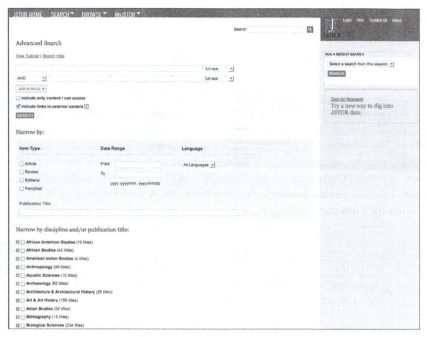

FIGURE 19.4 The advanced search page for *JSTOR*. While the search pages for each database differs, the skills you need to conduct a successful search are similar to those needed for other electronic searches (see pp. 264–68 for more on searching electronically).

Taking Notes and Paraphrasing Material

There are many ways of taking notes, but a few things are clear. Because your notes should facilitate, not hinder, your writing of the final research essay, you will need a systematic way of handling your notes. The best way is to develop a method whereby you will be able to see all your notes together, laid out in front of you. If you are taking handwritten notes, you can achieve simultaneous viewability by using note cards. If you have never used cards before, you might profit from consulting any one of a number of handbooks and special workbooks on research. The principal advantage of cards is the ease with which you can see them at a glance when you lay them out on a desk or other large surface. Cards are also sturdy and will easily maintain their physical integrity as you handle them and assign them to their relevant piles. As a result, cards may be easily classified. They may be numbered and renumbered; shuffled; tried out in one place, rejected, and then used in another place (or thrown away); and arranged in order when you start to write. If you prefer taking notes on a computer, it is these same qualities—viewability and ease of finding, classifying, and reordering notes without losing information—that you should aim for in a filing system. When taking notes on the computer, you might want to consider either keeping them in one large file or organizing them in separate files by source or by topic. No matter how you decide to take notes, follow the guidelines in the next section to ease your research process and avoid plagiarism.

Taking Complete and Accurate Notes

Write the Source of Each Note You Take Be especially diligent about writing the source of your information on each card or computer note. This might seem bothersome, but it is easier than going back to the library to locate the correct source after you have begun your essay. You can save time if you take the complete data on one card or computer file—a "master card" for that source—and then create an abbreviation for the separate notes you take from the source. Here is an example, which also includes the location where the reference was originally found (e.g., library catalogue, research database, Internet search, bibliography in a book, *MLA Bibliography*, etc.). Observe that the author's last name goes first.

Donovan, Josephine, ed. <u>Feminist Literary Criticism: Explorations in Theory</u>. 2nd ed. Lexington: UP of Kentucky. 1989	PN 98 W64 F4
DONOVAN	
Card Catalog, "Women"	

If you take many notes from this book, the name "Donovan" will serve as identification. Be sure not to lose your master group of references because you will need them when you prepare your list of works cited. If you are working with a computer, record the complete bibliographical data in a computer file.

Record the Page Number for Each Note It would be hard to guess how much exasperation has been caused by failure to record page numbers in notes. Be sure to write the page number down first, before you begin to take your note; to be doubly sure, write the page number again at the end of your note. If the detail goes from one page to the next in your source, record the exact spot where the page changes, as in the following example.

> Heilbrun and Stimson, in DONOVAN, pp. 63–64
>
> [63] After the raising of the feminist consciousness it is necessary to develop/[64] "the growth of moral perception" through anger and the "amelioration of social inequities."

The reason for such care is that you might wish to use only a part of a note you have taken, and when there are two pages, you will need to be accurate in locating what goes where.

Record Only One Fact or Opinion on a Card Record only one major detail on each card—one quotation, one paraphrase, one observation—*never two or more*. You might be tempted to fill up the entire card with many separate but unrelated details, but such a try at economy often gets you into trouble because you might want to use some of the details in other places. If you have only one entry per card, you will avoid such problems and also retain the freedom you need.

Use Quotation Marks for All Quoted Material In taking notes, it is extremely important—vitally important—to distinguish copied material from your own words. *Always put quotation marks around every direct quotation you copy verbatim from a source.* Put the quotation marks in *immediately, before you forget,* so that you will always know that the words of your notes within quotation marks are the words of another writer.

Often, as you take a note, you might use some of your own words and some of the words from your source. In cases like this, you should be even more cautious. Put quotation marks around *every word* that you take directly from the source, even if that makes your note look like a picket fence. Later, when you begin writing your essay, your memory of what is yours and not yours will be dim, and *if you use another's words in your own essay without proper acknowledgment, you are risking the charge of plagiarism.* Much of the time, plagiarism is caused not by deliberate deception but rather by sloppy note taking.

If Your Source Is Long, Make a Brief and Accurate Paraphrase When you take notes, it is best to paraphrase the sources. A paraphrase is a restatement in your own words, and because of this, it is actually a first step in the writing of your essay. A big problem in paraphrasing is to capture the idea in the source without copying the words verbatim. The best way is to read and reread the passage you are noting. Turn over the book or journal—or put your computer screen to sleep—and write out the idea in your own words as accurately as you can. Once you have completed this note, compare it with the original and make corrections to improve your thought and emphasis. Add a short quotation if you believe it is needed, but be sure to use quotation marks. If your paraphrase is too close to the original, throw out the note and write another one. This effort may have its own reward because often you can transfer some or even all of your note, word for word, directly to the appropriate place in your research essay.

Plagiarism: An Embarrassing But Vital Subject—and a Danger to Be Overcome

When you are using sources as the substance of many of the details in your essay, you run the risk of *plagiarism*—using the words and ideas of other writers without their consent and without acknowledgment. Recognizing the source means being clear about the identity of other authors, together with the name or names of the works from which one gets details and ideas. When there is no recognition, readers, and the intellectual world generally, are deceived. They assume that the material they are reading is the original work and the intellectual property of the writer. When there is no recognition, the plagiarizing author is committing intellectual theft.

This is no small matter. In the world of publications, many people who have committed plagiarism have suffered irreparable damage to their credibility and reputations as writers and authorities. Some well-known writers have found it hard if not impossible to continue their careers because of the wide knowledge of their plagiarism. It does not end there. A plagiarist might be open to legal actions and might, if the situation is grave enough, be required to supply financial restitution to the author or authors whose work has been illegally appropriated. In schools and colleges, students who plagiarize may face academic discipline. Often, the discipline is a failure for the course, but it might also include suspension and expulsion.

Because of the serious nature of this issue, you must be constantly aware that you need to distinguish between the sources you are using and your own work. Your readers will assume that everything you write is your own unless you indicate otherwise. Therefore, when blending your words with the ideas from sources, **be clear about proper acknowledgments**. Most commonly, if you are simply presenting details and facts, you can write straightforwardly and let parenthetical references suffice as your authority, as in the following sentence from the illustrative research essay:

> Marvin Magalaner, using "Miss Brill" as an example, speaks of Mansfield's weaving of "a myriad of threads into a rigidly patterned whole" (39). Also noting Mansfield's control over form, Cheryl Hankin suggests that Mansfield's structuring is perhaps more "instinctive" than deliberate (474).

Here, there can be no question about plagiarism, for the names of the authors of the critical sources are fully acknowledged, the page numbers are specific, and the quotation marks clearly distinguish the words of the critics from the words of the essay writer. If you grant recognition as recommended here, no confusion can result about the authority underlying your essay. The linking words obviously belong to the writer of the essay, but the parenthetical references clearly indicate that the sentence is based on two sources.

If you use an interpretation that is unique to a particular writer or if you rely on a significant quotation from your source, you should make your acknowledgment an essential part of your discussion, as in this sentence:

> Saralyn Daly, referring to Miss Brill as one of Mansfield's "isolatoes"—that is, solitary persons cut off from normal human contacts—fears that the couple's callous insults have caused Miss Brill to face the outside world with her fur piece "perhaps for the very last time" (88, 90).

Here, the idea of the critic is singled out for special acknowledgment. If you recognize your sources in this way, no confusion can arise about how you have used them.

Please always keep foremost in your mind that *the purpose of research is to acquire knowledge and details through which to advance your own thoughts and interpretations*. You should consider your research discoveries as a kind of springboard from which you can launch yourself into your own written work. Thus, research should be creative. A test of how you use research is to determine how well you move from the details you are using to the development of your own ideas. Once you have gone forth in this way, you are using research correctly and creatively. Plagiarism will then no more be even a remote issue for you.

To see the problems of paraphrasing, let us look at a paragraph of criticism and then see how a student doing research might take notes on it. The paragraph is by Richard F. Peterson, from an essay entitled "The Circle of Truth: The Stories of Katherine Mansfield and Mary Lavin," published in *Modern Fiction Studies* 24 (1978): 383–394. In the passage to be quoted, Peterson is considering the structures of two Mansfield stories, "Bliss" and "Miss Brill":

> "Bliss" and "Miss Brill" are flawed stories, but not because the truth they reveal about their protagonists is too brutal or painful for the tastes of the common reader. In each story, the climax of the narrative suggests an arranged reality that leaves a lasting impression, not of life, but of the author's cleverness. This strategy of arrangement for dramatic effect or revelation, unfortunately, is common in Katherine Mansfield's fiction. Too often in her stories a dropped remark at the right or wrong moment, a chance meeting or discovery, an intrusive figure in the shape of a fat man at a ball or in the Cafe de Madrid, a convenient death of a hired man or a stranger dying aboard a ship, or a *deus ex machina* in the form of two doves, a dill pickle, or a fly plays too much of a role in /[386] creating a character's dilemma or deciding the outcome of the narrative. 385–386

Because taking notes forces a shortening of this or any criticism, it also requires you to discriminate, judge, interpret, and select; good note taking is not easy. There are some things to guide you, however, when you go through the many sources you uncover.

Think About the Purpose of Your Research You might not know exactly what you are "fishing for" when you start to take notes, for you cannot prejudge what your essay will contain. Research is a form of discovery. But soon you will notice subjects and issues that your sources constantly explore. If you can accept one of these as your major topic, or focus of interest, you can use that as your guide in all further note taking.

For example, suppose that you start to take notes on criticism about Katherine Mansfield's "Miss Brill," and after a certain amount of reading, you decide to focus on the story's structure. This decision guides your further research and note taking. Thus, for example, Richard Peterson criticizes Mansfield's technique of arranging climaxes in her stories. With your topic being structure, it would, therefore, be appropriate to take a note on Peterson's judgment. The following note is adequate as a brief reminder of the content in the passage:

Peterson 385   structure: negative

Peterson claims that Mansfield creates climaxes
that are too artificial, too unlifelike, giving the
impression not of reality but of Mansfield's own
"cleverness." 385

Let us now suppose that you want a fuller note, in the expectation that you need not just Peterson's general idea but also some of his supporting detail. Such a note might look like this:

Peterson 385   structure: negative

Peterson thinks that "Bliss" and "Miss Brill" are "flawed"
because they have contrived endings that give the impression "not of life but of" Mansfield's "cleverness." She
arranges things artificially, according to Peterson, to cause
the endings in many other stories. Some of these things are
chance remarks, discoveries, or meetings, together with
other unexpected or chance incidents and objects. These
contrivances make their stories imperfect. 385

In an actual research essay, any part of this note would be useful. The words are almost all the note taker's own, and the few quotations are within quotation marks. Note that Peterson, the critic, is properly recognized as the source of the criticism, so you could adapt the note easily when you are doing your writing. The key here is that your note taking should be guided by your developing plan for your essay.

Note taking is part of your thinking and composing process. You might not always know whether you will be able to use each note that you take, and you will always exclude many notes when you write your essay. You will find, however, that taking notes is easier once you have determined your purpose.

Give Your Notes Titles To help plan and develop the various parts of your essay, write a title for each of your notes, as in the examples in this chapter. This practice is a form of outlining. Let us continue discussing the structure of Mansfield's "Miss Brill," the actual subject of the illustrative research essay (pp. 284–90). As you do your research, you discover that there is a divergence of critical thought about how the ending of the story should be understood. Here is a note about one of the diverging interpretations:

Daly 90   Ending of the story

Miss Brill's "complete" "identification" with the shabby fur piece at the very end may cause readers to conclude that she is the one in tears but bravely does not recognize this fact, and also to conclude that she may never use the fur in public again because of her complete defeat. Everything may be for "perhaps the very last time."

Notice that the title classifies the topic of the note. If you use such classifications, a number of like-titled cards could underlie a section in your essay about how to understand the concluding sentence of "Miss Brill." In addition, once you decide to explore the last sentence, the topic itself will guide you in further study and notetaking. (See the illustrative essay on pp. 288–89, in which paragraphs 14 and 15 concern this topic.)

Write Down Your Own Original Thoughts, and Mark Them as Your Own As you take notes, you will be developing your own observations and thoughts. Do not push these aside in your mind, on the chance of remembering them later, but write them down immediately. Often, you may notice a detail that your source does not mention, or you may get a hint for an idea that the critic does not develop. Often, too, you may get thoughts that can serve as "bridges" between details in your notes or as introductions or concluding observations. Be sure to title your comments and to mark them as your own thought. Here is such a note, which is on the emphasis on character as opposed to action in "Miss Brill":

My Own	Ending of the story

It seems that action as such was less significant in Mansfield's scheme for the story than the sympathetic evocation of reactions and moods. Mansfield wanted to reveal feeling and character.

Observe that on page 285 of the illustrative essay, the idea of this note is the basis of the development in paragraph 3—that the day's scenes and actions have led Miss Brill to her "emotional pain" as she returns to her "little dark room." The third paragraph of the finished essay has been shaped by the original note about the importance of feeling and character.

Classify Your Cards and Group Them Accordingly

If you do a careful and thorough job of taking notes, your essay will already have been forming in your mind. The titles of your cards will suggest areas to be developed as you do your planning and initial drafting. Once you have assembled a stack of note cards derived from a reasonable number of sources (your instructor may have assigned an approximate number or a minimum number), you can sort them into groups according to the topics and titles. For the illustrative essay, after some shuffling and retitling, the cards were assembled in the following groups:

General structure
Specific structures: season, time of day, levels of cruelty, Miss Brill's own "hierarchies"
    of unreality
The concluding paragraphs, especially the last sentence

If you look at the major sections of the illustrative essay, you will see that the topics are closely adapted from these groups of cards. In other words, *the arrangement of the cards is an effective means of helping you organize and outline a research essay.*

Make Logical Arrangements of the Cards in Each Group

There is still much to do with each group of cards. You cannot use the details as they happen to fall randomly in your stack. You need to decide which notes are relevant. You might also need to retitlesome cards and use them elsewhere. Those that remain will have to be arranged in a logical order for you to find use for them in your essay.

Once you have your cards in order, you can write whatever comments or transitions are needed to move from detail to detail. Write this material directly on the cards, and be sure to use a different color ink for your comments so that you can distinguish later between the original note and what you add. Here is an example of such a "developed" note card:

Magalaner 39   Structure, general

Speaking of Mansfield's sense of form and referring to "Miss Brill" as an example, Magalaner states that Mansfield has power to put together stories from "a myriad of threads into a rigidly patterned whole." 39

Some of these "threads" are the fall season, the time of day, examples of unkindness, the park bench sitters from the cupboards, and Miss Brill's stages of unreality (see Thorpe 661). Each of these is separate, but all work together to unify the story.

By adding such commentary to your note cards, you are also simplifying the writing of your first draft. In many instances, the note and the comment may be moved directly into the paper with minor adjustments (some of the content of this note appears in paragraph 1 of the illustrative research essay, and almost all the topics introduced here are developed in paragraphs 4–12).

Be Creative and Original Even Though You Are Doing Research

You will not always transfer your notes directly into your essay. The major trap to avoid in a research paper is that your use of sources can become an end in itself and, therefore, a shortcut for your own thinking and writing. Often, students make the mistake of introducing details the way a master of ceremonies introduces performers in a variety show. This is unfortunate because it is the *student* whose essay will be judged, even though the sources, like the performers, do all the work. It is important to be creative and original in a research essay and to do your own thinking and writing, even though you are relying heavily on your sources. Here are five ways in which research essays may be original:

1. **Your selection of material is original with you.** In each major part of your essay, you will include many details from your sources. To be creative, you should select different but related details and avoid overlapping or repetition. Your completed essay will be judged on the basis of the thoroughness with which you make your points with different details (which in turn will represent the completeness of your research). Even though you are relying on published materials and cannot be original on that score, your selection can be original because you bring these materials together for the first time and because you emphasize some details and minimize others. Inevitably, your assemblage of details from your sources will be unique and, therefore, original.

2. **Your development of your essay is yours alone.** Your arrangement of your various points is an obvious area of originality: One detail seems naturally to precede another, and certain conclusions stem from certain details. As you pres-

ent the details, conclusions, and arguments from your sources, you can add an original stamp by introducing supporting details that are different from those in the source material. You can also emphasize particular points in a way that is not found in your sources.

3. **The words are yours and yours alone.** Naturally, the words that you use will be original because they are yours. Your topic sentences, for example, will all be your own. As you introduce details and conclusions, you will need to write "bridges" to get yourself from point to point. These can be introductory remarks or transitions. In other words, as you write, you are not just stringing your notes together; rather, you are actively assembling and arranging your notes and thoughts in creative and unique ways.

4. **Explaining and contrasting controversial views is an original presentation of material.** Closely related to your selection is that in your research, you may have found conflicting or differing views on a topic. If you make a point to describe and distinguish these views and explain the reasons for the differences, you are presenting material originally. To see how differing views can be handled, see paragraph 14 of the illustrative essay.

5. **Your own insights and positions are uniquely your own.** There are three possibilities here, all related to how well you have learned the primary texts on which your research in secondary sources is based.
   a. *Weave your own interpretations and ideas into your essay.* An important part of taking notes is to make your own points *precisely when they occur to you.* Often, you can expand these as truly original parts of your essay. Your originality does not need to be extensive; it may consist of no more than a single insight. Here is such a card, which was written during research on the structure of "Miss Brill."

My Own   Miss Brill's unreality

It is ironic that the boy and girl sit down on the bench next to Miss Brill just when she is at the height of her fancies. By allowing her to overhear their insults, they almost slap her with the harshness of reality. She is then plunged instantly from the height of rapture to the depth of pain.

The originality here is built around the contrast between Miss Brill's exhilaration and her rapid and cruel deflation. This observation is not unusual or startling, but it nevertheless represents original thought about the story. When modified and adapted, much of this card is is used as an important part of paragraph 13 of the illustrative essay below. You can see that your writing a "My Own" note card can be vital to you in the development of your own thoughts.

   b. *Filling gaps in the sources enables you to present original thoughts and insights.* As you read your secondary sources, you might realize that a conclusion that seems obvious to you is not being made or that an important detail is not being stressed. Here is an area that you can develop on your own. Your conclusions may involve a particular interpretation or major point of comparison, or they may rest on a particularly important but understressed word or fact. For example, paragraphs 10–13 in the illustrative essay form an argument based on observations that critics have overlooked, or have neglected to mention, about the conclusion of "Miss Brill." In your research, whenever you find such a critical "vacuum" (assuming that you cannot read all the articles about some of your topics, in which your discovery may already have been made a number of times), it is right to include whatever is necessary to fill it.

c. *By disputing your sources with your own arguments, you are being original.* Your sources may present arguments that you wish to dispute. As you develop your disagreement, you will be arguing originally, for you will be using details in a different way from that of the critic or critics whom you are disputing, and your conclusions will be your own. This area of originality is similar to the laying out of controversial critical views, except that you furnish one of the opposing views yourself. The approach is limited because it is difficult to find many substantive points of interpretation on which there are not already clearly delineated opposing views. Paragraph 13 of the illustrative essay shows how a disagreement can lead to a different, if not original, interpretation.

Documenting Your Work

It is necessary and essential to acknowledge—to *document*—all sources from which you have *quoted or paraphrased* factual and interpretive information. Because of the need to avoid being challenged for plagiarism, this point cannot be overemphasized. As the means of documentation, various reference systems use parenthetical references, footnotes, or endnotes. Whatever system is used, documentation almost always includes a carefully prepared bibliography, or list of works cited.

We will first discuss the list of works cited and then review the two major reference systems for use in a research paper. Parenthetical references, preferred by the Modern Language Association (MLA) since 1984, are described in Joseph Gibaldi, *MLA Handbook for Writers of Research Papers*, Seventh Edition, published in 2009. Footnotes or endnotes, recommended by the MLA before 1984, are still required by many instructors. *Always consult your instructor regarding which documentation system to use.*

Include All the Works You Have Used in a List of Works Cited (Bibliography)

The key to any reference system is a carefully prepared list of works cited that is included at the end of the essay. "Works cited" means exactly that; the list should include just those books and articles you have actually *used* in your essay. If your instructor requires that you use footnotes or endnotes, however, you can extend your concluding list to be a complete bibliography both of works cited and of works consulted but not actually used. *Always, always, always, follow your instructor's directions.*

The list of works cited should include the following information, in each entry, in the form indicated. If you are using a word processor with the capacity to make italics, you can italicize book and article titles rather than underline them.

For a Book

1. The author's name: last name first, followed by first name and middle name or initial. Period.
2. The title, italicized or underlined. Period.
3. The city of publication (not the state or nation), colon; publisher (easily recognized abbreviations or key words can be used unless they seem awkward or strange; see the *MLA Handbook*, pp. 247–49), comma; year of publication. Period.
4. The medium of publication (Print. Web. etc.) Period.

For an Article

1. The author's name: last name first, followed by first name and middle name or initial. Period.
2. The title of the article in quotation marks. Period.
3. The title of the journal or periodical, italicized or underlined, followed by the volume number in Arabic (*not* Roman) numbers with no punctuation, then the year of publication within parentheses. Colon. For a daily paper or weekly magazine, omit the parentheses and cite the date in the British style followed by a colon (day, month, year, as in *2 Feb. 2005*:). Inclusive page numbers (without any preceding *p*. or *pp*.). Period.
4. The medium of publication (print, Web, DVI, etc.). Period.
5. If your article was obtained through a database, include the database name. If your article was obtained electronically, either through a database or on the Internet, include the date you visited the site. Period.

For a Web Publication

1. The author's name: last name first, followed by first name and middle name or initial. Period.
2. The title of work/site. Italicize if the document is independent or use quotation marks if it is a part of a larger work. Period.
3. Web site's name, italicized (if this is different than above). Period.
4. Publisher. Comma. Publication Date. Use "n.d." if no publication date is available. Period.
5. The medium of publication (Print, Web, etc…). Period.
6. The access date, meaning the date you viewed the site. Period.
7. The URL (uniform resource locator). The MLA specifies the URLs should no longer accompany works cited entries unless the URL is essential to locating the site. If you determine that the URL is necessary, include the full address (be absolutely accurate in reproducing the URL) and place angle brackets (< >) before and after. Period. (Note: When a URL continues from one line to the next, break it *before* punctuation.)

The works you are citing should be listed alphabetically according to the last names of authors, with unsigned articles included in the list alphabetically by titles. Bibliographical lists are begun at the left margin, with subsequent lines in hanging indentation, so that the key locating word—the author's last name or the first title word of an unsigned article—can be easily seen. Many unpredictable and complex combinations, including ways to describe works of art, musical or other performances, and films, are detailed extensively in the *MLA Handbook* (123–212). Here are two model entries:

> **Book:** Alpers, Antony. *The Life of Katherine Mansfield*. New York: Viking, 1980. Print.

> **Article:** Hankin, Cheryl. "Fantasy and the Sense of an Ending in the Work of Katherine Mansfield." *Modern Fiction Studies* 24 (1978): 465–74. Print.

Refer to Works Parenthetically as You Draw Details from Them

Within your research essay, use parentheses in referring to works from which you are using facts and conclusions. This parenthetical citation system is recommended in the *MLA Handbook*, Seventh Edition (213–32), and its principle is to provide documentation without asking readers to interrupt their reading to find footnotes or endnotes. Readers who want to see the complete reference can easily find it in your list of works cited. With this system, you incorporate the author's last name and the relevant page number or numbers directly, whenever possible, into the body of your essay. If the author's name is mentioned in your discussion, you need to give only the page number or numbers in parentheses. Here are two examples:

> Alexander Pope believed in the idea that the universe is a whole, a totally unified body, which provides a "viable benevolent system for the salvation of everyone who does good" (Kallich 24).

> Martin Kallich draws attention to Alexander Pope's belief in the idea that the universe is a whole, a totally unified body, which provides a "viable benevolent system for the salvation of everyone who does good" (24).

Footnotes and Endnotes—Formal and Traditional Reference Formats

As long as all you want from a reference is the page number of a quotation or paraphrase, the parenthetical system described briefly in the previous section—and detailed fully in the *MLA Handbook*—is the most suitable and convenient one you can use. However, you might wish to use footnotes (references at the bottom of each page) or endnotes (references listed numerically at the end of the essay) if you need to add more details, provide additional explanations, or refer your readers to other materials that you are not using.

Whatever method you follow, *you must always acknowledge sources properly*. Remember that whenever you begin to write and cite references, you might forget a number of specific details about documentation, and you will certainly discover that you have many questions. Be sure, then, to ask your instructor, who is your final authority.

Organize Your Research Essay

Introduction In your research essay, you might wish to expand your introduction more than usual because of the need to relate the problem of research to your topic. You may wish to bring in relevant historical or biographical information (see, for example, paragraph 1 of the illustrative research essay on p. 284). You might also wish to summarize critical opinion or describe critical problems about your topic. The idea is to lead your reader into your topic by providing interesting and significant materials that you have found.

Because of the length of most research essays, some instructors require a topic outline, which is in effect a brief table of contents. This pattern is used in the illustrative research essay below. *Because the inclusion of an outline is a matter of the instructor's choice, be sure to learn whether your instructor requires it.*

Body and Conclusion As you write the body and conclusion of your research essay, your development will be governed by your choice of topic. Consult the relevant chapters in this book about what to include for whatever approach or approaches you select (setting, ideas, point of view, character, tone, or any other).

In length, the research essay can be anywhere from five to fifteen or more pages, depending on your instructor's assignment. Obviously, an essay on a single work will be shorter than one based on several. If you narrow the scope of your topic, as suggested in the approaches described at the beginning of this chapter, you can readily keep your essay within the assigned length. The following illustrative research essay, for example, illustrates approach 1 (p. 263) by being limited to only one character in one story. Were you to write on characters in a number of other stories by Mansfield or any other writer (approach 2), you could limit your total number of pages by stressing comparative treatments and by avoiding excessive detail about problems pertaining to only one work.

Although you limit your topic yourself in consultation with your instructor, you may encounter problems because you will deal not with one source alone but with many. Naturally, the sources will provide you with details and trigger many of your ideas. The problem is to handle the many strands without piling on too many details and without being led into digressions. It is, therefore, important to keep your central idea foremost; the constant stressing of your central idea will help you nor only to select relevant materials but also to reject irrelevant ones.

Illustrative Research Essay

The Structure of Katherine Mansfield's "Miss Brill"[1]

Outline

I.   Introduction. The parallel structures of "Miss Brill"
II. Season and time as structure
III. Insensitive or cruel actions as structure
IV. Miss Brill's "hierarchy of unrealities" as structure
V.   The story's conclusion
VI. Conclusion

[1]   In the story "Miss Brill," Mansfield creates an aging and emotion-ally vulnerable character, Miss Brill (we are not told her first name), whose good feelings are dashed when she overhears a number of cruel and shattering personal insults. In accord with Miss Brill's emotional deflation, the story is developed through a parallel number of struc-tures. This parallelism demonstrates Mansfield's power generally over tight narrative control. Marvin Magalaner, using "Miss Brill" as an example, speaks of Mansfield's weaving "a myriad of threads into a rigidly patterned whole" (39). Also noting Mansfield's control over form, Cheryl Hankin suggests that Mansfield's control over structure is perhaps more "instinctive" than deliberate (474). Either of these observations is great praise for Mansfield. The complementary parallels, threads, stages, or "levels" of "unequal length" (Harmat uses the terms "niveaux" and "longueur inégale," 49, 51) are the fall season, the time of day, insensitive or cruel actions, Miss Brill's own unreal perceptions, and the final section or dénouement.[2]

[2]   An important aspect of structure in "Miss Brill" is Mansfield's use of the season of the year. Autumn, with its propulsion toward winter, is integral to the deteriorating life of the heroine. In the first paragraph, we learn that there is a "faint chill" in the air (is the word "chill" chosen to rhyme with "Brill"?), and this phrase is

---

[1]See MyLiteratureLab for this story.
[2]Thesis sentence.

repeated in the third paragraph of the story (FMN1–1). Thus, the author establishes autumn and the approaching year's end as the beginning of the downward movement toward dashed hopes. This seasonal reference is also carried out when we read that "yellow leaves" are "down drooping" in the local *Jardins Publiques* (FMN1–2) and that leaves are drifting "now and again" from almost "nowhere, from the sky" (FMN1–1). It is the autumn cold that has caused Miss Brill to wear her shabby fur piece, which later the young girl considers the object of contempt. The chill, together with the fur, forms a structural setting for both the action and the mood of the story. Sewell notes that "Miss Brill" both begins and ends with reference to the fur, which is the direct cause of the heroine's deep hurt at the conclusion.

Like the seasonal structuring, the times of day parallel Miss Brill's darkening existence. At the beginning, the speaker points out that the day is "brilliantly fine—the blue sky powdered with gold" and that the light is "like white wine." This figurative language suggests the brightness and crispness of full sunlight. In paragraph (FMN1–2), where we also learn of the yellow leaves, "the blue sky with gold-veined clouds" indicates that time has been passing as clouds accumulate during late afternoon. By the story's end, Miss Brill has returned in sadness to her "little dark room" (FMN1–3). In other words, the time moves from day to evening, from light to darkness, as a virtual accompaniment to Miss Brill's emotional pain.   [3]

Mansfield's most significant structural device, which is not emphasized by critics, is the introduction of insensitive or cruel actions. It is as though the hurt felt by Miss Brill on the bright Sunday afternoon is also being felt by many others. Because she is the spectator who is closely related to Mansfield's narrative voice, Miss Brill is the filter through whom these negative examples reach the reader. Considering the patterns that emerge, one may conclude that Mansfield intends that the beauty of the day and the joyousness of the band be taken as an ironic contrast to the pettiness and insensitivity of the people in the park.   [4]

[5]   The first of these people are the silent couple on Miss Brill's bench (FMN1–1) and the incompatible couple of the week before (FMN1–1).Because these seem no more than ordinary, they do not at first appear to be part of the story's pattern of cruelty and rejection. But their incompatibility, suggested by their silence and one-way complaining, establishes a structural parallel with the young and insensitive couple who later insult Miss Brill. Thus, the first two couples prepare the way for the third, and all show increasing insensitivity and cruelty.

[6]   Almost unnoticed as a second level of negation is the vast group of "odd, silent, nearly all old" people filling "the benches and green chairs" (FMN1–2). They seem to be no more than a normal part of the Sunday afternoon landscape. But these people are significant structurally because the "dark little rooms—or even cupboards" that Miss Brill associates with them also, ironically, describe the place where she lives (FMN1–2, FMN1–3). The reader may conclude from Miss Brill's quiet eavesdropping that she herself is one of these nameless and faceless ones who lead similarly dreary lives.

[7]   After Mansfield sets these levels for her heroine, she introduces characters experiencing additional rejection and cruelty. The beautiful woman who throws down the bunch of violets is the first of these (FMN1–2). The story does not explain the causes of this woman's scorn, and Miss Brill does not know what to make of the incident; but the woman's actions suggest that she has been involved in a relationship that has ended in anger and bitterness.

[8]   The major figure involved in rejection, who is important enough to be considered a structural double of Miss Brill, is the woman wearing the ermine toque (FMN1–2). It is clear that she, like Miss Brill, is one of "the lonely and isolated women in a hostile world" that Mansfield is so skillful in portraying (Gordon 6). This woman tries to please the "gentleman in grey," but this man insults her by blowing smoke in her face. It could be, as Peter Thorpe observes, that she is "obviously a prostitute" (661). But it is more likely that the "ermine toque" woman has had a broken relationship with the gentleman or perhaps even no relationship. Being familiar with his Sunday habits,

she comes to the park to meet him, as though by accident, to attempt to renew contact. After her rejection, her hurrying off to meet someone "much nicer" (there is no such person, for Mansfield uses the phrase "as though" to introduce "ermine toque's" departure) is her way of masking her hurt. Regardless of the exact situation, however, Mansfield makes it plain that the encounter shows not only vulnerability, unkindness, and pathos but also a certain amount of self defense.

Once Mansfield establishes this major incident, she introduces two additional examples of insensitivity. At the end of the story's eighth paragraph (FMN1–2), the hobbling old man "with long whiskers" is nearly knocked over by the group of four girls, who show arrogance if not contempt toward him. The final examples involve Miss Brill herself. These are her recollections of the apparent indifference of her students and of the old invalid "who habitually sleeps" when she reads to him.   [9]

Although "Miss Brill" is a brief story, Mansfield establishes a number of structural parallels to the sudden climax brought about by the boorishly insensitive young couple. The boy and girl do not appear until the very end, in other words (FMN1–3), but extreme insults like theirs have been fully anticipated in the story's earlier parts. Mansfield's speaker does not take us to the homes of the other people in the park, as she does when we follow Miss Brill to her wretched room. Instead, the narrative invites us to conclude that the silent couple, the complaining wife and long-suffering husband, the unseen man rejected by the young woman, the "ermine toque" woman, and the funny gentleman, not to mention the many silent and withdrawn people sitting like statues in the park, all return to loneliness and personal pain that are comparable to the feelings of Miss Brill.   [10]

The intricacy of the structure of "Miss Brill" does not end here. Of great importance is the structural development of the protagonist herself. Peter Thorpe notes a "hierarchy of unrealities" that govern the reader's increasing awareness of Miss Brill's plight (661). By this measure, the story's actions progressively bring out Miss Brill's failures of perception and understanding—failures that in this respect make her like her namesake fish, the lowly brill (Gargano).   [11]

[12]   These unrealities begin with Miss Brill's fanciful but harmless imaginings about her shabby fur piece. This beginning sets up the pattern of her pathetic inner life. When she imagines that the park band is a "single, responsive, and very sensitive creature" (Thorpe 661), we realize that she is unrealistically making too much out of a mediocre band of ordinary musicians. Although she cannot interpret the actions of the beautiful young woman with the violets, she does see the encounter between the "ermine toque" woman and the gentleman in grey as a vision of rejection. Her response is correct, but then her belief that the band's drumbeats are sounding out "The Brute! The Brute!" indicates her vivid overdramatization of the incident. The "top of the hierarchy of unrealities" (Thorpe 661) is her fancy that Miss Brill herself is an actor with a vital part in a gigantic drama played by all the people in the park. The most poignant aspect of her daydream is her unreal thought that someone would miss her if she were to be absent.

[13]   In light of this hierarchical structure of unrealities, it is ironic that the boy and girl sit down next to her just when she is at the height of her fancy about her own importance. When she hears the girl's insults, the couple has introduced objective reality to her with a vengeance, and she is plunged from rapture to pain. The concluding two paragraphs of "Miss Brill," hence, form a rapid dénouement to reflect her loneliness and solitude.

[14]   Of unique importance in the structure of "Miss Brill" are these final two paragraphs, describing how Miss Brill, all alone, returns to her wretched little room. Saralyn Daly, referring to Miss Brill as one of Mansfield's "isolatoes"—that is, solitary persons cut off from normal human contacts—fears that the couple's callous insults have caused Miss Brill to face the outside world with her fur piece "perhaps for the very last time" (88, 90). Sydney Kaplan adds a political dimension to Miss Brill's defeat, asserting that here and in other stories Mansfield is expressing "outrage" against "a society in which privilege is . . . marked by indifference" to situations like those of Miss Brill (192).

It is clear that Mansfield is asking readers not only to consider   [15]
Miss Brill alone but also to note her similarity to the many park
inhabitants who are like her. Miss Brill's grim existence exemplifies a
common personal pattern in which the old are destroyed "by
loneliness and sickness, by fear of death, by the thoughtless energy
of the younger world around them" (Zinman 457). More generally,
Mansfield herself considered such negative situations as "the snail
under the leaf," which implies that a gnawing fate is waiting for
everyone, not just those who are old (Meyers 213). With such a
crushing experience for the major character, "Miss Brill" may be
fitted to the structuring of Mansfield's stories described by André
Maurois: "moments of beauty suddenly broken by contact with
ugliness, cruelty, or death" (342–43).

Works Cited

Daly, Saralyn R. *Katherine Mansfield*. New York: Twayne, 1965. Print.

Gargano, James W. "Mansfield's Miss Brill." *Explicator* 19. 2 (1960)
    n.p. Print.

Gordon, Ian A. "Katherine Mansfield: Overview." *Reference Guide
    to English Literature*, 2nd ed. Ed. D. L. Kirkpatrick. London:
    St. James Press, 1991. *InfoTrac*. Web. 26 March 2010.

Hankin, Cheryl. "Fantasy and the Sense of an Ending in the Work
    of Katherine Mansfield." *Modern Fiction Studies* 24 (1978):
    465–74. Print.

Harmat, Andrée-Marie. "Essai D'Analyse Structurale d'une Nouvelle
    Lyrique Anglaise: 'Miss Brill' de Katherine Mansfield." *Les
    Cahiers de la Nouvelle* 1 (1983): 49–74. Print.

Kaplan, Sydney Janet. *Katherine Mansfield and the Origins of Modernist Fiction*. Ithaca and London: Cornell UP, 1991. *Google Books*. Web. 26 March 2010. Print.

Magalaner, Marvin. *The Fiction of Katherine Mansfield*. Carbondale: Southern Illinois UP, 1971. Print.

———. *The Short Stories of Katherine Mansfield*. New York: Knopf, 1967. Print.

Mansfield, Katherine. "Miss Brill." *MyLiteratureLab.com*. Pearson: 2010. 23 Sept. 2011.

Maurois, André. *Points of View from Kipling to Graham Greene*. 1935. New York: Ungar, 1968. Print.

McLaughlin, Ann L. "The Same Job: The Shared Writing Aims of Katherine Mansfield and Virginia Woolf." *Modern Fiction Studies* 24 (1978): 369–82. *Questia*. Web. 26 March 2010.

Meyers, Jeffrey. *Katherine Mansfield: A Darker View*. 1978. New York: Cooper Square Press, 2002. Print.

Sewell, Arthur. *Katherine Mansfield: A Critical Essay*. Auckland: Unicorn, 1936. Print.

Thorpe, Peter. "Teaching 'Miss Brill.'" *College English* 23 (1962): 661–63. *JSTOR*. Web. 2010 March 26.

Zinman, Toby Silverman. "The Snail Under the Leaf: Katherine Mansfield's Imagery." *Modern Fiction Studies* 24 (1978): 457–64. Print.

Commentary on the Essay

This essay fulfills an assignment of 1500–2000 words with ten to fifteen sources. (There are actually fifteen.) The bibliography was developed from a college library catalogue, references in books of criticism (Magalaner, Daly), the *MLA International Bibliography*; the *Essay and General Literature Index*, and the Literature Resource Center available through the Internet and a county library system (www.wls.lib .ny.us). The sources themselves were found in a college library with selective holdings, in a local public library, and in online resources. There is only one rare source, an article (Harmat) obtained in photocopy through interlibrary loan from one of only two U.S. libraries holding the journal in which it appears. The location was made through the national Online Computer Library Center (OCLC). For most semester-long or quarter-long courses, you will probably not have time to add to your sources by such a method, but the article in question refers specifically to "Miss Brill," and it was, therefore, desirable to examine it.

The sources consist of books, articles, and chapters or portions of books. One article (Sewell) has been published as a separate short monograph. Also, one of the sources is the story "Miss Brill" itself (with locations made by paragraph and page numbers), together with a collection of her stories. The sources are used for facts, interpretations, conclusions, and general guidance and authority.

All necessary thematic devices, including overall organization and transitions, are unique to the essay. The essay also contains passages that take issue with certain conclusions in a few of the sources. Additional particulars about the handling of sources and developing a research essay are included in the discussion of note taking and related matters in this chapter.

The central idea of the essay (paragraph 1) is built out of this idea, explaining that the movement of emotions in the story is accompanied by an intricate and complementary set of structures. Paragraphs 2 through 13 examine various elements of the story for their structural relationship to Miss Brill's emotions.

Paragraphs 2 and 3 detail the structural uses of the settings of autumn and times of day, pointing out how they parallel her experiences.

The longest part, paragraphs 4 through 10, is based on an idea not found in the sources: that a number of characters are experiencing difficulties and cruelties such as those that befall Miss Brill. Paragraph 5 cites the three couples of the story, paragraph 6 the silent old people, and paragraph 7 the scornful woman with violets. Paragraph 8 is developed in contrast to one of the sources, showing how an essay involving research may be original even though the sources form the basis of discussion. Paragraph 9 contains additional examples of insensitivity—two of them involving Miss Brill herself. Paragraph 10 summarizes the story's instances of insensitivity and cruelty, once again emphasizing parallels to Miss Brill's situation.

Paragraphs 11 through 13 are based on ideas about the story's structure found in one of the sources (Thorpe). It is, hence, more derivative than paragraphs 4 through 10. Paragraphs 14 and 15, the concluding paragraphs of the essay, are devoted to the story's dénouement and to the broader application of the story: Miss Brill is to be considered an example of the anonymous "isolatoes" who inhabit the park. Because they are comparable to Miss Brill, their lives are unlikely just as sad and anguishing as hers is.

The list of works cited is the basis of all references in the essay, in accord with the *MLA Handbook for Writers of Research Papers,* 7th ed. (2009). By locating these references, a reader might readily examine, verify, and study any of the ideas and details drawn from the sources and developed in the essay.

Writing Topics for Research Essays

In beginning research on any of the following topics, follow the steps described in this chapter:

1. Common themes in a number of stories by Hawthorne, Poe, Hardy, or Mansfield.
2. Various critical views of Chekhov's *The Bear*.
3. Glaspell's use of the narrative material in *Trifles*.
4. Hawthorne's use of religious and moral topic material.
5. Shakespeare's imagery in the Sonnets.
6. Views about women in Chopin, Glaspell, Mansfield, and Keats.
7. Poe's view of the short story as represented in "The Cask of Amontillado" and a number of other stories.

Appendix A

Critical Approaches Important in the Study of Literature

Fiction, Poetry, and Drama

A number of critical theories or approaches for understanding and interpreting literature are available to critics and students alike.[1] Many of these were developed during the twentieth century to create a discipline of literary studies comparable with disciplines in the natural and social sciences. Literary critics have often borrowed liberally from other disciplines (e.g., history, psychology, politics, anthropology) but have aimed primarily at developing literature as a study in its own right.

At the heart of the various critical approaches are many fundamental questions: What is literature? What does it do? Is its concern primarily to tell stories, to divert attention, to entertain, to communicate ideas, to persuade, and to teach, or is it to describe and interpret reality, or to explore and explain emotions—or is it all of these? To what degree is literature an art, as opposed to a medium for imparting knowledge? What more does it do than express ideas? How does it get its ideas across? What can it contribute to intellectual, artistic, political, and social thought and history? How is literature used, and how and why is it misused? Is it private? Public? What theoretical and technical expertise may be invoked to enhance literary studies? How valuable was literature in the past, and how valuable is it now? To what degree should literature be in the vanguard of social and political change?

Questions such as these indicate that criticism is concerned not only with reading and interpreting stories, poems, and plays, but also with establishing theoretical understanding. Because of such extensive aims, a full explanation and illustration of the approaches would fill the pages of a long book. The following descriptions are, therefore, intended as no more than brief introductions. Bear in mind that in the hands of skilled critics, the approaches can be so subtle, sophisticated, and complex that they are not only critical stances but also philosophies.

Although the various approaches provide widely divergent ways to study literature and literary problems, they reflect major tendencies rather than absolute straitjacketing. Not every approach is appropriate for every work, nor are the approaches always mutually exclusive. Even the most devoted practitioners of the methods do not pursue

---

[1]Some of the approaches described in this chapter are presented in Chapter 1 of this book as basic study techniques for writing about literary works.

them rigidly. In addition, some of the approaches are more "user friendly" than others for certain types of discovery. To a degree, at least, most critics, therefore, take a particular approach but utilize methods that technically belong to one or more of the other approaches. A critic stressing the topical/historical approach, for example, might introduce the close study of a work that is associated with the method of the New Criticism. Similarly, a psychoanalytical critic might include details about archetypes. In short, a great deal of criticism is *pragmatic* or *eclectic* rather than rigid.

The approaches to be considered here are these: *moral/intellectual*; *topical/historical*; *New Critical/formalist*; *structuralist*; *feminist/gender studies/ queer theory*; *economic determinist/Marxist*; *psychological/psychoanalytic*; *archetypal/symbolic/mythic*; *deconstructionist*; and *reader-response*.

The object of learning about these approaches, like everything else in this book, is to help you develop your own capacities as a reader and writer. Accordingly, following each of the descriptions is a brief paragraph showing how Hawthorne's story "Young Goodman Brown" (p. 317, Appendix C) might be considered in the light of the particular approach. The illustrative paragraph following the discussion of structuralism, for example, shows an application of the structuralist approach to Goodman Brown and his story, and so with the feminist approach, the economic determinist approach, and the others. In the Twelfth Edition, these paragraphs are followed by additional paragraphs illustrating the same approaches based on other literary works. Whenever you are doing your own writing about literature, you are free to use the various approaches as part or all of your assignment if you believe the approach may help you.

Moral/Intellectual

The **moral/intellectual critical approach** is concerned with content, ideas, and values. The approach is as old as literature itself, for literature is a traditional mode of inculcating thought, morality, philosophy, and religion. The concern in moral/intellectual criticism is not only to discover meaning, but also to determine whether works of literature are both *true* and *significant*.

To study literature from the moral/intellectual perspective is, therefore, to determine whether a work conveys a lesson or a message and whether it can help readers to lead better lives and improve their understanding of the world. What ideas does the work contain? How strongly does the work bring forth its ideas? What application do the ideas have to the work's characters and situations? How may the ideas be evaluated intellectually? Morally? Discussions based on such questions do not imply that literature is primarily a medium of moral and intellectual exhortation. Ideally, moral/intellectual criticism should differ from sermonizing to the degree to which readers should always be left with their own decisions about whether to assimilate the ideas of a work and about whether the ideas—and values—are personally or morally acceptable.

Sophisticated critics have sometimes denigrated the moral/intellectual approach on the grounds that "message hunting" reduces a work's artistic value by treating it like a sermon or political speech; but, the approach will be valuable as long as readers expect literature to be applicable to their own lives.

Example: Hawthorne's "Young Goodman Brown"

"Young Goodman Brown" raises the issue of how an institution designed for human elevation, such as the religious system of colonial Salem, can be so ruinous. Does the failure result from the system itself or from the people who misunderstand it? Is what is true of religion as practiced by Brown also true of social and political institutions? Should any religious or political philosophy be given greater significance than good will and mutual trust? One of the major virtues of "Young Goodman Brown" is that it provokes questions like these but at the same time provides a number of satisfying answers. A particularly important one is that religious and moral beliefs should not be used to justify the condemnation of others. Another important answer is that attacks made from the refuge of a religion or group, such as Brown's Puritanism, are dangerous because the judge may condemn without thought and without personal responsibility.

Topical/Historical

The **topical/historical critical approach** stresses the relationship of literature to its historical period, and for this reason, it has had a long life. Although much literature may be applicable to many places and times, much of it also directly reflects the intellectual and social worlds of the authors. When was the work written? What were the circumstances that produced it? What major issues does it deal with? How does it fit into the author's career? Keats's poem "On First Looking into Chapman's Homer" (p. 356), for example, is his excited response to his reading of one of the major literary works of Western civilization. Hardy's "Channel Firing" (p. 353) is an ironically acerbic response to continued armament and preparation for war in the past, in the present, and in the future.

The topical/historical approach investigates relationships of this sort, including the elucidation of words and concepts that today's readers might not immediately understand. Obviously, the approach may require the assistance of footnotes, dictionaries, library catalogues, histories, online searches, and handbooks.

A common criticism of the topical/historical approach is that, in the extreme, it deals with background knowledge rather than with literature itself. It is possible, for example, for a topical/historical critic to describe a writer's life, the period of the writer's work, and the social and intellectual ideas of the time—all without ever considering the meaning, importance, and value of any of that writer's works themselves.

A reaction against such an unconnected use of historical details is the so-called **New Historicism**. This approach justifies the parallel reading of both literary and non-literary works to bring an informed understanding of the context of a literary work. The New Historicist assumes that history is not a fixed essence but a literary construction. As such, history is a prism through which a society views itself; a work of literature is given resonance by seeing the nonobjective context in which it was produced. This approach justifies the introduction of historical knowledge by integrating it with the understanding of particular texts. Readers of Arnold's "Dover Beach" (p. 347), for example, sometimes find it difficult to follow the meaning of Arnold's statement "The Sea of Faith / Was once, too, at the full." Historical background has a definite role to play here.

In Arnold's time, there developed a method of treating the Bible as a historical document rather than a divinely inspired revelation. This approach has been called the "Higher Criticism" of the Bible, and to many thoughtful people, the Higher Criticism undermined the concept that the Bible was divine, infallible, and inerrant. Therefore, Arnold's idea is that the "Sea of Faith" is no longer at full tide but is now rather at an ebb. Because the introduction of such historical material is designed to facilitate the reading of the poem—and the reading of other literature of the period—the New Historicism represents an integration of knowledge and interpretation. As a principle, New Historicism entails the acquisition of as much historical information as possible because our knowledge of the relationship of literature to its historical period can never be complete. The practitioner of historical criticism must always seek new information on the grounds that it may prove relevant to the understanding of various literary works.

Example: Hawthorne's "Young Goodman Brown"

"Young Goodman Brown" is an allegorical story by Nathaniel Hawthorne (1804–1864), the major New England writer who probed deeply into the relationship between religion and guilt. His ancestors had been involved in religious persecutions, including the Salem witch trials, and he, living 150 years afterward, wanted to analyze the weaknesses and uncertainties of the sin-dominated religion of the earlier period, a tradition of which he was a resentful heir. Not surprisingly, therefore, the story about "Young Goodman Brown" takes place in Salem during Puritan times, and Hawthorne's implied judgments are those of a severe critic of how the harsh old religion destroyed personal and family relationships. Although the immediate concerns of the story belong to a vanished age, Hawthorne's treatment is still valuable because it is still timely.

New Critical/Formalist

The **New Critical/formalist critical approach**, also known as the New Criticism, has been a dominant force in modern literary studies. It focuses on literary texts as formal works of art, and for this reason, it can be seen as a reaction against the topical/historical approach. The objection raised by New Critics is that as topical/historical critics consider literary history, they evade direct contact with actual texts.

The inspiration for the New Critical/formalist approach was the French practice of *explication de texte*, a method that emphasizes detailed examination and explanation. The New Criticism is at its most brilliant in the formal analysis of smaller units such as entire poems and short passages. For the analysis of larger structures, the New Criticism also utilizes a number of techniques that have been selected as the basis of chapters in this book. Discussions of point of view, tone, plot, character, and structure, for example, are formal ways of looking at literature that are derived from the New Criticism.

The aim of the formalist study of literature is to provide readers not only with the means of explaining the content of works (what, specifically, does a work say?), but also with the insights needed for evaluating the artistic quality of individual works and writers (how well is it said?). A major aspect of New Critical thought is that content and form—including all ideas, ambiguities, subtleties, and even apparent contradictions—

were originally within the conscious or subconscious control of the author. There are no accidents. It does not necessarily follow, however, that today's critic is able to define the author's intentions exactly, for such intentions require knowledge of biographical details that are irretrievably lost. Each literary work, therefore, takes on its own existence and identity, and the critic's work is to discover a reading or readings that explain the facts of the text. Please note that the New Critic does not claim infallible interpretations and does not exclude the validity of multiple readings of the same work.

Dissenters from the New Criticism have noted a tendency by New Critics to ignore relevant knowledge that history and biography can bring to literary studies. In addition, the approach has been subject to the charge that stressing the explication of texts alone fails to deal with literary value and appreciation. In other words, the formalist critic, in explaining the meaning of literature, sometimes neglects the reasons for which readers find literature interesting, stimulating, and valuable.

Example: Hawthorne's "Young Goodman Brown"

A major aspect of Hawthorne's "Young Goodman Brown" is that the details are so vague and dreamlike that many readers are uncertain about what is happening. The action is a nighttime walk by the protagonist, Young Goodman Brown, into a deep forest where he encounters a mysterious satanic ritual that leaves him bitter and misanthropic. This much seems clear, but the precise nature of Brown's experience is not clear, nor is the identity of the stranger (father, village elder, devil) who accompanies Brown as he begins his walk. At the story's end, Hawthorne's narrator states that the whole episode may have been no more than a dream or nightmare. Yet when morning comes, Brown walks back into town as though returning from an overnight trip, and he recoils in horror from his fellow villagers, including his wife Faith (317, 70). Could his attitude result from nothing more than a nightmare?

Even at the story's end, these uncertainties remain. For this reason, one may conclude that Hawthorne deliberately creates the uncertainties to reveal how people like Brown build defensive walls of judgment around themselves. The story thus implies that the real source of Brown's anger is as vague as his nocturnal walk, but he doesn't understand it in this way. Because Brown's vision and judgment are absolute, he rejects everyone around him, even if the cost is a life of bitter suspicion and spiritual isolation.

Structuralist

The principle of the **structuralist critical approach** stems from the attempt to find relationships and connections among elements that appear to be separate and unique. Just as physical science reveals unifying universal principles of matter such as gravity and the forces of electromagnetism (and is constantly searching for a "unified field theory"), the structuralist critic attempts to discover the forms unifying all literature. Thus, a structuralist description of Maupassant's "The Necklace" stresses that the main character, Mathilde, is an *active* protagonist who undergoes a *test* (or series of tests) and emerges with a victory, though not the kind she had originally hoped for. The same might be said of Smirnov and Mrs. Popov in Chekhov's play *The Bear*. If this same kind of structural view is applied to Hawthorne's

"Young Goodman Brown" (p. 317), the protagonist is defeated in the test. Generally, the structuralist approach applies such patterns to other works of literature to determine that certain protagonists are active or submissive, that they pass or fail their tests, that they succeed or fail at other encounters, or that they might fail one kind of test but are victorious in another. The key is that many apparently unrelated works reveal many common patterns or contain similar structures with important variations.

The structuralist approach is important because it enables critics to discuss works from widely separate cultures and historical periods. In this respect, critics have followed the leads of modern anthropologists, most notably Claude Lévi-Strauss (1908–1990). Along such lines, critics have undertaken the serious examination of folktales and fairy tales. Some of the groundbreaking structuralist criticism, for example, was devoted to the structural analysis of themes, actions, and characters to be found in Russian folktales. The method also bridges popular and serious literature, making little distinction between the two insofar as the description of the structures is concerned. Indeed, structuralism furnishes an ideal approach for comparative literature; the method also enables critics to consolidate genres such as modern romances, detective tales, soap operas, and sitcoms.

Like the New Criticism, structuralism aims at comprehensiveness of description, and many critics would insist that the two are complementary and not separate. A distinction is that New Criticism is at its best in dealing with smaller units of literature, whereas structuralist criticism is best in the analysis of narratives and, therefore, larger units such as novels, myths, stories, plays, and films. Because structuralism shows how fiction is organized into various typical situations, the approach merges with the *archetypal* approach (see below, p. 302), and at times, it is difficult to find any distinctions between structuralist and archetypal criticism.

Structuralism, however, deals not just with narrative structures but also with structures of any type, wherever they occur. For example, structuralism makes considerable use of linguistics. Modern linguistic scholars have determined that there is a difference between "deep structures" and "surface structures" in language. A structuralist analysis of style, therefore, emphasizes how writers utilize such structures. The structuralist interpretation of language also perceives distinguishing types or "grammars" of language that are recurrent in various types of literature. Suppose, for example, that you encounter opening passages like the following:

1. Once upon a time a young prince fell in love with a young princess. He was in love so deeply that he wanted to declare his love for her, and early one morning, he left his castle on his white charger, along with his retainers and servants, riding toward her castle home high in the distant and cloud-topped mountains.
2. Early that morning, Alan found himself thinking about Anne. He had thought that she was being ambiguous when she said she loved him, and his feelings about her were not certain. His further thought left him still unsure.

The words of these two passages create different and distinct frames of reference. One is a fairy tale of the past; the other is a modern internalized reflection of feeling. The passages, therefore, demonstrate how language itself fits into predetermined patterns or structures. Similar uses of language structures can be associated with other types of literature.

Example: Hawthorne's "Young Goodman Brown"

Young Goodman Brown is a hero who is passive, not active. He is a *witness*, a *receiver* rather than a *doer*. His only action—taking his trip in the forest—occurs at the story's beginning. After that point, he no longer acts but instead is acted upon, and his reactions to what he sees around him put his life's beliefs to a test. Of course, many protagonists undergo similar testing (such as rescuing victims and overcoming particularly terrible dragons), and they emerge as heroes or conquerors. Not so with Goodman Brown. He is a responder who allows himself to be victimized by his own perceptions—or misperceptions. Despite all his previous experiences with his wife and with the good people of his village, he generalizes too hastily. He lets the single disillusioning experience of his nightmare govern his entire outlook on others, and, thus, he fails his test and turns his entire life into darkness.

Feminist Criticism, Gender Studies, and Queer Theory

Feminist criticism, **gender studies**, and **queer theory** display divergent interests drawing insights from many disciplines. These are still evolving and rich fields of inquiry. Feminist criticism had its genesis in the women's movement of the 1960s, shares many of its concerns, and has applied them to the study of literature. One of the early aims of feminist critics was to question the traditional canon and claim a place in it for neglected women writers. Writers such as Mary Shelley, Elizabeth Gaskell, Christina Rossetti, Kate Chopin, Charlotte Perkins Gilman, and Anita Scott Coleman have been given great critical attention as a result. Feminist critics also delineate the ways both male and female characters are portrayed in literature, looking at how societal norms about sexual difference are either enforced or subverted, and focusing partly on patriarchal structures and institutions such as marriage. As early as the beginning of the twentieth century, Virginia Woolf questioned whether there was a feminine/masculine divide in writing styles, a contentious subject among feminist critics to this day. Feminist critics are also interested in how interpretation of texts differs between the sexes. For instance, in *A Map for Rereading* (1980), the critic Annette Kolodny analyzes how men and women read the same stories differently.

Gender studies, a more recent critical approach, brings attention to gender rather than to sexual differences. Gender studies critics see the masculine/feminine divide as socially constructed and not innate. Drawing partly on the works of the French philosopher Michel Foucault (1926–1984) such as *The History of Sexuality* and *Madness and Civilization*, which explore the way in which powerful institutions organize our society and way of thinking, gender studies critics apply Foucault's ideas to understanding patriarchal structures and their representations in literature. Many studies have also built on the insights of psychoanalysis and deconstruction, questioning Freud's male-oriented categories and seeking insights into the way in which language is constructed and the way in which it affects our thinking. In the essay "The Laugh of the Medusa" (1975), Hélène Cixous applies deconstructionist insights about binary oppositions to a study of discourse about women, showing how this discourse disparages women.

A more recent critical orientation, which came to prominence in the early 1990s, is queer theory, which also appropriates many of the insights of deconstruction, particularly its understanding that binary oppositions are relative and that thinking about matters such as sexual orientation is partly ideological and partly social. Many queer theorists see the heterosexual/homosexual divide as less distinct than has typically been believed. Queer theorists are interested in how homosexuals are portrayed in literature and whether they write or read literature differently than heterosexuals do. Queer theory has brought attention to recent literary works that deal explicitly with lesbian and gay themes, along with attention to sometimes veiled references to the same themes in writers whose works make up the standard canon.

Example Hawthorne's "Young Goodman Brown"

At the beginning of "Young Goodman Brown," Brown's wife, Faith, is seen only peripherally. In the traditional patriarchal spirit of wife-as-adjunct, she tells her new husband of her fears and then asks him to stay at home and take his journey at some other time. Hawthorne does not give her the intelligence or dignity, however, to let her explain her concern (or might he not have been interested in what she had to say?), and she, therefore, remains in the background with her pink hair ribbon as her distinguishing symbol of submissive inferiority. During the mid-forest satanic ritual, she appears again and is given power, but only the power to cause her husband to go astray. Once she is led in as a novice in the practice of demonism, her husband falls right in step. Unfortunately, by following her, Brown can conveniently excuse himself from guilt by claiming that "she" had made him do it, just as Eve, in some traditional views of the fall of humankind, compelled Adam to eat the apple (Genesis 3:16–17). Hawthorne's attention to the male protagonist, in other words, permits him to neglect the independence and integrity of a female protagonist.

Economic Determinist/Marxist

The concept of cultural and economic determinism is one of the major political ideas of the nineteenth century. Karl Marx (1818–1883) emphasized that the primary influence on life was economic, and he saw society as being enmeshed in a continuous conflict between capitalist oppressors and oppressed working people. The literature that emerged from this kind of analysis often features individuals who are coping with the ill effects of economic disadvantage. Sometimes called "proletarian" literature, it focuses on people of the lower class—the poor and oppressed who spend their lives in endless drudgery and misery and whose attempts to rise to the top usually result in renewed oppression.

Marx's political ideas were never widely accepted in the United States and have faded still more since the breakup of the Soviet Union, but the idea of economic determinism (and the related term *Social Darwinism*) is still credible. As a result, much literature can be judged from an economic perspective even though the economic critics may not be Marxian: What is the economic status of the characters? What happens to them as a result of this status? How do they fare against economic and political odds? What other conditions stemming from their class does the writer emphasize (e.g., poor education, poor nutrition, poor health care, inadequate opportunity)? To what extent does the work fail by overlooking the economic, social, and political implications of its material? In what other ways does economic determinism affect the work? How should readers consider the story in today's developed or underdeveloped world? Seemingly, Hawthorne's story "Young Goodman Brown," which we have used for analysis in these discussions, has no major economic implications, but an **economic determinist/ Marxist critical approach** might take the following turns.

Example: Hawthorne's "Young Goodman Brown"

"Young Goodman Brown" is a fine story just as it is. It deals with the false values instilled by the skewed acceptance of sin-dominated religion, but it overlooks the economic implications of this situation. One might suspect that the real story in Goodman Brown's Salem should be about the disruption caused by an alienated member of society. In other words, after Brown's condemnation and distrust of others forces him into his own shell of sick imagination, Hawthorne does not consider how such a disaffected character would injure the economic and public life of the town. Consider this, just for a moment: Why would the people from whom Brown recoils in disgust want to deal with him in business or personal matters? In town meetings, would they want to follow his opinions on crucial issues of public concern and investment? Would his preoccupation with sin and damnation make him anything more than a horror in his domestic life? Would his wife, Faith, be able to discuss household management with him or ask him about methods of caring for the children? All these questions, of course, are pointed toward another story—a story that Hawthorne did not write. They also indicate the shortcomings of Hawthorne's approach, because it is clear that the major result of Young Goodman Brown's selfish preoccupation with evil would be a serious disruption of the economic and political affairs of his small community.

Psychological/Psychoanalytic

The scientific study of the mind is a product of psychodynamic theory as established by Sigmund Freud (1856–1939) and of the psychoanalytic method practiced by his followers. Psychoanalysis provided a new key to the understanding of character by claiming that behavior is caused by hidden and unconscious motives. It was greeted as a revelation with far-reaching implications for all intellectual pursuits. Not surprisingly, it has had a profound and continuing effect on post-Freudian literature.

In addition, its popularity produced the **psychological/psychoanalytic approach** to criticism.[2] Some critics use the approach to explain fictional characters, as in the landmark interpretation by Freud and Ernest Jones that Shakespeare's Hamlet suffers from an Oedipus complex. Still other critics use it as a way of analyzing authors and the artistic process. For example, John Livingston Lowes's study *The Road to Xanadu* presents a detailed examination of the mind, reading, and neuroses of Coleridge, the author of "Kubla Khan" (p. 350).

---

[2]See Chapter 4, "Writing About Character: The People in Literature."

Critics using the psychoanalytic approach treat literature somewhat like information about patients in therapy. In the work itself, what are the obvious and hidden motives that cause a character's behavior and speech? How much background (e.g., repressed child-hood trauma, adolescent memories) does the author reveal about a character? How purposeful is this information with regard to the character's psychological condition? How much is important in the analysis and understanding of the character?

In the consideration of authors, critics utilizing the psychoanalytic model consider questions like these: What particular life experiences explain characteristic subjects or preoccupations? Was the author's life happy? Miserable? Upsetting? Solitary? Social? Can the death of someone in the author's family be associated with melancholy situations in that author's work? All eleven brothers and sisters of the English poet Thomas Gray, for example, died before reaching adulthood. Gray was the only one of the twelve to survive. In his poetry, Gray often deals with death, and he is, therefore, considered one of the "Graveyard School" of eighteenth-century poets. A psychoanalytical critic might make much of this connection.

Example: Hawthorne's "Young Goodman Brown"

At the end of "Young Goodman Brown," Hawthorne's major character is no longer capable of normal existence. His nightmare should be read as a symbol of what in real-ity would have been lifelong mental subjection to the type of puritanical religion that emphasizes sin and guilt. Such preoccupation with sin is no hindrance to psychological health if the preoccupied people are convinced that God forgives them and grants them mercy. In their dealings with others, they remain healthy as long as they believe that other people have the same sincere trust in divine forgiveness. If their own faith is weak and uncertain, however, and if they cannot believe in forgiveness, then they are likely to transfer their own guilt—really a form of personal terror—to others. They re-main conscious of their own sins, but they find it easy to claim that others are sinful—even those who are spiritually spotless, and even their own family, who should be dear-est to them. When this process of projection or transference occurs, such people have created the rationale of condemning others because of their own guilt. The price that they pay is a life of gloom, a fate that Hawthorne designates for Goodman Brown after his nightmare about demons in human form.

Archetypal/Symbolic/Mythic

The **archetypal/symbolic/mythic critical approach**, derived from the work of the Swiss psychoanalyst Carl Jung (1875–1961), presupposes that human life is built up out of patterns, or *archetypes* ("first molds" or "first patterns") that are similar throughout various cultures and historical times.[3] The approach is similar to the structuralist analysis of literature, for both approaches stress the connections that may be discovered in literature that is written in different times and in vastly different locations in the world.

In literary evaluation, the archetypal approach is used to support the claim that the very best literature is grounded in archetypal patterns. The archetypal critic, therefore,

---

[3]Symbolism is also considered in Chapter 11.

looks for archetypes such as God's creation of human beings, the sacrifice of a hero, or the search for paradise. How does an individual story, poem, or play fit into any of the archetypal patterns? What truths does this correlation provide (particularly truths that cross historical, national, and cultural lines)? How closely does the work fit the archetype? What variations can be seen? What meaning or meanings do the connections have?

The most tenuous aspect of archetypal criticism is Jung's assertion that the recurring patterns provide evidence for a "universal human consciousness" that all of us, by virtue of our humanity, still retain in our minds and in our very blood.

Not all critics accept the hypothesis of a universal human consciousness, but they nevertheless consider the approach important for comparisons and contrasts (see Chapter 15, p. 210). Many human situations, such as adolescence, dawning love, the search for success, the reconciliation with one's mother and father, and the encroachment of age and death, are similar in structure and can be analyzed as archetypes. For example, the following situations can be seen as a pattern or archetype of initiation: A young man discovers the power of literature and understanding (Keats's "On First Looking into Chapman's Homer," p. 153, 356); a man determines the importance of truth and fidelity amidst uncertainty (Arnold's "Dover Beach," p. 347); a man and a woman fall in love despite their wishes to remain independent (Chekhov's *The Bear*); a woman gains strength and integrity because of previously unrealized inner resources (Maupassant's "The Necklace"). The archetypal approach encourages the analysis of variations on the same theme, as in Glaspell's *Trifles* and O'Connor's "First Confession" (p. 332) when characters ignore the imposition of a particular moral (or legal) standard (one sort of initiation) and instead assert their own individuality and freedom (another sort of initiation).

Example: Hawthorne's "Young Goodman Brown"

In the sense that Young Goodman Brown undergoes a change from psychological normality to rigidity, the story is a reverse archetype of the initiation ritual. According to the archetype of successful initiation, initiates seek to demonstrate their worthiness to become full-fledged members of society. Telemachus in Homer's *Odyssey*, for example, is a young man who in the course of the epic goes through the initiation rituals of travel, discussion, and battle. But in "Young Goodman Brown," we see initiation in reverse, for just as there is an archetype of successful initiation, Brown's initiation leads him into failure. In the private areas of life on which happiness depends, he falls short. He sees evil in his fellow villagers, condemns his minister, and shrinks even from his own family. His life, therefore, becomes filled with despair and gloom. His suspicions are those of a Puritan of long ago, but the timeliness of Hawthorne's story is that the archetype of misunderstanding and condemnation has not changed. Today's headlines of misery and war are produced by the same kind of intolerance that is exhibited by Goodman Brown.

Deconstructionist

The **deconstructionist critical approach**—which deconstructionists explain not as an approach but rather as a performance or as a strategy of reading—was developed by the French philosopher Jacques Derrida (1930–2004). In the 1970s and 1980s, it became a major mode of criticism by critiquing the "logocentric" Western philosophical tradition. Logocentrism is the belief that speech is a direct expression of a speaker's intention, that it has a direct correspondence to reality, and that it is, therefore, the privileged arbiter of interpretation. Derrida, by exposing what he saw as the fallacious assumptions of logocentrism, sought to undermine the basis of stable meanings derivable from language. The implications for reading and, therefore, for literary studies were far reaching.

Deconstructionist critics begin literary analysis by assuming the instability of language and the impossibility of arriving at a fixed standard to anchor interpretation. The dictum, in Derrida's *Of Grammatology*, that "There is nothing outside the text" indicates the denial of any authoritative referent outside of words. Texts are always self-contradictory because they can always be reread to undermine an apparently stable interpretation. In part, this is due to how meaning is derived from binary oppositions such as speech/writing, male/female, good/evil. Each word of the pair obtains its significance by contrast with the other, so its meaning is relative, not absolute. A female may, therefore, be defined as lacking male features or a male as lacking female traits. In addition, each set of opposites has been arranged hierarchically. Speech, for instance, is considered more immediate and, therefore, closer to reality than writing; therefore, speech is the privileged member of the set of speech/writing. These pairings are social constructs, and form part of our way of thinking, even if they do not necessarily reflect reality.

Other strategies for undermining the stability of texts are to see how they have "gaps," or missing pieces of information, or how the words of texts have several meanings and connotations, all of which "de-center" the meaning of the texts. While a poem might seem to mean one thing when our habitual, formalistic reading strategies are applied to it, it can be shown to have a completely different meaning as well. Additional readings will yield still other meanings. The text is, therefore, said to "deconstruct" itself, as the reading strategies applied to it are merely pointing out contradictory elements that inhere in the nature of language itself.

While formalist critics aim at resolving contradictions and ambiguities to form a unified literary work, deconstructionists aim to find disunity and disruptions in the language of a text. The typical deconstructionist strategy is to start with a standard formalistic reading of a text and then undermine that interpretation to yield a new one. The deconstructionist does not deny that interpretations are possible, only that there is no basis for appealing to final, absolute ones. Deconstruction has yielded some new, imaginative readings of canonical literature. Some critics of deconstruction argue that the "initial" formalistic readings of the deconstructionist strategy are the most rewarding and that deconstructionist interpretations are often incoherent.

Example: Hawthorne's "Young Goodman Brown"

There are many uncertainties in the details of "Young Goodman Brown." If one starts with the stranger on the path, one might conclude that he could be Brown's father, because he recognizes Brown immediately and speaks to him jovially. On the other hand, the stranger could be the devil (he is recognized as such by Goody Cloyse) because of his wriggling walking stick. After disappearing, the stranger also takes on the characteristics of an omniscient cult leader and seer, because at the satanic celebration he knows all the secret sins committed by Brown's neighbors and the community of greater New England. Additionally, he might represent a perverted conscience whose aim is to mislead and befuddle people by steering them into the holier-than-thou judgmental attitude that Brown adopts. This method would be truly diabolical—to use religion in order to bring people to their own damnation. That the stranger is an evil force is, therefore, clear, but the pathways of his evil are not as clear. He seems to work his mission of damnation by reaching the souls of persons like Goodman Brown through means ordinarily attributed to conscience. If the stranger represents a satanic conscience, what are we to suppose that Hawthorne is asserting about what is considered real conscience?

Reader-Response

The **reader-response critical approach** is rooted in *phenomenology*, a branch of philosophy that deals with the understanding of how things appear. The phenomenological idea of knowledge is based on the separation of the reality of our thoughts from the reality of the world. Our quest for truth is to be found not in the external world itself but rather in our mental *perception* and interpretation of externals. All that we human beings can know—actual *knowledge*—is our collective and personal understanding of the world and our conclusions about it.

As a consequence of the phenomenological concept, reader-response theory holds that the reader is a necessary third party in the author-text-reader relationship that constitutes the literary work. In other words, the work is not fully created until readers make a *transaction* with it by assimilating it and *actualizing* it in the light of their own knowledge and experience. The representative questions of the theory are these: What does this work mean to me, in my present intellectual and moral makeup? How can the work improve my understanding and widen my insights? How can my increasing understanding help me to understand the work more deeply? The theory is that the free interchange or transaction that such questions bring about leads toward interest and growth, so readers can assimilate literary works and accept them as parts of their lives and as parts of the civilization in which they live.

As an initial way of reading, the reader-response method may be personal and anecdotal. In addition, by stressing response rather than interpretation, one of the leading exponents of the method, Stanley Fish, has raised the extreme question about whether texts, by themselves, have objective identity. These aspects have been cited as both a shortcoming and an inconsequentiality of the method.

It is, therefore, important to stress that the reader-response theory is *open*. It permits beginning readers to bring their own personal reactions to literature, but it also aims to increase their discipline and skill. The more that readers bring to literature through their interests and disciplined studies, the more "competent" and comprehensive their "transactions" will be. It is possible, for example, to explain the structure of a work not according to commonly recognized categories such as exposition and climax, but rather according to the personal reactions of disciplined readers. The contention is that structure, like other topics of study such as tone or the comprehension of figurative language, refers to the clearly definable responses of readers "transacting" with works.

By such means, literature is subject not only to outward and objective analysis, but also to inward and psychological responses.

The reader-response approach, thus, lends an additional dimension to the critical awareness of literature. If literary works imply that readers should possess special knowledge in fields such as art, politics, science, philosophy, religion, or morality, then disciplined readers will seek out such knowledge and utilize it in developing their responses. Also, because students experience many similar intellectual and cultural disciplines, it is logical to conclude that responses will tend not to diverge but rather to coalesce; agreements result not from personal but from cultural similarities. The reader-response theory, then, can and should be an avenue toward informed and detailed understanding of literature, but the initial emphasis is the *transaction* that readers make with literary works.

Example: Hawthorne's "Young Goodman Brown"

"Young Goodman Brown" is worrisome because it shows so disturbingly that good intentions may cause harmful results. I think that a person with too high a set of expectations is ripe for disillusionment, just as Goodman Brown is. When people don't measure up to this person's standard of perfection, they can be thrown aside as though they are worthless. They may be good people, but whatever past mistakes they have made can make it impossible for the person with high expectations to endure them. Goodman Brown makes the same kind of misjudgment, expecting perfection and turning sour when he learns about flaws. It is not that he is not a good man, because he is shown at the start as a person of belief and stability. He uncritically accepts his nightmare revelation that everyone else is evil, however (including his parents), and he finally distrusts everyone because of this baseless suspicion. He cannot look at his neighbors without avoiding them like an "anathema," and he turns away from his own wife "without a greeting" (326). Brown's problem is that he equates being human with being unworthy. By such a distorted standard of judgment, all of us fail, and that is what makes the story so disturbing.

Appendix B

MLA Recommendations for Documenting Sources

Fiction, Poetry, and Drama

This appendix provides general guidelines for making source citations. For general information on citation recommendations by the Modern Language Association (MLA), please see the *MLA Handbook for Writers of Research Papers,* Seventh Edition (New York: MLA, 2009).

The following examples show the formats you are likely to use most often, for both nonelectronic and electronic references.

(Nonelectronic) Books, Articles, Poems, Letters, Reviews, Recordings, Programs

Book by One Author

Fitzgerald, F. Scott. *The Great Gatsby*. New York: Scribners, 1925. Print.

Book with No Author Listed

The Pictorial History of the Guitar. New York: Random, 1992. Print.

Book by Two (or Three) Authors

Clemens, Samuel L., and Charles Dudley Warner. *The Gilded Age: A Tale of Today*. Hartford: American, 1874. Print.

Book by Four or More Authors

Guerin, Wilfred L., Earle Labor, Lee Morgan, Jeanne C. Reesman, and John R. Willingham. *A Handbook of Critical Approaches to Literature*. New York: Oxford UP, 2004. Print.

or

Guerin, Wilfred L., et al. *A Handbook of Critical Approaches to Literature*. New York: Oxford UP, 2004. Print.

Citing a Work in an Anthology

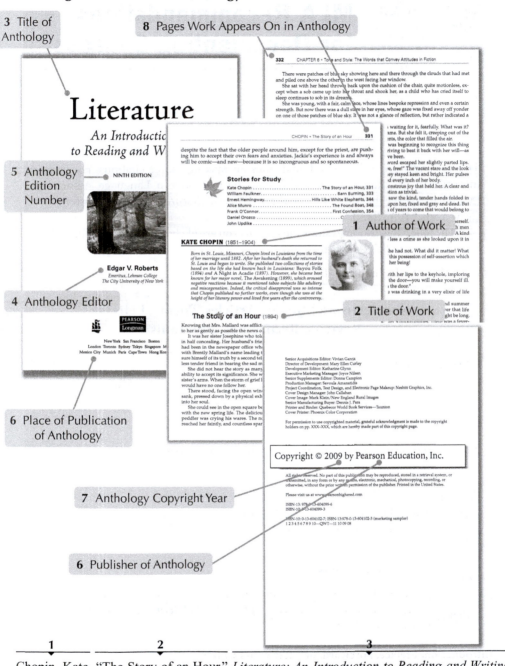

3 Title of Anthology

8 Pages Work Appears On in Anthology

5 Anthology Edition Number

4 Anthology Editor

1 Author of Work

2 Title of Work

6 Place of Publication of Anthology

7 Anthology Copyright Year

6 Publisher of Anthology

————— —————   —————
    1   2   3

Chopin, Kate. "The Story of an Hour." *Literature: An Introduction to Reading and Writing.*

Ed. Edgar V. Roberts. 9th ed. New York: Pearson Longman 2009. 331–32. Print.

—— —— ——   —— ——
  4   5   6   7   8

Two Books by the Same Author

Reynolds, David S. *Beneath the American Renaissance*. Cambridge: Harvard UP, 1988. Print.

——. *Walt Whitman's America: A Cultural Biography*. New York: Knopf, 1995. Print.

Book with an Editor

Scharnhorst, Gary, ed. *Selected Letters of Bret Harte*. Norman: U of Oklahoma P, 1997. Print.

Book with Two Editors

Dionne, Craig, and Steve Mentz, eds. *Rogues and Early Modern English Culture*. Ann Arbor: U of Michigan P, 2004. Print.

Book with an Author and an Editor

De Quille, Dan. *The Fighting Horse of the Stanislaus*. Ed. Lawrence I. Berkove. Iowa City: U of Iowa P, 1990. Print.

Translated Book

Cervantes Saavedra, Miguel de. *Don Quixote de la Mancha*. Trans. Charles Jarvis. New York: Oxford UP, 1999. Print.

Long Poem Published as a Book

Homer. *The Odyssey*. Trans. Robert Fitzgerald. New York: Vintage, 1990. Print.

Collection of Poetry Published as a Book

Mueller, Lisel. *Alive Together: New and Selected Poems*. Baton Rouge: Louisiana State UP, 1996. Print.

Literary Work in an Anthology

Chopin, Kate. "The Storm." *Fiction 100: An Anthology of Short Fiction*. Ed. James H. Pickering. 10th ed. Upper Saddle River: Pearson, 2004. 226–29. Print.

Introduction, Preface, Foreword, or Afterword in a Book

Pryse, Marjorie. Introduction. *The Country of the Pointed Firs and Other Stories*. By Sarah Orne Jewett. New York: Norton, 1981. v–xix. Print.

Article in a Reference Book

Gerber, Phillip. "Naturalism." *The Encyclopedia of American Literature.* Ed. Steven
  Serafin. New York: Continuum, 1999. 808–09. Print.

Article in a Journal with Continuous Paging

Rhodes, Chip. "Satire in Romanian Literature." *Humor* 8 (1995): 275–86. Print.

Article in a Journal That Pages Each Issue Separately

Kruse, Horst. "The Motif of the Flattened Corpse." *Studies in American Humor* 4
  (Spring, 1997): 47–53. Print.

Signed Book Review

Bird, John. Rev. of *The Singular Mark Twain*, by Fred Kaplan. *Mark Twain Annual.* 2
  (2004): 57–61. Print.

Unsigned Book Review

Rev. of *Canons by Consensus: Critical Trends and American Literature Anthologies*,
  by Joseph Csicsila. *Essays in Arts and Sciences* 24 (2000): 69–74. Print.

Article in a Newspaper

Album, Mitch. "Longing for Another Slice of Dorm Pizza." *Detroit Free Press,* 3
  April 2005: C1. Print.

Editorial

"Death Penalty Debate Finally Produces Useful Result." Editorial. *USA Today.* 22
  June, 2005: A15. Print.

Letter to the Editor

Mulder, Sara. Letter. *New York Times.* 27 September 2005, late ed., sec 2:5. Print.

Article in a Magazine

McDermott, John R. "The Famous Moustache That Was." *Life* 20 Dec. 1968: 53–56. Print.

Article in an Encyclopedia

"Afghanistan." *Encyclopaedia Britannica. 2009 Student and Home Edition.* Chicago:
  Encyclopaedia Britannica. 2009. Web.

Dictionary Entry

"Apricot." *The American Heritage Dictionary of the English Language*. 4th ed. 2000. Print.

Government Publication

United States. Cong. Joint Committee on the Investigation of Land Use in the Midwest. *Hearings*. 105th Cong., 2nd sess. 4 vols. Washington GPO, 1997. Print.

Lecture

Kaston Tange, Andrea. "The Importance of American Literature." Literature 100 class lecture. Eastern Michigan University, 5 Nov. 2002. Lecture.

Letter

Hosko, John. Letter to the author. 23 Sept. 2000.

Email

Judd, Professor Jacob. E-mail to the author. 19 May 2009. E-mail.

Interview

Stipe, Michael. Personal interview. 10 Nov. 2004.

Film

Napoleon Dynamite. Dir. Jared Hess. Fox Searchlight, 2004. Film.

Television Program

"The Parking Garage." *Seinfeld*. NBC. WDIV, Detroit. 23 July 1994. Television.

Sound Recording

Strauss, Richard. *Vier letzte Lieder (Four Last Songs)*. *Tod und Verklärung*. *Metamorphosen*. Herbert von Karajan, Cond. Gundula Janowitz, Soprano. Rec. Nov. 1972, Aug. 1969. Musical Heritage Society, 1997. CD.

Song on a Recording

Graham, Susan. "Le spectre de la rose." By Hector Berlioz. *Susan Graham, Berlioz, Les Nuits D'été*. London, 1997. CD.

Music Video

Outkast. "Hey Ya." *Speakerboxxx/The Love Below.* Dir. Bryan Barber. La Face, 2003.
    Music video.

The Citation of Electronic Sources

Both students and instructors can now take advantage of the technology available to
assist in research. While many libraries offer varied databases that enable researchers to
locate information easily, the main thrust of technology is now the World Wide Web.
At one time, it was necessary, in the search of electronic sources, to type the letters,
numbers, symbols, dots, underlines, and spaces. That is no longer true. Through the
use of various search engines, such as Google and Yahoo!, you simply need to type in
the name of an author, a title, or a topic, hit Enter, and you will be linked to a host of
resources from all over the world—Web sites of specific authors and literary organizations and works on various topics by contemporary writers. You'll find a good deal of
what you're searching for at the touch of your keys. As you perform your search, electronic references will appear on your screen with the proper Uniform Resource Loca-
tors (URL) intact, so you may conveniently ignore the basically unreadable collections
of letters, periods, and signs contained in each URL and simply click on the link.

  An important caveat is that many sources still remain in printed journals and
magazines that may or, more probably, may not be on the Web. To make your searches
thorough, therefore, *you must never neglect to search for printed information.*

MLA Style Guidelines for Electronic Sources

  Many of the guidelines that the MLA has authorized for the citation of electronic
sources overlap with the MLA recommendations for printed sources, but to avoid ambiguity, a number of recommendations bear repetition. Electronic materials are to be
documented in basically the same style as printed sources. According to the seventh
edition of the *MLA Handbook*, which illustrates virtually all the situations you could
ever encounter, the following items need to be included if they are available. Because
most word-processing programs now support the use of italics, you can routinely use
italics in your citations of electronic sources.

  1. The name of the author, editor, compiler, or translator of the source (if available and
      relevant), last name first, followed by an abbreviation, such as *ed.*, if appropriate.
  2. If no author is listed in the source, you should list the title first: the title of a
      poem, short story, article, or similar short work within a scholarly project, data-
      base, or periodical (in quotation marks) or the title of a posting to a discussion
      list or forum (taken from the subject line and enclosed by quotation marks),
      concluded by the phrase "Online posting."
  3. The title of a book, italicized.
  4. The name of the editor, compiler, or translator of the text (if relevant and if not cited
      earlier), preceded by (not followed by) any necessary abbreviations, such as *Ed.*
  5. Publication information for any printed version of the source.

6. The title of the scholarly project, database, periodical, or professional or personal site, italicized, or, for a professional or personal site with no title, a description such as "Home Page."
7. The name of the editor of the scholarly project or database (if available).
8. The version number of the source (if not part of the title), or, for a journal, the volume number, issue number, or other identifying number. All numbers should be in Arabic numerals, not Roman numerals.
9. The date of publication or posting that you find in your source. Sometimes the original date is no longer available because it has been replaced with an update; if so, cite that. Dates should be arranged by (a) day of the month, (b) month (the names of longer months may be abbreviated), and (c) year.
10. For a work from a subscription service, the name of the service (and name, city, and state abbreviation if the subscriber is a library).
11. For a posting to a discussion list or forum, the name of the list or forum.
12. The number range or total number of pages, paragraphs, or other sections, if they are numbered. If you do your own numbering, include your numbers within square brackets [ ], and be sure to indicate what you have numbered.
13. The name of any institution or organization sponsoring or associated with the Web site.
14. The date on which you consulted the source. If you have looked at the site a number of times, include the most recent date of use. The principle here is that the date immediately before the uniform resource locator (URL) will mark the last time you used the source.
15. The electronic address or URL of the source in angle brackets < >. Many programs now automatically include the angle brackets. If the URL is too long to fit on one line, it should be divided at a slash (/) if possible—do not introduce hyphens into the URL as these may be mistaken for actual significant characters in that address.

Book

Shaw, Bernard. *Pygmalion.* 1916, 1999. Bartleby Archive. Web. 10 July 2009.
<http://www.bartleby.com/138/>

Poem

Carroll, Lewis. *The Hunting of the Snark.* 1876. *Literature.org.* Web. 10 July 2009.
<http://www.literature.org/authors/carroll-lewis/the-hunting-of-the-snark/>

Play

Shakespeare, William. *Hamlet.* ca. 1601. Project Gutenberg. Web. 10 July 2009.
<http://www.gutenberg.org/etext/1524>

Journal Article

Hart, D. Alexis. "Creating a Canvas of Knowledge: An Interview with Larry Sanger." *Kairos* 13.2 (Spring 2009). Multiple Sections. Web. 10 July 2009.
<http://kairos.technorhetoric.net/13.2/interviews/hart/index.html>

Magazine Article

Playbill Arts Staff. "Photo Update: DiDonato and Wheelchair Go On With the
    Show." *Playbilarts.com* July 8, 2009. Web. 10 July 2009.
    <http://www.playbillarts.com/features/article/8048.html>

Posting to a Discussion List

van Veen, Johan. "North German Music of the 17th Century." Online posting.
    Google Groups. 8 June 2009. Web. 10 July 2009. <http://groups.google
    .com/group/alt.music.j-s-bach/browse_thread/thread/e6469cd684b3747d#>

Scholarly Project

Voice of the Shuttle: Web Site for Humanities Research. Ed. Alan Liu. 10 July 2009.
    U of California Santa Barbara. Web. 10 July 2009. <http://vos.ucsb.edu/>

Professional Site

Nobel Museum. The Nobel Foundation. 2009. Web. 10 July 2009.
    <http://www.nobelmuseum.se/zino.aspx?lan=en-us>

Personal Site

Barrett, Dan. *The Gentle Giant Home Page.* 25 April 2009. Web. 10 July 2009.
    <http://blazemonger.com/GG/Gentle_Giant_Home_Page>

Appendix C

Works Used in the Text for Illustrative Essays and References

The following selections are referenced throughout *Writing About Literature*, but do not physically appear in the text:

However, these selections are available in the eAnthology featured in MyLiteratureLab (www.myliteraturelab.com), along with more than 200 additional literary works. Please refer to the inside front and back cover for a complete listing of available selections. For more information on packaging this text with *MyLiteratureLab*, refer to page xvi.

STORIES

Kate Chopin (1851–1904)

The Story of an Hour (1894)

Knowing that Mrs. Mallard was afflicted with a heart trouble, great care was taken to break to her as gently as possible the news of her husband's death.

It was her sister Josephine who told her, in broken sentences: veiled hints that revealed in half concealing. Her husband's friend Richards was there, too, near her. It was he who had been in the newspaper office when intelligence of the railroad disaster was received, with Brently Mallard's name leading the list of "killed." He had only taken the time to assure himself of its truth by a second telegram, and had hastened to forestall any less careful, less tender friend in bearing the sad message.

She did not hear the story as many women have heard the same, with a paralyzed inability to accept its significance. She wept at once, with sudden, wild abandonment, in her sister's arms. When the storm of grief had spent itself she went away to her room alone. She would have no one follow her.

There stood, facing the open window, a comfortable, roomy armchair. Into this she sank, pressed down by a physical exhaustion that haunted her body and seemed to reach into her soul.

5   She could see in the open square before her house the tops of trees that were all aquiver with the new spring life. The delicious breath of rain was in the air. In the street below a peddler was crying his wares. The notes of a distant song which some one was singing reached her faintly, and countless sparrows were twittering in the eaves.

There were patches of blue sky showing here and there through the clouds that had met and piled one above the other in the west facing her window.

She sat with her head thrown back upon the cushion of the chair, quite motionless, except when a sob came up into her throat and shook her, as a child who has cried itself to sleep continues to sob in its dreams.

She was young, with a fair, calm face, whose lines bespoke repression and even a certain strength. But now there was a dull stare in her eyes, whose gaze was fixed away off yonder on one of those patches of blue sky. It was not a glance of reflection, but rather indicated a suspension of intelligent thought.

There was something coming to her and she was waiting for it, fearfully. What was it? She did not know; it was too subtle and elusive to name. But she felt it, creeping out of the sky, reaching toward her through the sounds, the scents, the color that filled the air.

10   Now her bosom rose and fell tumultuously. She was beginning to recognize this thing that was approaching to possess her, and she was striving to beat it back with her will—as powerless as her two white slender hands would have been.

When she abandoned herself a little whispered word escaped her slightly parted lips. She said it over and over under her breath: "free, free, free!" The vacant stare and the look of terror that had followed it went from her eyes. They stayed keen and bright. Her pulses beat fast, and the coursing blood warmed and relaxed every inch of her body.

She did not stop to ask if it were or were not a monstrous joy that held her. A clear and exalted perception enabled her to dismiss the suggestion as trivial.

She knew that she would weep again when she saw the kind, tender hands folded in death; the face that had never looked save with love upon her, fixed and gray and dead. But she saw beyond that bitter moment a long procession of years to come that would belong to her absolutely. And she opened and spread her arms out to them in welcome.

There would be no one to live for during those coming years; she would live for herself. There would be no powerful will bending hers in that blind persistence with which men and women believe they have a right to impose a private will upon a fellow-creature. A kind intention or a cruel intention made the act seem no less a crime as she looked upon it in that brief moment of illumination.

And yet she had loved him—sometimes. Often she had not. What did it matter!   15 What could love, the unsolved mystery, count for in face of this possession of self asser- tion which she suddenly recognized as the strongest impulse of her being!

"Free! Body and soul free!" she kept whispering.

Josephine was kneeling before the closed door with her lips to the keyhole, implor- ing for admission. "Louise, open the door! I beg; open the door—you will make your- self ill. What are you doing, Louise? For heaven's sake open the door."

"Go away. I am not making myself ill." No; she was drinking in a very elixir of life through that open window.

Her fancy was running riot along those days ahead of her. Spring days, and summer days, and all sorts of days that would be her own. She breathed a quick prayer that life might be long. It was only yesterday she had thought with a shudder that life might be long.

She arose at length and opened the door to her sister's importunities. There was a   20 feverish triumph in her eyes, and she carried herself unwittingly like a goddess of Vic- tory. She clasped her sister's waist, and together they descended the stairs. Richards stood waiting for them at the bottom.

Some one was opening the front door with a latchkey. It was Brently Mallard who entered, a little travel-stained, composedly carrying his grip-sack and umbrella. He had been far from the scene of accident, and did not even know there had been one. He stood amazed at Josephine's piercing cry: at Richards' quick motion to screen him from the view of his wife.

But Richards was too late.

When the doctors came they said she had died of heart disease—of joy that kills.

Nathaniel Hawthorne (1804–1864)

Young Goodman Brown (1835)

Young Goodman Brown came forth at sunset, into the street of Salem village,° but put his head back, after crossing the threshold, to exchange a parting kiss with his young wife. And Faith, as the wife was aptly named, thrust her own pretty head into the street, letting the wind play with the pink ribbons of her cap, while she called to Goodman Brown.

°*Salem village:* in Massachusetts, about fifteen miles north of Boston. The time of the story is the seven- teenth or early eighteenth century.

"Dearest heart," whispered she, softly and rather sadly, when her lips were close to his ear, "prithee, put off your journey until sunrise, and sleep in your own bed tonight. A lone woman is troubled with such dreams and such thoughts, that she's afeared of herself, sometimes. Pray, tarry with me this night, dear husband, of all nights in the year!"

"My love and my Faith," replied young Goodman Brown, "of all nights in the year; this one night must I tarry away from thee. My journey, as thou callest it, forth and back again, must needs be done 'twixt now and sunrise. What, my sweet, pretty wife, dost thou doubt me already, and we but three months married!"

"Then God bless you!" said Faith with the pink ribbons, "and may you find all well, when you come back."

5   "Amen!" cried Goodman Brown. "Say thy prayers, dear Faith, and go to bed at dusk, and no harm will come to thee."

So they parted; and the young man pursued his way, until, being about to turn the corner by the meeting-house, he looked back and saw the head of Faith still peeping after him, with a melancholy air, in spite of her pink ribbons.

"Poor little Faith!" thought he, for his heart smote him. "What a wretch am I, to leave her on such an errand! She talks of dreams, too. Methought, as she spoke, there was trouble in her face, as if a dream had warned her what work is to be done tonight. But no, no! 'twould kill her to think it. Well, she's a blessed angel on earth; and after this one night, I'll cling to her skirts and follow her to Heaven."

With this excellent resolve for the future, Goodman Brown felt himself justified in making more haste on his present evil purpose. He had taken a dreary road, darkened by all the gloomiest trees of the forest, which barely stood aside to let the narrow path creep through, and closed immediately behind. It was all as lonely as could be; and there is this peculiarity in such a solitude, that the traveller knows not who may be concealed by the innumerable trunks and the thick boughs overhead; so that, with lonely footsteps, he may yet be passing through an unseen multitude.

"There may be a devilish Indian behind every tree," said Goodman Brown to himself; and he glanced fearfully behind him, as he added, "What if the devil himself should be at my very elbow!"

10   His head being turned back, he passed a crook of the road, and looking forward again, beheld the figure of a man, in grave and decent attire, seated at the foot of an old tree. He arose at Goodman Brown's approach, and walked onward, side by side with him.

"You are late, Goodman Brown," said he. "The clock of the Old South° was striking, as I came through Boston; and that is full fifteen minutes agone."

"Faith kept me back a while," replied the young man, with a tremor in his voice, caused by the sudden appearance of his companion, though not wholly unexpected.

It was now deep dusk in the forest, and deepest in that part of it where these two were journeying. As nearly as could be discerned, the second traveller was about fifty years old, apparently in the same rank of life as Goodman Brown, and bearing a considerable resemblance to him, though perhaps more in expression than features. Still, they might have been taken for father and son. And yet, though the elder person was as

---

°*Old South:* The Old South Church, in Boston, is still there.

simply clad as the younger, and as simple in manner too, he had an indescribable air of one who knew the world, and would not have felt abashed at the governor's dinner-table, or in King William's* court, were it possible that his affairs should call him thither. But the only thing about him that could be fixed upon as remarkable, was his staff, which bore the likeness of a great black snake, so curiously wrought, that it might almost be seen to twist and wriggle itself like a living serpent. This, of course, must have been an ocular deception, assisted by the uncertain light.

"Come, Goodman Brown!" cried his fellow-traveller, "this is a dull pace for the beginning of a journey. Take my staff, if you are so soon weary."

"Friend," said the other, exchanging his slow pace for a full stop, "having kept covenant by meeting thee here, it is my purpose now to return whence I came. I have scruples, touching the matter thou wot'st of."† 15

"Sayest thou so?" replied he of the serpent, smiling apart. "Let us walk on, nevertheless, reasoning as we go, and if I convince thee not, thou shalt turn back. We are but a little way in the forest, yet."

"Too far, too far!" exclaimed the goodman, unconsciously resuming his walk. "My father never went into the woods on such an errand, nor his father before him. We have been a race of honest men and good Christians, since the days of the martyrs.° And shall I be the first of the name of Brown that ever took this path and kept—"

"Such company, thou wouldst say," observed the elder person, interrupting his pause. "Well said, Goodman Brown! I have been as well acquainted with your family as ever a one among the Puritans; and that's no trifle to say. I helped your grandfather, the constable, when he lashed the Quaker woman so smartly through the streets of Salem. And it was I that brought your father a pitch-pine knot, kindled at my own hearth, to set fire to an Indian village, in King Philip's war.* They were my good friends, both; and many a pleasant walk have we had along this path, and returned merrily after midnight. I would fain be friends with you, for their sake."

"If it be as thou sayest," replied Goodman Brown, "I marvel they never spoke of these matters. Or, verily, I marvel not, seeing that the least rumor of the sort would have driven them from New England. We are a people of prayer, and good works to boot, and abide no such wickedness."

"Wickedness or not," said the traveller with twisted staff, "I have a very general acquaintance here in New England. The deacons of many a church have drunk the communion wine with me; the selectmen, of divers towns, make me their chairman; and a majority of the Great and General Court are firm supporters of my interest. The governor and I, too—but these are state secrets." 20

King William: William III was king of England from 1688 to 1701 (the time of the story). William IV was king from 1830 to 1837 (the period when Hawthorne wrote the story). †*thou wot'st:* you know (thou knowest). °*days of the martyrs:* the period of martyrdom of Protestants in England during the reign of Queen Mary (1553–1558). *King Philip's war:* This war (1675–1676), infamous for the atrocities committed by the New England settlers, resulted in the suppression of Indian tribal life and prepared the way for unlimited settlement of New England by European immigrants. "Philip" was the English name of Chief Metacomet of the Wampanoag tribe.

"Can this be so!" cried Goodman Brown, with a stare of amazement at his undisturbed companion. "Howbeit, I have nothing to do with the governor and council; they have their own ways, and are no rule for a simple husbandman like me. But, were I to go on with thee, how should I meet the eye of that good old man, our minister, at Salem village? Oh, his voice would make me tremble, both Sabbath-day and lecture-day!"

Thus far, the elder traveller had listened with due gravity, but now burst into a fit of irrepressible mirth, shaking himself so violently, that his snakelike staff actually seemed to wriggle in sympathy.

"Ha! ha! ha!" shouted he, again and again; then composing himself, "Well, go on, Goodman Brown, go on; but, prithee, don't kill me with laughing!"

"Well, then, to end the matter at once," said Goodman Brown, considerably nettled, "there is my wife, Faith. It would break her dear little heart; and I'd rather break my own!"

25 "Nay, if that be the case," answered the other, "e'en go thy ways, Goodman Brown. I would not, for twenty old women like the one hobbling before us, that Faith should come to any harm."

As he spoke, he pointed his staff at a female figure on the path, in whom Goodman Brown recognized a very pious and exemplary dame, who had taught him his catechism in youth, and was still his moral and spiritual adviser, jointly with the minister and Deacon Gookin.

"A marvel, truly, that Goody° Cloyse should be so far in the wilderness, at nightfall!" said he. "But, with your leave, friend, I shall take a cut through the woods, until we have left this Christian woman behind. Being a stranger to you, she might ask whom I was consorting with, and whither I was going."

"Be it so," said his fellow-traveller. "Betake you to the woods, and let me keep the path."

Accordingly, the young man turned aside, but took care to watch his companion, who advanced softly along the road, until he had come within a staff's length of the old dame. She, meanwhile, was making the best of her way, with singular speed for so aged a woman, and mumbling some indistinct words, a prayer, doubtless, as she went. The traveller put forth his staff, and touched her withered neck with what seemed the serpent's tail.

30 "The devil!" screamed the pious old lady.

"Then Goody Cloyse knows her old friend?" observed the traveller, confronting her, and leaning on his writhing stick.

"Ah, forsooth, and is it your worship, indeed?" cried the good dame. "Yea, truly is it, and in the very image of my old gossip,* Goodman Brown, the grandfather of the silly fellow that now is. But, would your worship believe it? My broomstick hath strangely disappeared, stolen, as I suspect, by that unhanged witch, Goody Cory,† and that, too, when I was all anointed with the juice of smallage and cinquefoil and wolf's-bane—"°°

°*Goody:* shortened form of "goodwife," a respectful name for a married woman of low rank. "Goody Cloyse" was one of the women sentenced to execution by Hawthorne's great-grandfather, Judge John Hawthorne.
gossip: from "good sib" or "good relative." †*Goody Cory:* the name of a woman who was also sentenced to execution by Judge John Hawthorne. °°*smallage and cinquefoil and wolf's-bane:* plants commonly used by witches to make ointments.

"Mingled with fine wheat and the fat of a new-born babe," said the shape of old Goodman Brown.

"Ah, your worship knows the recipe," cried the old lady, cackling aloud. "So, as I was saying, being all ready for the meeting, and no horse to ride on, I made up my mind to foot it; for they tell me there is a nice young man to be taken into communion to-night. But now your good worship will lend me your arm, and we shall be there in a twinkling."

"That can hardly be," answered her friend. "I will not spare you my arm, Goody Cloyse, but here is my staff, if you will." 35

So saying, he threw it down at her feet, where, perhaps, it assumed life, being one of the rods which its owner had formerly lent to the Egyptian Magi.** Of this fact, however, Goodman Brown could not take cognizance. He had cast up his eyes in astonishment, and looking down again, beheld neither Goody Cloyse nor the serpentine staff, but his fellow-traveller alone, who waited for him as calmly as if nothing had happened.

"That old woman taught me my catechism!" said the young man; and there was a world of meaning in this simple comment.

They continued to walk onward, while the elder traveller exhorted his companion to make good speed and persevere in the path, discoursing so aptly, that his arguments seemed rather to spring up in the bosom of his auditor, than to be suggested by himself. As they went he plucked a branch of maple, to serve for a walking-stick, and began to strip it of the twigs and little boughs, which were wet with evening dew. The moment his fingers touched them, they became strangely withered and dried up, as with a week's sunshine. Thus the pair proceeded, at a good free pace, until suddenly, in a gloomy hollow of the road, Goodman Brown sat himself down on the stump of a tree, and refused to go any farther.

"Friend," said he, stubbornly, "my mind is made up. Not another step will I budge on this errand. What if a wretched old woman do choose to go to the devil, when I thought she was going to Heaven! Is that any reason why I should quit my dear Faith, and go after her?"

"You will think better of this by and by," said his acquaintance, composedly. "Sit 40 here and rest yourself a while; and when you feel like moving again, there is my staff to help you along."

Without more words, he threw his companion the maple stick, and was as speedily out of sight as if he had vanished into the deepening gloom. The young man sat a few moments by the roadside, applauding himself greatly, and thinking with how clear a conscience he should meet the minister, in his morning walk, nor shrink from the eye of good old Deacon Gookin. And what calm sleep would be his, that very night, which was to have been spent so wickedly, but purely and sweetly now, in the arms of Faith! Amidst these pleasant and praiseworthy meditations, Goodman Brown heard the tramp of horses along the road, and deemed it advisable to conceal himself within the verge of the forest, conscious of the guilty purpose that had brought him thither, though now so happily turned from it.

**lent to the Egyptian Magi: See Exodus 7:10–12.

On came the hoof-tramps and the voices of the riders, two grave old voices, conversing soberly as they drew near. These mingled sounds appeared to pass along the road, within a few yards of the young man's hiding-place; but owing, doubtless, to the depth of the gloom, at that particular spot, neither the travellers nor their steeds were visible. Though their figures brushed the small boughs by the wayside, it could not be seen that they intercepted, even for a moment, the faint gleam from the strip of bright sky, athwart which they must have passed. Goodman Brown alternately crouched and stood on tiptoe, pulling aside the branches, and thrusting forth his head as far as he durst, without discerning so much as a shadow. It vexed him the more, because he could have sworn, were such a thing possible, that he recognized the voices of the minister and Deacon Gookin, jogging° along quietly, as they were wont to do, when bound to some ordination or ecclesiastical council. While yet within hearing, one of the riders stopped to pluck a switch.

"Of the two, reverend Sir," said the voice like the deacon's, "I had rather miss an ordination dinner than tonight's meeting. They tell me that some of our community are to be here from Falmouth and beyond, and others from Connecticut and Rhode Island; besides several of the Indian powwows,* who, after their fashion, know almost as much deviltry as the best of us. Moreover, there is a goodly young woman to be taken into communion."

"Mighty well, Deacon Gookin" replied the solemn old tones of the minister. "Spur up, or we shall be late. Nothing can be done, you know, until I get on the ground."

The hoofs clattered again, and the voices, talking so strangely in the empty air, passed on through the forest, where no church had ever been gathered, nor solitary Christian prayed. Whither, then, could these holy men be journeying, so deep into the heathen wilderness? Young Goodman Brown caught hold of a tree, for support, being ready to sink down on the ground, faint and over-burthened with the heavy sickness of his heart. He looked up to the sky, doubting whether there really was a Heaven above him. Yet, there was the blue arch, and the stars brightening in it.

"With Heaven above, and Faith below, I will yet stand firm against the devil!" cried Goodman Brown.

While he still gazed upward, into the deep arch of the firmament, and had lifted his hands to pray, a cloud, though no wind was stirring, hurried across the zenith, and hid the brightening stars. The blue sky was still visible, except directly overhead, where this black mass of cloud was sweeping swiftly northward. Aloft in the air, as if from the depths of the cloud, came a confused and doubtful sound of voices. Once, the listener fancied that he could distinguish the accents of town's people of his own, men and women, both pious and ungodly, many of whom he had met at the communion-table, and had seen others rioting at the tavern. The next moment, so indistinct were the sounds, he doubted whether he had heard aught but the murmur of the old forest, whispering without a wind. Then came a stronger swell of those familiar tones, heard daily in the sunshine, at Salem village, but never, until now, from a cloud at night. There was one voice, of a young woman, uttering lamentations, yet with an uncertain

---

°*jogging:* riding a horse at a slow trot; not to be confused with the current meaning of "jogging," which refers to running slowly on foot.   *powwows:* a Narragansett Indian word describing a ritual ceremony of dancing, incantation, and magic.

sorrow, and entreating for some favor, which, perhaps, it would grieve her to obtain. And all the unseen multitude, both saints and sinners, seemed to encourage her onward.

"Faith!" shouted Goodman Brown, in a voice of agony and desperation; and the echoes of the forest mocked him, crying—"Faith! Faith!" as if bewildered wretches were seeking her, all through the wilderness.

The cry of grief, rage, and terror was yet piercing the night, when the unhappy husband held his breath for a response. There was a scream, drowned immediately in a louder murmur of voices fading into far-off laughter, as the dark cloud swept away, leaving the clear and silent sky above Goodman Brown. But something fluttered lightly down through the air, and caught on the branch of a tree. The young man seized it and beheld a pink ribbon.

"My Faith is gone!" cried he, after one stupefied moment. "There is no good on earth, and sin is but a name. Come, devil! for to thee is this world given."   50

And maddened with despair, so that he laughed loud and long, did Goodman Brown grasp his staff and set forth again, at such a rate, that he seemed to fly along the forest path, rather than to walk or run. The road grew wilder and drearier, and more faintly traced, and vanished at length, leaving him in the heart of the dark wilderness, still rushing onward, with the instinct that guides mortal man to evil. The whole forest was peopled with frightful sounds; the creaking of the trees, the howling of wild beasts, and the yell of Indians; while, sometimes, the wind tolled like a distant church bell, and some-times gave a broad roar around the traveller, as if all Nature were laughing him to scorn. But he was himself the chief horror of the scene, and shrank not from its other horrors.

"Ha! ha! ha!" roared Goodman Brown, when the wind laughed at him. "Let us hear which will laugh loudest! Think not to frighten me with your deviltry! Come witch, come wizard, come Indian powwow, come devil himself! and here comes Goodman Brown. You may as well fear him as he fear you!"

In truth, all through the haunted forest, there could be nothing more frightful than the figure of Goodman Brown. On he flew, among the black pines, brandishing his staff with frenzied gestures, now giving vent to an inspiration of horrid blasphemy, and now shouting forth such laughter, as set all the echoes of the forest laughing like demons around him. The fiend in his own shape is less hideous than when he rages in the breast of man. Thus sped the demoniac on his course, until, quivering among the trees, he saw a red light before him, as when the felled trunks and branches of a clearing have been set on fire, and throw up their lurid blaze against the sky, at the hour of midnight. He paused, in a lull of the tempest that had driven him onward, and heard the swell of what seemed a hymn, rolling solemnly from a distance, with the weight of many voices. He knew the tune. It was a familiar one in the choir of the vil-lage meeting-house. The verse died heavily away, and was lengthened by a chorus, not of human voices, but of all the sounds of the benighted wilderness, pealing in awful harmony together. Goodman Brown cried out; and his cry was lost to his own ear, by its unison with the cry of the desert.

In the interval of silence, he stole forward, until the light glared full upon his eyes. At one extremity of an open space, hemmed in by the dark wall of the forest, arose a rock, bearing some rude, natural resemblance either to an altar or a pulpit, and surrounded by four blazing pines, their tops aflame, their stems untouched, like candles at an evening meeting. The mass of foliage, that had overgrown the summit of the rock, was all on fire, blazing high into the night, and fitfully illuminating the whole field. Each pendent twig and leafy festoon was in a blaze. As the red light arose and fell, a numerous congregation alternately shone forth, then disappeared in shadow, and again grew, as it were, out of the darkness, peopling the heart of the solitary woods at once.

55 "A grave and dark-clad company!" quoth Goodman Brown.

In truth, they were such. Among them, quivering to-and-fro, between gloom and splendor, appeared faces that would be seen, next day, at the council-board of the province, and others which, Sabbath after Sabbath, looked devoutly heavenward, and benignantly over the crowded pews, from the holiest pulpits in the land. Some affirm that the lady of the governor was there. At least, there were high dames well known to her, and wives of honored husbands, and widows a great multitude, and ancient maidens, all of excellent repute, and fair young girls, who trembled lest their mothers should espy them. Either the sudden gleams of light, flashing over the obscure field, bedazzled Goodman Brown, or he recognized a score of the church members of Salem village, famous for their especial sanctity. Good old Deacon Gookin had arrived, and waited at the skirts of that venerable saint, his reverend pastor. But, irreverently consorting with these grave, reputable, and pious people, these elders of the church, these chaste dames and dewy virgins, there were men of dissolute lives and women of spotted fame, wretches given over to all mean and filthy vice, and suspected even of horrid crimes. It was strange to see, that the good shrank not from the wicked, nor were the sinners abashed by the saints. Scattered, also, among their pale-faced enemies, were the Indian priests, or powwows, who had often scared their native forest with more hideous incantations than any known to English witchcraft.

"But, where is Faith?" thought Goodman Brown; and, as hope came into his heart, he trembled.

Another verse of the hymn arose, a slow and mournful strain, such as the pious love, but joined to words which expressed all that our nature can conceive of sin, and darkly hinted at far more. Unfathomable to mere mortals is the lore of fiends. Verse after verse was sung, and still the chorus of the desert swelled between, like the deepest tone of a mighty organ. And, with the final peal of that dreadful anthem, there came a sound, as if the roaring wind, the rushing streams, the howling beasts, and every other voice of the unconverted wilderness were mingling and according with the voice of guilty man, in homage to the prince of all. The four blazing pines threw up a loftier flame, and obscurely discovered shapes and visages of horror on the smoke-wreaths, above the impious assembly. At the same moment, the fire on the rock shot redly forth, and formed a glowing arch above its base, where now appeared a figure. With reverence be it spoken, the apparition bore no slight similitude, both in garb and manner, to some grave divine of the New England churches.

"Bring forth the converts!" cried a voice, that echoed through the field and rolled into the forest.

60 At the word, Goodman Brown stepped forth from the shadow of the trees, and approached the congregation, with whom he felt a loathful brotherhood, by the sympathy of all that was wicked in his heart. He could have well-nigh sworn, that the shape of

his own dead father beckoned him to advance, looking downward from a smoke-wreath, while a woman, with dim features of despair, threw out her hand to warn him back. Was it his mother? But he had no power to retreat one step, nor to resist, even in thought, when the minister and good old Deacon Gookin seized his arms, and led him to the blazing rock. Thither came also the slender form of a veiled female, led between Goody Cloyse, that pious teacher of the catechism, and Martha Carrier, who had received the devil's promise to be queen of hell. A rampant hag was she! And there stood the proselytes, beneath the canopy of fire.

"Welcome, my children," said the dark figure, "to the communion of your race! Ye have found, thus young, your nature and your destiny. My children, look behind you!"

They turned; and flashing forth, as it were, in a sheet of flame, the fiend-worshippers were seen; the smile of welcome gleamed darkly on every visage.

"There," resumed the sable form, "are all whom ye have reverenced from youth. Ye deemed them holier than yourselves, and shrank from your own sin, contrasting it with their lives of righteousness and prayerful aspirations heavenward. Yet, here are they all, in my worshipping assembly! This night it shall be granted you to know their secret deeds; how hoary-bearded elders of the church have whispered wanton words to the young maids of their households; how many a woman, eager for widow's weeds, has given her husband a drink at bedtime, and let him sleep his last sleep in her bosom; how beardless youths have made haste to inherit their father's wealth; and how fair damsels—blush not, sweet ones!—have dug little graves in the garden, and bidden me, the sole guest, to an infant's funeral. By the sympathy of your human hearts for sin, ye shall scent out all the places—whether in church, bed-chamber, street, field, or forest—where crime has been committed, and shall exult to behold the whole earth one stain of guilt, one mighty blood-spot. Far more than this! It shall be yours to penetrate, in every bosom, the deep mystery of sin, the fountain of all wicked arts, and which inexhaustibly supplies more evil impulses than human power—than my power, at its utmost!—can make manifest in deeds. And now, my children, look upon each other."

They did so; and, by the blaze of the hell-kindled torches, the wretched man beheld his Faith, and the wife her husband, trembling before that unhallowed altar.

"Lo! there ye stand, my children," said the figure, in a deep and solemn tone, almost sad, with its despairing awfulness, as if his once angelic nature° could yet mourn for our miserable race. Depending upon one another's hearts, ye had still hoped that virtue were not all a dream! Now are ye undeceived!—Evil is the nature of mankind. Evil must be your only happiness. Welcome, again, my children, to the communion of your race!"

"Welcome!" repeated the fiend-worshippers, in one cry of despair and triumph.

And there they stood, the only pair, as it seemed, who were yet hesitating on the verge of wickedness, in this dark world. A basin was hollowed, naturally, in the rock. Did it contain water, reddened by the lurid light? or was it blood? or, perchance, a liquid flame? Herein did the Shape of Evil dip his hand, and prepare to lay the mark

65

°*once angelic nature:* Lucifer ("light carrier"), another name for the Devil, led the traditional revolt of the angels and was thrown into hell as his punishment. See Isaiah 14:12–15.

of baptism upon their foreheads, that they might be partakers of the mystery of sin, more conscious of the secret guilt of others, both in deed and thought, than they could now be of their own. The husband cast one look at his pale wife, and Faith at him. What polluted wretches would the next glance show them to each other, shuddering alike at what they disclosed and what they saw!

"Faith! Faith!" cried the husband. "Look up to Heaven, and resist the Wicked One!"

Whether Faith obeyed, he knew not. Hardly had he spoken, when he found himself amid calm night and solitude, listening to a roar of the wind, which died heavily away through the forest. He staggered against the rock, and felt it chill and damp, while a hanging twig, that had been all on fire, besprinkled his cheek with the coldest dew.

70   The next morning, young Goodman Brown came slowly into the street of Salem village staring around him like a bewildered man. The good old minister was taking a walk along the grave-yard, to get an appetite for breakfast and meditate his sermon, and bestowed a blessing, as he passed, on Goodman Brown. He shrank from the venerable saint, as if to avoid an anathema. Old Deacon Gookin was at domestic worship, and the holy words of his prayer were heard through the open window. "What God doth the wizard pray to?" quoth Goodman Brown. Goody Cloyse, that excellent old Christian, stood in the early sunshine, at her own lattice, catechising a little girl, who had brought her a pint of morning's milk. Goodman Brown snatched away the child, as from the grasp of the fiend himself. Turning the corner by the meetinghouse, he spied the head of Faith, with the pink ribbons, gazing anxiously forth, and bursting into such joy at the sight of him that she skipt along the street, and almost kissed her husband before the whole village. But Goodman Brown looked sternly and sadly into her face, and passed on without a greeting.

Had Goodman Brown fallen asleep in the forest, and only dreamed a wild dream of a witch-meeting?

Be it so, if you will. But, alas! it was a dream of evil omen for young Goodman Brown. A stern, a sad, a darkly meditative, a distrustful, if not a desperate man did he become, from the night of that fearful dream. On the Sabbath day, when the congregation were singing a holy psalm, he could not listen, because an anthem of sin rushed loudly upon his ear, and drowned all the blessed strain. When the minister spoke from the pulpit, with power and fervid eloquence, and with his hand on the open Bible, of the sacred truths of our religion, and of saint-like lives and triumphant deaths, and of future bliss or misery unutterable, then did Goodman Brown turn pale, dreading lest the roof should thunder down upon the gray blasphemer and his hearers. Often, awaking suddenly at midnight, he shrank from the bosom of Faith, and at morning or eventide, when the family knelt down in prayer, he scowled, and muttered to himself, and gazed sternly at his wife, and turned away. And when he had lived long, and was borne to his grave, a hoary corpse, followed by Faith, an aged woman, and children and grandchildren, a goodly procession, besides neighbors not a few, they carved no hopeful verse upon his tombstone; for his dying hour was gloom.

Shirley Jackson (1919–1965)

The Lottery (1948)

The morning of June 27th was clear and sunny, with the fresh warmth of a full summer day; the flowers were blossoming profusely and the grass was richly green. The people of the village began to gather in the square, between the post office and the bank, around ten o'clock; in some towns there were so many people that the lottery took two days and had to be started on June 26th, but in this village, where there were only about three hundred people, the whole lottery took less than two hours, so it could begin at ten o'clock in the morning and still be through in time to allow the villagers to get home for noon dinner.

The children assembled first, of course. School was recently over for the summer, and the feeling of liberty sat uneasily on most of them; they tended to gather together quietly for a while before they broke into boisterous play, and their talk was still of the classroom and the teacher, of books and reprimands. Bobby Martin had already stuffed his pockets full of stones, and the other boys soon followed his example, selecting the smoothest and roundest stones; Bobby and Harry Jones and Dickie Delacroix—the villagers pronounced this name "Dellacroy"—eventually made a great pile of stones in one corner of the square and guarded it against the raids of the other boys. The girls stood aside, talking among themselves, looking over their shoulders at the boys, and the very small children rolled in the dust or clung to the hands of their older brothers or sisters.

Soon the men began to gather, surveying their own children, speaking of planting and rain, tractors and taxes. They stood together, away from the pile of stones in the corner, and their jokes were quiet and they smiled rather than laughed. The women, wearing faded house dresses and sweaters, came shortly after their menfolk. They greeted one another and exchanged bits of gossip as they went to join their husbands. Soon the women, standing by their husbands, began to call to their children, and the children came reluctantly, having to be called four or five times. Bobby Martin ducked under his mother's grasping hand and ran, laughing, back to the pile of stones. His father spoke up sharply, and Bobby came quickly and took his place between his father and his oldest brother.

The lottery was conducted—as were the square dances, the teen-age club, the Halloween program—by Mr. Summers, who had time and energy to devote to civic activities. He was a round-faced, jovial man and he ran the coal business, and people were sorry for him, because he had no children and his wife was a scold. When he arrived in the square, carrying the black wooden box, there was a murmur of conversation among the villagers, and he waved and called, "Little late today, folks." The postmaster, Mr. Graves, followed him, carrying a three-legged stool, and the stool was put in the center of the square and Mr. Summers set the black box down on it. The villagers kept their distance, leaving a space between themselves and the stool, and when Mr. Summers said, "Some of you fellows want to give me a hand?" there was a hesitation before two men, Mr. Martin and his oldest son, Baxter, came forward to hold the box steady on the stool while Mr. Summers stirred up the papers inside it.

5   The original paraphernalia for the lottery had been lost long ago, and the black box now resting on the stool had been put into use even before Old Man Warner, the oldest man in town, was born. Mr. Summers spoke frequently to the villagers about making a new box, but no one liked to upset even as much tradition as was represented by the black box. There was a story that the present box had been made with some pieces of the box that had preceded it, the one that had been constructed when the first people settled down to make a village here. Every year, after the lottery, Mr. Summers began talking again about a new box, but every year the subject was allowed to fade off without anything's being done. The black box grew shabbier each year; by now it was no longer completely black but splintered badly along one side to show the original wood color, and in some places faded or stained.

Mr. Martin and his oldest son, Baxter, held the black box securely on the stool until Mr. Summers had stirred the papers thoroughly with his hand. Because so much of the ritual had been forgotten or discarded, Mr. Summers had been successful in having slips of paper substituted for the chips of wood that had been used for generations. Chips of wood, Mr. Summers had argued, had been all very well when the village was tiny, but now that the population was more than three hundred and likely to keep on growing, it was necessary to use something that would fit more easily into the black box. The night before the lottery, Mr. Summers and Mr. Graves made up the slips of paper and put them in the box, and it was then taken to the safe of Mr. Summers' coal company and locked up until Mr. Summers was ready to take it to the square next morning. The rest of the year, the box was put away, sometimes one place, sometimes another; it had spent one year in Mr. Graves's barn and another year underfoot in the post office, and sometimes it was set on a shelf in the Martin grocery and left there.

There was a great deal of fussing to be done before Mr. Summers declared the lottery open. There were the lists to make up—of heads of families, heads of households in each family, members of each household in each family. There was the proper swearing-in of Mr. Summers by the postmaster, as the official of the lottery; at one time, some people remembered, there had been a recital of some sort, performed by the official of the lottery, a perfunctory, tuneless chant that had been rattled off duly each year; some people believed that the official of the lottery used to stand just so when he said or sang it, others believed that he was supposed to walk among the people, but years and years ago this part of the ritual had been allowed to lapse. There had been, also, a ritual salute, which the official of the lottery had had to use in addressing each person who came up to draw from the box, but this also had changed with time, until now it was felt necessary only for the official to speak to each person approaching. Mr. Summers was very good at all this; in his clean white shirt and blue jeans, with one hand resting carelessly on the black box, he seemed very proper and important as he talked interminably to Mr. Graves and the Martins.

Just as Mr. Summers finally left off talking and turned to the assembled villagers, Mrs. Hutchinson came hurriedly along the path to the square, her sweater thrown over her shoulders, and slid into place in the back of the crowd. "Clean forgot what day it was," she said to Mrs. Delacroix, who stood next to her, and they both laughed softly. "Thought my old man was out back stacking wood," Mrs. Hutchinson went on, "and then I looked out the window and the kids was gone, and then I remembered it was the twenty-seventh and came a-running." She dried her hands on her apron, and Mrs. Delacroix said, "You're in time, though. They're still talking away up there."

Mrs. Hutchinson craned her neck to see through the crowd and found her husband and children standing near the front. She tapped Mrs. Delacroix on the arm as a farewell and began to make her way through the crowd. The people separated good-humoredly to let her through; two or three people said, in voices just loud enough to be heard across the crowd, "Here comes your Missus, Hutchinson," and "Bill, she made it after all." Mrs. Hutchinson reached her husband, and Mr. Summers, who had been waiting, said cheerfully, "Thought we were going to have to get on without you, Tessie." Mrs. Hutchinson said, grinning, "Wouldn't have me leave m'dishes in the sink, now, would you, Joe?," and soft laughter ran through the crowd as the people stirred back into position after Mrs. Hutchinson's arrival.

"Well, now," Mr. Summers said soberly, "guess we better get started, get this over with, so's we can go back to work. Anybody ain't here?"   10

"Dunbar," several people said. "Dunbar, Dunbar."

Mr. Summers consulted his list. "Clyde Dunbar," he said. "That's right. He's broke his leg, hasn't he? Who's drawing for him?"

"Me, I guess," a woman said, and Mr. Summers turned to look at her. "Wife draws for her husband," Mr. Summers said. "Don't you have a grown boy to do it for you, Janey?" Although Mr. Summers and everyone else in the village knew the answer perfectly well, it was the business of the official of the lottery to ask such questions formally. Mr. Summers waited with an expression of polite interest while Mrs. Dunbar answered.

"Horace's not but sixteen yet," Mrs. Dunbar said regretfully. "Guess I gotta fill in for the old man this year."

"Right," Mr. Summers said. He made a note on the list he was holding. Then he   15
asked, "Watson boy drawing this year?"

A tall boy in the crowd raised his hand. "Here," he said. "I'm drawing for m'mother and me." He blinked his eyes nervously and ducked his head as several voices in the crowd said things like "Good fellow, Jack," and "Glad to see your mother's got a man to do it."

"Well," Mr. Summers said, "guess that's everyone. Old Man Warner make it?"

"Here," a voice said, and Mr. Summers nodded.

A sudden hush fell on the crowd as Mr. Summers cleared his throat and looked at the list. "All ready?" he called. "Now, I'll read the names—heads of families first—and the men come up and take a paper out of the box. Keep the paper folded in your hand without looking at it until everyone has had a turn. Everything clear?"

The people had done it so many times that they only half listened to the directions;   20
most of them were quiet, wetting their lips, not looking around. Then Mr. Summers raised one hand high and said, "Adams." A man disengaged himself from the crowd and came forward. "Hi, Steve," Mr. Summers said, and Mr. Adams said, "Hi, Joe." They grinned at one another humorlessly and nervously. Then Mr. Adams reached into the black box and took out a folded paper. He held it firmly by one corner as he turned and went hastily back to his place in the crowd, where he stood a little apart from his family, not looking down at his hand.

"Allen," Mr. Summers said. "Anderson.... Bentham."

"Seems like there's no time at all between lotteries any more," Mrs. Delacroix said to Mrs. Graves in the back row. "Seems like we got through with the last one only last week."

"Time sure goes fast," Mrs. Graves said.

"Clark ... Delacroix."

25 "There goes my old man," Mrs. Delacroix said. She held her breath while her husband went forward.

"Dunbar," Mr. Summers said, and Mrs. Dunbar went steadily to the box while one of the women said, "Go on, Janey," and another said, "There she goes."

"We're next," Mrs. Graves said. She watched while Mr. Graves came around from the side of the box, greeted Mr. Summers gravely, and selected a slip of paper from the box. By now, all through the crowd there were men holding the small folded papers in their large hands, turning them over and over nervously. Mrs. Dunbar and her two sons stood together, Mrs. Dunbar holding the slip of paper.

"Harburt.... Hutchinson."

"Get up there, Bill," Mrs. Hutchinson said, and the people near her laughed.

30 "Jones."

"They do say," Mr. Adams said to Old Man Warner, who stood next to him, "that over in the north village they're talking of giving up the lottery."

Old Man Warner snorted. "Pack of crazy fools," he said. "Listening to the young folks, nothing's good enough for *them*. Next thing you know, they'll be wanting to go back to living in caves, nobody work any more, live *that* way for a while. Used to be a saying about 'Lottery in June, corn be heavy soon.' First thing you know, we'd all be eating stewed chickweed and acorns. There's *always* been a lottery," he added petulantly. "Bad enough to see young Joe Summers up there joking with everybody."

"Some places have already quit lotteries," Mrs. Adams said.

"Nothing but trouble in *that*," Old Man Warner said stoutly. "Pack of young fools."

35 "Martin." And Bobby Martin watched his father go forward. "Overdyke.... Percy."

"I wish they'd hurry," Mrs. Dunbar said to her older son. "I wish they'd hurry."

"They're almost through," her son said.

"You get ready to run tell Dad," Mrs. Dunbar said.

Mr. Summers called his own name and then stepped forward precisely and selected a slip from the box. Then he called, "Warner."

40 "Seventy-seventh year I been in the lottery," Old Man Warner said as he went through the crowd. "Seventy-seventh time."

"Watson." The tall boy came awkwardly through the crowd. Someone said, "Don't be nervous, Jack," and Mr. Summers said, "Take your time, son."

"Zanini."

After that, there was a long pause, a breathless pause, until Mr. Summers, holding his slip of paper in the air, said, "All right, fellows." For a minute, no one moved, and then all the slips of paper were opened. Suddenly, all the women began to speak at once, saying, "Who is it?" "Who's got it?" "Is it the Dunbars?" "Is it the Watsons?" Then the voices began to say, "It's Hutchinson. It's Bill," "Bill Hutchinson's got it."

"Go tell your father," Mrs. Dunbar said to her older son.

45 People began to look around to see the Hutchinsons. Bill Hutchinson was standing quiet, staring down at the paper in his hand. Suddenly, Tessie Hutchinson

shouted to Mr. Summers, "You didn't give him time enough to take any paper he wanted. I saw you. It wasn't fair!"

"Be a good sport, Tessie," Mrs. Delacroix called, and Mrs. Graves said, "All of us took the same chance."

"Shut up, Tessie," Bill Hutchinson said.

"Well, everyone," Mr. Summers said, "that was done pretty fast, and now we've got to be hurrying a little more to get done in time." He consulted his next list. "Bill," he said, "you draw for the Hutchinson family. You got any other households in the Hutchinsons?"

"There's Don and Eva," Mrs. Hutchinson yelled. "Make *them* take their chance!"

"Daughters draw with their husbands' families, Tessie," Mr. Summers said gently. 50
"You know that as well as anyone else."

"It wasn't *fair*," Tessie said.

"I guess not, Joe," Bill Hutchinson said regretfully. "My daughter draws with her husband's family, that's only fair. And I've got no other family except the kids."

"Then, as far as drawing for families is concerned, it's you," Mr. Summers said in explanation, "and as far as drawing for households is concerned, that's you, too. Right?"

"Right," Bill Hutchinson said.

"How many kids, Bill?" Mr. Summers asked formally. 55

"Three," Bill Hutchinson said. "There's Bill, Jr., and Nancy, and little Dave. And Tessie and me."

"All right, then," Mr. Summers said. "Harry, you got their tickets back?"

Mr. Graves nodded and held up the slips of paper. "Put them in the box, then," Mr. Summers directed. "Take Bill's and put it in."

"I think we ought to start over," Mrs. Hutchinson said, as quietly as she could. "I tell you it wasn't *fair*. You didn't give him time enough to choose. *Every-body saw that.*" 60

Mr. Graves had selected the five slips and put them in the box, and he dropped all the papers but those onto the ground, where the breeze caught them and lifted them off.

"Listen, everybody," Mrs. Hutchinson was saying to the people around her.

"Ready, Bill?" Mr. Summers asked, and Bill Hutchinson, with one quick glance around at his wife and children, nodded.

"Remember," Mr. Summers said, "take the slips and keep them folded until each person has taken one. Harry, you help little Dave." Mr. Graves took the hand of the little boy, who came willingly with him up to the box. "Take a paper out of the box, Davy," Mr. Summers said. Davy put his hand into the box and laughed. "Take just *one* paper," Mr. Summers said. "Harry, you hold it for him." Mr. Graves took the child's hand and removed the folded paper from the tight fist and held it while little Dave stood next to him and looked up at him wonderingly.

"Nancy next," Mr. Summers said. Nancy was twelve, and her school friends breathed heavily as she went forward, switching her skirt, and took a slip daintily from the box. "Bill, Jr.," Mr. Summers said, and Billy, his face red and his feet over-large, nearly knocked the box over as he got a paper out. "Tessie," Mr. Summers said. She hesitated for a minute, looking around defiantly, and then set her lips and went up to the box. She snatched a paper out and held it behind her.

65   "Bill," Mr. Summers said, and Bill Hutchinson reached into the box and felt around, bringing his hand out at last with the slip of paper in it.

The crowd was quiet. A girl whispered, "I hope it's not Nancy," and the sound of the whisper reached the edges of the crowd.

"It's not the way it used to be," Old Man Warner said clearly. "People ain't the way they used to be."

"All right," Mr. Summers said. "Open the papers. Harry, you open little Dave's."

Mr. Graves opened the slip of paper and there was a general sigh through the crowd as he held it up and everyone could see that it was blank. Nancy and Bill, Jr., opened theirs at the same time, and both beamed and laughed, turning around to the crowd and holding their slips of paper above their heads.

70   "Tessie," Mr. Summers said. There was a pause, and then Mr. Summers looked at Bill Hutchinson, and Bill unfolded his paper and showed it. It was blank.

"It's Tessie," Mr. Summers said, and his voice was hushed. "Show us her paper, Bill."

Bill Hutchinson went over to his wife and forced the slip of paper out of her hand. It had a black spot on it, the black spot Mr. Summers had made the night before with the heavy pencil in the coal-company office. Bill Hutchinson held it up, and there was a stir in the crowd.

"All right, folks," Mr. Summers said. "Let's finish quickly."

Although the villagers had forgotten the ritual and lost the original black box, they still remembered to use stones. The pile of stones the boys had made earlier was ready; there were stones on the ground with the blowing scraps of paper that had come out of the box. Mrs. Delacroix selected a stone so large she had to pick it up with both hands and turned to Mrs. Dunbar. "Come on," she said. "Hurry up."

75   Mrs. Dunbar had small stones in both hands, and she said, gasping for breath, "I can't run at all. You'll have to go ahead and I'll catch up with you."

The children had stones already, and someone gave little Davy Hutchinson a few pebbles.

Tessie Hutchinson was in the center of a cleared space by now, and she held her hands out desperately as the villagers moved in on her. "It isn't fair," she said. A stone hit her on the side of the head.

Old Man Warner was saying, "Come on, come on, everyone." Steve Adams was in the front of the crowd of villagers with Mrs. Graves beside him.

"It isn't fair, it isn't right," Mrs. Hutchinson screamed, and then they were upon her.

Frank O'Connor (1903–1966)

First Confession (1951)

All the trouble began when my grandfather died and my grandmother—my father's mother—came to live with us. Relations in the one house are a strain at the best of times, but, to make matters worse, my grandmother was a real old countrywoman and quite unsuited to the life in town. She had a fat, wrinkled old face, and, to Mother's great indignation, went round the house in bare feet—the boots had her crippled, she said. For dinner she had a jug of porter° and a pot of potatoes with—sometimes—a bit of salt fish, and she poured out the potatoes on the table and ate them slowly, with great relish, using her fingers by way of a fork.

Now, girls are supposed to be fastidious, but I was the one who suffered most from this. Nora, my sister, just sucked up to the old woman for the penny she got every Friday out of the old-age pension, a thing I could not do. I was too honest, that was my trouble; and when I was playing with Bill Connell, the sergeant-major's son, and saw my grandmother steering up the path with the jug of porter sticking out from beneath her shawl I was mortified. I made excuses not to let him come into the house, because I could never be sure what she would be up to when we went in.

When Mother was at work and my grandmother made the dinner I wouldn't touch it. Nora once tried to make me, but I hid under the table from her and took the bread-knife with me for protection. Nora let on to be very indignant (she wasn't, of course, but she knew Mother saw through her, so she sided with Gran) and came after me. I lashed out at her with the bread-knife, and after that she left me alone. I stayed there till Mother came in from work and made my dinner, but when Father came in later Nora said in a shocked voice: "Oh, Dadda, do you know what Jackie did at dinner time?" Then, of course, it all came out; Father gave me a flaking; Mother interfered, and for days after that he didn't speak to me and Mother barely spoke to Nora. And all because of that old woman! God knows, I was heart-scalded.

Then, to crown my misfortune, I had to make my first confession and communion. It was an old woman called Ryan who prepared us for these. She was about the one age with Gran; she was well-to-do, lived in a big house on Montenotte, wore a black cloak and bonnet, and came every day to school at three o'clock when we should have been going home, and talked to us of hell. She may have mentioned the other place as well, but that could only have been by accident, for hell had the first place in her heart.

She lit a candle, took out a new half-crown, and offered it to the first boy who would hold one finger—only one finger!—in the flame for five minutes by the school clock. Being always very ambitious I was tempted to volunteer, but I thought it might look greedy. Then she asked were we afraid of holding one finger—only one finger!—in a little candle flame for five minutes and not be afraid of burning all over in roasting hot furnaces for all eternity. "All eternity! Just think of that! A whole lifetime goes by and it's nothing, not even a drop in the ocean of your sufferings." The woman was really interesting about hell, but my attention was all fixed on the half-crown. At the end of the lesson she put it back in her purse. It was a great disappointment; a religious woman like that, you wouldn't think she'd bother about a thing like a half-crown.

Another day she said she knew a priest who woke one night to find a fellow he didn't recognize leaning over the end of his bed. The priest was a bit frightened—naturally enough—but he asked the fellow what he wanted, and the fellow said in a deep, husky voice that he wanted to go to confession. The priest said it was an awkward time and wouldn't it do in the morning, but the fellow said that last time he went to confession, there was one sin he kept back, being ashamed to mention it, and now it was

5

°*porter:* a dark-brown beer.

always on his mind. Then the priest knew it was a bad case, because the fellow was after making a bad confession and committing a mortal sin. He got up to dress, and just then the cock crew in the yard outside, and—lo and behold!—when the priest looked round there was no sign of the fellow, only a smell of burning timber, and when the priest looked at his bed didn't he see the print of two hands burned in it? That was because the fellow had made a bad confession. This story made a shocking impression on me.

But the worst of all was when she showed us how to examine our conscience. Did we take the name of the Lord, our God, in vain? Did we honour our father and our mother? (I asked her did this include grandmothers and she said it did.) Did we love our neighbours as ourselves? Did we covet our neighbour's goods? (I thought of the way I felt about the penny that Nora got every Friday.) I decided that, between one thing and another, I must have broken the whole ten commandments, all on account of that old woman, and so far as I could see, so long as she remained in the house I had no hope of ever doing anything else.

I was scared to death of confession. The day the whole class went I let on to have a toothache, hoping my absence wouldn't be noticed; but at three o'clock, just as I was feeling safe, along comes a chap with a message from Mrs. Ryan that I was to go to confession myself on Saturday and be at the chapel for communion with the rest. To make it worse, Mother couldn't come with me and sent Nora instead.

Now, that girl had ways of tormenting me that Mother never knew of. She held my hand as we went down the hill, smiling sadly and saying how sorry she was for me, as if she were bringing me to the hospital for an operation.

10   "Oh, God help us!" she moaned. "Isn't it a terrible pity you weren't a good boy? Oh, Jackie, my heart bleeds for you! How will you ever think of all your sins? Don't forget you have to tell him about the time you kicked Gran on the shin."

"Lemme go!" I said, trying to drag myself free of her. "I don't want to go to confession at all."

"But sure, you'll have to go to confession, Jackie," she replied in the same regretful tone. "Sure, if you didn't the parish priest would be up to the house, looking for you. 'Tisn't, God knows, that I'm not sorry for you. Do you remember the time you tried to kill me with the bread-knife under the table? And the language you used to me? I don't know what he'll do with you at all, Jackie. He might have to send you up to the bishop."

I remember thinking bitterly that she didn't know the half of what I had to tell—if I told it. I knew I couldn't tell it, and understood perfectly why the fellow in Mrs. Ryan's story made a bad confession; it seemed to me a great shame that people wouldn't stop criticizing him. I remember that steep hill down to the church, and the sunlit hillsides beyond the valley of the river, which I saw in the gaps between the houses like Adam's last glimpse of Paradise.°

Then, when she had maneuvered me down the long flight of steps to the chapel yard, Nora suddenly changed her tone. She became the raging malicious devil she really was.

°*Adam's last glimpse of Paradise:* Genesis 3:23–24.

"There you are!" she said with a yelp of triumph, hurling me through the church   15
door. "And I hope he'll give you the penitential psalms, you dirty little caffler."

I knew then I was lost, given up to eternal justice. The door with the coloured-glass
panels swung shut behind me, the sunlight went out and gave place to deep shadow,
and the wind whistled outside so that the silence within seemed to crackle like ice under
my feet. Nora sat in front of me by the confession box. There were a couple of old
women ahead of her, and then a miserable-looking poor devil came and wedged me in
at the other side, so that I couldn't escape even if I had the courage. He joined his hands
and rolled his eyes in the direction of the roof, muttering aspirations in an anguished
tone, and I wondered had he a grandmother too. Only a grandmother could account
for a fellow behaving in that heartbroken way, but he was better off than I, for he at least
could go and confess his sins; while I would make a bad confession and then die in the
night and be continually coming back and burning people's furniture.

Nora's turn came, and I heard the sound of something slamming, and then her
voice as if butter wouldn't melt in her mouth, and then another slam, and out she came.
God, the hypocrisy of women! Her eyes were lowered, her head was bowed, and her
hands were joined very low down on her stomach, and she walked up the aisle to the
side altar looking like a saint. You never saw such an exhibition of devotion, and I remembered the devilish malice with which she had tormented me all the way from our
door, and wondered were all religious people like that, really. It was my turn now. With
the fear of damnation in my soul I went in, and the confessional door closed of itself
behind me.

It was pitch-dark and I couldn't see the priest or anything else. Then I really began
to be frightened. In the darkness it was a matter between God and me, and He had all
the odds. He knew what my intentions were before I even started; I had no chance. All
I had ever been told about confession got mixed up in my mind, and I knelt to one wall
and said: "Bless me, father, for I have sinned; this is my first confession." I waited for a
few minutes, but nothing happened, so I tried it on the other wall. Nothing happened
there either. He had me spotted all right.

It must have been then that I noticed the shelf at about one height with my head.
It was really a place for grown-up people to rest their elbows, but in my distracted state
I thought it was probably the place you were supposed to kneel. Of course, it was on the
high side and not very deep, but I was always good at climbing and managed to get up
all right. Staying up was the trouble. There was room only for my knees, and nothing
you could get a grip on but a sort of wooden moulding a bit above it. I held on to the
moulding and repeated the words a little louder, and this time something happened all
right. A slide was slammed back; a little light entered the box, and a man's voice said:
"Who's there?"

"'Tis me, father," I said for fear he mightn't see me and go away again. I couldn't   20
see him at all. The place the voice came from was under the moulding, about level with
my knees, so I took a good grip of the moulding and swung myself down till I saw the
astonished face of a young priest looking up at me. He had to put his head on one side
to see me, and I had to put mine on one side to see him, so we were more or less talking
to one another upside-down. It struck me as a queer way of hearing confessions, but I
didn't feel it my place to criticize.

"Bless me, father, for I have sinned; this is my first confession," I rattled off all in one breath, and swung myself down the least shade more to make it easier for him.

"What are you doing up there?" he shouted in an angry voice, and the strain the politeness was putting on my hold of the moulding, and the shock of being addressed in such an uncivil tone, were too much for me. I lost my grip, tumbled, and hit the door an unmerciful wallop before I found myself flat on my back in the middle of the aisle. The people who had been waiting stood up with their mouths open. The priest opened the door of the middle box and came out, pushing his biretta back from his forehead; he looked something terrible. Then Nora came scampering down the aisle.

"Oh, you dirty little caffler!" she said. "I might have known you'd do it. I might have known you'd disgrace me. I can't leave you out of my sight for one minute."

Before I could even get to my feet to defend myself she bent down and gave me a clip across the ear. This reminded me that I was so stunned I had even forgotten to cry, so that people might think I wasn't hurt at all, when in fact I was probably maimed for life. I gave a roar out of me.

25   "What's all this about?" the priest hissed, getting angrier than ever and pushing Nora off me. "How dare you hit the child like that, you little vixen?"

"But I can't do my penance with him, father," Nora cried, cocking an outraged eye up to him.

"Well, go and do it, or I'll give you some more to do," he said, giving me a hand up. "Was it coming to confession you were, my poor man?" he asked me.

"'Twas, father," said I with a sob.

"Oh," he said respectfully, "a big hefty fellow like you must have terrible sins. Is this your first?"

30   "'Tis, father," said I.

"Worse and worse," he said gloomily. "The crimes of a lifetime. I don't know will I get rid of you at all today. You'd better wait now till I'm finished with these old ones. You can see by the looks of them they haven't much to tell."

"I will, father," I said with something approaching joy.

The relief of it was really enormous. Nora stuck out her tongue at me from behind his back, but I couldn't even be bothered retorting. I knew from the very moment that man opened his mouth that he was intelligent above the ordinary. When I had time to think, I saw how right I was. It only stood to reason that a fellow confessing after seven years would have more to tell than people that went every week. The crimes of a lifetime, exactly as he said. It was only what he expected, and the rest was the cackle of old women and girls with their talk of hell, the bishop, and the penitential psalms. That was all they knew. I started to make my examination of conscience, and barring the one bad business of my grandmother it didn't seem so bad.

The next time, the priest steered me into the confession box himself and left the shutter back the way I could see him get in and sit down at the further side of the grille from me.

35   "Well, now," he said, "what do they call you?"

"Jackie, father," said I.

"And what's a-trouble to you, Jackie?"

"Father," I said, feeling I might as well get it over while I had him in good humour,

"I had it all arranged to kill my grandmother."

He seemed a bit shaken by that, all right, because he said nothing for quite a while.

"My goodness," he said at last, "that'd be a shocking thing to do. What put that into your head?"   40

"Father," I said, feeling very sorry for myself, "she's an awful woman."

"Is she?" he asked. "What way is she awful?"

"She takes porter, father," I said, knowing well from the way Mother talked of it that this was a mortal sin, and hoping it would make the priest take a more favourable view of my case.

"Oh, my!" he said, and I could see he was impressed.

"And snuff, father," said I.

"That's a bad case, sure enough, Jackie," he said.   45

"And she goes round in her bare feet, father," I went on in a rush of self-pity, "and she knows I don't like her, and she gives pennies to Nora and none to me, and my da sides with her and flakes me, and one night I was so heartscalded I made up my mind I'd have to kill her."

"And what would you do with the body?" he asked with great interest.

"I was thinking I could chop that up and carry it away in a barrow I have," I said.

"Begor, Jackie," he said, "do you know you're a terrible child?"   50

"I know, father," I said, for I was just thinking the same thing myself. "I tried to kill Nora too with a bread-knife under the table, only I missed her."

"Is that the little girl that was beating you just now?" he asked.

"'Tis, father."

"Someone will go for her with a bread-knife one day, and he won't miss her," he said rather cryptically. "You must have great courage. Between ourselves, there's a lot of people I'd like to do the same to but I'd never have the nerve. Hanging is an awful death."

"Is it, father?" I asked with the deepest interest—I was always very keen on hang-   55
ing. "Did you ever see a fellow hanged?"

"Dozens of them," he said solemnly. "And they all died roaring."

"Jay!" I said.

"Oh, a horrible death!" he said with great satisfaction. "Lots of fellows I saw killed their grandmothers too, but they all said 'twas never worth it."

He had me there for a full ten minutes talking, and then walked out the chapel yard with me. I was genuinely sorry to part with him, because he was the most entertaining character I'd ever met in the religious line. Outside, after the shadow of the church, the sunlight was like the roaring of waves on a beach; it dazzled me; and when the frozen silence melted and I heard the screech of trams on the road my heart soared. I knew now I wouldn't die in the night and come back, leaving marks on my mother's furniture. It would be a great worry to her, and the poor soul had enough.

Nora was sitting on the railing, waiting for me, and she put on a very sour puss   60
when she saw the priest with me. She was made jealous because a priest had never come out of the church with her.

"Well," she asked coldly, after he left me, "what did he give you?"

"Three Hail Marys," I said.

"Three Hail Marys," she repeated incredulously. "You mustn't have told him anything."

"I told him everything," I said confidently.

65 "About Gran and all?"

"About Gran and all."

(All she wanted was to be able to go home and say I'd made a bad confession.)

"Did you tell him you went for me with the bread-knife?" she asked with a frown.

"I did to be sure."

70 "And he only gave you three Hail Marys?"

"That's all."

She slowly got down from the railing with a baffled air. Clearly, this was beyond her. As we mounted the steps back to the main road she looked at me suspiciously.

"What are you sucking?" she asked.

"Bullseyes."

75 "Was it the priest gave them to you?"

"'Twas."

"Lord God," she wailed bitterly, "some people have all the luck! 'Tis no advantage to anybody trying to be good. I might just as well be a sinner like you."

Mark Twain (1835–1910)

Luck* (1891)

It was at a banquet in London in honor of one of the two or three conspicuously illustrious English military names of this generation. For reasons which will presently appear, I will withhold his real name and titles and call him Lieutenant-General Lord Arthur Scoresby, V.C., K.C.B., etc., etc. What a fascination there is in a renowned name! There sat the man, in actual flesh, whom I had heard of so many thousands of times since that day, thirty years before, when his name shot suddenly to the zenith from a Crimean battlefield to remain forever celebrated. It was food and drink to me to look, and look, and look at that demigod; scanning, searching, noting: the quietness, the reserve, the noble gravity of his countenance; the simple honesty that expressed itself all over him; the sweet unconsciousness of his greatness—unconsciousness of the hundreds of admiring eyes fastened upon him, unconsciousness of the deep, loving, sincere worship welling out of the breasts of those people and flowing toward him.

The clergyman at my left was an old acquaintance of mine—clergyman now, but had spent the first half of his life in the camp and field and as an instructor in the military school at Woolwich. Just at the moment I have been talking about a veiled and singular light glimmered in his eyes and he leaned down and muttered confidentially to me—indicating the hero of the banquet with a gesture:

"Privately—he's an absolute fool."

---

*This is not a fancy sketch. I got it from a clergyman who was an instructor at Woolwich forty years ago, and who vouched for its truth. [Twain's note.]

This verdict was a great surprise to me. If its subject had been Napoleon, or Socrates, or Solomon, my astonishment could not have been greater. Two things I was well aware of: that the Reverend was a man of strict veracity and that his judgment of men was good. Therefore I knew, beyond doubt or question, that the world was mistaken about this hero: he *was* a fool. So I meant to find out, at a convenient moment, how the Reverend, all solitary and alone, had discovered the secret.

Some days later the opportunity came, and this is what the Reverend told me: 5

About forty years ago I was an instructor in the military academy at Woolwich. I was present in one of the sections when young Scoresby underwent his preliminary examination. I was touched to the quick with pity, for the rest of the class answered up brightly and handsomely, while he—why, dear me, he didn't know *anything*, so to speak. He was evidently good, and sweet, and lovable, and guileless; and so it was exceedingly painful to see him stand there, as serene as a graven image, and deliver himself of answers which were veritably miraculous for stupidity and ignorance. All the compassion in me was aroused in his behalf. I said to myself, when he comes to be examined again he will be flung over, of course; so it will be simply a harmless act of charity to ease his fall as much as I can. I took him aside and found that he knew a little of Caesar's history; and as he didn't know anything else, I went to work and drilled him like a galley-slave on a certain line of stock questions concerning Caesar which I knew would be used. If you'll believe me, he went through with flying colors on examination day! He went through on that purely superficial "cram," and got compliments too, while others, who knew a thousand times more than he, got plucked. By some strangely lucky accident—an accident not likely to happen twice in a century— he was asked no question outside of the narrow limits of his drill.

It was stupefying. Well, all through his course I stood by him, with something of the sentiment which a mother feels for a crippled child; and he always saved himself— just by miracle, apparently.

Now, of course, the thing that would expose him and kill him at last was mathematics. I resolved to make his death as easy as I could; so I drilled him and crammed him, and crammed him and drilled him, just on the line of questions which the examiners would be most likely to use, and then launched him on his fate. Well, sir, try to conceive of the result: to my consternation, he took the first prize! And with it he got a perfect ovation in the way of compliments.

Sleep? There was no more sleep for me for a week. My conscience tortured me day and night. What I had done I had done purely through charity, and only to ease the poor youth's fall. I never had dreamed of any such preposterous results as the thing that had happened. I felt as guilty and miserable as Frankenstein. Here was a wooden-head whom I had put in the way of glittering promotions and prodigious responsibilities, and but one thing could happen: He and his responsibilities would all go to ruin together at the first opportunity.

The Crimean War° had just broken out. Of course there had to be a war, I said to   10 myself. We couldn't have peace and give this donkey a chance to die before he is found out. I waited for the earthquake. It came. And it made me reel when it did come. He was

---

°*Crimean War:* In the Crimean War (1853–1856), England was one of the allies that fought against Russia.

actually gazetted to a captaincy in a marching regiment! Better men grow old and gray in the service before they climb to a sublimity like that. And who could ever have foreseen that they would go and put such a load of responsibility on such green and inadequate shoulders? I could just barely have stood it if they had made him a cornet; but a captain—think of it! I thought my hair would turn white.

Consider what I did—I who so loved repose and inaction. I said to myself, I am responsible to the country for this, and I must go along with him and protect the country against him as far as I can. So I took my poor little capital that I had saved up through years of work and grinding economy, and went with a sigh and bought a cornetcy in his regiment, and away we went to the field.

And there—oh, dear, it was awful. Blunders?—why he never did anything but blunder. But, you see, nobody was in the fellow's secret. Everybody had him focused wrong, and necessarily misinterpreted his performance every time. Consequently they took his idiotic blunders for inspirations of genius. They did, honestly! His mildest blunders were enough to make a man in his right mind cry; and they did make me cry—and rage and rave, too, privately. And the thing that kept me always in a sweat of apprehension was the fact that every fresh blunder he made increased the luster of his reputation! I kept saying to myself, he'll get so high that when discovery does finally come it will be like the sun falling out of the sky.

He went right along, up from grade to grade, over the dead bodies of his superiors, until at last, in the hottest moment of the battle of————down went our colonel, and my heart jumped into my mouth, for Scoresby was next in rank! Now for it, said I: we'll all land in Sheol in ten minutes, sure.

The battle was awfully hot; the allies were steadily giving way all over the field. Our regiment occupied a position that was vital; a blunder now must be destruction. At this crucial moment, what does this immortal fool do but detach the regiment from its place and order a charge over a neighboring hill where there wasn't a suggestion of an enemy! "There you go!" I said to myself; "This is the end at last."

15   And away we did go, and were over the shoulder of the hill before the insane movement could be discovered and stopped. And what did we find? An entire and unsuspected Russian army in reserve! And what happened? We were eaten up? That is necessarily what would have happened in ninety-nine cases out of a hundred. But no; those Russians argued that no single regiment would come browsing around there at such a time. It must be the entire English army, and that the sly Russian game was detected and blocked, so they turned tail, and away they went, pell-mell, over the hill and down into the field, in wild confusion, and we after them; they themselves broke the solid Russian center in the field, and tore through, and in no time there was the most tremendous rout you ever saw, and the defeat of the allies was turned into a sweeping and splendid victory! Marshall Canrobert looked on, dizzy with astonishment, admiration, and delight; and sent right off for Scoresby, and hugged him, and decorated him on the field in presence of all the armies!

And what was Scoresby's blunder that time? Merely the mistaking his right hand for his left—that was all. An order had come to him to fall back and support our right; and, instead, he fell *forward* and went over the hill to the left. But the name he won that day as a marvelous military genius filled the world with his glory, and that glory will never fade while history books last.

He is just as good and sweet and lovable and unpretending as a man can be, but he doesn't know enough to come in when it rains. Now that is absolutely true. He is the supremest ass in the universe; and until half an hour ago nobody knew it but himself and me. He has been pursued, day by day and year by year, by a most phenomenal astonishing luckiness. He has been a shining soldier in all our wars for a generation; he has littered his whole military life with blunders, and yet has never committed one that didn't make him a knight or a baronet or a lord or something. Look at his breast; why, he is just clothed in domestic and foreign decorations. Well, sir, every one of them is the record of some shouting stupidity or other; and, taken together, they are proof that the very best thing in all this world that can befall a man is to be born lucky. I say again, as I said at the banquet, Scoresby's an absolute fool.

Eudora Welty (1909–2001)

A Worn Path (1941)

It was December—a bright frozen day in the early morning. Far out in the country there was an old Negro woman with her head tied in a red rag, coming along a path through the pinewoods. Her name was Phoenix Jackson. She was very old and small and she walked slowly in the dark pine shadows, moving a little from side to side in her steps, with the balanced heaviness and lightness of a pendulum in a grandfather clock. She carried a thin, small cane made from an umbrella, and with this she kept tapping the frozen earth in front of her. This made a grave and persistent noise in the still air, that seemed meditative like the chirping of a solitary little bird.

She wore a dark striped dress reaching down to her shoe tops, and an equally long apron of bleached sugar sacks, with a full pocket: all neat and tidy, but every time she took a step she might have fallen over her shoelaces, which dragged from her unlaced shoes. She looked straight ahead. Her eyes were blue with age. Her skin had a pattern all its own of numberless branching wrinkles and as though a whole little tree stood in the middle of her forehead, but a golden color ran underneath, and the two knobs of her cheeks were illuminated by a yellow burning under the dark. Under the rag her hair came down on her neck in the frailest of ringlets, still black, and with an odor like copper.

Now and then there was a quivering in the thicket. Old Phoenix said, "Out of my way, all you foxes, owls, beetles, jack rabbits, coons and wild animals! … Keep out from under these feet, little bob-whites…. Keep the big wild hogs out of my path. Don't let none of those come running my direction. I got a long way." Under her small black-freckled hand her cane, limber as a buggy whip, would switch at the brush as if to rouse up any hiding things.

On she went. The woods were deep and still. The sun made the pine needles almost too bright to look at, up where the wind rocked. The cones dropped as light as feathers. Down in the hollow was the mourning dove—it was not too late for him.

The path ran up a hill. "Seem like there is chains about my feet, time I get this far," she said, in the voice of argument old people keep to use with themselves. "Something always take a hold of me on this hill—pleads I should stay."   5

After she got to the top she turned and gave a full, severe look behind her where she had come. "Up through pines," she said at length. "Now down through oaks."

Her eyes opened their widest, and she started down gently. But before she got to the bottom of the hill a bush caught her dress.

Her fingers were busy and intent, but her skirts were full and long, so that before she could pull them free in one place they were caught in another. It was not possible to allow the dress to tear. "I in the thorny bush," she said. "Thorns, you doing your appointed work. Never want to let folks pass, no sir. Old eyes thought you was a pretty little *green* bush."

Finally, trembling all over, she stood free, and after a moment dared to stoop for her cane.

10   "Sun so high!" she cried, leaning back and looking, while the thick tears went over her eyes. "The time getting all gone here."

At the foot of this hill was a place where a log was laid across the creek.

"Now comes the trial," said Phoenix.

Putting her right foot out, she mounted the log and shut her eyes. Lifting her skirt, leveling her cane fiercely before her, like a festival figure in some parade, she began to march across. Then she opened her eyes and she was safe on the other side.

"I wasn't as old as I thought," she said.

15   But she sat down to rest. She spread her skirts on the bank around her and folded her hands over her knees. Up above her was a tree in a pearly cloud of mistletoe. She did not dare to close her eyes, and when a little boy brought her a plate with a slice of marble-cake on it she spoke to him. "That would be acceptable," she said. But when she went to take it there was just her own hand in the air.

So she left that tree, and had to go through a barbed-wire fence. There she had to creep and crawl, spreading her knees and stretching her fingers like a baby trying to climb the steps. But she talked loudly to herself: she could not let her dress be torn now, so late in the day, and she could not pay for having her arm or leg sawed off if she got caught fast where she was.

At last she was safe through the fence and risen up out in the clearing. Big dead trees, like black men with one arm, were standing in the purple stalks of the withered cotton field. There sat a buzzard.

"Who you watching?"

In the furrow she made her way along.

20   "Glad this is not the season for bulls," she said, looking sideways, "and the good Lord made his snakes to curl up and sleep in the winter. A pleasure I don't see no two-headed snake coming around that tree, where it come once. It took a while to get by him, back in the summer."

She passed through the old cotton and went into a field of dead corn. It whispered and shook and was taller than her head. "Through the maze now," she said, for there was no path.

Then there was something tall, black, and skinny there, moving before her.

At first she took it for a man. It could have been a man dancing in the field. But she stood still and listened, and it did not make a sound. It was as silent as a ghost.

"Ghost," she said sharply, "who be you the ghost of? For I have heard of nary death close by."

But there was no answer—only the ragged dancing in the wind.   25

She shut her eyes, reached out her hand, and touched a sleeve. She found a coat and inside that an emptiness, cold as ice.

"You scarecrow," she said. Her face lighted. "I ought to be shut up for good," she said with laughter. "My senses is gone. I too old, I the oldest people I ever know. Dance, old scarecrow," she said, "while I dancing with you."

She kicked her foot over the furrow, and with mouth drawn down, shook her head once or twice in a little strutting way. Some husks blew down and whirled in steamers about her skirts.

Then she went on, parting her way from side to side with the cane, through the whispering field. At last she came to the end, to a wagon track where the silver grass blew between the red ruts. The quail were walking around like pullets, seeming all dainty and unseen.

"Walk pretty," she said. "This is the easy place. This the easy going."   30

She followed the track, swaying through the quiet bare fields, through the little strings of trees silver in their dead leaves, past cabins silver from weather, with the doors and windows boarded shut, all like old women under a spell sitting there. "I walking in their sleep," she said, nodding her head vigorously.

In a ravine she went where a spring was silently flowing through a hollow log. Old Phoenix bent and drank. "Sweet-gum makes the water sweet," she said, and drank more. "Nobody know who made this well, for it was here when I was born."

The track crossed a swampy part where the moss hung as white as lace from every limb. "Sleep on, alligators, and blow your bubbles." Then the track went into the road.

Deep, deep the road went down between the high green-colored banks. Overhead the live-oaks met, and it was as dark as a cave.

A black dog with a lolling tongue came up out of the weeds by the ditch. She was   35
meditating, and not ready, and when he came at her she only hit him a little with her cane. Over she went in the ditch, like a little puff of milkweed.

Down there, her sense drifted away. A dream visited her, and she reached her hand up, but nothing reached down and gave her a pull. So she lay there and presently went to talking. "Old woman," she said to herself, "that black dog come up out of the weeds to stall you off, and now there he sitting on his fine tail smiling at you."

A white man finally came along and found her—a hunter, a young man, with his dog on a chain.

"Well, Granny!" he laughed. "What are you doing there?"

"Lying on my back like a June-bug waiting to be turned over, mister," she said, reaching up her hand.

He lifted her up, gave her a swing in the air, and set her down. "Anything broken,   40
Granny?"

"No sir, them old dead weeds is springy enough," said Phoenix, when she had got her breath. "I thank you for your trouble."

"Where do you live, Granny?" he asked, while the two dogs were growling at each other.

"Away back yonder, sir, behind the ridge. You can't even see it from here."

"On your way home?"

45   "No sir, I goin to town."

"Why, that's too far! That's as far as I walk when I come out myself, and I get something for my trouble." He patted the stuffed bag he carried, and there hung down a little closed claw. It was one of the bob-whites, with its beak hooked bitterly to show it was dead. "Now you go on home, Granny!"

"I bound to go to town, mister," said Phoenix. "The time come around."

He gave another laugh, filling the whole landscape. "I know you old colored people! Wouldn't miss going to town to see Santa Claus!"

But something held old Phoenix very still. The deep lines in her face went into a fierce and different radiation. Without warning, she had seen with her own eyes a flashing nickel fall out of the man's pocket onto the ground.

50   "How old are you, Granny?" he was saying.

"There is no telling, mister," she said, "no telling."

Then she gave a little cry and clapped her hands and said, "Git on away from here, dog! Look! Look at that dog!" She laughed as if in admiration. "He ain't scared of nobody. He a big black dog." She whispered, "Sic him!"

"Watch me get rid of that cur," said the man. "Sic him, Pete! Sic him!"

Phoenix heard the dogs fighting, and heard the man running and throwing sticks. She even heard a gunshot. But she was slowly bending forward by that time, further and further forward, the lids stretched down over her eyes, as if she were doing this in her sleep. Her chin was lowered almost to her knees. The yellow palm of her hand came out from the fold of her apron. Her fingers slid down and along the ground under the piece of money with the grace and care they would have in lifting an egg from under a setting hen. Then she slowly straightened up, she stood erect, and the nickel was in her apron pocket. A bird flew by. Her lips moved. "God watching me the whole time. I come to stealing."

55   The man came back, and his own dog panted about them. "Well, I scared him off that time," he said, and then he laughed and lifted his gun and pointed it at Phoenix.

She stood straight and faced him.

"Doesn't the gun scare you?" he said, still pointing it.

"No sir. I seen plenty go off closer by, in my day, and for less than what I done," she said, holding utterly still.

He smiled, and shouldered the gun. "Well, Granny," he said, "you must be a hundred years old, and scared of nothing. I'd give you a dime if I had any money with me. But you take my advice and stay home, and nothing will happen to you."

60   "I bound to go on my way, mister," said Phoenix. She inclined her head in the red rag. Then they went in different directions, but she could hear the gun shooting again and again over the hill.

She walked on. The shadows hung from the oak trees to the road like curtains. Then she smelled wood-smoke, and smelled the river, and she saw a steeple and the cabins on their steep steps. Dozens of little black children whirled around her. There ahead was Natchez shining. Bells were ringing. She walked on.

In the paved city it was Christmas time. There were red and green electric lights strung and crisscrossed everywhere, and all turned on in the daytime. Old Phoenix would have been lost if she had not distrusted her eyesight and depended on her feet to know where to take her.

She paused quietly on the sidewalk where people were passing by. A lady came along in the crowd, carrying an armful of red-, green-, and silver-wrapped presents; she gave off perfume like the red roses in hot summer, and Phoenix stopped her.

"Please, missy, will you lace up my shoe?" She held up her foot.

"What do you want, Grandma?"   65

"See my shoe," said Phoenix. "Do all right for out in the country, but wouldn't look right to go in a big building."

"Stand still then, Grandma," said the lady. She put her packages down on the sidewalk beside her and laced and tied both shoes tightly.

"Can't lace 'em with a cane," said Phoenix. "Thank you, missy. I doesn't mind asking a nice lady to tie up my shoe, when I gets out on the street."

Moving slowly and from side to side, she went into the big building, and into a tower of steps, where she walked up and around and around until her feet knew to stop.

She entered a door, and there she saw nailed up on the wall the document that had   70
been stamped with the gold seal and framed in the gold frame, which matched the dream that was hung up in her head.

"Here I be," she said. There was a fixed and ceremonial stiffness over her body.

"A charity case, I suppose," said an attendant who sat at the desk before her.

But Phoenix only looked above her head. There was sweat on her face, the wrinkles in her skin shone like a bright net.

"Speak up, Grandma," the woman said, "What's your name? We must have your history, you know. Have you been here before? What seems to be the trouble with you?"

Old Phoenix only gave a twitch to her face as if a fly were bothering her.   75

"Are you deaf?" cried the attendant.

But then the nurse came in.

"Oh, that's just old Aunt Phoenix," she said. "She doesn't come for herself—she has a little grandson. She makes these trips just as regular as clockwork. She lives away back off the Old Natchez Trace." She bent down. "Well, Aunt Phoenix, why don't you just take a seat? We won't keep you standing after your long trip." She pointed.

The old woman sat down, bolt upright in the chair.

"Now, how is the boy?" asked the nurse.   80

Old Phoenix did not speak.

"I said, how is the boy?"

But Phoenix only waited and stared straight ahead, her face very solemn and withdrawn into rigidity.

"Is his throat any better?" asked the nurse. "Aunt Phoenix, don't you hear me? Is your grandson's throat any better since the last time you came for the medicine?"

With her hands on her knees, the old woman waited, silent, erect, and motionless,   85
just as if she were in armor.

"You mustn't take up our time this way, Aunt Phoenix," the nurse said. "Tell us quickly about your grandson, and get it over. He isn't dead, is he?"

At last there came a flicker and then a flame of comprehension across her face, and she spoke.

"My grandson. It was my memory had left me. There I sat and forgot why I made my long trip."

"Forgot?" the nurse frowned. "After you came so far?"

90   Then Phoenix was like an old woman begging a dignified forgiveness for waking up frightened in the night. "I never did go to school, I was too old at the Surrender," she said in a soft voice. "I'm an old woman without an education. It was my memory fail me. My little grandson, he is just the same, and I forgot it in the coming."

"Throat never heals, does it?" said the nurse, speaking in a loud, sure voice to old Phoenix. By now she had a card with something written on it, a little list. "Yes. Swallowed lye. When was it—January—two, three years ago—"

Phoenix spoke unasked now. "No missy, he not dead, he just the same. Every little while his throat begin to close up again, and he not able to swallow. He not get his breath. He not able to help himself. So the time come around, and I go on another trip for the soothing medicine."

"All right. The doctor said as long as you came to get it, you could have it," said the nurse. "But it's an obstinate case."

"My little grandson, he sit up there in the house all wrapped up, waiting by himself," Phoenix went on. "We is the only two left in the world. He suffer and it don't seem to put him back at all. He got a sweet look. He going to last. He wear a little patch quilt and peep out holding his mouth open like a little bird. I remembers so plain now. I not going to forget him again, no, the whole enduring time. I could tell him from all the others in creation."

95   "All right." The nurse was trying to hush her now. She brought her a bottle of medicine. "Charity," she said, making a check mark in a book.

Old Phoenix held the bottle close to her eyes, and then carefully put it into her pocket.

"I thank you," she said.

"It's Christmas time, Grandma," said the attendant. "Could I give you a few pennies out of my purse?"

"Five pennies is a nickel," said Phoenix stiffly.

100   "Here's a nickel," said the attendant.

Phoenix rose carefully and held out her hand. She received the nickel and then fished the other nickel out of her pocket and laid it beside the new one. She stared at her palm closely, with her head on one side.

Then she gave a tap with her cane on the floor.

"This is what come to me to do," she said, "I going to the store and buy my child a little windmill they sells, made out of paper. He going to find it hard to believe there such a thing in the world. I'll march myself back where he waiting, holding it straight up in this hand."

She lifted her free hand, gave a little nod, turned around, and walked out of the doctor's office. Then her slow step began on the stairs, going down.

POEMS

Matthew Arnold (1822–1888)

Dover Beach (1849)

The sea is calm tonight.
The tide is full, the moon lies fair
Upon the straits:—on the French coast the light
Gleams and is gone; the cliffs of England stand,
Glimmering and vast, out in the tranquil bay.   5
Come to the window, sweet is the night air!
Only, from the long line of spray
Where the sea meets the moon-blanched land,
Listen! You can hear the grating roar
Of pebbles which the waves draw back, and fling,   10
At their return, up the high strand,
Begin, and cease, and then again begin,
With tremulous cadence slow, and bring
The eternal note of sadness in.

Sophocles long ago   15
Heard it on the Ægean, and it brought
Into his mind the turbid ebb and flow
Of human misery; we
Find also in the sound a thought,
Hearing it by this distant northern sea.   20
The Sea of Faith
Was once, too, at the full, and round earth's shore
Lay like the folds of a bright girdle furled.
But now I only hear
Its melancholy, long, withdrawing roar,   25
Retreating, to the breath
Of the night wind, down the vast edges drear
And naked shingles of the world.

Ah, love, let us be true
To one another! for the world, which seems   30
To lie before us like a land of dreams,
So various, so beautiful, so new,
Hath really neither joy, nor love, nor light,
Nor certitude, nor peace, nor help for pain;
And we are here as on a darkling plain   35
Swept with confused alarms of struggle and flight
Where ignorant armies clash by night.

William Blake (1757–1827)

The Tyger° (1794)

Tyger! Tyger! burning bright
In the forests of the night,
What immortal hand or eye
Could frame thy fearful symmetry?

In what distant deeps or skies   5
Burnt the fire of thine eyes?
On what wings dare he aspire?
What the hand, dare seize the fire?

And what shoulder, & what art,
Could twist the sinews of thy heart?   10
And when thy heart began to beat,
What dread hand? & what dread feet?

What the hammer? what the chain?
In what furnace was thy brain?
What the anvil? what dread grasp   15
Dare its deadly terrors clasp?

When the stars threw down their spears,
And water'd heaven with their tears,
Did he smile his work to see?
Did he who made the Lamb make thee?   20

Tyger! Tyger! burning bright
In the forests of the night,
What immortal hand or eye
Dare frame thy fearful symmetry?

Gwendolyn Brooks (1917–2000)

We Real Cool (1959)

**The Pool Players.
Seven at the Golden Shovel.**

We real cool. We
Left school. We

°*Tyger:* Tyger here means not only a tiger but also a lion or similarly large and ferocious cat.

Lurk late. We
Strike straight. We

Sing sin. We   5
Thin gin. We

Jazz June. We
Die soon.

Robert Browning (1812–1889)

My Last Duchess (1842)

That's my last Duchess painted on the wall,
Looking as if she were alive. I call
That piece a wonder, now: Frà Pandolf's° hands
Worked busily a day, and there she stands.
Will't please you sit and look at her? I said   5
"Frà Pandolf" by design, for never read
Strangers like you that pictured countenance,
The depth and passion of its earnest glance,
But to myself they turned (since none puts by
The curtain I have drawn for you, but I)   10
And seemed as they would ask me, if they durst,*
How such a glance came there; so, not the first
Are you to turn and ask thus. Sir, 'twas not
Her husband's presence only, called that spot
Of joy into the Duchess' cheek: perhaps   15
Frà Pandolf chanced to say "Her mantle laps
Over my lady's wrist too much," or "Paint
Must never hope to reproduce the faint
Half-flush that dies along her throat": such stuff
Was courtesy, she thought, and cause enough   20
For calling up that spot of joy. She had
A heart—how shall I say?—too soon made glad,
Too easily impressed; she liked whate'er
She looked on, and her looks went everywhere.
Sir, 'twas all one! My favor at her breast,   25
The dropping of the daylight in the West,
The bough of cherries some officious fool
Broke in the orchard for her, the white mule

°*Frà Pandolf:* an imaginary painter and a monk.   **durst:* dared.

She rode with round the terrace—all and each
Would draw from her alike the approving speech,   30
Or blush, at least. She thanked men—good! But thanked
Somehow—I know not how—as if she ranked
My gift of a nine-hundred-years-old name
With anybody's gift. Who'd stoop to blame
This sort of trifling? Even had you skill   35
In speech—(which I have not)—to make your will
Quite clear to such a one, and say, "Just this
Or that in you disgusts me; here you miss,
Or there exceed the mark"—and if she let
Herself be lessoned so, nor plainly set   40
Her wits to yours, forsooth, and made excuse
—E'en then would be some stooping; and I choose
Never to stoop. Oh sir, she smiled, no doubt,
Whene'er I passed her; but who passed without
Much the same smile? This grew, I gave commands;   45
Then all smiles stopped together. There she stands
As if alive. Will't please you rise? We'll meet
The company below, then. I repeat,
The Count your master's known munificence
Is ample warrant that no just pretense   50
Of mine for dowry will be disallowed;
Though his fair daughter's self, as I avowed
At starting, is my object. Nay, we'll go
Together down, sir. Notice Neptune,° though,
Taming a sea horse, thought a rarity,   55
Which Claus of Innsbruck* cast in bronze for me!

Samuel Taylor Coleridge (1772–1834)

Kubla Khan (1816)

In Xanadu did Kubla Kahn
A stately pleasure dome decree:
Where Alph, the sacred river, ran
Through caverns measureless to man
    Down to a sunless sea.   5
So twice five miles of fertile ground
With walls and towers were girdled round:
And there were gardens bright with sinuous rills,
Where blossomed many an incense-bearing tree;

°*Neptune:* statue of the Roman Sea God.   *Claus of Innsbrook:* an imaginary sculptor.

And here were forests ancient as the hills,   10
Enfolding sunny spots of greenery.

But oh! that deep romantic chasm which slanted
Down the green hill athwart a cedarn cover!
A savage place! as holy and enchanted
As e'er beneath a waning moon was haunted   15
By woman wailing for her demon lover!
And from this chasm, with ceaseless turmoil seething,
As if this earth in fast thick pants were breathing,
A mighty fountain momently was forced:
Amid whose swift half-intermitted burst   20
Huge fragments vaulted like rebounding hail,
Or chaffy grain beneath the thresher's flail;
And 'mid these dancing rocks at once and ever
It flung up momently the sacred river.
Five miles meandering with a mazy motion   25
Through wood and dale the sacred river ran,
Then reached the caverns measureless to man,
And sank in tumult to a lifeless ocean:
And 'mid this tumult Kubla heard from far
Ancestral voices prophesying war!   30
    The shadow of the dome of pleasure
    Floated midway on the waves;
    Where was heard the mingled measure
    From the fountain and the caves.
It was a miracle of rare device,   35
A sunny pleasure dome with caves of ice!
    A damsel with a dulcimer
    In a vision once I saw:
    It was an Abyssinian maid,
    And on her dulcimer she played,   40
    Singing of Mount Abora.
Could I revive within me
Her symphony and song,
To such a deep delight 'twould win me,
That with music loud and long,   45
I would build that dome in air,
That sunny dome! those caves of ice!
And all who heard should see them there,
And all should cry, Beware! Beware!
His flashing eyes, his floating hair!   50
Weave a circle round him thrice,
And close your eyes with holy dread,
For he on honeydew hath fed,
And drunk the milk of Paradise.

John Donne (1572–1631)

Holy Sonnet 10: Death Be Not Proud (1633)

Death, be not proud, though some have callèd thee
Mighty and dreadful, for thou art not so;
For those whom thou think'st thou dost overthrow
Die not, poor Death, nor yet canst thou kill me.
From rest and sleep, which but thy pictures° be,   5
Much pleasure; then from thee much more must flow,
And soonest our best men with thee do go,
Rest of their bones, and soul's delivery.
Thou art slave to fate, chance, kings, and desperate men,
And dost with poison, war, and sickness dwell,   10
And poppy* or charms can make us sleep as well
And better than thy stroke; why swell'st† thou then?
One short sleep past, we wake eternally°°
And death shall be no more; death, thou shalt die.

Robert Frost (1875–1963)

Desert Places (1936)

Snow falling and night falling fast, oh, fast
In a field I looked into going past,
And the ground almost covered smooth in snow,
But a few weeds and stubble showing last.

The woods around it have it—it is theirs.   5
All animals are smothered in their lairs.
I am too absent-spirited to count;
The loneliness includes me unawares.

And lonely as it is that loneliness
Will be more lonely ere it will be less—   10
A blanker whiteness of benighted snow
With no expression, nothing to express.

They cannot scare me with their empty spaces
Between stars—on stars where no human race is.
I have it in me so much nearer home   15
To scare myself with my own desert places.

°*pictures*: imitations.   *poppy*: opium.   †*swell'st*: puff up with pride.   °°*we wake eternally*: we will live eternally.

Thomas Hardy (1840–1928)

Channel Firing (1914)

That night your great guns unawares,
Shook all our coffins as we lay,
And broke the chancel window squares.
We thought it was the Judgment-day

And sat upright. While drearisome   5
Arose the howl of wakened hounds:
The mouse let fall the altar-crumb,
The worms drew back into the mounds.

The glebe° cow drooled. Till God called, "No;
It's gunnery practice out at sea   10
Just as before you went below;
The world is as it used to be:

"All nations striving strong to make
Red war yet redder. Mad as hatters
They do no more for Christés sake   15
Than you who are helpless in such matters.

"That this is not the judgment-hour
For some of them's a blessed thing,
For if it were they'd have to scour
Hell's floor for so much threatening . . .   20

"Ha, ha. It will be warmer when
I blow the trumpet (if indeed
I ever do; for you are men,
And rest eternal sorely need)."

So down we lay again. "I wonder,   25
Will the world ever saner be,"
Said one, "than when He sent us under
In our indifferent century!"

And many a skeleton shook his head.
"Instead of preaching forty year,"   30
My neighbor Parson Thirdly said,
"I wish I had stuck to pipes and beer."

°*glebe:* the land and cemetery surrounding and belonging to a church. Cows were kept there to keep the grass short.

Again the guns disturbed the hour,
Roaring their readiness to avenge,
As far inland as Stourton Tower,   35
And Camelot, and starlit Stonehenge.*

The Man He Killed (1902)

"Had he and I but met
By some old ancient inn,
We should have sat us down to wet
Right many a nipperkin!°

"But ranged as infantry,   5
And staring face to face,
I shot at him as he at me,
And killed him in his place.

"I shot him dead because—
Because he was my foe.   10
Just so: my foe of course he was;
That's clear enough; although

"He thought he'd 'list,* perhaps,
Off-hand like—just as I—
Was out of work—had sold his traps†   15
No other reason why.

"Yes; quaint and curious war is!
You shoot a fellow down
You'd treat if met where any bar is
Or help to half-a-crown."°°   20

Laugston Hughes (1902–1967)

Negro (1958)

I am a Negro:
    Black as the night is black,
    Black like the depths of my Africa.

---

*Stourton Tower . . . Stonehenge: places in the south of England associated with ancient Druids and also
with the mythical King Arthur.   °nipperkin: a half-pint of ale. *'list: enlist. †traps: personal possessions.
°°half-a-crown: perhaps as much as $10 or $20.

I've been a slave:
>
>> Caesar told me to keep his door-steps clean.
>> I brushed the boots of Washington.

I've been a worker:
>
>> Under my hand the pyramids arose.
>> I made mortar for the Woolworth Building.

I've been a singer:
>
>> All the way from Africa to Georgia
>> I carried my sorrow songs.
>> I made ragtime.

I've been a victim:
>
>> The Belgians cut off my hands in the Congo.
>> They lynch me still in Mississippi.

I am a Negro:
>
>> Black as the night is black,
>> Black like the depths of my Africa.

John Keats (1795–1821)

Bright Star (1819)

Bright star! would I were steadfast as thou art—
Not in lone splendor hung aloft the night,
And watching, with eternal lids apart,
Like Nature's patient, sleepless eremite,**
The moving waters at their priestlike task
Of pure ablution round earth's human shores,
Or gazing on the new soft-fallen mask
Of snow upon the mountains and the moors;
No—yet still steadfast, still unchangeable,
Pillowed upon my fair love's ripening breast,
To feel forever its soft fall and swell,
Awake forever in a sweet unrest,
Still, still to hear her tender-taken breath,
And so live ever—or else swoon to death.

**eremite: hermit.

On First Looking into Chapman's Homer° (1816)

Much have I travell'd in the realms of gold,°	*the world of great art*
And many goodly states and kingdoms seen:	
Round many western islands° have I been	*much ancient literature*
Which bards in fealty to Apollo° hold.	
Oft of one wide expanse° had I been told	5
That deep-brow'd Homer ruled as his demesne°;	*realm, estate*
Yet did I never breathe its pure serene°	*epic poetry*
Till I heard Chapman speak out loud and bold:	
Then felt I like some watcher of the skies	
When a new planet swims into his ken°;	10
Or like stout Cortez° when with eagle eyes	
He star'd at the Pacific—and all his men	*range of vision*
Look'd at each other with a wild surmise°—	
Silent, upon a peak in Darien.	*conjecture, supposition*

Irving Layton (1912–2006)

Rhine Boat Trip° (1977)

The castles on the Rhine
are all haunted
by the ghosts of Jewish mothers
looking for their ghostly children

And the clusters of grapes   5
in the sloping vineyards
are myriads of blinded eyes
staring at the blind sun

The tireless Lorelei*
can never comb from their hair   10
the crimson beards
of murdered rabbis

°George Chapman (c. 1560–1634) published his translations of Homer's *Iliad* in 1612 and *Odyssey* in 1614–15.   4 *bards . . . Apollo*: writers who are sworn subjects of Apollo, the Greek god of light, music, poetry, prophecy, and the sun.   7 *serene*: a clear expanse of air; also grandeur, clarity; rulers were also sometimes called "serene majesty."   11 *Cortez*: Hernando Cortés (1485–1547), a Spanish general and the conqueror of Mexico. Keats confuses him with Vasco de Balboa (c. 1475–1519), the first European to see the Pacific Ocean (in 1510) from Darien, an early name for the Isthmus of Panama.   °*Rhine Boat Trip*: The Rhine, Germany's best-known river, is virtually synonymous with German national history.
Lorelei: mythical shore nymphs who lured passing rivermen to their doom; subject of a famous poem by Heinrich Heine (1797–1856).

However sweetly they sing
one hears only
the low wailing of cattle-cars[†]   15
moving invisibly across the land

Amy Lowell (1874–1925)

Patterns (1916)

I walk down the garden paths,
And all the daffodils
Are blowing, and the bright blue squills.
I walk down the patterned garden-paths
In my stiff, brocaded gown.   5
With my powdered hair and jewelled fan,
I too am a rare
Pattern. As I wander down
The garden paths.

My dress is richly figured,   10
And the train
Makes a pink and silver stain
On the gravel, and the thrift
Of the borders.
Just a plate of current fashion   15
Tripping by in high-heeled, ribboned shoes.
Not a softness anywhere about me,
Only whalebone° and brocade.
And I sink on a seat in the shade

Of a lime tree. For my passion   20
Wars against the stiff brocade.
The daffodils and squills
Flutter in the breeze
As they please.
And I weep;   25
For the lime-tree is in blossom
And one small flower has dropped upon my bosom.
And the plashing of waterdrops

---

†*cattle-cars:* During the Holocaust in World War II, the Nazis crowded their victims together into cattle-cars and transported them by rail to concentration and extermination camps in Germany and neighboring countries.   °*whalebone:* Baleen from whales was used to make corsets for women because it was strong and flexible, like an early plastic.

In the marble fountain
Comes down the garden-paths.   30
The dripping never stops.
Underneath my stiffened gown
Is the softness of a woman bathing in a marble basin,
A basin in the midst of hedges grown
So thick, she cannot see her lover hiding.   35
But she guesses he is near,

And the sliding of the water
Seems the stroking of a dear
Hand upon her.
What is Summer in a fine brocaded gown!   40

I should like to see it lying in a heap upon the ground.
All the pink and silver crumpled up on the ground.
I would be the pink and silver as I ran along the paths,
And he would stumble after,
Bewildered by my laughter.   45
I should see the sun flashing from his sword-hilt and
buckles on his shoes.
I would choose
To lead him in a maze along the patterned paths,
A bright and laughing maze for my heavy-booted lover.
Till he caught me in the shade,   50
And the buttons of his waistcoat bruised my body
as he clasped me,
Aching, melting, unafraid.
With the shadows of the leaves and the sundrops,
And the plopping of the waterdrops,
All about us in the open afternoon—   55
I am very like to swoon
With the weight of this brocade,
For the sun sifts through the shade.

Underneath the fallen blossom
In my bosom,   60
Is a letter I have hid.
It was brought to me this morning by a rider from the Duke.
Madam, we regret to inform you that Lord Hartwell
Died in action Thursday se'nnight.°
As I read it in the white, morning sunlight,   65
The letters squirmed like snakes.
"Any answer, Madam," said my footman.

°*se'nnight*: on a Thursday, seven days before last Thursday.

"No," I told him.
"See that the messenger takes some refreshment.

No, no answer."   70
And I walked into the garden.
Up and down the patterned paths,
In my stiff, correct brocade.
The blue and yellow flowers stood up proudly in the sun,
Each one.   75
I stood upright too,
Held rigid to the pattern
By the stiffness of my gown.
Up and down I walked.
Up and down.   80
In a month he would have been my husband.
In a month, here, underneath this lime,
We would have broken the pattern;
He for me, and I for him,
He as Colonel, I as Lady,   85
On this shady seat.
He had a whim
That sunlight carried blessing.
And I answered, "It shall be as you have said."
Now he is dead.   90

In Summer and in Winter I shall walk
Up and down
The patterned garden-paths
In my stiff, brocaded gown.
The squills and daffodils   95
Will give place to pillared roses, and to asters, and to snow.
I shall go
Up and down,
In my gown.
Gorgeously arrayed,   100
Boned and stayed.
And the softness of my body will be guarded from embrace
By each button, hook, and lace.
For the man who should loose me is dead,
Fighting with the Duke in Flanders,°   105
In a pattern called a war.
Christ! What are patterns for?

°*Flanders:* a place of frequent warfare in Belgium (e.g., the Duke of Marlborough's Flanders campaigns of 1702–1710; The Battle of Waterloo, 1815, under the Duke of Wellington; battles with the Germans during World War I, 1914–1915).

John Masefield (1878–1967)

Cargoes (1902)

Quinquereme* of Nineveh† from distant Ophir,°°
Rowing home to haven in sunny Palestine,
With a cargo of ivory,
And apes and peacocks,°
Sandalwood, cedarwood,* and sweet white wine.   5

Stately Spanish galleon coming from the Isthmus,†
Dipping through the Tropics by the palm-green shores,
With a cargo of diamonds,
Emeralds, amethysts,
Topazes, and cinnamon, and gold moidores.°°   10

Dirty British coaster with a salt-caked smoke-stack,
Butting through the Channel in the mad March days,
With a cargo of Tyne coal,**
Road-rails, pig-lead,
Firewood, iron-ware, and cheap tin trays.   15

Wilfred Owen (1893–1918)

Anthem for Doomed Youth (1920)

What passing-bells†† for these who die as cattle?
Only the monstrous anger of the guns.
Only the stuttering rifles' rapid rattle
Can patter out their hasty orisons.°°°

No mockeries for them from prayers or bells,   5
Nor any voice of mourning save the choirs—
The shrill, demented choirs of wailing shells;
And bugles calling for them from sad shires.***

What candles may be held to speed them all?
Not in the hands of boys, but in their eyes   10
Shall shine the holy glimmers of good-byes.
The pallor of girls' brows shall be their pall;

---

*quinquereme: largest of the ancient ships, with three tiers of oars operated by five men at each vertical oar station. †Nineveh: the capital of ancient Assyria. °°Ophir: Ophir, known for its gold, probably was in Africa. °apes and peacocks: 1 Kings 10:22 and 2 Chronicles 9:21. *cedarwood: 1 Kings 9:11. †Isthmus: the Isthmus of Panama. °°moidores: coins (in Portugal and Brazil). **Tyne coal: coal from Newcastle upon Tyne, England. ††passing-bells: church bells that are tolled at the entry of a funeral cortege into a church cemetery. °°°orisons: prayers. ***shires: British counties.

Their flowers the tenderness of patient minds,
And each slow dusk a drawing-down of blinds.

Christina Rossetti (1830–1894)

Echo (1854)

Come to me in the silence of the night;
   Come in the speaking silence of a dream;
Come with soft rounded cheeks and eyes as bright
    As sunlight on a stream
      Come back in tears,   5
     O memory, hope, love of finished years.

O dream how sweet, too sweet, too bitter sweet,
   Whose wakening should have been in paradise,
Where souls brimful of love abide and meet;
    Where thirsty longing eyes   10
      Watch the slow door
     That opening, letting in, lets out no more.

Yet come to me in dreams, that I may live
   My very life again though cold in death;
Come back to me in dreams, that I may give   15
    Pulse for pulse, breath for breath:
      Speak low, lean low,
     As long ago, my love, how long ago!

William Shakespeare (1564–1616)

*Sonnet 30: When to the Sessions
of Sweet Silent Thought* (1609)

When to the sessions° of sweet silent thought   *holding of court*
I summon° up remembrance of things past,
I sigh the lack of many a thing I sought,
And with old woes new wail my dear time's waste:°
Then can I drown an eye (un-used to flow)   5
For precious friends hid in death's dateless° night,   *endless*
And weep afresh love's long since canceled° woe,   *paid in full*
And moan th'expense° of many a vanished sight.   *cost, loss*
Then can I grieve at grievances foregone,

°2 *summon:* to issue a summons to appear at a legal hearing.   4 *old woes . . . waste:* revive old sorrows about
lost opportunities and express sorrow for them again.

And heavily° from woe to woe tell° o'er   *sadly; count*   10
The sad account of fore-bemoanéd moan,
Which I new pay, as if not paid before.
      But if the while I think on thee (dear friend)
      All losses are restored, and sorrows end.

*Sonnet 73: That Time of Year Thou May'st
in Me Behold* (1609)

That time of year thou may'st in me behold
When yellow leaves, or none, or few, do hang
Upon those boughs which shake against the cold,
Bare ruined choirs,° where late the sweet birds sang.
In me thou see'st the twilight of such day   5
As after sunset fadeth in the west;
Which by and by black night doth take away,
Death's second self,° that seals up all in rest.
In me thou see'st the glowing of such fire,
That on the ashes of his° youth doth lie,   *its*   10
As the death-bed whereon it must expire,
Consumed with that which it was nourished by.°
This thou perceivest, which makes thy love more strong,
To love that well which thou must leave ere long.

Walt Whitman (1819–1892)

Reconciliation (1865, 1881)

Word over all, beautiful as the sky,
Beautiful that war and all its deeds of carnage must in time be utterly lost,
That the hands of the sisters Death and Night incessantly softly wash again, and ever
      again, this soiled world;
For my enemy is dead, a man divine as myself is dead,   5
I look where he lies white-faced and still in the coffin—I draw near,
Bend down and touch lightly with my lips the white face in the coffin.

°4 *choirs:* the part of a church just in front of the altar.   8 *Death's . . . self:* That is, night is a mirror image of
death inasmuch as it brings the sleep of rest just as death brings the sleep of actual death.   12 *Consumed . . .
by:* That is, the ashes of the fuel burned at the fire's height now prevent the fire from continuing, and in
fact extinguish it.

William Wordsworth (1770–1850)

Lines Written in Early Spring (1798)

I heard a thousand blended notes,
While in a grove I sat reclined,
In that sweet mood when pleasant thoughts
Bring sad thoughts to the mind.

To her fair works did Nature link   5
The human soul that through me ran;
And much it grieved my heart to think
What man has made of man.

Through primrose tufts, in that green bower,
The periwinkle trailed its wreaths;   10
And 'tis my faith that every flower
Enjoys the air it breathes.

The birds around me hopped and played,
Their thoughts I cannot measure—
But the least motion which they made,   15
It seemed a thrill of pleasure.

The budding twigs spread out their fan,
To catch the breezy air;
And I must think, do all I can,
That there was pleasure there.   20

If this belief from heaven be sent,
If such be Nature's holy plan,
Have I not reason to lament
What man has made of man?

William Butler Yeats (1865–1939)

The Second Coming° (1920)

Turning and turning in the widening gyre*
The falcon cannot hear the falconer;
Things fall apart; the center cannot hold;
Mere anarchy is loosed upon the world.
The blood-dimmed tide† is loosed, and everywhere   5

The ceremony of innocence is drowned;
The best lack all conviction, while the worst
Are full of passionate intensity.
Surely some revelation is at hand;

Surely the Second Coming is at hand.   10
The Second Coming! Hardly are those words out
When a vast image out of *Spiritus Mundi°*
Troubles my sight; somewhere in sands of the desert
A shape with lion body and the head of a man,*
A gaze blank and pitiless as the sun,   15
Is moving its slow thighs, while all about it
Reel shadows of the indignant desert birds.
The darkness drops again; but now I know

That twenty centuries of stony sleep
Were vexed to nightmare by a rocking cradle,   20
And what rough beast, its hour come round at last
Slouches towards Bethlehem to be born?

°*Second Coming:* the return of Jesus Christ for the salvation of believers, as described in the Book of Revelation, which foretold that Christ's return would be preceded by famine, epidemics, war, and civil disturbances. Yeats believed that human history could be measured in cycles of 2,000 years (approx.) and that Jesus's birth ended the Greco-Roman cycle. In 1919 when Yeats wrote "The Second Coming," he thought the Christian period was ending. The New Testament expectation was that Jesus would reappear, but Yeats held that the disruptions of the twentieth century were preceding a takeover by the forces of evil.
gyre: a radiating spiral, cone, or vortex. Yeats refers to the intersection of two of these shapes as a visual symbol of his cyclic theory. As one gyre spiraled, widened, and disintegrated, a period of history would be ending. At the same time a new gyre would be beginning a reverse spiral:

The falcon is at the broadest, centrifugal point of the old gyre, symbolizing the end of a historic cycle. The desert birds "reel" in a tighter circle, symbolizing the beginning of the new age in the new gyre.   †*Blood-dimmed tide:* See Shakespeare's *Macbeth,* 2.2.60–63.   °*Spiritus Mundi:* "the spirit of the world," a collective human consciousness that furnished a common fund of images and symbols; Yeats referred to it as "a great memory passing on from generation to generation."   *lion body and the head of a man:* a description of an Egyptian sphinx, which symbolized the Pharaoh as a sun spirit. Here the sphinx represents a monstrous satanic figure.

A Glossary of Important Literary Terms

This glossary presents brief definitions of terms that are significant in the text. Page references indicate where readers may find additional detail and illustration, together with discussions about how the concepts may be used in writing about literature.

accent, or **beat**   The heavy stresses or accents in lines of poetry. Because heavy stresses are paired with *light stresses* to compose metrical *feet*, the numbers of accents or beats in a line usually govern the meter of the line (five feet in a *pentameter* line, four feet in a *tetrameter* line, etc.). 193

accented rhyme   See *heavy-stress rhyme*.

accented syllable   A syllable that receives a major, or heavy, *stress*. 193

action   What characters do within a work of literature; the things they undertake in order to solve problems and overcome situations. 3, 83, 123, and ideas, 130, 134

acute accent   In some forms of poetic scansion, the prime mark (´) indicating a heavy *stress*. 193

allegory   A complete narrative that may also be applied to a parallel set of moral, philosophical, political, religious, or social situations.   Chapter 11: 162–78

allusion   Unacknowledged references and quotations that authors make with the assumption that readers will recognize the original sources and relate their meanings to the new context. Allusions are hence compliments that authors pay to readers for their perceptiveness, knowledge, and awareness.   166

analytical sentence outline   A scheme or plan for an essay, arranged according to topics (A, B, C, etc.) and with the topics expressed in sentences.   36

analyzed rhyme   See *inexact rhyme*.

anapest   Sometimes spelled **anapaest.** A three-syllable foot consisting of two light stresses and a heavy stress, as in "*and bright STARS*" and "*ear-ly LIGHT*."   194

antagonist   (i.e., one who struggles against.) The person, idea, force, or general set of circumstances opposing the *protagonist*; an essential element of *plot*.   86

anticipation   See *procatalepsis*.

archetypal/symbolic/mythic critical approach   An interpretive literary approach explaining literature in terms of archetypal patterns (e.g., God's creation of human beings, the sacrifice of a hero, the search for paradise, the initiation or "test" of a young person).   302

argument   The development of a pattern of interpretation or thought with an intent to persuade. In most writing about literature, the persuasive situation is to show the validity of a particular idea or circumstance in a story, poem, or play. More broadly, the term *argument* applies to any situation about which there may be disagreement. Although argumentative discourse may sometimes become disputatious, one should never forget that true arguments should stem from the logical and reasonable interpretation of correct and accurate data.   31, 46

assertion   A sentence putting an idea or argument (the subject) into operation (the predicate); necessary for both developing and understanding the idea. 128

assonance   The repetition of identical vowel sounds in different words in close proximity, as in the d*ee*p gr*ee*n s*ea.*

atmosphere, or mood   The emotional aura invoked by a work. 121, 123

auditory images   References to sounds. 143

authorial symbol   See *contextual symbol.*

authorial voice   The *voice* or *persona* used by authors when seemingly speaking for themselves. The use of the term makes it possible to discuss a narration or presentation without identifying the ideas absolutely as those of the author. See also *point of view, speaker,* and *third-person point of view.* 71

ballad, ballad measure   A narrative poem, originally a popular form, composed of quatrains in *ballad measure*—that is, a pattern of iambic tetrameter alternating with iambic trimeter and rhyming *x-a-x-a.* 3, 196

beast fable   A narrative or poem attributing human characteristics to animals, including powers of thought and speech. 166

beat   See *accent.*

blank verse   Unrhymed iambic pentameter. Most of the poetry in Shakespeare's plays is blank verse, as is the poetry of Milton's *Paradise Lost* and many of Wordsworth's longer poems. 3

brainstorming   The exploration and discovery of details to be developed in a composition. 19

central idea, central argument, or central statement   (1) The thesis or main idea of an essay. (2) The *theme* of a literary work. 30

character   An extended verbal representation of a human being, the inner self that determines thought, speech, and behavior. 3, 21, Ch. 4: 82–94, 123; and ideas, 134

chronology   Meaning the **"logic of time,"** the sequence of events in a work, with emphasis on the intertwining of cause and effect. 58

cliché rhyme   A rhyme that is typically easy and unoriginal, such as the word "breeze" being followed by "trees." 193

climax   Meaning **"ladder"** in Greek, the high point of *conflict* and tension preceding the resolution of a story or play; the point of decision, of inevitability and no return. The climax is sometimes merged with the *crisis* in the consideration of dramatic and narrative structure. 108

close reading   The detailed study of a poem or passage, designed to explain characters, motivations, situations, ideas, style, organization, word selections, settings, similarities, and contrasts of sound, etc. Ch 5: 95–106

comparison-contrast analysis   A technique of analyzing two or more works to determine similarities and differences in topic, treatment, and quality. Ch. 15

complication   A stage of narrative and dramatic structure in which the major *conflicts* are brought out; the rising action of a *drama.* 107

conflict   The opposition between two characters, between large groups of people, or between *protagonists* and larger forces such as natural objects, ideas, modes of behavior, and public opinion. Conflict may also be internal and psychological, involving choices facing a *protagonist.* The resolution of conflict is the essence of *plot.* 58

consonant sounds, or consonant segments   Consonant sounds (i.e., sounds that accompany ["con"= "with"] the sound ["sonant," = vowel sounds]). They are produced as a result of the touching or close proximity of the tongue or the lips in relation to the teeth or palate (e.g., *m, n, p, f, sh, ch*); to be compared and contrasted with *vowel sounds, q.v.* 192

contextual, private, or **authorial symbol**   A symbol that is not derived from common historical, cultural, or religious materials but is developed within the context of an individual work. See also *cultural, or universal, symbol.* 163, 166

continuant consonant sounds   Consonants that may be sustained by a stream or flow of breath while the consonant position is being held, unlike the stop sounds (*p, t, k, b, d, g*), which require an instant release of breath. The continuants are *m, n, ng* (as in you*ng*), *l, r, th* (as in *Th*ursday), *th* (as in wea*th*er), *f, v, s, z, sh, zh* (as in measure). 192

cosmic irony, or **irony of fate**   Situational irony that is connected to a pessimistic or fatalistic view of life. 183

couplet   Two lines that may be unified by rhyme or, in biblical poetry, by content. 3

creative nonfiction   A type of literature that is technically nonfiction, such as diaries, journals, and news features, but that nevertheless exhibits high degrees of imaginative and literary skill. 4

crisis   The point of uncertainty and tension—the turning point—that results from the *conflicts* and difficulties brought about through the *complications* of the plot. The crisis leads to the *climax*—that is, to the attempts made by the protagonist to resolve the conflict. Sometimes the crisis and the climax are considered as two elements of the same stage of *plot* development. 108

critical approaches   Appendix A, pp. 293–306

cultural context   See *historical context.*

cultural, or **universal, symbol**   A symbol that is recognized and shared as a result of a common political, social, and cultural heritage. See also *contextual, private, or authorial symbol.* 163, 167

dactyl   A three-syllable foot consisting of a heavy stress followed by two light stresses, as in the words *HAP-pi-ness, EV-i-dent,* and *LIB-er-ty.* 194

dactylic rhyme   Rhyming dactyls, such as *spillable* and *syllable* or *mortify* and *fortify.* Also called *triple rhyme.* 194

deconstructionist critical approach   An interpretive literary approach that rejects absolute interpretations and stresses ambiguities and contradictions. 303

dénouement (untying), or **resolution**   The final stage of plot development, in which mysteries are explained, characters find their destinies, lovers are united, sanity is restored, and the work is completed. Usually the dénouement is done as speedily as possible, because it occurs after all conflicts are ended and little that is new can be introduced to hold the readers' interest. 108

dialogue   What characters say to each other, especially in drama. 3; and ideas, 134

dilemma   A situation presenting a character with two choices, each one of which is unacceptable, dangerous, or even lethal. 108, 183

documentation   Granting recognition to the ideas and words of others, whether through textual, parenthetical, or footnote references. 280

double entendre   Meaning "**double meaning**" in French, deliberate ambiguity, usually humorous, and often sexual. 183

double rhyme   See *trochaic rhyme.*

drama   An individual play; also plays considered as a group. One of the three major genres of *imaginative literature.* 4

dramatic irony   A special kind of *situational irony* in which a character is ignorant of his or her true plight, or may perceive it in a limited way, whereas readers and the audience—and perhaps one or more of the other characters—understand it fully. 184

dramatic, or **objective, point of view**   A *third-person narration* reporting speech and action but excluding commentary about the actions and thoughts of the characters. 71

dying rhyme   See *falling rhyme.*

dynamic character   A character who tries to assert control by recognition, adjustment, and change. Dynamic changes may be shown in (1) an action or actions, (2) the realization of new strength and, therefore, the affirmation of previous decisions, (3) the acceptance of new conditions and the need for making changes and improvements, (4) the discovery of unrecognized truths, or (5) the reconciliation of the character with adverse conditions. In a *short story*, there is usually only one dynamic character, whereas in a *novel* there may be many. See *static character.* 86

economic determinist/Marxist critical approach   An interpretive literary approach based on the theories of Karl Marx (1818–1883), stressing that literature is to be judged from the perspective of economic and social class inequality and oppression. 300

elegy   A poem of lamentation about a death. Often an elegy takes the form of a pastoral poem. 3

enclosing setting   See *framing setting.*

epic poem   A long narrative poem elevating character, speech, and action. Some of the earliest surviving literary works are epics about the exploits of Gilgamesh, the Wrath of Achilles, and the Wanderings of Odysseus. 3

epigram   A short and witty poem, often in couplets, that makes a comic or satiric point. 3

essay   In writing about literature, an essay is a short and tightly organized written composition dealing with a topic such as character, a major idea, or point of view. Broadly, essays also deal with any and all conceivable topics. 24, *passim* (regularly, throughout the book)

exact rhyme   Sometimes called *perfect rhyme.* Exact rhyme is the placement of rhyming words or syllables in which both the vowel and concluding consonant sounds, if any, are identical, as in "done" and "run" and in "see" and "be." It is important to judge rhymes on the basis of *sound* rather than spelling, as in these examples. Words do not have to be spelled the same way to be exact rhymes. 192

examination   A written or oral test or inquiry designed to discover a person's understanding of and capacity to deal successfully with a particular topic or set of topics. Ch. 18: 251–61

exposition   The stage of dramatic or narrative structure that introduces all things necessary for the development of the plot. 107

eye rhyme or sight rhyme   Words that seem to rhyme because parts of them are spelled identically even though they are pronounced differently (e.g., *bear, fear; fury, bury; shove, stove; wonder, yonder; clover, hover*). 193, 195

fable   A brief *story* illustrating a moral truth, most often associated with the ancient Greek writer Aesop. See also *beast fable.* 166

falling rhyme   Trochaic rhymes, such as *dying* and *crying,* and multisyllabic rhymes, such as *flattery* and *battery* and *listening* and *glistening.* See *trochee.* 196

feet   See *foot.*

feminist criticism   An interpretive literary approach designed to raise consciousness about the importance and unique nature of women in literature. 299

fiction   *Narratives* based in the imagination of the author, not in literal, reportorial, or historical facts; one of the three major genres of imaginative literature. 4

figurative devices   See *figurative language.*

figurative language   An organized pattern of comparison that deepens, broadens, extends, illuminates, and emphasizes meaning, and that conforms to particular patterns or forms such as *metaphor, simile,* and *parallelism.* 151

figures   See *figurative language.*

figures of speech   See *figurative language.*

first-person point of view   The use of an "I," or first-person, speaker or narrator who tells about things that he or she has seen, done, spoken, heard, thought, and learned about in other ways.   69, 73, 75

flashback   Also called *selective recollection.* A method of *narration* in which past events are introduced into a present action.   109

flat character   A character, usually minor, who is not individual but is useful and structural, static and unchanging; distinguished from *round character, q.v.*   86

foot   A poetic foot consists of the measured combination of heavy and light *stresses,* such as the *iamb,* which contains a light stress followed by a heavy stress (e.g., "*of YEAR*"). In poetic scansion, the feet are separated by a *virgule* or single slash mark (/), as in the first line of Shakespeare's Sonnet 73: "*That TIME / of YEAR / thou MAY'ST / in ME / be - HOLD.*"

formalist critical approach   See *New Critical/Formalist critical approach.*

framing (enclosing) setting   The same features of topic or setting used at both the beginning and ending of a work so as to "frame" or "enclose" the work.   121

free verse   Poetry based on the natural rhythms of phrases and normal pauses, not metrical feet.   3

freewriting   See *brainstorming.*

gender studies   See *Feminist Criticism, Gender Studies, and Queer Theory.*

genre   One of the major forms of literature, such as the genres of *fiction* and *poetry.* Also, a type of work, such as the genres of detective fiction, comedy, epic poetry, or tragedy.   3

guidelines for reading   Systematic procedures for recording responses and ideas during the reading process. An essential step toward the development of analytical thought.   14

gustatory images   References to sensations and impressions of taste.   143

haiku   A poetic form derived from Japanese literature, traditionally containing three lines of five, seven, and five syllables, in that order, and generally treating topics derived from nature.   3

half rhyme   See *inexact rhyme.*

heavy stress   See *accent.*

heavy-stress rhyme, or rising rhyme, or accented rhyme   A rhyme, such as rhyming iambs or anapests, ending with a strong stress. The rhymes may be produced with one-syllable words, such as *EARTH* and *DEARTH,* or with multisyllabic words in which the accent falls on the final syllable, such as *deCLINE* and *conFINE.*   193

hero, heroine   The major male and female *protagonists* in a narrative or drama. The terms are often used to describe leading characters in adventures and romances.   86

historical context (also **cultural context** and **intellectual context**)   The historical time when a work was written, together with the intellectual and cultural ideas of this period. To study a work of literature in this perspective is to determine the degree to which the work not only spoke to people of its own time but also continues to speak to people of the present time (and perhaps to people of all time).   22, Ch. 16: 228–38

historical critical approach   See *topical/historical critical approach.*

humor   The feature or features of a situation or expression that are designed to provoke laughter and amusement.   181–82

hymn   A religious song, consisting usually of a number of replicating stanzas, designed for religious services.   3

hyperbole, or overstatement   A rhetorical figure in which emphasis is achieved through exaggeration.   183

iamb   A two-syllable *foot* consisting of a light stress followed by a heavy stress (e.g., *the WINDS, have FELT, of MAY*). The iamb is the most common metrical foot in English poetry inasmuch as it closely resembles natural speech but is also determined by measured poetic accents. 193

iambic rhyme   A *heavy-stress rhyme* that is built from rhyming *iambs* such as *the WEST* and *in REST*, or from rhyming two-syllable words such as *ad - MIRE* and *de - SIRE*. 193

idea, or theme   A concept, thought, opinion, or belief; in literature, a unifying, centralizing conception or theme. 23, Ch. 8: 128–40

identical rhyme   The use of the same words in rhyming positions, such as *VEIL* and *VEIL*, or *STONE* and *STONE*. 193, 195

image, imagery   Images are references that trigger the mind to fuse together memories of sights (*visual*), sounds (*auditory*), tastes (*gustatory*), smells (*olfactory*), and sensations of touch (*tactile*). "Image" refers to a single mental creation. "Imagery" refers to images throughout a work or throughout the works of a writer or group of writers. Images may be *literal* (descriptive and pictorial) or *metaphorical* (figurative and suggestive). 3, Ch. 9: 141–50

imaginative literature   *Literature* based in the imagination of the writer. The genres of imaginative literature are *fiction, poetry,* and *drama*. 2, *passim*

incidents   See *action*.

incongruity   A discrepancy between what is ordinarily or normally expected and what is actually experienced. The resulting gap is a major cause of amusement. 181

inexact rhyme   Rhymes that are created from words with similar but not identical sounds. In most of these instances, either the vowel segments are different while the consonants are the same, or vice versa. This type of rhyme is variously called *slant rhyme, near rhyme, half rhyme, off rhyme, analyzed rhyme,* or *suspended rhyme*. 194

intellectual critical approach   See *moral/intellectual critical approach*.

internal rhyme   The occurrence of rhyming words within a single line of verse, as with Poe's "can ever dissever" in *Annabel Lee*. 194

irony   A major aspect of literary tone, based on the proposition that even the simplest events in human life may be seen in multiple ways. Irony, therefore, deals with contradictions and ambiguities—the shadows underlying human existence. It is conveyed through indirection both in situations and in language. See *cosmic irony, dramatic irony, situational irony,* and *verbal irony*. 121, 182–84

irony of fate   See *cosmic irony*.

irony of situation   See *situational irony*.

journal   A notebook or word-processor file for recording responses and observations that, for purposes of writing, may be used in the development of essays. 14–17

kinesthetic images   Words describing human or animal motion and activity. 144

kinetic images   Words describing general motion. 144

limerick   A brief comic poem with set line lengths and rhyming patterns. More often than not, limericks are risqué. 3

limited point of view, limited third-person point of view, or limited-omniscient point of view   A third-person narration in which the actions, thoughts, and speeches of the protagonist are the primary focus of attention. 72

line   The basic unit of length of a poem, appearing as a row of words on a page, or sometimes as a single word or even part of a word making up the line, and cohering grammatically through phrases and sentences. Lines in closed-form poetry are composed of determinable numbers of metrical feet, such as five, four, or three. Lines in open-form poetry are variable, changing with the poet's subject matter and rhythmical speech patterns. 192

literary devices   See *figurative language*.

literary research   See *research, literary*.

literature   Written or oral compositions that tell stories, dramatize situations, express emotions, analyze and advocate ideas, and express ideals. Literature is designed to engage readers emotionally as well as intellectually, the major genres being *fiction, poetry, drama,* and *nonfiction prose* with many separate sub forms. 1, *passim*

lyric   A short and concentrated poem or song, usually meditative, often personal, and sometimes philosophical. Traditional lyrics follow a fixed stanzaic form, having been originally intended for a musical setting, such as hymns or texts of dramatic arias. The lyrics of many modern poets, however, are comparatively free and unrestricted, and many modern lyrics are designed not for music at all but rather for silent reading or spoken delivery. 3, *passim*

major mover   A primary participant in a work's action who either causes things to happen or is the subject of major events. If the first-person narrator is also a major mover, such as the *protagonist*, that fact gives firsthand authenticity to the narration. 67

malapropism   The comic use of an improperly pronounced word so that what comes out is a real but also an incorrect word. Examples are *odorous* for *odious* (Shakespeare) or *pineapple* for *pinnacle* (Sheridan). The new word must be close enough to the correct word that the resemblance is immediately recognized, along with the error. 181

Marxist critical approach   See *economic determinist/Marxist critical approach.*

mechanics of verse   See *prosody.*

metaphor   Meaning **"carrying out a change,"** *figurative language* that describes something as though it actually were something else, thereby enhancing understanding and insight. 3, Ch. 10: 151–61

metaphorical language   See *figurative language.*

metrical foot   See *foot.*

metrics   See *prosody.*

mood   See *atmosphere.*

moral/intellectual critical approach   An interpretive literary approach that is concerned primarily with content and values. 294

music of poetry   See *prosody.*

myth, mythology, mythos   A *myth* is a story that deals with the relationships of gods to humanity or with battles among heroes. A myth may also be a set of beliefs or assumptions among societies. *Mythology* refers collectively to the stories and beliefs of either a single group or number of groups. A system of beliefs and religious or historical doctrine is a *mythos.* 2, 166

mythic critical approach   See *archetypal/symbolic/mythic critical approach.*

narration, narrative fiction   The relating or recounting of a sequence of events or actions. Whereas a narration may be reportorial and historical, *narrative fiction* is primarily creative and imaginative. See also *creative nonfiction* and *prose fiction* . 2

narrative fiction   See *prose fiction.*

narrator   See *speaker.*

near rhyme   See *inexact rhyme.*

New Critical/formalist critical approach   An interpretive literary approach based on the French method of *explication de texte* (the [detailed] explanation of a text), stressing the form, details, and meanings of literary works. 296

New Historicism   A type of literary criticism that treats literature as a functional and integrated part of culture and history. 295

nonfiction prose   A *genre* consisting of essays, articles, and books about real rather than fictional occurrences and objects; one of the major *genres* of literature. 3

novel   A long work of prose fiction. 2

objective point of view   See *dramatic point of view.*

ode   A stanzaic poem with varying line lengths and often intricate rhyme schemes that contrast it with songs and hymns. 3

off rhyme   See *inexact rhyme.*

olfactory imagery   Images referring to impressions of smell. 143

omniscient point of view   A *third-person narrative* in which the *speaker* or *narrator*, with no apparent limitations, may describe intentions, actions, reactions, locations, and speeches of any or all of the characters and may also describe their innermost thoughts (when necessary). 71

onomatopoeia   A blending of consonant and vowel sounds designed to imitate or suggest the object or activity being described, as in line 357 of Pope's *An Essay on Criticism*: "That like a wounded Snake, drags its slow length along." 197

outline   See *analytical sentence outline.*

overstatement   See *hyperbole.*

parable   A short *allegory* designed to illustrate a religious truth, most often associated with Jesus as recorded in the Gospels. 2, 166

pastoral   A traditional poetic form with topical material drawn from the idealized lives and vocabularies of rural and shepherd life. Famous English pastoral poems are Arnold's *Thyrsis* (1867), Milton's *Lycidas* (1637), Pope's *Pastorals* (1709), Shelley's *Adonais* (1821), and Spenser's *The Shepheardes Calendar* (1579). 4

pentameter   A poetic line of five metrical *feet*. 195

perfect rhyme   See *exact rhyme.*

persona   See *speaker.*

phonetic, phonetics   The actual pronunciation of sounds, as distinguished from spelling or *graphics*. Thus *bear, eat,* and *ear* are each spelled or graphed with an *ea* vowel combination, but phonetically the words are pronounced differently. 193

plagiarism   A writer's use of the language and ideas of another writer or writers without proper acknowledgment. Plagiarism is an exceedingly serious breach of academic honor; some call it intellectual theft, and others call it an academic crime. 273–74

plausibility   See *probability.*

plot   The plan or groundwork for a story or a play, with the actions resulting from believable and authentic human responses to a *conflict*. It is causality, conflict, response, opposition, and interaction that make a plot out of a series of actions. Aristotle's word for plot was *muthos*, from which our modern English word *myth* was derived. Ch. 2: 58–64, 107

poem, poet, poetry   Poetry is a variable literary genre that is, foremost, characterized by the rhythmical qualities of language. Whereas poems may be short (including *epigrams* and *haiku* of just a few lines) or long (*epics* of thousands of lines), the essence of poetry is compression, economy, and force, in contrast with the logic and expansiveness of prose. There is no bar to the topics that poets may consider, and poems may range from the personal and lyric to the public and discursive. A *poem* is one poetic work. A *poet* is a person who writes poems. *Poetry* may refer to the poems of one writer, to poems of a number of writers, to all poems generally, or to the aesthetics of poetry considered as an art. 3, *passim*

point of view   The *speaker, voice, narrator,* or *persona* of a work; the position from which details are perceived and related; a centralizing mind or intelligence; not to be confused with *opinion* or *belief.* Ch. 3: 65–81

point-of-view character   The central figure or *protagonist* in a *limited-point-of-view narration*, the character about whom events turn, the focus of attention in the narration. 72

presupposal   See *procatalepsis.* 204

private, or **contextual, symbol**   See *cultural symbol.*

probability or **plausibility**   The standard that literature should be concerned with what is likely, common, normal, and usual. 87

problem   A question or issue about the interpretation or understanding of a work. Ch. 14: 202–209

procatalepsis, or anticipation   A rhetorical strategy whereby the writer raises an objection and then answers it; the idea is to strengthen an argument by anticipating and thereby forestalling objections. Also called a figure of *presumptuousness* or *presupposal.* 204

prose fiction   *Imaginative* prose narratives (*short stories* and *novels*) that focus on one or a few characters who undergo a change or development as they interact with other characters and deal with their problems. 2

prosody   Metrics and versification; the sounds, rhythms, rhymes, and general qualities of poetic technique; the relationships between content and sound in poetry. 3, Ch. 13: 192–201

protagonist   The central character and focus of interest in a narrative or drama. 86

psychological/psychoanalytic critical approach   An interpretive literary approach that stresses how psychology may be used in the explanation of both authors and their works. 301

quatrain   (1) A four-line stanza or poetic unit. (2) In an *English* or *Shakespearean* sonnet, a group of four lines, usually united by rhyme. 3, 196

queer theory   An interpretive literary approach based on the idea that sexual orientation is partly ideological and partly social. A number of queer theorists see the heterosexual/homosexual divide as less distinct than has traditionally been understood. The application of the theory is the discovery, often previously ignored, that many works contain either obvious or submerged homosexual elements. 299

reader-response critical approach   An interpretive literary approach based on the proposition that literary works are not fully created until readers make transactions with them by actualizing the works in the light of their own particular knowledge and experience. 305

realism, or **verisimilitude**   The use of true, lifelike, or probable situations and concerns. Also, the theory underlying the depiction of reality in literature. 120

reliable narrator   A speaker who is untainted by self-interest or other limitations, who, therefore, has no reason to hide details and make misstatements. This speaker's narration is, therefore, to be accepted at face value; contrasted with an *unreliable narrator.* 69, 73

representative character   A *flat character* with the qualities of all other members of a group (e.g., clerks, cowboys, detectives, etc.); a *stereotype character,* a *stock character.* 87

research, literary   The systematic use of primary and secondary sources for assistance in studying and writing about a literary *problem.* Ch. 19: 262–92

resolution   See *dénouement.*

response   A reader's intellectual and emotional reactions to a literary work. 14

review   A free-ranging essay on a literary work. Reviews may be designed for general readers and for readers with specific fields of interest (e.g., politics, religion, history, science, family life). Ch. 17: 239–50

rhetorical figures   See *figurative language.*

rhyme   The repetition of identical or closely related sounds in the syllables of different words, usually in concluding syllables at the ends of lines, such as Shakespeare's *day* and *away* ("Sonnet 18") and Swinburne's *forever* and *never* ("The Garden of Proserpine"). See also *internal rhyme.* Ch. 13: 192–201

rhyme scheme   A pattern of *rhyme,* usually indicated by the assignment of a letter of the alphabet to each rhyming sound, as in *a b b a* as the rhyming pattern of the first quatrain of an Italian or Petrarchan sonnet. 195

rising rhyme See *heavy-stress rhyme.*

romance (1) Lengthy Spanish and French stories of the sixteenth and seventeenth centuries. (2) Modern formulaic stories describing the growth of an impulsive, passionate, and powerful love relationship. 2

round character A literary character, usually but not necessarily the *protagonist* of a story or play, who is three-dimensional, rounded, authentic, memorable, original, and true to life. A round character is the center of our attention and is both individual and unpredictable. The round character also profits from experience and, in the course of a story or play, undergoes change or development. See *dynamic character.* 85

second-person point of view A narration in which a second-person listener ("you") is the protagonist and the speaker is someone (e.g., doctor, parent, rejected lover) who has knowledge that the protagonist does not possess or understand about his or her own actions. Sometimes the "you" of the second person is used popularly and vaguely to signify persons in a general audience, including the speaker. 70, 74, 75

segment The smallest meaningful unit of sound, such as the *l, uh,* and *v* sounds making up the word "love." Segments are to be distinguished from spellings. Thus, the *oo* segment may be spelled as *ui* in "fruit," *u* in "flute," *oo* in "foolish," *o* in "lose," *uu* in "vacuum," or *ou* in "troupe." 192

selective recollection See *flashback.*

setting The natural, manufactured, and cultural environment in which characters live and move, including all their possessions, homes, ways of life, and assumptions. Ch. 7: 118–27

short story A compact, concentrated work of *narrative fiction* that may also contain description, dialogue, and commentary. Poe used the term "brief prose tale" for the short story and emphasized that it should create a powerful and unified impact. 2

sight rhyme See *eye rhyme.*

simile A figure of comparison, using "like" with nouns and "as" with clauses, as in "the trees were bent by the wind *like actors bowing after a performance,"* Ch. 10: 151–61

situation The special circumstances or encounters that characters face within a literary work, especially in drama and fiction. 3; and ideas, 130

situational irony, or irony of situation A type of *irony* emphasizing that particular characters are enmeshed in forces that greatly exceed their perception, comprehension, and control. See *irony.* 183

slant rhyme A *near rhyme* in which the concluding consonant sounds (but not the vowels) are identical, as in *should* and *food, slim* and *ham.* See also *inexact rhyme.* 193, 195

song See *lyric.*

sonnet A poem of fourteen lines originally designed to be spoken (not sung) in iambic pentameter. 3

speaker The *narrator* of a story or poem, the *point of view,* often an independent character who is completely imagined and consistently maintained by the author. In addition to narrating the essential events of the work (justifying the status of narrator), the speaker may introduce other aspects of his or her knowledge and may express judgments and opinions. Often the character of the speaker is of as much interest in the story as are the *actions* or *incidents.* 65

speech The individual talk or spoken interchange between characters in various forms of literature, especially in drama. 3

stanza A group of poetic lines corresponding to paragraphs in prose; stanzaic meters and rhymes are usually repeating and systematic. 196

static character A character who undergoes no change, a *flat character;* contrasted with a *dynamic character* or *round character.* 86

stereotype character   A character who is so ordinary and unoriginal that he or she seems to have been cast in a mold; a *representative character*. 87

stock character   A *flat character* in a standard role with standard *traits*, such as the irate police captain, the bored hotel clerk, or the sadistic criminal; a *stereotype*. 86

story   A *narrative*, usually fictional and usually centering on a major character and rendering a complete action. 3

structuralist critical approach   An interpretive literary approach that attempts to find relationships and similarities among elements that appear to be separate and discrete. 297

structure   The arrangement and placement of materials in a work. Ch. 6: 107–117; and ideas, 134

suspended rhyme   See *inexact rhyme.*

symbol, symbolism   A specific word, idea, or object that may stand for ideas, values, persons, or ways of life. 48, Ch. 11: 162–78

symbolic literary approach   See *archetypal/symbolic/mythic critical approach*

tactile imagery   *Images* of touch and responses to touch. 143

tenor   The ideas that are conveyed in a *metaphor* or *simile*. See also *vehicle.* 155

tense   Besides embodying reports of actions and circumstances, verbs possess altering forms—*tenses*—that signify the times when things occur, whether past, present, or future. Perfect and progressive tenses indicate completed or continuing activities. Tense is an important aspect of *point of view* because the notation of time influences the way in which events are perceived and expressed. Narratives are usually told in the past tense, but many recent writers of fiction prefer the present tense for conveying a sense of immediacy. No matter when a sequence of actions is presumed to have taken place, the introduction of dialogue changes the action to the present. See *point of view.* 72, 76

tercet or **triplet**   a three-line unit or stanza of poetry, usually rhyming *a a a, b c b, c d c,* etc. 3

theme   (1) The major or central idea of a work. (2) An essay, a short composition developing an interpretation or advancing an argument. (3) The main point or idea that a writer of an essay asserts and illustrates. 129

thesis sentence, or **thesis statement**   An introductory sentence that names the topics to be developed in the body of an essay. 32

third-person objective point of view   See *dramatic point of view.*

third-person point of view   A third-person method of *narration* (i.e., *she, he, it, they, them,* etc.) in which the *speaker* or *narrator* is not a part of the story, unlike the involvement of the narrator of a *first-person point of view*. Because the third-person speaker may exhibit great knowledge and understanding, together with other qualities of character, he or she is often virtually identified with the author, but this identification is not easily decided. See also *authorial voice, omniscient point of view.* 71, 74, 75

tone   The techniques and modes of presentation that reveal or create attitudes. Ch. 12: 179–91

topic sentence   The sentence that determines or introduces the subject matter of a paragraph. 33

topical/historical critical approach   An interpretive literary approach that stresses the relationship of literature to its historical period. 295

trait, traits   A typical mode of behavior; the study of major traits provides a guide to the description of *character*. 82

triple rhyme   See *dactylic rhyme.*

trochaic (double) rhyme   Rhyming trochees such as *FLOW-er* and *TOW-er.* 194

trochee, trochaic   A two-syllable foot consisting of a heavy stress followed by a light stress (e.g., *RUN-ning, SING-ing, EAT-ing*). 193

understatement   Rhetorically, the deliberate underplaying or undervaluing of an assertion or idea to create emphasis; a form of *irony*. 182

universal symbol   See *cultural symbol*.

unreliable narrator   A speaker who through ignorance, self-interest, deviousness, or lack of capacity may tell lies and otherwise distort truth. For the reader to locate truth in the unreliable narrator's story requires careful judgment and not inconsiderable skepticism. See also *reliable narrator*. 69, 73

value, values   The attachment of worth, significance, and desirability to an *idea* so that the idea is judged not only for its significance as thought but also for its importance as a goal, ideal, or standard. 129

vehicle   The image or reference of figures of speech, such as a *metaphor* or *simile*; it is the vehicle that carries or embodies the *tenor*. See also *tenor*. 155

verbal irony   Language stressing the importance of an idea by stating the opposite of what is meant. Verbal irony may convey humor, but as often as not it also reflects serious criticism and even bitterness and mockery of particular facets of life and the universe. See *irony*. 182

verisimilitude   Meaning **"like truth,"** a characteristic whereby the setting, circumstances, characters, dialogue, actions, and outcomes in a work are designed to seem true, lifelike, real, plausible, and probable. See *realism*. 87

versification   See *prosody*.

villanelle   A poem of nineteen lines, composed of five *tercets* and a concluding *quatrain*. The villanelle as a form requires that whole lines be repeated in a specific order and that only two rhyming sounds occur throughout. 3

visual image   Language describing visible objects and situations. 142

voice   See *speaker*.

vowel rhyme   The use of any vowels in rhyming positions, regardless of pronunciation, such as *sigh* and *say*, or *fee* and *foe*. The use of vowel rhyme, generally, is a means of stretching the applicability of English vocabulary to poetic use. 195

vowel sounds, or vowel segments   Meaningful sounds produced by the continuant resonation of the voice in the space between the tongue and the top of the mouth, such as the *ay* in "pray," the *ee* in "feel," the *i* in "fine," the *oh* in "flow," and the *oo* in "cool." 192

Credits

Boston University's Library Catalog. "Advanced Keyword Search," from Boston University Libraries. Reprinted with permission.

Boston University's Library Catalog. "Results: Katherine Mansfield and Criticism," from Boston University Libraries. Reprinted with permission.

Brooks, Gwendolyn. "We Real Cool" from *Blacks* by Gwendolyn Brooks. Reprinted by permission of Brooks Permissions.

Frost, Robert. "Desert Places" and "The Road Not Taken" from the book *The Poetry of Robert Frost,* edited by Edward Connery Lathem. Copyright ©1923, 1969 by Henry Holt and Company, Copyright ©1936 by Robert Frost, Copyright ©1964 by Lesley Frost Ballantine. Reprinted by permission of Henry Holt and Company, LLC.

Hughes, Langston. "Negro" from *The Collected Poems of Langston Hughes*, edited by Arnold Rampersad with David Roessel, Associate Editor. Copyright ©1994 by the Estate of Langston Hughes. Used by permission of Alfred A. Knopf, a division of Random House, Inc.

Jackson, Shirley. "The Lottery" from *The Lottery*. Copyright ©1948, 1949 by Shirley Jackson. Copyright © 1948, 1949 by Shirley Jackson. Copyright © renewed 1976, 1977 by Laurence Hyman, Barry Hyman, Mrs. Sarah Webster, and Mrs. Joanne Schnurer. Reprinted by permission of Farrar, Straus and Giroux, LLC.

JSTOR, Advanced Search Page. Reprinted with permission.

Layton, Irving. "Rhine Boat Trip" from *The Selected Poems of Irving Layton,* Copyright ©1977 by New Directions Publishing Corp. Copyright ©1982, 2004 by Irving Layton. Copyright ©2007 by The Estate of Irving Layton. Reprinted by permission of New Directions Publishing Corp., McClelland & Stewart Ltd., and the Estate of Irving Layton.

Masefield, John. "Cargoes." Reprinted by permission of The Society of Authors as the literary representative of the Estate of John Masefield.

Maupassant, Guy de. "The Necklace" translated by Edgar V. Roberts

MLA International Bibliography. Basic search for "Katherine Mansfield." Reprinted by permission of the Modern Language Association of America from MLA International Bibliography.

O'Connor, Frank. "First Confession" from *The Collected Stories of Frank O'Connor* by Frank O' Connor. Copyright ©1981 by Harriet O'Donovan Sheehy, Executrix of the Estate of Frank O'Connor. Used by permission of Alfred A. Knopf, a division of Random House, Inc. and Jennifer Lyons Literary Agency as agent for the proprietor.

Walker, Alice. "Everyday Use" from *In Love & Trouble: Stories of Black Women*. Copyright ©1973 by Alice Walker. Reprinted by permission of Harcourt, Inc.

Welty, Eudora. "A Worn Path" from *A Curtain of Green and Other Stories*. Copyright ©1941 and renewed 1969 by Eudora Welty. Reprinted by permission of Houghton Mifflin Harcourt Publishing Company.

Index of Authors and Titles, Topics, References, and Chapter Titles

Authors are listed alphabetically, followed by the titles of their works. In some instances, such as *The Oxford Companions*, the books are listed by title. Anonymous works are indexed under the titles. For brief definitions of important terms and concepts used in the text, please consult the preceding Glossary.